Advance Praise for

# THE FILE

"San Charles Haddad's *The File* skillfully unearths some of the most deeply hidden roots of the horrendous 'Black September' massacre that overshadowed the 1972 Munich Olympic Games. On the basis of awesomely extensive archival research, Haddad stages a historical drama of the formation of the Palestine Olympic Committee, in 1934, on the eve of Berlin's 'Nazi Olympics,' to which the POC was destined to send no team. It is, in fact, with a dramatist's keen sense of character and action that Haddad delves into the work of a handful of dedicated idealistic organizers who struggled to bring together all the mutually antagonistic Palestinian sports organizations during the years of British Mandate rule. Among the most important of the many dramatis personae are the Zionist sports enthusiast Yosef Yekutieli and Jerusalem's YMCA director Waldo Heinrichs. Their stories are told with loving detail—against the dark backdrop of Palestinian Nazis determined to prevent any kind of cooperation between Jews and Arabs, on or off the fields of play. It is a shame that *The File* is not twice as long as its 368 pages."

—ALLEN GUTTMANN, author of
*The Olympics: A History of the Modern Games*

# THE FILE

# THE FILE

## ORIGINS OF THE MUNICH MASSACRE

## SAN CHARLES HADDAD

Post Hill
PRESS

A POST HILL PRESS BOOK

The File:
Origins of the Munich Massacre
© 2020 by San Charles Haddad
All Rights Reserved

ISBN: 978-1-64293-026-9
ISBN (eBook): 978-1-64293-027-6

Cover art by Rob Rice
Interior design and composition by Greg Johnson, Textbook Perfect

**Post Hill Press**
New York • Nashville
posthillpress.com

Published in the United States of America

*For Blair and Wesley*

# Dedication & Epigraph

*To the memory of those who died at the Games of the XX Olympiad in Munich, Germany, as a result of the events of 5–6 September 1972, and to those in Palestinian sport who emboldened me to reconsider our divided past, and our shared future.*

**Israel Olympic Committee Delegation Members**

Moshe Weinberg, Wrestling Coach (d. 1972)

Yossef Romano, Weightlifter (d. 1972)

Ze'ev Friedman, Weightlifter (d. 1972)

David Berger, Weightlifter (d. 1972)

Yakov Springer, Weightlifting Judge (d. 1972)

Eliezer Halfin, Wrestler (d. 1972)

Yossef Gutfreund, Wrestling Referee (d. 1972)

Kehat Shorr, Shooting Coach (d. 1972)

Mark Slavin, Wrestler (d. 1972)

Andre Spitzer, Fencing Coach (d. 1972)

Amitzur Shapira, Track Coach (d. 1972)

**West German Police**

Anton Fliegerbauer, German Police Officer (d. 1972)

**Palestine Olympic Committee**

Omar Hussein Shuweikeh, Secretary General, Palestine Olympic Committee (d. 2007)

Khalil Hassan Jaber, Secretary General of Palestine Amateur Athletics Federation (d. 2008)

Akram Daher, Head of International Affairs, Palestine Olympic Committee (d. 2009)

## Ecclesiastes 9:11-12[1]

[11] I have further observed under the sun that
The race is not won by the swift,
Nor the battle by the valiant;
Nor is bread won by the wise,
Nor wealth by the intelligent,
Nor favor by the learned.
For the time of mischance comes to all.
[12] And a man cannot even know his time. As fishes are enmeshed in a fatal net, and as birds are trapped in a snare, so men are caught at the time of calamity, when it comes upon them without warning.

## 1 Corinthians 9:24-27[2]

[24] Do you not know that those who run in a race all run, but one receives the prize? Run in such a way that you may obtain it. [25] And everyone who competes for the prize is temperate in all things. Now they do it to obtain a perishable crown, but we for an imperishable crown. [26] Therefore I run thus: not with uncertainty. Thus I fight: not as one who beats the air. [27] But I discipline my body and bring it into subjection, lest, when I have preached to others, I myself should become disqualified.

## Surah al-Hadid 57:20[3]

57:20 Know that the life of the world is only play, and idle talk, and pageantry, and boasting among you, and rivalry in respect of wealth and children; as the likeness of vegetation after rain, whereof the growth is pleasing to the husbandman, but afterward it drieth up and thou seest it turning yellow, then it becometh straw. And in the Hereafter there is grievous punishment, and (also) forgiveness from Allah and His good pleasure, whereas the life of the world is but matter of illusion.

---

[1] Berlin, Adele, Marc Zvi Brettler, and Michael Fishbane, eds. 2004. The Jewish Study Bible. Jewish Publication Society. Oxford: Oxford University Press.

[2] Scripture taken from the New King James Version®. Copyright © 1982 by Thomas Nelson, Inc. Used by permission. All rights reserved.

[3] Mohammed Marmaduke Pickthall. The Holy Qur'an: Transliteration in Roman Script. 1930.

# Contents

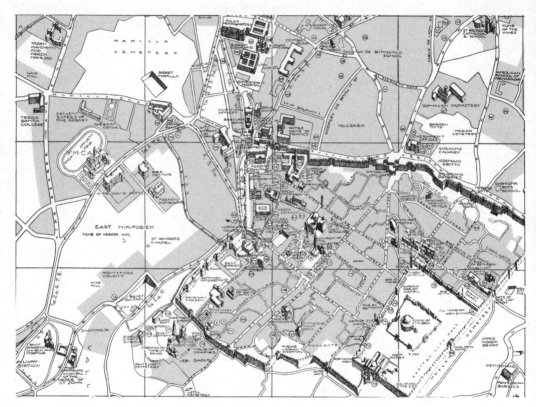

*Section of a sports map of Jerusalem published by the Jerusalem YMCA for and distributed at its Dedication event on April 18, 1933.*

# PREFACE

# Context and Background

"Sports will not make angels of brutes, but there is a great possibility that they will temper that brutality, giving the individual a bit of self control. That, at least, is something!"[1] So wrote Pierre de Coubertin, the spiritual founder of the modern Olympic Games, in early 1935.

But what if the brute were not an athlete?

Adolf Hitler, the fascist dictator of the "New Germany", certainly was not the sporting type. He was more on the pathway to becoming a demon. Hitler did not waste time philosophizing the values of sport. While an ailing Coubertin (d. 1937) was writing commentary for a Belgian sport newspaper, Hitler was focused on bringing to fruition his aspirations for a new German empire. The creation of his Third Reich would bring about the deaths of tens of millions between September 1939 and May 1945.

Hitler's priorities were exhibited in some of the key strategic policy benchmarks that he achieved during the raging debate on whether to withdraw the Olympic hosting rights from Germany after the Nazis seized full control of the country on January 30, 1933. These benchmarks included: the Enabling Act (March 1933), which gave Hitler the right to pass laws without the approval of the German parliament; the Reichs-konkordat (July 1933), in which the Vatican consented to the restriction of the German clergy's political activity; the reintegration of the Saar region into the territory of Germany (January 1935); his massive rearmament campaign and reintroduction of conscription (March 1935);

introduction of the anti-Semitic and racial Nuremberg Laws (September 1935); and the remilitarization of the Rhineland (March 1936) in violation of the Treaty of Versailles (which had formalized the end of the First World War). This is the national context in Germany in the lead-up to the Berlin Games that influenced the behaviors and decisions of this book's protagonists and other characters.

The fate and values of Coubertin's cherished Olympic Movement hung in the balance. So did the lives of European Jews. The Nazis assumed full control of Germany on January 30, 1933. In doing so, they inherited the hosting rights of the Games of the XI Olympiad. The Nazis' actions (versus words) made it clear that Jews were not welcome at the Games. Arguments raged in the American Olympic Association, among worldwide socialists and communists, and within global Jewry. These arguments presented the very real threat that the Games might be boycotted.

For Joseph Goebbels, Hitler's Reich Minister of Public Enlightenment and Propaganda, there would be no boycott. He was determined to make the Games one of his greatest propaganda successes. Indeed, three hundred million people around the world would eventually tune in on the radio to follow the Games.[2] And what a success they were! Despite their dark undertones, these Games established benchmarks to which the modern Olympic festival still adheres, the most famous (and ironic) of which is the torch relay that carries the Olympic flame—the symbol of the Olympic Truce—from Ancient Olympia in Greece to the host stadium.

Today, the "Nazi Olympics" are often remembered as the Games that should have been boycotted, but were not. Nazi ideology was an affront to the internationalist, peaceful mission of the Olympic Movement, so how could the International Olympic Committee (IOC) and its associated national Olympic committees rubber-stamp the Nazi regime? This regime's intent was to break rather than fortify the links between the Olympic rings.

In fact, Spain did boycott, but its decision was not purely out of principle against the Nazis or because the country's politicians favored the Olympic ideals. The country's leftist government was interested in using sport for its own propaganda in support of leftist causes. It organized the People's Olympiad in Barcelona as a leftist demonstration against the Olympics in Berlin. Those games never took place because of the Spanish Civil War.

But there was one small country that actually took the final public stand against Berlin: Palestine.

This is the story of the first Palestine Olympic Committee, which existed from 1930 until 1948 and was the supreme Olympic authority in the territory administered during the British Mandate for Palestine (1920–1948). David Margolick[3] once suggested that epic sport stories worth immortalizing in a book are in short supply, with events like the "Nazi Olympics" pretty much picked clean. This is one story that has been mysteriously left on the bone.

Complicated and purposefully concealed or forgotten, the history in this book sometimes raises more questions than it provides answers. I believe that the Munich Massacre, in which eleven Israelis, one German policeman, and a number of Palestinian attackers died at the Games of the XX Olympiad in 1972, is the reason for the story's obscurity. If Munich had not happened, I suspect that the story would have been told a long time ago. Its time has arrived.

## 2.

I constructed this book with alternating segments that present the actions of the two camps: Jewish and Arab national sport, with the Jerusalem Young Men's Christian Association (YMCA) representing the organizational interests and competency development of the latter camp. I introduce the three main characters in the order that I perceive them to be chronologically and historically important to the corresponding national sport files.

Yosef Yekutieli is arguably the most important person in the history of Jewish and Israeli sports as both the founder of the Maccabi Games (historically considered the Jewish Olympics) and the architect of Mandate Palestine's earliest internationally-recognized national sport governing bodies, the Federation of the Amateur Sports Clubs of Palestine (FASCP), and the Palestine Olympic Association (POA). His colleague Frederick Kisch is in some ways incidental, except that he was the political figurehead of the Palestine Olympic body and an extremely important figure of the time, so much so that members of the International Olympic Committee considered his joining its board before the Second World War. Without Kisch in the role of president, in 1934, the IOC could never have recognized the POA. In the case of Waldo Heinrichs Sr., he could have been more important in the history of Arab Palestinian sport in Mandate Palestine if not for his unfortunate removal in a Nazi campaign reinforced by some of the Christian Arabs on the board of the Jerusalem YMCA. Yet it is in Heinrichs that we see more than anyone else the stance that sound principles count for something in this world and that if we stick to them, we can alter the course of history. That, along with his long covered-up story, is why I chose to weave him throughout the book, even though he was in Jerusalem for barely two years.

## 3.

People who would eventually become very senior Israeli government officials after the establishment of the State of Israel had affiliations with the Maccabi sports movement. It was Yekutieli who drew for them the movement's logo, sometime between the Stockholm Olympic Games of 1912 and the restructuring of the Maccabi Movement in 1921. Using a pencil and a sheet of carbon copy paper, he took the four letters of the Hebrew word *Maccabi*[4]—a *mim, kaph, bet*, and *yod*—and fashioned them into the Star of David, what the Jewish community refers to as the Magen David, or Shield of David.

In ancient times, King David carried a six-pointed shield into battle. The modern Maccabis adopted this symbol as a reflection of their disciplined commitment to Zionism and readiness to defend Jews. Maccabi sport clubs around the world still wear Yekutieli's logo as a badge of honor, whereas the Nazis purposely took the Shield of David and tried to make it a mark of shame. It is not a star, but a deep connection to an ancient Jewish military history. Since the Shield of David is a relatively recent symbol for Jews in the religious and political sense, religious scholars are not certain who introduced its association as a unifying symbol for and of Jews. But there is no doubt that Yekutieli saw in it a form around which the Jewish sports movement could unite. In his pamphlet *The Jewish State*, Theodor Herzl described how it was the condition of the Diaspora—the dispersal of the Jews from their historic land and disconnection from one another—that prevented them "from conducting their political affairs for themselves."[5]

On November 24, 1895, more than one year before the First Zionist Congress, Herzl presented his strategy for a Jewish state to the Order of Ancient Maccabeans,[6] an Anglo-Jewish friendly society and avowedly Zionist order. He won the Order's support for his plan. Major figures were associated with this Order. Its Grand Commander was Herbert Bentwich, whose son Norman became a close associate of Kisch. Other major figures in the Order were Chaim Weizmann, Israel's first president, and the renowned mathematician Selig Brodetsky, who became the president of the Maccabi World Union after it moved from Germany to London because of the rise of Nazism.

It is based on these connections and for these reasons that one can find Zionist and Jewish leaders who were associated with the Maccabi Movement writing books like president of Israel Chaim Herzog's *Heroes of Israel: Profiles of Jewish Courage*. In this book, modern Israeli leaders are profiled with ancient Jewish leaders, including Judah the Maccabi (the "Hammer") who led a critical campaign of the ancient Maccabean Wars against the Seleucids. These wars lasted from 167 to 37 BCE. The wars' end took place in the final defeat of the last standing Jewish fortress at Betar in the Bar Kochba revolt. The torch-lighting ceremony for the Maccabi Games occurs at the site of the Hasmonean tombs in Modi'in. The Hasmoneans were the Jewish dynasty that led the revolt against the Romans, and Modi'in (where they are buried) is their ancestral town.

It would be a mistake to interpret this history as mere propaganda, even though it has been used to coalesce a modern Jewish identity for state-building. For early Zionists especially, this was simply history. Their mission as a group was to reveal it to Jews who, in the words of Max Nordau (Herzl's close associate who inspired the Maccabi Movement with his concept of "Muscular Jewry"), had rabbis who "expunged from Prayer books what has become to them a meaningless hope—'Next year in Jerusalem!'"[7] To leaders like those in the Order of Ancient Maccabeans, the ancient Maccabean Wars were fought specifically to preserve Jewish identity against what was seen as an increasingly assimilated, Hellenistic (Greek) Jewish culture. Zionism sought to reverse assimilation, but not based on ancient religious perceptions; rather, it was an antidote to the very real problem of anti-Semitism faced by the Jews in Europe and the Diaspora.

There are many ideologies within Zionism, and it would be inappropriate to overstate the Maccabis' power within the state today or within the broader global Jewish community. But the Maccabis were very important in that they gave a broad Jewish emotive connection point to Zionism that helped enable its business strategy and political structure in a way that still binds so many Jews together, even if they are not Israelis. To say that Zionism is one thing—racism, Nazism, apartheid, colonialism, and so forth—is oversimplification to the extreme, as well as ignorant, which is why the charge of anti-Semitism is leveled against such statements. This language can be very harmful, even if it is a reaction to the very distressing facts of life for Palestinians today. Statecraft is perfectly legitimate in today's global order—even if its tactics are morally abhorrent to some—and the affairs of states or states-in-formation are highly complicated as well as subjective.

For this reason, it is important to stress that the Maccabi Movement was never exclusively Jewish. It simply has always been centered on and inspired by Jewish identity, and its primary clientele is Jewish youth. There is nothing exceptional or nefarious about Jewish sport organizing itself globally or in Mandate Palestine historically: this is how everyone in sport arranged their affairs, especially before the Second World War. Communists formed communist clubs, Greek Orthodox formed Orthodox clubs, Muslims formed Islamic clubs, the military had military teams, and so on.

Sport from its inception has been organized on an identity model much like nations. Acknowledging the constraints of that model, it's probably better to have these groups let off steam on the field of play instead of on the battlefield. This was a central desired outcome of Coubertin's Olympic ideal. Despite the legitimate critique of some of its shortcomings, the Olympic Movement has broken down a lot of the identity model historically present in sport, even though it also struggles to manage some within its ranks who promote national identification excessively.

## 4.

The Zionists' "Muscular Judaism" was preceded by its Christian version, "Muscular Christianity." This found its fullest expression in the global network of YMCAs. Although the YMCA Movement did not seek to build specifically Christian nation states through its activity, "Muscular Christianity" perceived sports as "a source of moral education…and a moral code of honor based on 'sportsmanship.'"[8] Humphrey Bowman was the chair of the board of directors of the Jerusalem YMCA during our story and promoted such an ideal. He was also the director of the Education Department for the government of Palestine. He presided over two entities—one governmental and one non-governmental—that sought to unify the communities through education and sport.

Thus, Jewish and Christian sport movements were emulating one another, albeit through different identity and value lenses. It should come as no surprise that the Muslim inhabitants of Palestine would follow suit. In 1926 in Egypt, a Young Men's Muslim Association was founded.[9] Its branch in Haifa, Palestine, was headed by Izz ad-Din al-Qassam, the Syrian sheikh who emigrated to Palestine in the early 1920s and tried to organize a peasant revolt. This picture demonstrates that all major actors were utilizing sport to assert identity and express political ambitions, a fact that must be recognized in order to digest the story in the "file."

The key differentiating factor between the Jewish, YMCA, and non-Jewish Palestinian sport movements as it related to Olympic affiliation was the degree to which any of them was willing to suppress some of the more overt private agendas and adopt the IOC's internationalist agenda, which insisted that Olympic governing bodies work across ethnic and religious lines. As the three camps fought it out in the early 1930s and petitioned international sport for membership, the international system would have an increasingly hard time sorting it all out. Even the IOC would be confronted by its own leaders gravitating in one direction or another.

In 1920, the International Committee of YMCAs (IC/YMCA) reached out to the IOC at the Games of the VII Olympiad. At an appearance before the committee in Antwerp, Elwood Brown, who was the Director of Physical Education for the IC/YMCA, presented a plan to collaborate with the IOC. Back then, it was actually the YMCA that had the more global reach and was leading the way in the development of sport outside of Europe, especially in Asia.

Brown extolled the virtues of the YMCA's promotion machine. It had nearly one hundred trained physical directors in twenty-five countries and its work was "in harmony with Olympic standards."[10] He argued that the YMCA could "quickly increase the number of countries for sending qualified competitors to the quadrennial contests." While the IOC organized the Olympic Games, it was the YMCA that was organizing sport at the continental level. This gave the YMCA real power and influence.

Brown gave three examples of the YMCA's work in organizing regional or continental games: the Far Eastern Games,[11] the South American International Games,[12] and the Indian Empire Games (which later became the British Empire Games and then the Commonwealth Games). In the case of all three games, Brown stressed that all of the promotion work was done by the YMCA.[13] He asked the IOC to consider six suggestions, including that the Far Eastern Games be recognized by the IOC and incorporated into its global program. More importantly for the "file", Brown wanted the IOC to work with the YMCA Movement to "[i]nvite countries which are not represented on the International Olympic Committee and have never sent an athlete to the Olympic Games to send one or more observers to the 1924 Games"[14] in Paris. Although he did not specifically reference Palestine, we begin to see movement in the "file" around the Paris Games, first by Maccabi Palestine. By 1930, the Jerusalem YMCA also asserted itself as a representative of Palestinian Olympic interests, and the Maccabis and Zionists engaged the Association (and Arab sport constituents that it represented) to form a Palestine Olympic Games Association (POGA). Such associations characterized some of the early Olympic activity around the world. They would convene before an Olympic Games to handle the administrative and financial requirements associated with sending a team to the Games. Unfortunately, the POGA never came to fruition. This context of failure is critical to understanding why Waldo Heinrichs was so important to a Palestine Olympic initiative. It might also explain why he was targeted by the Nazis.

# Author's Note on Presentation
## of Referenced Sources

I targeted this book at a general audience with the desire that it also be useful to traditional academic researchers. There were so many unpublished sources for the book that, throughout the text, I placed their numeric markers in unconventional locations. For example, such instances appear when I introduce a historical document or event based on a rich diary entry or long correspondence. This source might receive a single reference. Several sentences then follow the initial reference that describe the event or scene. In many cases, I used the same words found in the source document without quotation marks, relying upon the reference marker to disclose the source for the corresponding statements in a given passage. I did this to suppress the overall number of pages that would be required for the endnotes at the back of the book (the number of endnotes exceeding sixteen hundred in their condensed form) to simplify reading for the general public. This approach was not an attempt to plagiarize or paraphrase. I simply wanted to facilitate the reading experience for the nonacademic reader while staying true (to the greatest extent possible) to the historical value of the text. Readers will also note a number of reference markers that appear immediately after a nominal currency value. Their corresponding endnote gives the reader a sense of the real dollar value (2019) of the financial amounts shared in the chapters. These conversions were obtained from two online sites that I accessed in the year 2019: https://www.uwyo.edu/numimage/currency.htm and https://futureboy.us/fsp/dollar.fsp. All web links were valid at the time of submission of the manuscript for publication. Regarding the three passages of scripture in the Epigraph, I chose to use translations so as not to increase the risk of a printing error in the original languages. Readers should refer to the original languages and source texts for the most accurate meaning of the three passages. In the case of Yosef Yekutieli, in the narrative I used his Hebrew name, but the archives that bear his name use the anglicized version of it (Joseph Yekutieli).

I recognize that my approach might create some disagreement in terms of method of construction, but it was an editorial decision that, in the end, I was comfortable with (after providing this disclosure). Readers may consult the archives identified in the relevant appendix to review the original documents. In many cases, the archives digitized the material after I accessed it and it is now available online. Inquiries about and reactions to the the book can be sent electronically to TheFile1936@outlook.com.

I compiled Appendix 2 using sources obtained in the archives consulted (see Appendix 1) as well as from Kisch (1938), Bentwich and M. Kisch (1966), Mandell (1971), Guttmann (1984), Segev (1991), Wasserstein (1991), Wigoder (ed.) (1994), Segev (1999), Brenner and Reuveni (eds.) (2006), Mendelsohn (ed.) (2008), Wawrzyn (2013), the New York Times, Jewish Daily Bulletin, Jewish Telegraphic Agency, Associated Press, Jewish Virtual Library (jewishvirtuallibrary.org), and Wikipedia (wikipedia.org).

The views or opinions expressed in this book, and the context in which the images are used, do not necessarily reflect the views or policy of, nor imply approval or endorsement by, the United States Holocaust Memorial Museum, and any other organization, archives, or person.

# CHAPTER 1

# Soldier Sons

Exactly forty years before the Munich Massacre, three men would begin cooperating on the formation of a representative national sport governing body for Palestine. Two were ardent Zionists, the third a Christian who was deeply religious by nature yet equally radical on social progress. All three had served in the First World War, formidable heroes and personalities in their own right. All three loved sports, each dedicated to its practice irrespective of race, creed, or nationality.

Their conversations appear to have caught the attention of the darker emerging forces of the 1930s. In the ongoing efforts to defeat the boycott campaign against the 1936 Berlin Games and admit Palestine to the International Olympic Committee, a veritable cesspool of charges, collusion, and intrigue emerged from a Nazi cell that became active in Jerusalem in the lead-up to the Games. Although defeated in war, the legacy of the Nazis' actions seems to have affected Olympic history for decades. So deeply rooted was the Arab refusal of cooperation with Jews on joint sport governance (Olympic or otherwise) that it altered the course of sport history.

This is a cautionary tale about what could have been in sport, told for the benefit of all those who seek to learn from the past and yearn for a more positive future on the field of play. Everyone is an ideologue; what counts is how we control and share our ideologies. Time is a valuable lens through which we can better understand our past and try to change course for the future. The time has arrived for an Olympic Truce in the Israeli-Palestinian conflict.

# Yosef Yekutieli,
## The Maccabi Soldier[1]

It was mid-1934 and the world was tumbling toward new darkness. The invitation to the Games of the XI Olympiad in Berlin finally arrived at P.O. Box 129, Tel Aviv, Palestine. But this invitation was special. It had the attention of Hitler's Reich Minister of Propaganda, Joseph Goebbels.

To open or not to open? The president of the Olympic Committee and his honorary secretary Yosef Yekutieli discussed how to respond. Rumors were already circulating in the press that the president had come to some type of arrangement with senior Nazi officials,[2] and he wanted the matter cleared up.

Some saw Yekutieli as an angel of God[3] destined to bring the light out from the east[4] and shine it on this dark world. It was his purpose. It was why he was born. Swarthy[5] and rough-hewn, he was the sage of the Maccabi Jewish sports movement in British Palestine. Armed with a volley of inspirational words, words meant to pierce the hearts of Jewish youth,[6] he would now direct his arrows at the International Olympic Committee for what he perceived to be its failure in its duty to withdraw the hosting rights for the Olympic Games from Germany. He would let the IOC know the position of the Jews of Palestine. The time had arrived for the "Maccabi Soldier."[7]

First a number of quiet meetings needed to take place, correspondences sent. All following accepted protocol, diplomatic channels, a quiet but commanding strategy. The fate of Jews in Germany—loyal citizens being stripped of their rights every day—hung in the balance. The boat could not be rocked too much. When Yekutieli and the Palestine Olympic Committee's president finished settling the words of the official correspondence, Palestine's position was clear: it would decline to go to the Berlin Games. It would boycott.

A few weeks after Palestine formally declined the invitation, Yekutieli's door of opportunity to speak more frankly opened. He received a private letter in January 1935[8] from Sigfrid Edström, the president of the International Amateur Athletic Federation (IAAF) and a member of the executive commission of the IOC. Yekutieli responded to him in March.[9]

He probably sat at his desk in his office at the Maccabi House, or *Bayt HaMaccabi* in Hebrew. It was the home of Maccabi Tel Aviv. The sports club was the most active Maccabi club in Mandate Palestine. From its humble two-story Bauhaus building in the White City, Yekutieli was helping to build the Jewish national home. In front of him might have been his typewriter. Surrounding him were probably shelves filled with folders, folders filled with words that had set in motion Palestine's various sport federations and their affiliations to international sport governing bodies. From here he had called forth the Jewish youth of the world to the shores of the eastern Mediterranean for the First Maccabiad (or *Maccabiah* in Hebrew), the first Jewish Olympics. From here he would tell the IOC that Palestine's Jews were not interested in the Nazi Olympics' concept of the equality of mankind.

Edström had appealed to Yekutieli on his private letterhead, which meant that Yekutieli could respond as he truly felt, without the formalities of his position. The Swede had tried to convince him of the better policy, for Palestine to participate in the Games, thereby strengthening the position of Jews in Germany. Yekutieli was not fooled.

Yekutieli pulled out a sheet of the stationery designed for the Federation of the Amateur Sports Clubs of Palestine (FASCP). He had been instrumental in founding the organization on December 26, 1931, at the annual meeting of Maccabi Palestine in Rehovot.[10]

He began his three-page reply to Edström. His fingers clicked at the keys.

He told Edström how pleased he was that someone of his caliber and standing in international sport had chosen to start a conversation on the equality of mankind. He proceeded to instruct Edström on how he and Mr. Avery Brundage, the president of the American Olympic Association, had been led astray[11] on their investigative trip to Germany. He asserted forcefully that Jewish sport associations in Germany could not possibly be relied upon to represent the facts under the fear of Nazi terror.[12] Yekutieli cited the example of severe punishment for a Catholic club that had allowed a Jew to stand on its field of play. He quoted the final summation of the German court to Edström: "He who cultivates such contemptible relations with the Jews is not worthy of the name 'German.'"[13]

He continued, referring Edström's attention to the signs hanging outside twenty-two of Germany's thirty-two stadiums that read "Jews, negros, and dogs are prohibited to enter."[14] And on top of all that, he reminded him of the Aryan paragraph, a new law aimed at "protecting" Aryan sportsmen from any competition by prohibiting their meeting with non-Aryans on the field of play.[15]

Yekutieli continued: In sports and the Olympic Games, the Jewish race had nothing to be afraid of. When the German tribes were wild and uncivilized, the Jewish King Hordus financed the 192nd ancient Olympic Games and was the sole judge and distributor of prizes to the winners. "Fate itself has made the farce shown of the Nazi teachings appear ridiculous, for even to-day at the head of the Olympic Committee stands the German Jew Lewald."[16] Then Yekutieli admitted that the explanation that the Palestine Olympic Committee was young was merely an excuse for not participating in the Olympic Games.[17]

After finishing his letter to Edström, Yekutieli probably went outside and stood at the edge of Maccabi Tel Aviv's tennis court. Through the chain-link fence, the setting sun would have bathed the emerging Bauhaus buildings of the White City with flaming hues.

## 2.

Yekutieli was born in modern-day Belarus in 1897 to a Zionist family. In 1908, his family emigrated to Ottoman Palestine (Eretz Israel) from the Russian Empire because of Zionism. At the time, the State of Israel as we know it today was only a dream in the minds of a few Jews, and the great fire of Zionism that built Israel was still only sparks and smoldering kindling. The small sliver of territory on the southeastern shores of the Mediterranean Sea was still under Turkish (Ottoman) rule. Nonetheless, Yekutieli was a believer in the words of Theodor Herzl, the author of *The Jewish State*. Herzl was a man considered by all to be the spiritual founder of Zionism, the organized movement to create a Jewish state. Herzl said: "If you will it, there is no legend."[18]

Yekutieli was the type who would will. Out of nothing, he would create the organizational architecture of the Zionist sport movement and prepare it for its affiliation to the IOC.

But before the First World War, Yekutieli could only be inspired by the 1912 Olympic Games in Stockholm, Sweden after reading a publication about them. He was just fifteen years old when these Olympics planted in him the dream of organizing a great Jewish Olympiad—what we know today as the Maccabi Games.

By 1917, Yekutieli had turned twenty years old. The First World War was on the threshold of its final year. Europe was preparing for the collapse of the Ottoman Empire. Friday, November 2, 1917, would be the most important Sabbath for Jews in nearly two thousand years. That day, the United Kingdom's foreign secretary, Arthur Balfour, wrote a letter to Lord Rothschild of the Jewish community in England. In it, he pledged support for the creation of a national home for Jews in Palestine. Known as the Balfour Declaration, its brevity and simplicity were no measure of the seismic shift that it would create. The Jewish state was no longer simply the dream it had been when Yekutieli arrived in Palestine in 1908. Suddenly, structural foundations for the emergence of it were firmly planted in an international order.

A mere forty-one days later, General Edmund Allenby, British commander of the Egyptian Expeditionary Force that defeated the German commander of Ottoman forces in Palestine, dismounted his horse and entered the Jaffa Gate of the walled city of Jerusalem at twelve noon. Allenby declared martial law, which lasted three and a half years.

In 1920, Yekutieli moved to Jerusalem to work for *HaMisrad HaEretz Israeli*. Known as the Palestine Office when Palestine was under Ottoman control, this organization eventually became the Palestine Zionist Executive in the early period of the British Mandate and, eventually, the Jewish Agency. In all its forms and before May 15, 1948, this organization represented Zionist interests to whomever was in charge in Palestine (whether an Ottoman, military, or British administration). Since the creation of the State of Israel, it has been known as the Jewish Agency for Israel.

In June 1920, a civil administration ended the military rule declared by Allenby. The League of Nations approved a British Mandate for Palestine and began work to set up a government that could represent the interests of Palestinian Muslims, Christians, and Jews. The Mandate recognized the Zionist organization for which Yekutieli worked as a

Jewish Agency. This agency would function as a public body to work with the British administration in the interests of the Jewish population in the country.[19] For Zionism and Zionists, this meant working constantly for the establishment of the Jewish national home. Yekutieli, an unapologetic Zionist, was undoubtedly energized and got straight to work on his sport dreams.

In 1924, Yekutieli married Yehudit Weiss, the daughter of Akiva Aryeh Weiss, the founder of Tel Aviv. He had met her at the city's club branch of the Maccabi sports movement. Maccabi Tel Aviv, from which Yekutieli would execute much of his voluntary sports work in support of Zionism, was central to his life and is central to the "file."

## 3.

The first Zionist sport club in Palestine was set up in 1906, two years before Yekutieli arrived in Palestine.[20] It was called the Jaffa Athletic Association "Rishon-le-Zion."[21] In 1907, this club moved to the Gymnasia Herzliya, the first Hebrew high school in Palestine,[22] where it introduced gymnastics into the curriculum.[23] In 1912, the Maccabi World Union (MWU) Palestine Branch was established.[24]

With Allenby's 1917 declaration of martial law by a British military administration, Zionist sport in Palestine finally could flourish. Yekutieli wasted no time. In 1919, he organized the first structured meeting of the MWU Palestine Branch,[25] to which eleven Zionist sport organizations affiliated. These Maccabi sport organizations were not the only organizations practicing sport activities or physical education of some kind in the territory; however, they were the first that had an ideological orientation toward the emerging global Olympic Movement.

This Olympic orientation found its roots in Yekutieli's dream of the Maccabiad. Although centered on the Jewish athlete, Yekutieli seemed intuitively cognizant of a possible convergence of Maccabi activity with Olympic interests. The Olympic Movement was still young, and the Zionist movement included many highly trained sport-minded Jews in European countries who were seminal to the birth of modern sport. The Maccabi Movement in Palestine, buttressed by this talent's emigration to the country, could help the Olympic Movement broaden its reach.

When the 1912 Stockholm Olympics inspired Yekutieli, four individuals were in attendance who would eventually become presidents of the IOC and govern it for the next sixty years.[26] Each would interact during his tenure as president with Yekutieli or an ambassador of his Maccabi sport dreams: Baron Pierre de Coubertin (P. 1896–1925), Count Henri de Baillet-Latour (P. 1925–1942), Sigfrid Edström (P. 1946-1952), and Avery Brundage (P. 1952–1972). In 1912, Brundage was a track athlete for the United States in Stockholm.[27]

Yekutieli's Olympic dreams would eventually become Brundage's worst nightmare. In September 1972, only seven days before the end of his tenure as IOC president, Brundage spoke in the Olympic stadium at the memorial service for eleven Israeli Olympic athletes killed by Palestinians in what has become known to many as the Munich Massacre.[28]

But, in earlier, happier times, Yekutieli's Jewish Olympics served as a key measure by which a Palestine Olympic Committee—or more accurately, a nascent Olympic Committee of Israel—would demonstrate its organizational capabilities and reliability as a custodian of the Olympic ideal. In 1934, the IOC recognized a Maccabi-dominated Palestine Olympic Committee as the official Olympic committee from British Mandate Palestine (in time for it to participate in the 1936 Berlin Games). Despite a tragic future at Munich, the seed that Stockholm planted in Yekutieli's heart and mind blossomed into a national sports movement that defined the rest of his life. Breathing the fresh air of his emerging country's Mediterranean freedom, Yekutieli pulled off the First Maccabiad. It all started like this...

## 4.

Yekutieli mounted the Sunbeam motorcycle[29] to get a feel for it. He chose it purposefully because of the reliable statistics he had read about its performance.[30] He needed a bike that would respond reliably to the strain of a 9,375-kilometer[31] round-trip transcontinental tour he was organizing between Tel Aviv and London. His team of eleven Maccabi riders planned to arrive by early June 1931. Yekutieli probably liked the Sunbeam because it was a gentleman's bike, something that would soften his harder Russian and oriental Palestinian profile in front of his

English hosts at the end of his journey in London. Perceptions were important.

Organizing the journey was not an easy task. The Palestine branch of the Maccabi sports movement was not exactly rich. The global financial crisis had affected everyone. Yekutieli needed to account for every penny spent. He even requested the Royal Automobile Club d'Egypte in Cairo to reimburse him for a few outstanding Palestine pounds when the team returned to Palestine.[32] (One Palestine pound in 1931 is equivalent to $119 today.)

Yekutieli worked hard to cut a deal with the Sunbeam's manufacturer. He sought free service, supply of parts, benzine, and oil at Sunbeam service stations along the journey's route.[33] In exchange, and as part of a lofty sales pitch, he extolled the values and scale of the Maccabi sport movement, noting that it had over 120,000 members worldwide.[34] Surely the tour could act as publicity for Sunbeam in this small yet significant emerging market? After all, the Sunbeam brand was meagerly represented in Palestine.[35] Perhaps the British company could benefit from the tour by selling more of its bikes into the emerging Jewish economy in Palestine. And what a sight the riders would be, racing across rugged terrain toward reception in London, towards recognition. He could feel the heat of high sun, the roar of their bikes, the smell of the fuel lingering on the air.

Unfortunately, Sunbeam did not accept the pitch. That was not going to stop Yekutieli. He organized his group of bikers, anyway, on a mixed fleet of motorcycles: FN, Saroléa, Indian, and Ariel.[36] He continued his efforts to obtain mechanical support for the tour, calling and corresponding with a number of companies including the Shell Oil Company of Palestine,[37] Vacuum Oil Company,[38] and the Asiatic Petroleum Company.[39] He was not very successful and the trip would be run on a shoestring.

Aside from the logistics of operating and maintaining the machines, Yekutieli also needed to navigate the emerging transnational road network between West Asia and Europe. The riders' route would take them to and through large Jewish communities. Along the way they would encourage these communities to send delegations to his dream of the First Maccabiad, scheduled to take place in Tel Aviv in

1932. Yekutieli had aligned the sports competition with the 1932 Levant Fair. This important trade exposition would highlight the full range of the emergent Jewish economy centered in Tel Aviv.

The motorcyclists carried Palestinian passports as they rode. They would cross the frontiers of Syria, Turkey, Bulgaria, Romania, Yugoslavia, Czechoslovakia, Germany, Poland, Lithuania, Latvia, Holland, Belgium, England, France, Switzerland, and Italy.[40] Yekutieli corresponded with the automobile clubs in these countries to obtain maps identifying the roads that were suitable for motorcycles.[41] He requested instructions regarding rites of passage and payment of customs, as well as the requirements surrounding international driver's licenses, road certificates, and triptyques (customized passes for importing motorized vehicles).[42] Of course, the team needed visas, available only from the consulates of each of the countries along the route.[43] The Automobil-Club der Schweiz (Switzerland) was particularly organized and thorough in its response to his request for information.[44] It provided details about motor traffic on Sundays and holidays, noting the speed limits between and within villages in all cantons of Switzerland (in typical Swiss organizational style and precision).

Yekutieli packed his business cards. He would grab the attention of athletes and spectators, of a world waiting for bigger sporting events and grander outcomes. He would build the First Maccabiad with paper, ink, and sweat equity. Yekutieli's business cards read:[45]

**JOSEPH YEKUTIELI**
Secretary of the 1st Maccabiad
(taking place in Tel-Aviv, spring 1932)
Captain of the Pro-Maccabia Motortrip
—TEL-AVIV – LONDON—
TEL-AVIV
P.O.B. 129

As the journey got underway, the motorcycle tour was followed by the press. They received an enthusiastic reception from the Jewish community in Salonika, Greece.[46] Yekutieli passed on the greetings of Mayor Dizengoff of the White City to Mayor Vamvakas of ancient Salonica, just a few weeks before the Camp Campbell pogrom there in which five hundred Jewish homes would be burned. Yekutieli could not have known of the destruction awaiting the quiet sun-soaked city.

The grueling leg to Sofia, Bulgaria, was next on the bikers' agenda. Shell decided to support this leg of the tour with fuel.[47] Another company gave lubricants.[48] The team departed at 4:00 a.m.,[49] crossing rolling mountains and sheer rock face, urging their bikes forward on narrow roadways past forests tall with age. They rode towards an uncertain outcome.

In Poland, some of the bikes began to break down. The strain of the trip was certain: the men and bikes would not continue without repair. Yekutieli worried about more than the bikes. Their visas were set to expire. More time in Poland meant legal trouble. Yekutieli's worries were well founded. The team was arrested.[50] Fortunately, the Polish authorities released the team after news coverage of their arrest circulated in the media. With the bikes repaired and their incarceration over, the team carried on to London.

On June 1, 1931, the *Manchester Evening Chronicle*[51] reported the imminent arrival of the Jewish sport ambassadors from Palestine. The team crossed into London on fumes of fatigue and satisfaction. They had made it. While in London, the Lord Mayor personally passed a letter to Yekutieli, which he asked to be read at the opening ceremony of the "great Jewish Olympiad to be held in the Holy Land"[52] the following year. Following "big programmes"[53] there, the riders continued on to Manchester on June 19.

Surely Yekutieli would have reflected with great satisfaction upon the completion of the tour. The First Maccabiad had been advertised to thousands of potential participants, and vital relationships were made for the Maccabi cause. Yekutieli and his team had accomplished an irrational, outsized task of cross-continental advertising unimaginable in their day and age. And for good cause.

Only ten years earlier, Yekutieli's emerging sporting zeal would only be matched by the arrival of another unsung hero, Frederick Hermann Kisch. Despite his extremely important role in Zionist history, Kisch is largely unrecognized among the pantheon of Zionist leaders that includes Herzl, Ben Gurion, and others. Perhaps it was because of his untimely death. Or perhaps because he became the president of the first Palestine Olympic Committee.

# Frederick Kisch,
# Soldier and Zionist[54]

On the pristine, spring morning of April 7, 1943, Colonel Kisch was the chief engineer of the Allies' Western Desert Forces in the North African campaign.[55] Known to friends and family as Fred, he was constructing a deviation in Wadi Akarit through minefields that German Axis forces had laid in the dry seasonal river bed.[56] Germany's Field Marshal Erwin Rommel, the Desert Fox, had staked out the elevated land just to the north of the *wadi* as a good defensive position.[57] By this time in the war, the Axis was struggling and would soon capitulate in Tunis.

For Kisch, clearing a few mines and building a small bridge were simple tasks. A recipient of the Croix de Guerre with Palm for his combat service in the First World War, he served from 1909[58] to 1919[59] in the British army and was an experienced sapper. He was well regarded as an innovator in the regularization of mine warfare and established the mine-marking system that was critical to the success of the North Africa campaign. When the Second World War broke out, Kisch reenlisted enthusiastically from the army reserve to combat the Nazis. He wrote: "However imperfectly we may deserve victory, the enemy most certainly deserve destruction, without which there is no future worth having for the world."[60]

As Kisch and three other officers worked to clear some of the mines, the calm of that morning belied the dangers of the task, the horrific battles fought there, and the effort to liberate those suffering in North Africa under Nazi occupation. German forces had quietly withdrawn from the *wadi* only hours before. Their retreat was the latest of several following their loss of the pivotal Second Battle of El Alamein. Considered the battle that turned the tide on the African front, during El Alamein, the Allies' Eighth Army and those of the German and Italian Axis faced off in the Egyptian desert.

The combined power of the opposing armies numbered conservatively over 300,000 men, 1,500 tanks, 600 armored cars, 1,500 planes, 1,400 pieces of artillery, and 2,000 antitank guns.[61] In the initial volley of fire that started the battle on the quiet autumn evening of October 23, 1942, over a thousand Allied guns rumbled for nearly six hours, firing an estimated half million shells across a forty-mile north–south front.[62] And that was just to soften up the Germans. The ensuing battle and resulting Allied victory on November 11, 1942, is what placed Kisch westward in this Tunisian *wadi* the following spring.

The calm of that morning might have allowed Kisch to reflect on his leading role as chief engineer in one of the largest logistical wartime operations ever, a role that helped tip the entire war in the Allies' favor. Winston Churchill is reported to have said of the battle, "It may almost be said, 'Before Alamein we never had a victory. After Alamein we never had a defeat.'"[63]

Kisch had ensured a more seamless supply of armaments, water, and fuel to the Eighth Army than had his counterparts to the Axis forces. This support was very personal to him as a Jew: only a few weeks prior, the Eighth Army had liberated Tripoli. On the Sabbath of January 30, the *Tripoli Times* noted the importance of Kisch's Jewishness (as a senior liberating soldier) to those who had been "so cruelly oppressed under the Nazi Fascist regime, among them leading representatives of Tripoli's 20,000 Jewish population…They said it was the happiest Sabbath of their lives."[64]

Furthermore, Kisch's engineering capabilities had also supported the first liberation of an Axis concentration camp, one of his happiest achievements in life: "Cyrenaica's 3,500 Jews had been deported to a camp at Gialdo in the desert, while the Jews of Tripoli had been pressed into labour gangs…[T]he inmates at Gialdo were the first of the few who survived Hitler's 'Final Solution,'"[65] the implementation of which had been secured at the Wannsee Conference on January 20, 1942. Compared to the eleven million estimated Jews that Adolf Eichmann presented at this meeting to Nazi colleagues as targets for liquidation, and the estimated six million who were in the process of being murdered under Nazi control across the Mediterranean in Europe, Kisch's role in saving a few tens of thousands of Jews in these North African provinces would be a small victory against evil.

Such noble and grand achievements in war. But what of his beginnings?

# 2.

Born in Darjeeling, India, in 1888, Frederick Hermann Kisch was the son of Hermann Kisch of the Indian Civil Service.[66] He was the descendant of a renowned Jewish family that had settled in Prague sometime in the eighteenth century.[67] His ancestors had acquired the House at the Two Golden Bears, named for its elaborate residential portal.[68]

Kisch's ancestor Benjamin established the English branch of the family when he emigrated to London and practiced as a physician.[69] His son Joseph followed the family practice, which allowed him to support five children, the youngest of which was Hermann, Frederick Kisch's father.[70] A successful graduate of Trinity College, Cambridge, Hermann Kisch entered the Indian Civil Service and was stationed in Bengal in 1873.[71] When Kisch was born, his father was the Postmaster-General of Bengal, eventually serving as the Director-General of the Postmaster of India.[72] Hermann Kisch was an early convert to Zionism, many years before the movement had gained widespread acceptance.[73] However, because Palestine was closed to Jewish immigration under the rule of the Ottomans, Kisch's father supported the concept of a national home for the Jews in Africa.[74]

The first site that Zionists considered for a Jewish state in Africa was Cyrenaica, but they abandoned it as an option because of lack of water.[75] Despite considering other options for a Jewish national home, Hermann Kisch always carried a map of Palestine in his pocket.[76] He died in early 1943, just weeks before Kisch found himself in Wadi Akarit. Kisch wrote about him: "I owe him my Jewish consciousness, which brought me to Palestine."[77]

In addition to obtaining his Jewish consciousness from his father, Kisch acquired two key skills growing up in India. The first was his language ability. As a young boy, it was reported that he spoke Hindustani better than English.[78] When, in 1910, he returned to India and joined the Military Works Service and India Public Works Department, Kisch easily picked up Baluchi, Persian, and Pashtu.[79] He was also capable in French, having been attached to the Paris Peace Conference[80] (which ended the First World War with the Treaty of Versailles on June 28, 1919). The second skill was the British administrative competency that

13

he used to manage the competing interests of multiethnic and religious communities. As a boy in India, he would have acquired an intuition regarding the distinctions between caste and religious affiliation and how they influenced politics. Both these skills would serve Kisch well in Palestine when he became chairman of the Palestine Zionist Executive. In Palestine, he would have to learn Hebrew and balance many competing interests.

Kisch was approached by the World Zionist Organization in part because of his well-received performance during his attachment to the Paris Peace Conference. Through this work, Kisch had met Lord Balfour, the author of the Balfour Declaration, and some other future Zionist leaders.[81] As a British Jew experienced in the British military and colonial administrations, Kisch was an ideal pick. Although he had briefly met the president of the World Zionist Organization, Dr. Chaim Weizmann, in June of 1917,[82] Kisch had never been affiliated with Zionist organizations and was well connected because of his colonial and war service.

In November 1922, only five years after the release of the Balfour Declaration, Kisch arrived in Palestine with Dr. Weizmann to take on the tasks of his new role as chairman of the Palestine Zionist Executive. In doing so, he became the official representative in Palestine of the World Zionist Organization, whose Congress (held every two years in Europe) was the supreme organ of the global Zionist movement that advanced the principle of the return of the Children of Israel to their ancient home.[83] Kisch's main task in Palestine was to use his administration skills and British contacts to coalesce the wide range of competing Zionist ideas regarding the kind of Zion to be created and the way to create it.[84] He was perceived as the personal representative of Dr. Weizmann himself in Palestine.[85]

Britain had only acquired the Mandate for Palestine months prior, and Kisch got straight to work. One cannot overstate the centrality and formative nature of Kisch's tenure as chairman for the eventual creation of the State of Israel. As a movement, Zionism was an incubator for some of the greatest social and political leaders of the twentieth century. But much like Yekutieli, Kisch is not often considered among this pantheon. Yet without Kisch's work in the critical period between 1922 and 1931—when the first civil administration in Palestine opened the doors for the realization of the Jewish national home—it could be argued that Israel's chances for emerging victorious in its 1948–1949 War of Independence would have been much slimmer.

As chairman of the Executive, Kisch was perfectly positioned to change the balance of forces on the ground. His role made him effectively the executor of the World Zionist Congress' financial account in Palestine. He oversaw the spending of every penny and was proud that an audit several months in length by Price, Waterhouse & Company resulted in a determination of the "unchallengeable correctness…of financial procedure and control."[86] The financial resources that Kisch oversaw undoubtedly supported Yekutieli's activities with the MWU Palestine Branch, over which Kisch was invited to preside.

Kisch was also in the position to negotiate with his counterparts in the British government of Palestine the quotas for entry visas of European Jews to Palestine. He presided over Zionist spending pertaining to the fourth Aliyah, the fourth wave of Jewish immigration to Palestine (1924–1928),[87] which provided the framework to absorb the approximately 225,000 Jews that fled Nazi persecution in Europe during the fifth Aliyah (1929–1936).[88] In a meeting with the British Zionist Federation after his retirement as chairman of the Palestine Zionist Executive, "[Kisch] pointed with justifiable pride to the growth of Jewish settlement during his term of office. In the nine years from 1922 to 1931, Palestine's Jewish population increased by 100,000 [which includes part of the third and fifth Aliyahs] and the proportion of the whole population made up by Jews rose from 11 to 17 per cent…"[89]

After leaving his post as chairman, Kisch decided to settle in Palestine, taking up the life of a civilian as a Palestinian citizen. He ran the Anglo-Palestine Fruit Export, Ltd. in which he lived out his belief of a pragmatic approach to the indigenous Arab population.[90] He employed Arabs in his company in near-equal numbers as a testament to his faith in the infinite possibilities of a broader Jewish-Arab cooperation.[91] This period of his life witnessed his many philanthropic and other social activities and engagements.

## 3.

Kisch was an active Mason in Palestinian lodges that brought together Jews, Arabs, and British.[92] He helped found the King Solomon Quarries Lodge of Master Masons in Jerusalem, whose proceedings took place in the ancient quarries of the Jerusalem Temple.[93] Kisch also loved music and drama, supported the Mordechai Golinkin opera company *Habimah* (a Hebrew language dramatic company from Russia), and was president of one of the committees associated with the Palestine Arts Theatre.[94] He was close friends with Bronislaw Huberman and helped him set up the Palestine Symphony Orchestra.[95]

Kisch remained active with the Jewish Agency in his civilian life. He chaired its Ben-Yehuda Memorial Trust, named after the Russian Jewish dreamer who modernized Hebrew for the emerging Jewish national home.[96] This trust completed the modern Hebrew lexicon. In media affairs, Kisch was chairman of the board of the *Palestine Post*,[97] the most significant English-language daily in Palestine.

All these associations and activities came to a sudden end with the outbreak of World War II in September 1939. Except two. The first was the Palestine Symphony Orchestra and is identified in Kisch's biography.[98] The second was his role as president of the Palestine Olympic Committee, which is not referenced in either his biography, his published *Palestine Diary*, the *Encyclopedia of Zionism*, or any other mainstream publication about him. From his residence in Haifa, Kisch directed the most sensitive of his projects. Immediately after his resignation from the Palestine Zionist Executive, Kisch became president of the Palestine Olympic Committee.

## 4.

As the president of the Palestine Olympic Committee worked with his three fellow soldiers to clear the mines in Wadi Akarit on that beautiful spring morning, "one of them kicked the trip wire of a picket mine. It killed them all."[99] Buried within one hundred yards of where they fell, their graves are still present to this day in Tunisia.[100]

At the time, Kisch's death was a shock and led to emotional tributes from the greatest Zionists.

Moshe Sharett, who played an important role in securing the immigration quotas for the Second Maccabiah and became Israel's foreign secretary (presiding over the state's integration into the United Nations), eulogized Kisch as follows: "Peace unto your dust in foreign soil, Jewish soldier! Your stout heart was beating for the redemption of Israel. Because of the contribution which you have made through your life's work for our Homeland, and because of your self-sacrifice, your name shall forever blossom in the memory of our people."[101]

Dr. Weizmann, Kisch's former boss in the World Zionist Organization and Israel's first president, remembered Kisch with the following words: "The modest, graceful-mannered young man, whom I had first met in Britain's War Office, travelled a long way during his comparatively short life. But he lived a full, harmonious life, and died a clean harmonious death. With his life and with his death he proved that one can be an excellent Zionist and a good patriotic Englishman, and thus, I hope, silenced those who still talk about 'divided loyalties' and 'inner conflicts.'"[102]

Yekutieli established a memorial track-and-field meet in Kisch's name in Tel Aviv. It was held annually until Israel's War of Independence (1948–1949). A gold medal from the competition, dated May 13, 1945, portrays the famous military portrait of Kisch on the obverse. On the reverse are the Olympic Symbol—its five interlocking rings—and the words "Palestine Olympic Committee" in English, Arabic, and Hebrew—although the Hebrew translation actually reads "Olympic Committee in the Land of Israel." Despite his glorious life replete with achievement and a heroic death, today many Zionists (especially those outside of Israel) do not know of Kisch and his Olympic accomplishments; this despite a collective agricultural settlement in the Lower Galilee,[103] a forest in the Judean hills,[104] and an electrical engineering lab at the Technion in Haifa[105] bearing his name.

Perhaps this has something to do with the Olympic office he moved from Tel Aviv to Haifa in 1938, and how his and Yekutieli's associations with the Olympic Movement were drenched in blood on the world stage in 1972. Kisch's role in Palestine Olympic history seems to have been scrubbed clean, perhaps as a way to sanitize a painful period for Israel in Olympic history. *The File* restores his rightful position in this history.

## Waldo Heinrichs Sr., Watchman—Jerusalem

He would be called the luckiest man in the First World War.[106] By July 8, 1918, the press was reporting the exploits of 1st Lieutenant Waldo Huntley Heinrichs, who would pursue enemy German planes until he exhausted his ammunition. Heinrichs, or "Fish" as he was called by family and friends,[107] was a fighter pilot with the 95th Aero Squadron, the "first to the front"[108] for the United States in aerial combat missions over German-held territory. Definitely a fighter, he suggested[109] the Kicking Mule design and insignia on the squadron's planes. The army mule was West Point's mascot.[110] The 95th Aero Squadron even bought a donkey that had been used for waste removal at the airfield and made it their live mascot, naming him Jake.[111]

But September 17, 1918, was not going to be a routinely success-ful day for Heinrichs, even if it would be his luckiest. He was about to become a "Fish" out of water.

After a late breakfast and a warm shave, Heinrichs was assigned to fly No. 1 right that afternoon.[112] The squadron's formation sighted eight Fokker D.VII-type German planes off in the distance.[113] With the sun behind the Americans, the pilots cruised at 1,800 meters over a broken layer of clouds.[114] Suddenly, Heinrichs spotted an additional six Fokkers behind him, who turned to attack.[115] His gun had just jammed[116] and he was a sitting duck. He began to drop altitude to head home but was confronted by a "Boche"[117,118] that opened fired.[119] In attempting to outmaneuver, Heinrichs flew directly into the line of fire of another enemy plane.

As he watched tracer bullets "spider web"[120] from the enemy muzzle, he felt a terrible blow to his left cheek as though his "whole lower jaw were shot away" and became a "gaping hole."[121] Heinrichs spat out a mouthful of teeth and blood and then felt another round pierce his left arm.[122] He tried to let open the throttle, but his machine would not respond. He looked down to troubleshoot and noticed his arm "dan-gling uselessly"[123] by his side. More bullets "came crashing through the machine"[124] as blood poured down his throat, choking him. He coughed and spat out another mouthful of teeth, only to have the wind blow them and his blood back into his face and over his goggles, effectively blinding him.[125] Then another round came through his fuselage, striking him in the thigh.[126] He gave the stick a sharp tug, his plane turtled, and he knew the game was up. With his engine hit, and outnumbered seven to one with a jammed gun, Heinrichs started a rapid dive, seriously injured.[127]

As he took off his goggles, he saw the bullet hole in his windshield, the spider-web[128] of cracks that testified to its passage, and the shredded leather interior of his cockpit.[129] It was a miracle that he was alive. Heinrichs "thanked heaven that the…[SPAD was]…the fastest machine on the front on a nose dive."[130] He snapped off his switch to reduce the possibility of a fire during his crash landing.[131] As he peacefully looked off into the distance at the lakes of La Chausée for the last time (which marked the front lines), he tasted his blood, felt the rush of wind entering his mouth through the hole in the side of his face, and knew that he would not make it back.

His SPAD hurtled to the ground, followed all the way down by one of the enemy planes.[132] He dodged a telegraph cable that suddenly appeared, and miraculously brought the plane down safely—his wing snapping a 4 x 4 pole as he rolled toward the edge of a wood.[133] Heinrichs reached for his matches to set the plane alight, but he could not hold the box. His useless left arm. Nor could he hold it in his teeth. They had been blown out of his mouth.[134] Heinrichs knew the attempt to torch was useless, although it might have been for the better: the Germans had a reputation for executing enemy pilots who torched their aircraft.

A group of German soldiers, rifles raised, approached Heinrichs from the wood as he slid out of his cockpit, one hand raised in the air in surrender.[135] After they dressed his wounds, one offered him cognac or schnapps, but he could not drink because his mouth "was burning terribly."[136] Heinrichs lay in the hot September sun,[137] clinging to life. Above him flew the "blue nosed striped Fokker"[138] that had given him pursuit. The soldiers standing around him cheered. As a German-American capable of understanding his enemies' words, Heinrichs overheard them confirm that the Fokker belonged to the Red Baron's squadron.[139]

Eventually, a German officer arrived on horseback to take charge. Heinrichs showed the soldiers his identity tag. "*Deutscher Amerikaner*," they exclaimed as they read his name.[140] One of the Germans piped in, "*Heinrichs? Ich bin Heinrichs auch* [I am Heinrichs, too]."[141] Heinrichs could not speak. He signaled the soldiers for paper and pencil. "*Ya, ya,*" one of the soldiers replied. By the time Heinrichs was being put on a stretcher, his plane had vanished on the officer's order.[142]

The Germans slid Heinrichs into a two-wheeled cart with room only for him.[143] A doctor at the dimly lit field dressing station asked Heinrichs if he could have the silver wings from his uniform. As he lay there on the operating table,[144] Heinrichs shook his head before they gave him morphine and he became hazy. He never saw his uniform again.

His captors eventually moved him to another building. They put him in a room filled with "seriously wounded men"[145] in which the orderly sneered at him as he slipped Heinrichs' watch off his wrist.[146] The night settled in. Then it dragged on. Heinrichs was too parched to keep up his constant calls for water.[147] He was also afraid to speak German for fear of letting on that he could understand his captors.[148] A German intelligence officer came in and approached a seriously wounded German in the corner of the room. A crowd gathered around a dim candle. As the soldier's breath became more rapid, shallow, and faint, the candle extinguished and the officers and orderlies left. Later in the night this happened again, with Heinrichs not understanding the significance of the extinguished candle and the departure of the German guests.[149]

The following morning, the Germans transferred Heinrichs to Lazarette St. Klemens. There he came under the care of Catholic nuns, one of whom the wounded had named "Sister Butcher."[150] She launched into a tirade when she learned of Heinrichs' nationality.[151] He was too weak to talk much. His mouth "burned like fire – a terrible, ugly, festering, sulphurous wound."[152] Another nun took charge of him. Schwester [Sister] Patagatha reminded Heinrichs of his mother. Although ruddy in the face and tough, she was kind and sweet to him as she helped save his life by feeding him warm milk four times a day through a tube that she would slide into the side of his face. The ward was filled with skeleton-thin Russians that the wounded soldiers called "Laggers,"[153] a moniker based on the German's heavy use of them in labor camps.

The doctors gave Heinrichs the formal summary of his injuries: bullet graze on left ankle; shrapnel in right hand; bullet cut to bone on right pinky finger; right heel cut by explosive bullet fragments; left elbow pierced by two bullets that blew a hole in his arm the size of his hand and caused a fracture of the left arm three inches above the elbow; explosive bullet from rear in back left of thigh with two-inch-deep flesh wound five inches in length; explosive bullet that entered left cheek, struck teeth, and exploded in his mouth, blowing out the right side of his face and leaving a nasty sulphur-poisoned wound and shredded lip and cheek; fracture of lower front jaw with loss of five front teeth with double hemorrhage of nose and an ear complication; fracture of upper jaw.[154]

After his first medical interventions, a German intelligence officer who resembled the "Hateful Hun" caricatures interrogated him.[155] Heinrichs refused to give him anything more than his "name and rank with squadron"[156] to which he was attached (so that news could be sent to the other side). English and German prisoners told him he was "very, very seriously wounded, too much so to live."[157] But she—Sister Patagatha—pulled him through.

On September 23, "Sister Butcher" came in to tell Heinrichs that his arm would have to come off.[158] He felt convinced, having witnessed himself the "masses of stinking matter" and the "terrible wound"[159] caused by the explosive bullet. So, he turned to Sister Diomedes, the "Sweet Sister," and asked her to cut off his ring finger once his arm was amputated and to return his "sweetheart's Wellesley class ring."[160] Providence intervened, and a decision was made to try cleaning the wound. Heinrichs would keep his arm, although he could not really use it effectively again.

Heinrichs wondered if word had gotten to the American Red Cross at Bern about his capture.[161] He was stabilizing, but was bored and needed to use his time. He managed to get "Sergeant Ya Ya" to deliver pencils and a small black notebook to him. With these simple but precious items, Heinrichs secretly began keeping a diary, which he would stuff into his blood-soaked mattress during the day and pull out at night when the orderlies left.

As the weeks dragged on, Heinrichs got to know the staff at the prison hospital in Metz: Schwester Lucia, more commonly known as

"Sister Butcher"; Schwester Patagatha or "Our Sister," who everyone liked; Schwester Diomedes or "Sweet Sister"; Ober Artz, short in stature and light on words; the "Young Doctor," a Jew; the "New Doctor," a handsome man always wearing a slim, tight-fitting blue overcoat—a perfect gentleman; "Sergeant Ya Ya," a barber in civilian life to whom the prisoners had given this nickname because he responded to every question with "*ya, ya*"; Sergeant Gaston, a French prisoner fluent in four languages and the "official" prison interpreter; Konstantin, a Russian prisoner who helped out with the dressings; and Peter, an African French colonial most proud of his three front teeth filed down to points like a tiger's teeth.[162]

One month after having his mouth and left arm blown open, Heinrichs was finally able to visit a dentist.[163] They gave him cocaine at the *kieferstation* (literally "jaw station")[164] and pulled out two more of his upper teeth ruined by the bullet. The dentist told Heinrichs that he had once visited Dayton. Heinrichs replied that he had played against the football team there while a student at Denison University. When they were done, the dentist told Heinrichs that he would need to come back for more work. He returned seven days later and had an additional three teeth pulled from his upper jaw, causing him to shake like a leaf by the time it was over.[165] The doctors looked over all his wounds and said, "He must have been an athlete before the war."[166]

Another month later came the Armistice. At the eleventh hour of the eleventh day of the eleventh month, the First World War was over. The doctors informed Heinrichs that he was no longer a prisoner and gave him a certificate of his injuries. Six days later, on November 17, 1918, ten weeks after he was shot down, there was a knock at the door. Cheers of joy went up as a secretary of the Young Men's Christian Association (YMCA) entered the ward in his khaki uniform to inform the prisoners of their release. Heinrichs would spend another year convalescing in Europe and New York, but he was well on his way home. He had made it back.[167]

Heinrichs was awarded the Croix de Guerre with Palm, like Kisch. He was honorably discharged a war hero on September 29, 1919.[168] These two war heroes would meet fifteen years later under the Jesus Tower of the Jerusalem YMCA, and Heinrichs would hold sensitive discussions with the highest echelons of the Zionist movement on forming a national governing body of sport in Palestine representative of Muslims, Christians, and Jews. The "New Germany" of Hitler would not be pleased.

2.
———

Who was this person who must have been an athlete before the war? From where did he get his fortitude? Character like this must come from somewhere.

Waldemar Huntley Heinrichs was the second of five children. He was born in Ongole, South India, on July 15, 1891, to Jacob Heinrichs Sr. and Lydia Victoria Conradina Fleischmann.[169] His father hailed from Allenstein, Germany (Prussia) and the family consisted of devout Baptist missionaries. Waldo, as he was called, had four siblings; an older brother named Edgar Jacob and three younger siblings named Doris Ana, Marie Margaret, and Leonard Conrad Fleischmann Heinrichs.[170] Doris would die at the tender age of fourteen. She was a year younger than Heinrichs. This probably strengthened Heinrichs' already inseparable relationship with his brother Edgar, who was a year his senior. They both loved sports and would eventually attend Denison and play football there.

At a young age, the boys were sent to attend First Baptist Bible School of Newton in Newton Center, Massachusetts.[171] Earning "NS" for "Not Satisfactory" in arithmetic on his third-grade report card as a member of "Class B,"[172] it is no surprise that Heinrichs would eventually drop engineering in college. However, this report card also identified that at a young age, Heinrichs was "Honest and Truthful,"[173] characteristics that would define him for the rest of his professional life. In fact, twelve years after Waldo Heinrichs' "homegoing" (how his father Jacob referred to death),[174] his widow, Dorothy Peterson Heinrichs, would write to their son "Junior" and tell them that "Dad blew his top and was totally frank at times…That was really part of his charm in a way."[175] Dishonesty really bothered Heinrichs.

By the ninth grade, Heinrichs was still only "Fair" in math, but he was promoted to the high school by schoolmaster E. M. Copeland.[176]

That year, Miss Barrett, who had watched over the boys at Newton Center, died. Conscious that his mother had been ill, Heinrichs wrote to his father to break the news, demonstrating tremendous maturity and a sensitivity for the feelings of others that was also part of his character.

In addition to football, Heinrichs played baseball and loved cross-country. Seated on the right in the first row of his 1907–1908 team photo at Newton, Heinrichs' white shorts and colored singlet (bearing the letters "c N c") reveal his sinewy legs and light frame as a high school senior. He was a young man of average height, standing just under six feet tall. The next year, he would follow in his brother Edgar's footsteps and attend Denison, where he would continue both his academic and sport pursuits.

In August 1910, Edgar wrote to Heinrichs irritated, having been close to his brother and noting that Heinrichs had not written to him during that summer's first period of separation since childhood. "Dear Fish, What in the name of thunder is the matter with you that you can't write a fellow[?] I have written several postals but never a word have I had from you."[177]

Only three months later, Edgar would be dead, killed in what the family suspected to be a freak football accident. He had his "home-going" and Heinrichs had to handle the burial affairs alone. The loss affected him profoundly, and over the years, Heinrichs would recall Edgar in his diaries. At the time of Edgar's death, Father Jacob and Mama Lydia were in India on missionary work. Jacob wrote to his son and daughter Margaret in sorrow. "Only you two to write to. The very thought makes my hand tremble as I write."[178] On December 13, 1910, he wrote again to Heinrichs. "Who would have thought that our strong and beautiful Edgar should ever occupy first the empty place in the... cemetery lot, which I purchased 3 years ago?"[179] Writing to the president of Denison on December 27, Jacob strongly disagreed with the result of the autopsy, which concluded that brain lesions it discovered from Edgar's bout with scarlet fever nine years prior to the football collision had been the culprit.[180]

When Heinrichs graduated, he got "the call", the term used to describe the dedication of one's life to service in the YMCA. Giving up engineering and the girl he loved, Heinrichs was committed to dedicate his young life and splendid gifts in the foreign service of the YMCA Movement.[181] His father wrote to him with tears in his eyes, quoting Matthew 19:29: "And every one that hath forsaken houses, or brethren, or sisters, or father, or mother, or children, or lands, for my name's sake, shall receive an hundred fold, and shall inherit ever-lasting life."[182] Naturally, his father was interested that Heinrichs return to Madras, India, the country in which Heinrichs was born. But first, Heinrichs had to go to Hawaii to accept the position of Fellowship Secretary in Honolulu.[183] On July 22, 1913, he traveled on the SS *Lurline* from San Francisco on voyage 61.[184] His impending arrival was announced in the local newspapers, and it was in Hawaii that he would meet his resilient wife, Dorothy Peterson.[185]

Heinrichs eventually moved to India, where he would serve faithfully in Madras and Lahore (before Lahore became part of Pakistan). He would build the Lahore YMCA into the leading association in India and help build the Punjab Olympic Association with his friend, Guru Dutt (G. D.) Sondhi, the secretary-general of the Indian Olympic Association. From Lahore, he received "the call" to be the secretary-general of the new Jerusalem YMCA, the largest physical plant of the movement in the world. Its design and construction costs exceeded $1 million—a staggering budget for the time, especially for a Christian mission project during the Depression. It was designed by the same architects as the Empire State Building. The International Committee of YMCAs of North America and Canada (IC/YMCA), which owned the project, was making a big gamble. Jerusalem was a city beginning to experience an economic miracle. The Mandate administration and Jewish Agency were pumping a lot of money into development and modernization. But tension was building between the religious communities, government, and secular Zionist Jews, the latter of whom were arriving in their tens of thousands and drastically changing the demographic and political landscape. Only the best of secretary-generals could be trusted to complete the project and dedicate the building. Little did Heinrichs know that the most thrilling job on earth[186] would become one of the greatest crises of his life.[187]

# CHAPTER 2

# The Starting Pistol

## 1.

The 1920s were not quite roaring for the "file." Palestine was undergoing major transition in the first part of the decade. The Turks had ruled over Palestine for just over four hundred years when, in 1917, General Allenby conquered Jerusalem and declared martial law. The military government, known as the Occupied Enemy Territory Administration (OETA), lasted until June 1920. In that month, the League of Nations transferred the Mandate for administering the territory to Great Britain, and the foundations of a civilian government emerged out of the war-torn country. There was a lot of work: the *New York Times*[1] reported Frederick Kisch's astonishment at finding the country as devastated as France at the end of the First World War.

Yet there were a few contacts between sport in Palestine and the International Olympic Committee (IOC). More importantly, as soon as Great Britain received the Mandate, the Zionist project took off rapidly. The sport and political developments of the latter half of the decade laid the foundation for an important cooperative effort in sport between Jews, Muslims, and Christians between 1930 and 1933. The Jerusalem YMCA spearheaded this effort with Maccabi Palestine, with the consent and active participation of the Arab sport leadership.

During the 1920s, Frederick Kisch was the head of the Palestine Zionist Executive. He was the most important Zionist official in Palestine. All key decisions about the Zionist project had to pass through him. He controlled the flow of money and information for Zionists between the World Zionist Organization (WZO), the Yishuv (Palestine's local Jewish leadership), and the British administration (the High Commissioner for Palestine and his staff in the Government of Palestine).

In the same period, Yosef Yekutieli was helping to build the Maccabi Movement in Palestine. The founding of the Maccabi World Union (Maccabi Weltverband) in Berlin[2] resulted in the restructuring of the Maccabi Movement worldwide, forming the foundations of Yekutieli's efforts, which he based largely out of Maccabi Tel Aviv (where he also served on the club's board).

Waldo Heinrichs was serving in the foreign work of the YMCA Movement in India. He married his fiancée Dorothy Peterson. They had one child, William, who died. But they were blessed with three more. They enjoyed their lives in service—first in Madras and then in Lahore—with their children, Waldo Jr. (referred to as "Junior") and Margaret ("Mary"). Their third child, Shirin, was born during their transition to Jerusalem in the early 1930s.

## 2.

Frederick Kisch captured the crucible of the 1920s in recollections he published in 1938. Twenty years after Allenby's triumphant entry into Jerusalem, Mandate Palestine was coming apart at the seams. A great Arab revolt had started in the spring of 1936 and showed no signs of abating. Investors and the Jewish community abroad were asking questions.[3] What had gone wrong? Why had there been a revolt? What did it mean for the Jewish national home? Kisch believed he could help answer such questions. He felt that complex circumstances needed to be explained[4] to the Jewish community outside the territory. Kisch had been the front-row witness to how things unraveled, especially between 1922 and 1929. After all, he had served as Zionism's chief executive in Palestine during this period. He had prepared the budgets, delivered the reports to help set policy, worked with the High Commissioner and his staff to convert these policies to law, and responded to the various crises. He had traveled the entire country and widely across the region. He had access to everyone. He was respected on all sides. Everyone opened their doors to Kisch, from the Arab peasant to the emirs. It was a testament to his character, calculation, and cordiality.

Like many high-profile men of his time, Kisch kept a diary. Not just a personal diary, but an office diary. People in positions of authority kept them as a way to leave a record of their work for the person who would eventually replace them; a method of record management. When he transferred his seat on the Zionist Executive to Chaim Arlosoroff in 1929, he transferred him the diary, too. Like Kisch, Arlosoroff supported enlarging the Jewish Agency. In 1927, he had traveled to the United States with Chaim Weizmann and Kisch to plan for the integration of America's non-Zionist Jewish population into the Zionist project. He was a leading Zionist, a future leader of Israel. But in 1933, shortly after several discussions with Heinrichs, Kisch, and the Va'ad Leumi (the local Jewish leadership in Mandate Palestine), he was assassinated. These discussions focused on the role of Heinrichs and the Jerusalem YMCA in bringing the different faith groups together through sport. Arlosoroff's assassination remains unsolved and is as controversial among Israelis as the Kennedy assassination is among Americans. In recent years, researchers have examined the potential role of Nazis in his death.

When Arlosoroff died, the office diary returned to Kisch. It is curious that Lloyd George, the British parliamentarian who openly supported appeasement of Hitler, wrote the foreword to the edited version of the diary. This reflects Kisch's ability—and willingness—to work across ideological lines as a politician, as well as the complex politics of the period.

Kisch did his last review of the postscript[5] for *Palestine Diary* just after[6] he returned from a meeting in Cairo with IOC president Count Henri de Baillet-Latour,[7] in which the men probably discussed Kisch's ascension as an IOC member.[8] In the postscript, Kisch reflected on the shortcomings of the tenure of the High Commissioner, Sir John Chancellor, with whom he had worked closely. Kisch noted that the subsequent seven years was a period of unparalleled prosperity under the watchful eye of the new High Commissioner, Sir Arthur Wauchope.[9] The influx of capital was critical to the blossoming of Palestinian sport, and Wauchope was patron of or attended many sport events like the Maccabiad and championships at the Jerusalem YMCA during this period.

Kisch published an edited version of his diary so that he could summarize for English-speaking Jews of America and England what had transpired with the Arabs. He felt that the Arabs' real grievance was that the British had a mandate over Palestine at all.[10] He considered the grievance regarding Jewish immigration as incidental. He felt that the 1936–1939 riots in Palestine were used as an excuse to rouse the people and that, without the policy pursued by Arab leaders, there would have been no uprising.

Kisch did not agree that the Mandate had become unworkable by 1938. He believed deeply that "only when terrorism and intimidation are definitely suppressed will moderate opinion among the Arabs, which has all along existed, be able to make itself heard and felt."[11] He was also critical of how the Mandate administration had been staffed and particularly so of its British employees who in Kisch's eyes had failed His Majesty's government, the Jews, and the Arabs: "[I]f [His Majesty's government] wish at last to make a reality of their desire to encourage cooperation between Arabs and Jews, they must see to it that they are served by men whose opinions and prejudices do not preclude the possibility of successful work to that end."[12]

Kisch concluded his postscript to *Palestine Diary* with a short story[13] about a group of young Jews who a few days prior had gone north to establish a colony on land that had been legally purchased by the Jewish National Fund. They were attacked and some mortally wounded in their defense of the colony. A few days later, as they were ploughing their fields, they discovered the remains of an ancient synagogue and, on the same day, were greeted in a friendly manner by the civilian leaders of two neighboring Arab villages. Kisch felt that this story summed up the situation in Palestine: the determination of Jews to resettle in Palestine, despite the obstacles; the readiness and ability to defend themselves; the refutation of the claim that Jews were alien to Palestine; and the natural relationship between Jewish and Arab peasantry.

Although Kisch worked primarily in the political domain in the 1920s, he included in *Palestine Diary* a number of references to his involvement in sport during this period. While on the Zionist Executive, he also served as honorary president of Maccabi Palestine. It is within this context that he would have come to work closely with Yekutieli.

## 3.

Kisch arrived in Palestine in November 1922. By spring, he was administering sport activity. He presided over a meeting to organize a Maccabi sports meet in Jerusalem at the end of September. In the meeting, the group appointed the necessary financial and organization subcommittees and decided to have two events open to non-Jews.[14] Early on, Kisch and the Maccabi Movement were open to incorporating Arab Palestinians into their sport activities. A short while later, Kisch attended another Maccabi event, this one the cutting of the sod for the Maccabean colony at Gezer. Herbert Bentwich was present. He was the father of Palestine's attorney general Norman Bentwich, and the Grand Commander of the Order of Ancient Maccabeans in London. Kisch was gratified "to see so many Arabs, most of them inhabitants of the neighboring villages, participating happily in such a ceremony under the shadow of the blue and white flag. No better answer could be given to the constantly repeated charge that all Arabs are opposed to Zionist work. As a matter of fact, the fellaheen [peasants] like having Jewish colonists as neighbors."[15]

Kisch also presided over the meeting of the Maccabi Palestine committee that dealt with the fund for developing the Maccabi sports ground in Jerusalem. He recorded the reason why he involved himself in such matters: "I attach much importance to sport here because: first, it teaches discipline which we need so much; secondly, both for the players and spectators it creates a reaction against the excessive strain of Palestinian life, and thirdly it tends to keep our youth away from politics."[16]

In the lead-up to the XIII Zionist Congress in Carlsbad, Czechoslovakia, Kisch asked his personal secretary Regina Copilon to write to Yekutieli to communicate urgently before Kisch departed.[17] He wanted to discuss sport during Sukkot, the autumn Jewish harvest festival that commemorates the Exodus and the Israelite tribes' dependence on God in the wilderness. Norman Bentwich, who was a close friend of Kisch, heard about it and intervened. Bentwich informed Kisch that in the preceding year the same event had turned into a Zionist demonstration and took on a propaganda form.[18] Kisch assured Bentwich that this would not recur: it was simply sports and not a political demonstration.[19] Copilon told Yekutieli that Kisch made him responsible for ensuring that no politics interfered in the sports meet at all.[20] Kisch had also exhibited a similar distaste for mixing politics and social clubs in a meeting with a group of former Jewish soldiers who were setting up the Menorah Club.[21] In that meeting, he insisted that the men put down in black and white that politics were prohibited at the club.

These small interactions, and even Kisch's presiding over Maccabi Palestine, were a distraction from his more important political work for the Zionist Executive. The XIII Zionist Congress in Carlsbad, Czechoslovakia was Kisch's first, and he was elected to the Executive for Palestine. Kisch recalled in a note[22] on the Congress (for the published version of the diary) that this Congress adopted a resolution regarding the desire of the Jewish people to build up their national home on an equal footing. The text of this resolution was quoted in an address made to King Hussein (of Mecca), and declared that Zionists were "determined to live with the Arab people on terms of concord and mutual respect, and together with them to make the common home into a prosperous land, the building-up of which may assure to each of its peoples undisturbed national development."[23]

The budget[24] approved at the Congress for the fiscal year 1924 was only £P 328,000.[25] To this could be added credits and investments of £P 124,000.[26] One can appreciate how careful Kisch had to be with resources. From these funds, he would have to build the Jewish national home, a modern Jewish state. In terms of the trust placed in him, he wrote that the numbers gave "no indication of my feelings at finding myself one of so small a group of Jews elected by delegates of more than half a million organized Zionists throughout the world to carry the great responsibility of directing the course of the Jewish national revival in Palestine."[27]

## 4.

Kisch started 1924 on the field of play, joining a field hockey match for the Jerusalem Sports Club against the army, which his team won.[28] That year, a Maccabi club in Europe, Hakoah Wien (Vienna), won the European football championship. This was a crucible moment for Jewish sport, and the team traveled to Palestine as part of a tour following its crowning achievement. Kisch attended the public reception for the team in Jerusalem on January 9 at Zion Hall, at which he delivered a short Hebrew speech on behalf of both the Palestine Zionist Executive and Maccabi Palestine.[29] This team would inspire Maccabi Palestine to tour with its sport teams in the near future. Despite its role as a beacon, many of Hakoah Wien's team members (along with the majority of European Jewish athletes) faced a tragic demise only twenty years later in the Nazi extermination campaign targeting Europe's Jews. (Hakoah Wien reestablished itself after the Second World War. Although it still inspires, it never reclaimed its global status.)

In April, Kisch joined High Commissioner Sir Herbert Samuel (Palestine's first High Commissioner) for the opening of a sports competition on the new Maccabi sports ground at Beth Hakerem.[30] He estimated five thousand people in attendance at the event. The Maccabis were getting noticed. Kisch then convened a meeting of the Palestine Macabbi Committee at his apartment to discuss moving the Maccabi World Union's headquarters to Palestine.[31] The World Union had made the proposal, but Kisch felt that his colleagues in Maccabi Palestine were not yet ready for such a move.

In early June, Kisch traveled to Nablus for the Agriculture Show and attended a local Arab sports meeting, enjoying the afternoon with a member of the Moslem Supreme Council.[32] At the end of June, he captained a cricket XI of the Jerusalem Sports Club, which traveled to Sarafand on the Mediterranean shore near Haifa for a match against the British Gendarmerie.

Of course, it was in the summer of 1924 that the Paris Olympic Games took place. Germany had been barred from the 1920 Games in Antwerp, Belgium, because of its role in the First World War. Much of that war had been fought on battlefields in Belgium and France. The

IOC allowed the Organizing Committee to decide whether or not the Germans could attend Paris, dodging the issue of boycotts. The French decided against German participation.[33]

Avery Brundage was not yet an IOC member in Paris, but since Antwerp, he had become involved in the American Olympic Association and was in Paris as a spectator.[34] The more important administrative development at Paris was that the IOC decided to establish an executive commission. Two persons on it would engage the Palestine Olympic file going forward: Baillet-Latour (who would become IOC president the next year) and Sigfrid Edström (who would take over from Baillet-Latour in 1942). Baillet-Latour would have to deal with the Palestine Olympic Association's request for membership in the 1930s. Later, Edström would deal with the challenging question of the change in name from Palestine to Israel and the Association's request to go to the 1948 Games in London.

It should come as no surprise that the Maccabis showed up at the Games in Paris for meetings. On June 9, 1924,[35] Kisch sent a letter to the Organizing Committee of the Games. Written on letterhead of the "Sports & Athletic Organisation of Eretz-Israel Maccabi Central Executive," he presented an Athletic Federation of Palestine, the Maccabi Organization, and expressed its desire to assist in international sport taking place that year. Kisch requested the Organizing Committee to provide the delegation whatever facilities were permissible and included the names of those in the delegation: Zvi Nishri, David Kleinmann, and Yehoshua Alouf (and his wife). A handwritten note from the French consul general introduced Kisch, extolling the friendly relations between the men and adding his hope that the requested facilities could be granted to the delegation.[36]

Kisch closed out 1924 by traveling to the United States on December 4, at a time when he was worried about growing Arab opposition to Zionist land purchases.[37] Kisch's purpose for his first trip to the United States was threefold. First, "[t]o secure the participation of American Jewry in the enlarged Jewish Agency for Palestine."[38] Jews of the world were to be responsible for the establishment of the Jewish national home,[39] and this was not easily achievable without the four and a half million Jews living in the United States. Second, to launch the annual campaign in the U.S. for Keren Hayesod (Palestine Foundation Fund), which was the chief financial instrument for funding the Jewish Agency. (In the United States, its activity was eventually replaced by that of United Jewish Appeal.) Third, to secure more support for the Hebrew University on Mount Scopus in advance of its inauguration in 1925, for which Lord Balfour, who had issued the Balfour Declaration, would travel to Palestine. Despite the increased pressure from the Arab Palestinians, Kisch remained optimistic in public on his talks in the United States. He attributed 1,800 years of stagnation in Palestine to misgovernment by the Turks[40] but withheld his concerns about increasing friction with the Arab inhabitants. In public, he expressed the belief that the connection between Jews and Arabs was stronger than politics and that, eventually, the Arabs would see the economic benefit of Jewish interest in the territory.[41]

## 5.

Kisch did not return from the United States until February 17, 1925. Back in Palestine, there were more indications of growing political tensions. Kisch felt that the concessions of the government to Arab hostility simply encouraged the Arabs.[42] One hot-button topic was the official reference to the country in Hebrew on official government artifacts (including, starting in 1927, on currency). On these artifacts, the country was referred to as "Palestine" in English, "*Falastin*" in Arabic, and "*Falastina*" in Hebrew. But the Hebrew was followed by parentheses that encapsulated two other Hebrew letters; *aleph* and *yud*. Kisch complained that he was being attacked in the Jewish press in Palestine, despite the fact that the letters represented the abbreviation for *Eretz Yisrael*, or the "Land of Israel."[43] Pressure was building. It was as if no action was suitable to any party.

Another major development of 1925 was the introduction of Palestinian citizenship,[44] a matter as controversial then as it is today, although for different reasons. Ottoman subjects (those in Palestine during Turkish rule) who were habitually resident in Palestine on August 1, 1925, automatically became Palestinian citizens. For others (and this affected Jews in particular who were coming from Europe), certificates of naturalization were available after two years of residence over a three-year period, but the clock started ticking only after the date of application. To set an example as chairman of the Palestine Zionist Executive, Kisch applied. He became a Palestinian citizen in 1926 and did not have his British passport returned to him until 1929 (when it was determined that he was still a British subject).

By the end of 1925, sport progress in Palestine was evident, as recorded in his diary: "It is astonishing how our boys here have learnt not only to play football, but to 'play the game.'"[45]

# 6.

The two big Maccabi events of 1926 were the re-internment of Max Nordau's remains in Palestine and the US tour of Hakoah Wien (Vienna). The Maccabis owed the very concept of "Muscular Jewry" to the Jewish philosopher, Nordau, and Kisch had the sad privilege of giving a speech at his re-internment.[46] The US tour by Hakoah Wien was a fitting homage to the philosopher and a testament both to how much attention Jewish sport was getting and how much "Muscular Jewry" had accomplished. The club's sport grounds in Vienna had capacity for thirty thousand fans and, in 1923 and 1924, the team had defeated the Egyptian Olympic team in Egypt while also winning the matches it played in Palestine during its tour.[47]

On the US tour, Hakoah Wien played a select team from the American Soccer League on May 1, 1926 with forty-six thousand spectators in attendance.[48] In the view of emerging American Zionists, "'thousands of speeches and nationalist reproofs' could not do as much as 'one [soccer] game to bring our youngsters back toward Jewishness.'"[49] The club's president, Ignatz Koerner, declared at a press conference in New York City that "'Jews from all over the world will be represented in the next famous Olympic Games.'"[50]

But the tour also caused some tension within the Jewish community in America. These related to the teams' playing on the Sabbath. Maccabi Palestine would also aggravate its relations with its more conservative and religious constituents in the Yishuv over the same matter.[51] Before one of the Hakoah matches in St. Louis, "two local Orthodox rabbis added their own plaintive calls. In a personal protest published in St. Louis' Yiddish-language *Jewish Record*…[the rabbis]…declared that the 'prestige' that Hakoah 'adds…to the Jews…cannot be attained at the price of the desecration of the Sabbath and with perverting the feelings of those to whom the Sabbath is holy.'"[52]

The visit of Hakoah Wien to Palestine and the United States inspired Maccabi Palestine to use its Jewish Palestinian football teams abroad. This step would be pivotal to establishing transnational activities in the emerging Palestinian Jewish sport movement. Such competitions would serve as evidence of Maccabi Palestine's reliability as a custodian of sport. The matches would form the foundation upon which an eventual Olympic effort could be built. In December 1926, Maccabi personnel held a meeting at the Egyptian Consulate in Jerusalem to further this agenda.[53] It wanted to arrange football matches with more Egyptian teams. On the occasion of this meeting, His Majesty's consul general of Egypt offered to approach the Egyptian federation to encourage it to enter into negotiations with Jewish football in Palestine, as well as to arrange on Palestine's behalf a side trip to the country for a visiting football team from Vienna.

## 7.

By 1927, the Zionists began electrifying Palestine with the Rutenberg hydroelectric power station, and Yekutieli was receiving his subscription to the IOC's new official bulletin. Palestine was not yet listed among recognized national Olympic committees.[54] Yekutieli began working hard to change that. He first needed a pathway into the coveted Olympic world. No other platform, except the League of Nations, would give broader exposure to the Zionist ideal and yearning for a Jewish national home than the international platform of the IOC. And none could provide legitimacy in the way the Olympic Movement could. If Palestine could get into the Olympics, then this would reinforce the cause of the Jewish national home. Arab Palestinians would feel the same way.

But how to find a way in? Consultations in Paris at the 1924 Games had not been productive. Nonetheless, relations had been made and information had been obtained to support next steps.

Yekutieli decided to start in the area of football. The International Football Federation (Fédération Internationale de Football Association/FIFA), although part of the Olympic Movement, had such a big footprint that it constituted a separate power base in global sport. Although FIFA was a smaller version of itself back then, football was still wildly popular and the main economic engine of an emerging sports market.

Yekutieli formed a provisional committee[55] to oversee the increasing number of football associations in Palestine and their rapid development. The committee consisted of Yekutieli and two friends, Asaf Grasowsky and Gideon Abulafia. This trio wanted to take "preliminary steps to form a federation whose object should be to coordinate all existing associations regardless of creed or race and to introduce a uniform system in the football game—a Federation which should be a credit to Palestine."[56] In order to form a federation, Yekutieli needed to collect data on who was actually organizing football in the form of a structured club activity. The committee asked the recipients[57] to whom it sent the circular to provide: (1) the name of their association, (2) when it was founded and whether it was already affiliated to an international organization, (3) the number of members of their association, (4) the number of teams belonging to them, (5) whether they possessed playing grounds compliant with international rules, and (6) whether the grounds were the property of the association or whether they were leased. The circular concluded with the request that people return the information as early as possible so that an assembly could be arranged "in the near future, thus enabling the Federation to start activities in the coming football season, activities in which all associations would be expected to take part."[58]

It is very telling that the return address of Yekutieli's circular was not P.O. Box 129 in Tel Aviv. The post office box was instead 456 and in Jerusalem. This was during the time that Yekutieli worked in Jerusalem for the Palestine Zionist Executive between 1920 and 1929. The emerging football grounds of Jerusalem were all relatively close to one another. Jerusalem was a small, intimate city, and teams would have known about one another's activities, especially with regards to organizing a federation. The post office box also reflects that there was a significant sport footprint and focus for football that extended beyond Maccabi Tel Aviv.

Yekutieli was aware of the historical Arab football presence in Jerusalem with which he needed to contend. However, this presence appears to have been based mostly in the schools. St. George's School and Rawdat Al Ma'aref school both established their teams in 1908.[59] As secondary school teams, they would not have been considered clubs in the sense needed to constitute a national federation recognized by FIFA. There also seems to have been a group of men who in 1910 fielded a team that would compete with foreign teams visiting Palestine, although which foreign teams is not clear.[60] A school team seems to have visited from Beirut in 1912 too, with news coverage in this case noting the involvement of Jewish youth on one of the two opposing teams.[61]

The British had one of the first real sport clubs as we might recognize them today—a free-standing, purpose-built facility for recreation with surrounding sport grounds—between 1920 and 1921[62] and called it the Jerusalem Sports Club. This would be the club of the British officers and elite Jerusalemites. Members of the Jerusalem YMCA would frequent it, too. Nearby and on the road leading to Government House (the home of the High Commissioner), a golf course was also laid out.[63] According to author Issam Khalidi, "by the start of the [1930s], Arab social athletic clubs numbered about 20 in Palestine."[64]

The Mandate administration was concerned about the nationalist tendencies of these Arab clubs from the outset.[65] When the cornerstone of the Jerusalem Sports Club was laid, Governor Sir Ronald Storrs of Jerusalem reiterated the typical English mantra of the necessity to promote participation "regardless of...religion or beliefs."[66] On April 12, 1921, the Arab-language newspaper *Falastin* reported that "the partisan athletic clubs in Egypt were a factor in the turmoil there, so this mistake must not be repeated in Palestine."[67]

By 1923, Orthodox Christian clubs organized a conference and decided to establish a number of clubs that would practice football: Jaffa (1924), Jerusalem (1926), Lod (1927), Ramla (1932), and Haifa (1937). In Jaffa, the Muslim community followed suit and established the Islamic Sports Club in 1926. One of its footballers eventually joined the Arab

Palestine Sports Federation (APSF) in 1944.[68] The APSF became the
eventual Arab organizational rival to Yekutieli's Federation of the
Amateur Sports Clubs of Palestine (FASCP).

But it was a land sale in late 1927 by the Greek Orthodox Church to
the Protestants in the West Nikiforieh district of Jerusalem that would
spur the biggest change in the city's Arab sport landscape. Maccabi Palestine needed to be attentive because a major player was moving into
town, one with the potential to disrupt Maccabi dreams: the Jerusalem International YMCA, underwritten with American capital, would
change the landscape of Jerusalem sports for decades.

By 1927, the finances of the Greek Orthodox Church were weak.
Formerly empowered by the Eastern Roman Empire, in which the
majority of the Western world's wealth had been stored, Constantinople fell to the Ottoman Turks in 1453. What had not been carried off by
the Latin Catholics in the sacking of Constantinople during the Fourth
Crusade was whittled away over nearly four hundred years of Ottoman
taxation and administrative constraints. And then there was the Russian
Revolution, which robbed the church in Russia of its remaining wealth.
This weak financial position spurred the Greek church to begin selling
property in the Holy Land. When the YMCA acquired the land from
the Greeks to build its new facility, it would also surrender its old headquarters to a new Arab Sports Club, which was founded in 1928.[69] This
club would become the center of Arab nationalist sport and political
interests in the city. Still, the real financial power and human capital in
sport lay with the Jerusalem YMCA.

The problem that Yekutieli faced in 1927 was that Jewish national
sport outside Tel Aviv often did not actually own the land on which its
activities took place. The White City was a Jewish city. The Jewish community owned it, ran it, and there were no headaches. In Jerusalem, the
Jewish community was distinct from the one in Tel Aviv. Politics were different. Religious attitudes were different. Everything was watched closely
by the High Commissioner, and Jewish sport did not have free rein.

In a document that Yekutieli titled "Memorandum of the Palestine Federation of Sports & Athletics 'Maccabi' World Organisation,"[70]
Yekutieli outlined Maccabi's aims and aspirations. He wrote how adequate sport facilities were still lacking. Some Jewish clubs had acquired

access to suitable grounds, but only on one- to two-year rental agreements from Arab landowners. This was financially inefficient and did not solve the serious long-term problem of owning sport infrastructure. The Palestine Federation of Sports & Athletics "Maccabi" World Organisation appears to have been the predecessor of Yekutieli's eventual FASCP (which he would establish in the 1930s).

Using the same organizational letterhead as this memorandum, Yekutieli wrote another letter to the Organizing Committee of the Games of the IX Olympiad in Amsterdam. He inquired about press tickets to watch the 1928 Games. The Organizing Committee did not grant them. Nonetheless, Yekutieli helped organize an international trip for footballers from Haguibor Maccabi, corresponding with the American Consular Service in Jerusalem to do so.[71] The *New York Times* covered the tour on July 20, 1927,[72] noting that it was the first Jewish team from Palestine to travel abroad. Clearly, Yekutieli was onto something with football activity. Whether or not he intended it, football would be Maccabi Palestine's breakthrough into international sport.

## 8.

In June 1928, Yekutieli began compiling a budget to send a Jewish football team to England.[73] The costs included travel expenses, room and board, indemnities for players in the eventuality of loss of employment of any of the players (subject to the decision of the Central Committee, presumably of the World Zionist Organization in London), the lease of grounds, and an English instructor. More important than the cost, Yekutieli was careful to calculate the expected income from ticket sales of the fifteen matches that he planned for the team to play in England. The projected revenue of £5,175[74] exceeded the cost of £4,735.[75] Jewish sport had to be a sustainable enterprise.

The same month, the Palestine Football Association sent a circular to all sport clubs (Jewish and non-Jewish) in Palestine informing them of Yekutieli's travel abroad to arrange "closer contact between our Association and other Associations and Clubs abroad."[76] Then, at the beginning of July, Yekutieli typed what is arguably the most important letter of his life.[77] He addressed it to Cornelis August Wilhelm

Hirschman, an influential Jewish Dutch banker who cofounded FIFA (along with representatives from six other European football federations). In it, Yekutieli asked for, on behalf of Maccabi Palestine Federation, the procedure for affiliating the Palestine Football Association to the international body. He requested the information in English and German. These were two languages that the Jews in Palestine could understand (Arabic was not yet a recognized language in international sport).[78]

In parallel, Yekutieli ramped up his cooperation with Egyptian sport bodies to fortify the reputation of the Palestine Football Association in the eyes of international sport organizers. These efforts had started with Egypt as early as 1927, following the example in 1924 of Hakoah Wien. In a letter[79] to the Société Sportif Orientale in Cairo, Yekutieli relayed that football was introduced to Palestine in 1912–1913 by the Maccabi Movement. He informed Cairo that the British had established, in 1922, a football challenge cup called the Palestine Football Competition Cup, which a Jewish team had won in 1927. Five British, one Arab, and six Jewish teams participated in the cup. Most importantly, Yekutieli identified the structure and composition of football in Palestine as it existed at the time. There were three divisions; A, B, and C.

Division A consisted of four British and eight Jewish teams (four Maccabi and four Hapoel). Yekutieli's distinction between Maccabi and Hapoel teams is important because it reflected the divide in the Jewish sport movement that lasted until 1951, when the IOC required the two to merge in order for Jewish sport to be re-affiliated to the Olympic Movement as Israel. In fact, in his letter to Cairo, Yekutieli specifically stated that Hapoel refused to join the Palestine Football Association "[on] the ground of being bound to their 'Labor Sport Organisation [sic]' in Lutzern [sic]."[80] Division B consisted of an unknown number of British teams, ten Maccabi teams, four Hapoel teams, and five Arab teams. Division C consisted of twenty Jewish Maccabi teams, eight Hapoel teams, and six Arab teams.

Toward the end of the decade, the Jewish sports movement had made significant strides and the future was looking bright. But big trouble was brewing around the Kotel, what is called the Wailing (or Western) Wall in English and Al Buraq in Arabic. After the destruction of the Second Temple by the Romans, Jews had venerated the Wall as a vestige of the Second Temple. It is considered the holiest site in Judaism for Jews, and the mount above it the third holiest site in Islam. Zionists were attempting to acquire it for the Jewish national home. The trouble at the Wall would make 1929 a very pivotal year in politics and sport in Mandate Palestine.

The International Committee of YMCAs of North America (IC/YMCA) sought to prevent such troubles from emerging. In July 1928, it laid the foundation stone of a massive YMCA in the heart of the New Jerusalem. Dubbed the Sermon in Stone, the project's goal was to bring together the communities of the three Abrahamic faiths. The High Commissioner of Palestine personally laid the stone. During his address[81] at the ceremony, he spoke of how the building would be one of the outstanding distinctive features of modern Jerusalem with facilities for study and recreation. Through engagement in its activities, the communities would come to recognize that they had many interests in common and that they could practice them without departing from their own tenets, principles, and traditions.

## 9.

It was a cold January day and the tugs guided the RMS *Aquitania* through the last stretch of icy waters on New York's west side. Kisch had traveled again to the United States to work on the "final arrangements for American participation in the Jewish Agency."[82] He would remain in the United States until his return to Palestine in early April 1929 and then travel in August to the XVI Zionist Congress in Zurich.

Felix Warburg[83] received Kisch on the docks in New York and hosted him during his stay. Warburg was a wealthy Jewish banker originally from Germany. Most American Jews were not Zionists, including Warburg. But after Chaim Weizmann suggested that Warburg visit Palestine, he returned to New York impressed with the Zionist project and decided to support the Zionist cause by representing non-Zionist Jews to the World Zionist Organization. The support of America's non-Zionist Jews was essential to Weizmann and Kisch's efforts to expand the Jewish Agency.

A press photo announced Kisch's arrival in New York. It referred to him as a "British War Hero and Diplomat."[84] New York City's mayor welcomed him at city hall.[85] Kisch crisscrossed New York for meetings, social events, and fund-raisers over the next several weeks. The trip was a great success in all three of its dimensions: (1) it laid the foundations for the incorporation of American Jewry into the enlarged Jewish Agency, (2) it launched the annual campaign for the Zionist fundraising organ Keren Hayesod, and (3) it secured more support for Hebrew University, which was preparing to open.[86]

Upon his return to Palestine, Kisch made final preparations for the XVI Zionist Congress in Zurich in August, which ultimately formalized the success of his trip to the United States and allowed for the adequate representation of non-Zionists in the Zionist effort.[87] The Jewish national home could not come to fruition without this strategic incorporation.

At about the same time as Kisch's return, Maccabi Palestine hosted its Fifth Annual Sports Meeting under the patronage of High Commissioner John Chancellor. The program[88] was entirely in Hebrew, except for its cover and the list of competitions on the first page. Lord Melchett's name was printed under that of the High Commissioner. Melchett was contributing substantial finances to Jewish sport in Palestine and by 1929 had replaced Kisch as Maccabi Palestine's honorary president. The Maccabis were building a relationship with Melchett and were already thinking of organizing the First Maccabiad, which needed the support of philanthropists like him.

The sports meeting that day included four programs of gymnastics, track and field, basketball, and handball. Four of these events were open to non-Maccabis. Basketball was reserved for the ladies. Men would compete in the other events. The program testified to the emerging micro-economy of the Jews in the country. It was filled with advertisements from companies selling bikes, football equipment, petroleum, chemicals, and cameras. The Citroën dealership on Herzl Street had even bought a full-page advertisement. The program's many pages of advertisements testify to the fairly early and robust revenue-generating mechanisms used by the Maccabis in organizing and funding their activities.

## 10.

The positivity and beauty of spring gave way to the long, hot summer. Jerusalem was particularly dry this time of year and increasingly agitated. Chancellor had departed for London to discuss the matter of establishing a Legislative Council for Palestine. His efforts would be scuttled by sensitivities around the Western Wall. Since 1926, Zionists had been exploring ways to acquire the Western Wall. This was causing tremendous tensions with Palestine's Muslims. Kisch had been deeply involved in these efforts (as was his eventual successor in the Palestine Olympic Association, Gad Frumkin—the only Jewish judge on Palestine's Supreme Court). For Zionists like Kisch and Frumkin, the Western Wall represented "a central, national shrine...[that would]... energize the Zionist movement and strengthen its position vis-à-vis the ultra-Orthodox and world Jewry."[89] The problem was that the British deemed the Wall and the small strip of road in front of it to be Arab property.[90] A status quo agreement meant no changes whatsoever could be made. On Yom Kippur in 1925 and 1928, Muslims had demanded the removal of chairs and other articles that had been brought to the Wall for Jewish devotions. Agitations continued and eventually exploded while Chancellor and Kisch were away in the summer of 1929.

Riots erupted in Jerusalem first. It was the last week of August. Soon the riots spread to the rest of the country. The worst atrocities would take place in Hebron. Although there were many Arab Palestinians who sheltered the majority of the Jews there in their homes,[91] the barbarity of the massacre of those who succumbed to the mobs was shocking beyond comprehension. Both Chancellor and Kisch rushed back from London, the latter having been abroad for the birth of his son.[92] It was as though the gates of hell had been opened in their absence.

Hebron is where the Tomb of the Patriarchs is located. Second only to the Wall in holiness for the Jews (and fourth in holiness for Muslims), the tombs of the Jewish and Muslim patriarch Abraham and his immediate family are in the cave of the field of Machpelah, purchased by Abraham over 3,500 years ago. Under Muslim control since the Islamic conquest, Hebron, like the Wall in Jerusalem, was becoming a dangerous flash point. The city had only one police commander, Raymond

Cafferata. He was assigned to Hebron from Jaffa only a couple of weeks before the riots broke out.[93] Under Cafferata's control were only eighteen constables on horseback and fifteen on foot.[94] These forces were way too few compared to the twenty thousand Arabs living in the city, most of them Muslim.[95] But Hebron was also home for eight hundred years to a Sephardic Jewish community.[96] A small Ashkenazi community inspired by the Zionists had also begun to settle there. In total, there were between six hundred and eight hundred Jews in Hebron.[97]

There was nothing Cafferata and his men could do to hold back the mob when it came that Sabbath morning looking for Jews to kill. The most notorious slaughter that day occurred at the home of Eliezer Dan, where a group of Jews had gathered for the Sabbath morning prayer. A surviving Jew by the name of Grodzinsky spoke of the horror unleashed by axes, swords, knives, clubs, and stones.[98] Cafferata heard a scream in one of the houses. He ran to it and entered. Later, he would describe during testimony that inside was an Arab cutting off a child's head with a sword.[99]

Grodzinsky gave further testimony during the investigation that followed the riots, detailing the sea of blood, knife and hatchet wounds, broken ribs, slashed stomachs and entrails, the indescribable look in the eyes of the dying, half-naked bodies of people barely alive, looting, and the feathers and blood-stained walls.[100] Seven men were castrated, one was burned to death, a woman was raped and killed, other Jews were strangled with rope, one was tied to a door and tortured to death, and a two-year-old had his head torn off.[101] Jews also committed atrocities in other parts of the country, with the Jewish Agency saying that, in some cases, Jews "shamefully went beyond the limits of self-defense."[102] There was at least one confirmed report of Jews entering a mosque and burning sacred books.[103]

Chancellor thought about bombing some Arab villages from the air as a response, but did not go through with the plans.[104] Of the seven hundred Arabs charged, Chancellor only signed the death warrants for three out of twenty-five death sentences, which were carried out by hanging.[105]

The severity of the situation was the greatest test of Kisch's leadership as chairman of the Palestine Zionist Executive. There were displaced

Jews all over the country, and a sense of fear gripped Palestine's Jewish community. Jews felt they had been defenseless and that the British had not stepped in to protect them. The Zionist Executive began receiving contributions through the Palestine Emergency Fund to aid the victims of the Arab attacks.[106] The attacks created an incredible sense of solidarity among Jews worldwide, particularly in the United States. Pogroms in Russia were understandable. But pogroms in Palestine…how could this be? The *New York Times* listed the names and amounts of daily contributions to the fund, along with appeals for other in-kind aid like clothing.[107] It also reported on the regular cables from Kisch regarding the security situation and how the contributions to the emergency fund were being used.[108] Plans to reconstruct Jewish villages that had been razed were announced by mid-September, as was the formation of the investigative commission that would look into the causes of the riots.[109] The Va'ad Leumi committed to Kisch that it would not sanction any other emergency funds through other organizations.[110] This was to be American Jewry's first broad support for the Jewish national home in its time of need. By the end of September, tens of thousands of dollars in relief funds were still pouring in daily.[111]

These were the political events that threw the Maccabis' sport efforts into high gear. Jews needed to be strong and capable of defending themselves. Come hell or high water, the Jewish national home would be built and capable of self-defense.

The aftermath of the riots hung over Jerusalem like an ash cloud spewing forth from a volcano of hate. This cloud threatened the YMCA's Sermon in Stone. The new building was rising out of the hilltop just to the west of the Old City. Would Jerusalem fall apart before it could be finished and carry out its mission? The grand and visionary project was suddenly also under-funded because of the stock market crash. Within this extremely unstable political and economic context, New York put out "the call" for Heinrichs in India.

# CHAPTER 3

# The Call

## 1.

Yekutieli grabbed a piece of letterhead for Maccabi Palestine.[1] He carefully placed the paper between the feed rollers and platen, grabbed the roller to his left, and wound it into his typewriter. He set the line selector to double-spaced and made sure that everything was aligned. This important letter would be neat.

Yekutieli cranked up the line and entered the number 129, the post office box he would use to affiliate Mandate Palestine to international sport. With each numeral, the ribbon vibrator would move up and down like a Zionist worker building the Jewish national home. Each clack of a key made the bell under the carriage hum softly. It was music. The typewriter had already made magic once: its ink had bonded the Palestine Football Association to FIFA. The chime signalling the end of each line would signal the carriage return needed to write the next line in the history of Jewish sport in Palestine.

It was January 2, 1930. Yekutieli addressed the letter to Major A. C. Berdez, the honorary secretary of the International Olympic Committee. After the 1929 riots, the Maccabi spirit of the Hasmonean dynasty burned in his heart with a new purpose. The word "Maccabi" means "hammer" and Yekutieli hammered out the first of Palestine's official Olympic correspondences that would lead to its affiliation to the Olympic Movement.[2] He explained that among the sporting clubs of Palestine, a question had arisen of forming a local Olympic committee. He requested the necessary information and steps required to form such a committee. He also wanted to know how Palestine could compete in the 1932 Olympic Games in Los Angeles. This historic letter made its way to Lausanne, arriving on January 10. But there was no time to waste. Before the IOC would prepare its reply, Yekutieli wrote another important letter.

This second letter went to Alice Milliat, the president of the Fédération Sportive Féminine Internationale (International Women's Sports Federation/FSFI). Yekutieli was impressed with Milliat. She was tough and persistent—a real thorn in one's side when she wanted to be. Milliat was fed up with the IOC's refusal to admit women to the Olympic Games. Pierre de Coubertin was steadfastly opposed to women in sport. He had reluctantly permitted their participation in Stockholm in 1912 in some swimming events, but he intended his call to the youth of the world for male youth and no one else.[3] He and Sigfrid Edström were a bulwark against women in track and field.

Much like Yekutieli, Milliat was someone who was not inclined to take no for an answer. She would find a way to show the IOC who was in charge. Milliat founded FSFI in October 1921, and this threatened to detract from the Olympic Games.[4] Then she organized the first Women's Olympiad in Paris in 1922.[5] Impressively, the event attracted twenty thousand spectators.[6] Clearly there was a market, and she could be a threat to the IAAF and IOC. Edström took note and decided to engage her, hoping that he could convince her to abandon her efforts.[7] Milliat was insistent and Edström conceded. He offered a compromise: in 1926, the two agreed that Milliat could control women's sport, but that it had to be managed under the rules of the IAAF.[8] Clearly there was something that Yekutieli could learn from Milliat. Surely someone with her zeal and determination would see in him his burning passion for Jewish sport. If Yekutieli approached her for the purpose of developing women's sport in Palestine, he would cultivate an ally. He dared to dream of a pathway to the Olympics for the Jewish national home.

When Milliat replied[9] to Yekutieli, she included all the necessary regulations for establishing statutes and rules for an athletics association for women in Palestine. She quoted him the fee of 125 French francs per year for membership, which would give one vote for Palestine in the FSFI Congress. She also invited him to attend the next Congress in

Prague and offered to procure for Maccabi Palestine the rule books for basketball, *hazena* (Czech handball, which had been incorporated as a sport under FSFI), and (regular) handball.

Shortly thereafter, Berdez at the IOC replied to Yekutieli's letter.[10] He provided Yekutieli the three steps required to create a national Olympic committee. First, all the associations playing a particular sport had to be grouped into a national federation. These then needed to affiliate to their corresponding international federations. Second, Yekutieli needed to form a national Olympic committee comprising delegates from the national federations, government, and persons in Palestine interested in the development of sport and physical education. Third, Yekutieli then had to submit an official request for recognition to the IOC. Specifically, Berdez instructed Yekutieli that "the Olympic Committee of Palestine will request that Palestine be admitted to participate, as an independent nation, in the Olympic Games."[11] Yekutieli kept on reading Berdez's reply. Berdez directed him to the Olympic statutes and regulations, pointing out that they would be modified at the next IOC Session in Berlin in May 1930.

As Yekutieli was writing these letters, the Zionists started making more stringent political demands of the English. The Jewish Agency held a regular session of its administrative committee in March 1930 at which it "declared that it was determined to do everything in its power for the realization for the Jewish national home in Palestine."[12,13] The meeting also adopted a unanimous resolution "asserting the principle that 'there shall be in Palestine no domination of Jews by Arabs or of Arabs by Jews.'"[14] The amazing budget of $3,500,000 was also confirmed at the meeting.[15] If the situation would just calm down, the 1930s could be good years for the Zionist project. Continued outreach was necessary to sustain the project, including for the Maccabiad: it is during this period that Yekutieli conceived his motorcycle tour across Europe and began coordinating its organization.[16]

Yekutieli was getting very busy. As a volunteer, he was now executing the administrative workflow for Maccabi Palestine, Palestine Football Association, Palestine women's sport, and the Palestine Olympic effort, as well as organizing the Maccabiad. The affairs of the PFA alone were complex and involved his smoothing out the amateur status of athletes who would arrive from Europe but had played there as professionals.[17] Each athlete had to be handled on a case-by-case basis.

Yekutieli worked feverishly to form a provisional commission for the formation of a Palestine Olympic Committee. He wrote to Berdez at the IOC[18] to update him about his efforts. He asked if the IOC could send him a copy of the statutes of any national Olympic committee that he could use as a model for Palestine. He also informed the IOC that Maccabi Palestine would affiliate to Milliat's FSFI and that it would send a delegation to the Olympic Games in Los Angeles. That's right: Palestine's first Olympians would be women. What successful propaganda that would be! Yekutieli wanted more guidance on that project. Unfortunately for him, Berdez said that FSFI was not invited to the Los Angeles Games because the invitations were directed to countries and not to international federations. Yekutieli still had a bit to learn. But at least he received the information he had requested from Berdez: the Olympic charter, sample statutes, and a copy of the regulations, protocol, and general rules of the Olympic Movement.[19] There was promise in the world of Palestinian sport.

On the political front, things were getting worse. The IOC required that the Palestine Olympic Committee represent Palestine as an independent nation. Palestine was not one. Britain had the Mandate to administer the territory, but it was not a part of the Empire like India (which could participate in the Games). In addition, the Passfield White Paper was released at exactly the same time that Yekutieli was writing to Berdez. This was a policy paper based on the findings of the investigation into the Wailing Wall riots. Rumors were circulating that even before its publication, Weizmann had tendered his resignation as chairman of the World Zionist Organization.[20] The paper proposed restricting Jewish immigration and tying the quotas to Arab labor rates. On behalf of the Jewish Agency, Frederick Kisch "called on the High Commissioner to express the indignation of Palestine Jewry at what it consider[ed] the virtual abolition of the Balfour declaration and the death knell of the Jewish homeland."[21] Reports like the Passfield White Paper surely influenced Berdez at the IOC. He warned Yekutieli that the eventual participation of Palestine could not be envisaged by the IOC until it could examine whether the Palestine Olympic Committee was constituted to its satisfaction. The IOC also wanted to study the conditions of the country.[22] It was clear to Yekutieli that the IOC was going to get into the politics of Palestine.

Toward the end of the year, Yekutieli completed the regulations of a Palestine Olympic body. At first referred to as the Olympic Organization of Palestine,[23] Yekutieli eventually decided to name it the Palestine Olympic Association.[24] He also updated the rules of the PFA's Orient Cup,[25] a regional football competition open to teams from neighboring countries. Regional sport competition would support any Olympic affiliation request. Finally, Yekutieli set up the Eretz Israel Sport Company, Ltd.[26] The company had twenty-one objectives that included acquisition of land, building of facilities, distribution of sport literature, investing of capital for sport purposes, and obtaining concessions from the government, to name a few. Such a company could easily function as a one-stop shop to coordinate all contracts with the upcoming Maccabiad.

Yekutieli's concerns about the IOC's suspicions were warranted. Because of Yekutieli's inquiry, the IOC checked in with the French Ministry of Foreign Affairs about the situation in Palestine. France was administering the Mandate in Syria (including what is now also Lebanon) just to the north of Palestine. The country was well positioned to inform IOC headquarters about the situation on the ground with its southern neighbor. Toward the end of 1930, the ministry sent a letter[27] to the IOC informing it that any invitation for the Games in Los Angeles would have to go to a Palestine Olympic Committee and not the government of Palestine. This could trigger a Syrian and Lebanese invitation, a situation that France would need to examine closely. It had spent a significant amount of time fighting a rebellion and did not need nationalistic sentiments inflamed by energetic southern sport neighbors.

## 2.

In the months after the riots of 1929, the Jerusalem YMCA worked hard on reconciliation. Its Physical Department was particularly active in trying to bring Jews, Muslims, and Christians together in the Holy City.

Jerusalem was a small capital, but it was fast becoming one of the most ethnically and religiously diverse cities in the world. Its cosmopolitan profile had increased with the British Mandate and influx of Zionist Jews. Although this enriched life in the city, it also created intercommunal tension.

One of the biggest strains was the city's skyrocketing real estate values. Ten years prior, prices per *dunum* (one quarter of an acre) were a small fraction of the value in 1930. Although the worldwide financial collapse had slowed projects down, Jerusalem's real estate had proven to be one of the best investments anyone could have made in the early 1920s. The British and Zionists were investing so much into the development of the New Jerusalem, located to the Old City's west and northwest, that land values were beginning to squeeze out locals from the market.

Although its real estate was growing costly, the city was an amazing destination. Jerusalem's climate was really delightful.[28] Situated at an altitude between 2,000 and 2,500 feet, the ancient mountains had soft curving edges. Terraced over millennia, the landscape of Jerusalem was a silvery green carpet of new and ancient olive trees that glistened in the sun. Those trees in the garden of Gethsemane had witnessed the arrest of Jesus by the Romans. Their giant twisted trunks had withstood numerous sieges that destroyed the city through the ages. Jerusalem winters were bracing, with some rain and occasional snow, and stimulating.[29] Although the summers were dry, summer evenings were glorious.[30] People had good homes, good servants, and a happy social life.[31]

More than an ancient capital, Jerusalem was becoming a modern city. The roads were well paved,[32] and it had received a railroad and station in the latter period of the Ottoman Empire. The British were installing a fully functional sewage system for the first time in its history, and electricity lit its roads at night. Commensurate with the city's stature, the IC/YMCA called on the services of the architectural firm that designed the Empire State Building to draw up the new Jerusalem YMCA building. The country was a gold mine of historical, religious, and archaeological attractions and generated a lot of money from tourism and religious pilgrimage.[33]

The Jerusalem YMCA's Physical Department was active in the summer of 1930 trying to heal the wounds of the preceding summer's riots. Olympic activity was attractive. In it, the department saw overlaps between Olympism's internationalist, peace-focused mission and the mission of the YMCA to bring Muslims, Christians, and Jews together. The wounds were still fresh, the blood barely dried. The Jerusalem YMCA sought to build new unity.

In 1930, the Jerusalem YMCA was still operating out of a humble building. It was a community-focused organization. It offered "very simple accommodations for social relationships, educational classes, indoor and outdoor games, Bible classes and religious meetings, and ha[d] a membership of 300, representing a score of nationalities."[34] Its crown jewel was a library of twenty thousand volumes that all communities used widely within its walls.[35]

In the summer of 1930, the Physical Department focused on tennis and track and field.[36] It founded the Jerusalem Tennis League with the Jewish Rehavia Tennis Club, the Jerusalem Tennis and Athletics Club, and its own YMCA team.[37] It organized the Richardson Challenge Cup[38] for this league, which the Jerusalem Tennis and Athletics Club won. The finals of the competition fell on a day that the Arab Executive (the Arabs' political leadership organ) had declared a strike. Still, about one hundred people representing different communities gathered on the new tennis courts. Newspapers were reluctant to cover the event so as not to arouse the displeasure and distrust of the more sensitive political elements, but the Physical Director of the Jerusalem YMCA and his wife went to a tea at the Arab National College and heard favorable reviews of the competition from members of the Arab Executive. The day before the finals, a young Muslim boy approached the Physical Director because his father had forbidden his participation. The Physical Director told him that the Association could not get involved in politics and that more good would come from his participation. He reminded the boy that he was one of the best players and, therefore, a role model. The boy decided to play and helped the Jerusalem YMCA win. His "good looks and splendid playing captivated all the young Jewesses."[39]

## 3.

The big news of 1930 was that the YMCA had organized a Palestine Olympic Games Association[40] to organize the Palestine Olympic Games in 1931.[41] This was not a national Olympic committee; rather, it was a working committee within the Jerusalem YMCA that was organizing a national Olympic activity. The YMCA Movement often organized such events around the world. Heinrichs was organizing similar Punjab Olympic Games in India during the same period. Although local, these games could be incubators for more serious Olympic activity and the crucible in which a national Olympic committee was forged.

The Palestine Olympic Games Association decided on the following sport program of activities, to take place mostly in Jerusalem: a fencing championship to be held in January, a cross-country run in March, water sports (at the Sea of Galilee one hundred miles to the north) in April, track and field in May, boxing and wrestling in June, and tennis in July.[42] Tennis was to have two tournaments, one only for Palestinians and the other open for foreigners.[43] The purpose was to help the Jerusalem YMCA determine who was actually the national champion of Palestine,[44] presumably to determine who might qualify to attend a real Olympic Games.

Unfortunately, it appears that the games never took place: the powder keg of politics that was emerging in the country seems to have derailed them. New York asked the Jerusalem YMCA's acting secretary-general, Nicholas Lattof, to prepare a report[45] on the general situation in the country and how it was affecting the Association's mission. Who was Lattof and how had he arrived in Jerusalem?

Lattof was a naturalized American[46] born to the head of the Reformed Presbyterian Mission in Tarsus, Syria. He had relatives in Alabama.[47] Frank Slack, in charge of the Palestine file for the IC/YMCA back in New York, once told Lattof, "You surprise me. I have met many students from all over Europe and other parts of the world, but I haven't met anyone like you. You are so completely and thoroughly Americanized."[48] When the First World War broke out, Lattof was sixteen and got a job at a factory that made clothing for the Turkish army (to avoid being conscripted into Christian labor corps, where the fatality rate was very high).[49] For his honesty, Lattof was quickly promoted to the role of paymaster for the whole factory.[50] When Turkey surrendered, he began work with the British army for nine months as an interpreter and then went to Mobile, Alabama to see his relatives.[51] In Alabama, he met Archie Harte, who inspired him to prepare for the secretaryship of the Jerusalem YMCA.[52] Because Lattof's father had worked for forty years among the Arabs and Lattof himself was multilingual, he felt well prepared as someone who knew the psychology of the region's inhabitants to assume such a role.[53] After finishing his training in Chicago at George Williams College, in 1928, Lattof moved to Jerusalem and became the acting secretary-general of the Association.[54]

When New York called upon Lattof to inform them about the emerging situation in Palestine, Item A in his report to headquarters was Zionism. Lattof described the political movement for the creation of the Jewish national home as a disturbing factor. "Here we see the conflict between two rights, two equally justifiable ideals, which seem to be entirely incompatible. No solution seems to be possible and the struggle continues. Generally speaking, some 660,000 Moslems and 80,000 Christians known as Arabs and composing five sixths of the population consider the 150,000 Jews as their enemies, and, in turn, the Jews reciprocate this feeling."[55] Lattof described a psychological effect manifesting "prejudice, antagonism, distrust, hatred, suspicion, and fanaticism."[56] The Arabs used boycotts to vent their frustration, but Lattof characterized the entire situation as a vicious cycle, saying, "[t]he pot boils continuously."[57]

Lattof gave an example of the trouble bubbling in sport. He had taken the liberty to send the photos of the 1930 tennis tournament to the IC/YMCA. Based in New York, it oversaw the YMCA Movement's foreign fieldwork in Palestine and managed much of its money. It sent Lattof a clipping in which the photos had been published, and Lattof put it on the bulletin board at the Association.[58] "It was not long before I learned that many of our members were indignant to know that the picture had been published in America. Why? Because it might give Americans the idea that Arabs and Jews in Palestine lived together peacefully! The Arabs wanted the world to know that there would be no peace in the country as long as the Jews lived here."[59] He then added,

"This feeling had much to do with the failure of the organization by our Physical Department of [an] Olympic Games Association and Athletics Championships for Palestine."[60]

Why did the Palestine Olympic Games Association and the Athletics Championship, the latter seemingly representative of all of Palestine's communities, fail?

It appears that the Jerusalem YMCA had established its Olympic committee independently of Jewish sport organizers in Palestine and in parallel with the efforts of Yekutieli. Yet even after the slaughter of Jews in Hebron, the Maccabis engaged the Association to cooperate on the Olympic "file" for Palestine. Other than complying with the Olympic charter, the Maccabis had no compelling reason to do so: their outreach occurred when the Jerusalem YMCA building project was stalled and before Heinrichs arrived. The Maccabis might even have approached the Association to incorporate it into their efforts to affiliate to the IAAF. Thus, the Maccabi position in negotiations appears to have been sincere, but the talks collapsed because Arab members of the Jerusalem YMCA were pressuring Lattof—an acting secretary-general—to boycott Jewish contact of any kind. The members even asked the Jerusalem YMCA not to purchase goods from Jews, despite Lattof explaining to them that the prices on Jewish products were 30 to 40 percent less than the alternatives in the market.[61] This pressure on Lattof led to the capitulation of the first round of talks to form a representative Palestine Olympic Association or athletics federation.

## 4.

Money drives progress. On March 4, 1930, the Jerusalem YMCA received a check for $650,000.[62] The correspondence with the check repeated the instructions of the fund from which the money came to "construct, equip and furnish a building or buildings in Jerusalem, Palestine, on premises now owned by you...to be used for the general purposes of the Young Men's Christian Association."[63] The money came from the Jarvie Commonwealth Fund.

James Jarvie had been a wealthy coffee magnate. He died in 1929, one year before the check arrived. His connections to the Jerusalem

YMCA went back to an encounter with Archie Harte shortly after the First World War while on a trip to Jerusalem.[64] At the time, Harte was the Jerusalem YMCA's secretary.[65] It was a very small outfit. He took Jarvie around the typical sites of Jerusalem that a Christian pilgrim would want to see.

On Jarvie's last day in Jerusalem, Harte took him to the summit of the Mount of Olives.[66] Harte and Jarvie looked down over the thousands of graves that dotted the mountainside like rubble. Their eyes traveled across the Kidron Valley with its ancient tombs, up the walls of the Old City to the Temple Mount, and beyond. Harte relayed to Jarvie how he had experienced something akin to a vision in the same location in 1888 while reading the Bible and soaking in his last summer sunset on a tour of the Holy Land.[67] He had traveled there after graduating from Wesleyan University.[68] Harte told Jarvie that he had felt called to establish a YMCA "worthy of the name Christian: a center where young men could meet on a basis of mutual understanding."[69] Jarvie asked him how much it would cost and Harte replied, "$400,000."[70] "That is a great deal of money," Jarvie said back.[71] One year later, at Christmas, the last present that Harte took off the tree was an envelope from an anonymous person that included a check for $400,000.[72]

The Jarvie Commonwealth Fund was established to support the initial cost of construction, but later contributions also established an endowment from which its operating costs would be paid. The business activities of the new campus would top up these operational costs and hopefully turn a profit, sustaining the Christian business and its mission for decades to come. Both Jarvie and Harte had a keen understanding that no place on earth was more split up into conflicting groups than Jerusalem.[73] Even the Christian groups were "at swords points with each other."[74] The building designed to address these problems was intended to be the most beautiful and attractive Association in the world.[75] The site measured eight acres, the project incorporated accommodations for seventy-five to a hundred men, and it would be fully outfitted for physical education, social, and religious work.[76] Money and vision were not the object. Running the place was going to be the challenge.

Back in New York, Fred W. Ramsey of the IC/YMCA was having to deal with such challenges. He wrote to Dr. Tawfiq Canaan, a member of the Jerusalem YMCA's board of directors and one of Jerusalem's most prominent doctors. Canaan was having trouble with New York's man in Cairo, Wilbert Smith. Ramsey could not understand why. He was anxious that Smith have the "complete confidence and good will"[77] of Canaan. Ramsey assured him that Smith was "a man of tested quality, of fine tact and judgement, and a very true Christian gentleman."[78] Yet Canaan had felt that Smith, who was in Cairo, was trying to take on additional responsibilities in Jerusalem in an unauthorized manner. Perhaps Canaan was exhibiting territorial behavior that eventually would contribute to a great conflict in the Association after the arrival of Heinrichs.

The enormous influx of cash and the magnificent building project that had gotten underway were starting to influence the behavior of the Arab Christians on the board and their relationship to the Association. This was no longer a small mission activity. It was becoming one of the biggest Association and sport projects in the world. In particular, Canaan had a power of attorney over the Association's affairs. In a crisis, he would be the one to yield final signatory power and to control vast sums of money. He also chaired its Building Committee, which meant he had ultimate access to the funds being distributed for its construction.

Ramsey assured Canaan that Smith had only sought additional responsibilities at the "urgent request"[79] of Ramsey. He was confused why a tested YMCA man of Smith's character would present a problem. But Canaan had been close to Harte. Harte and the IC/YMCA in New York had clashed so much over the project that it had led to Harte's dismissal (although it was announced as a resignation).[80] Perhaps Canaan had lost his mooring when Harte withdrew. Harte was refusing to return to Jerusalem—ever. The building project was souring long-standing relations between its sponsors, the YMCA Movement's foreign field workers, and the local Palestinian board and staff. A new leader needed to be brought in.

From his base in Cairo, Smith was formally advising the IC/YMCA in New York about the constantly evolving landscape in Jerusalem. He wrote to Frank Slack in New York on the need to find a good secretary-general. Slack was the secretary of the National Council of YMCAs in New York (NC/YMCA). Smith told Slack that Lattof had arrived in Jerusalem as acting secretary-general and that his wife would soon follow.[81] He seemed to like Lattof, but the way in which he had arrived in Jerusalem had "started some gossip."[82] Smith cautioned Slack that this would not make the path of the Jerusalem board or its members any easier "nor increase confidence in...[Lattof's]...judgement."[83] He concluded by telling Slack, "I am inclined to revise my previous opinion regarding the appointment of a General Secretary [sic]. Neither Lattof nor Auburn has had sufficient experience to enable them to handle the job that needs to be done now. As I feel now, we ought to find a permanent man before the end of this year."[84]

Auburn was Fred Auburn. He was the Physical Director of the Jerusalem YMCA, running sport activities like the attempted Palestine Olympic Games. Auburn was Armenian by birth and also a naturalized US citizen.[85] He had put in two years at the University of Pennsylvania and then transferred to Springfield College, from which he graduated successfully.[86] Auburn's wife was remarkably attractive and had been well educated in Boston. They had been in Jerusalem only thirteen months, but they had "made a remarkable showing in the work in the contacts with the community, especially among Moslem Arabs, and with the British officials."[87]

The IC/YMCA was not quite sure who to choose as a permanent secretary-general. Smith advised that they not select a British secretary[88] because he would not be perceived by the Arab community as sufficiently neutral. Even a Canadian would be considered too British.[89] Therefore, Smith advised that an "American could maintain the right relationships with both [sides] more easily."[90] The Palestinians would be more responsive, and the English members of the board had a good attitude towards Americans.[91] Because Smith understood the Jerusalem situation in all its nuances, he asked Slack to allow him an opinion on whoever was nominated to receive "the call".[92]

## 5.

Dorothy Heinrichs laid out the picnic blanket on the grassy slope of a Himalayan mountain. The group of friends had decided that this spot offered a splendid view of the surrounding mountain peaks. There was a lot of space for Junior to run around and play with the dog. Surrounded by the *deodar*—the renowned Himalayan cedar—they gathered to enjoy an afternoon of fresh air, friendship, and family.

Waldo Heinrichs glanced at his wife. She supported herself with her left arm, leaning slightly back as if to take in some mountain sun. Her short hair blew in the breeze. She was a corker,[93] a modern Wellesley woman. Twelve years earlier, Heinrichs had been wearing her class ring when he was shot down over enemy territory. When the doctors were planning to amputate his left arm, he had asked the Sweet Sister to cut off his finger to keep the ring. Luckily, he had kept the arm and ring, but his left limb never functioned that well after the war. That did not stop him from building and running an amazing YMCA program in Lahore.

Colleagues and the community in Lahore liked the Heinrichses. As they gathered together to take a photo, everyone sat down on the blanket except for one, who stood behind them. With the Heinrichses were Mr. and Mrs. Guru Dutt (G. D.) Sondhi, Mr. and Mrs. Henry Lal, Mr. and Mrs. Chatterji, and Miss Theo of the YWCA, the only other Westerner. Everyone else was an Indian friend and colleague.

Sondhi was a respected professor at Government College whose name is recognized in Pakistan and India to this day. He and Heinrichs were building Olympic sports in Punjab through the Punjab Olympic Association, which they had helped establish.[94] Sondhi was also secretary of the Indian Olympic Association. Although there were cultural differences, the two got along well and were friends. They served together on the Punjab University Sports Tournament Committee.[95] Heinrichs would often go to Sondhi's home for breakfast,[96] and in the evenings he would network with him at Masonic dinners at the Lodge of Hope and Perseverance—sometimes with Olympic officials from Switzerland.[97] As everyone got ready for Heinrichs to snap his photo, Sondhi put his curved calabash pipe in his mouth and proudly stuck out his chest, as if to emulate Sherlock Holmes.

Heinrichs loved his life in Lahore, especially its opportunities for sports. At the Punjab Olympic Games he served as marshal-announcer.[98] His voice boomed through the loudspeakers as he announced a new half-mile record by Bhalla. After distributing prizes, he could be seen darting off to the Lahore Flying Club for meetings or to give a lecture on aviation or war flying. On one occasion, he traveled hundreds of miles to southeast India to Moghalpura just to support their divisional sports championship.[99] Again he served as marshal-announcer. Realizing that all the other officials were "green at the game[, he] ran it off single handed and at various times was also timekeeper, judge, field judge, clerk of course and in fact all things as needed."[100] Once on the Sabbath, he went to Canal Bridge to run the swimming competitions in the Amritdhara Tournament.[101] The next day, he was refereeing the boxing between Islamic College and Forman College.[102] Then he would be at Chief's College for their Annual Sports (one of the big social events of the year) in conversation with His Excellency the Maharaja of Patiala (who will pop up again with Yekutieli in 1934).[103] Through the Lahore YMCA, Heinrichs organized the Punjab Open Badminton Tournament.[104] He regularly supported Islamic College's sports. He practically worked 24/7, 365 days a year.

But by 1930, the Heinrichses were approaching four and a half years of service, the standard term for a foreign deployment.[105] After such a period, YMCA foreign workers were eligible for nine months of furlough.[106] They loved Lahore, but India had also come with challenges. Heinrichs had attributed the loss of his first son, William, to India,[107] and their second son, Junior, had been healthy until arrival in Lahore. Heinrichs felt that Junior was in danger of contracting tuberculosis.[108] There were also complications back home in the United States. Dorothy Heinrichs was from Honolulu, so Lahore really was a long way away. Her mother had recently suffered a paralytic stroke, and Heinrichs' mother had suffered a cerebral hemorrhage.[109] They began the inevitable discussion of when to return to the United States.

Although Heinrichs had survived his war injuries, he felt that India had nearly exhausted his nervous energy.[110] After all, he had been shot numerous times and required six major surgeries in one year.[111] It was getting hard to do eight-mile walks on foot; they would leave him stiff.[112] He needed a break. When he had arrived in Lahore, the YMCA in the city was almost a dead association.[113] He spared "neither self, money or family to build up a city Association worthy of the name."[114] He was so proud that the Lahore YMCA was now ranked the number one YMCA building scheme in India.[115] He felt that he had helped Lahore on its transition to Dominion status.[116] "We love it, but we have felt we must leave it, for family and health reasons," he wrote.[117] Heinrichs felt that he had a feather in his cap anyway: he knew that he might receive "the call" to become the secretary-general in Honolulu. He had started his YMCA career there and met his wife there. Her family was well connected in Hawaii. Such a call would have been perfect for them, but Jerusalem would call instead, in the most unique way.

## 6.

In early September, Smith wrote to Slack in New York: "The suggestion of Waldo Heinrichs strikes me very favorably indeed…Jerusalem is a gossipy, cliquey, complicated situation and the man who would do the job must be able to steer his course in such a way as to win the confidence of all groups, the co-operation of most of them and avoid antagonism of at least the Christian elements."[118]

Slack replied[119] that Heinrichs had the business capacity and was a good program man, having done a fine job with the program of activities in Lahore. The Lahore YMCA building was filled with well-rounded activities. Although Heinrichs was outspoken, he was genuinely friendly. He was not as mellow as Alvah Miller (another candidate), but he was equally genuine and a first-class executive. Slack did not doubt Heinrichs' conviction of religion as the central factor of Association life.

Heinrichs did not know it yet, but soon someone from the YMCA Movement would be arriving in Lahore to check in on him and his wife. On December 1, Oliver Stanchfield, who used to be a YMCA secretary in Bangalore and was now head of Central Region Finance work, arrived for ten days. The Heinrichs showed him a busy week in the Lahore Association.[120] On his seventh day with the Heinrichses, Stanchfield said to him, "Well I think you have the only real YMCA I have yet seen in the East here at Lahore."[121] This message made it back to New York.

The very next day, Monday, December 8, 1930,[122] was Dorothy's thirty-fifth birthday. Heinrichs went to the office during the day but in the evening dutifully stayed home. Heinrichs intended for the evening to be about her. After enjoying her birthday dinner together, an astounding cable arrived from New York asking to propose his name as secretary-general for the "marvelous new $1,500,000 building"[123] in Jerusalem. Only one hour prior to the cable's arrival, Dorothy Heinrichs had been worrying about the future of the family. He had told her not to worry because there were a thousand things they could not control.[124]

Word of the cable had already spread at the Lahore YMCA. The cable had been opened before it was sent to Heinrichs, and word was spreading like wildfire before it arrived at Heinrichs' door. The role of secretary-general would be described as "The Most Thrilling Job on Earth."[125]

The cable was followed by a letter from Smith in Cairo.[126] There was a lot to cover, and he copied Slack in New York. Smith informed Heinrichs that, as he made his arrangements for furlough, he should consider stopping over in Jerusalem in March 1931. A visit might help the Heinrichses make their decision. Smith also went over five key topics: (1) the new building; (2) personnel; (3) the political, social, and religious environment; (4) the significance of the Jerusalem work; and (5) the living conditions and climate.

Smith explained that the construction work was entirely under the control of a local building committee. Canaan chaired this committee and worked closely with the Commissioner of Lands in the government. He explained to Heinrichs how Ramsey was the legal representative of the donor and that the IC/YMCA in New York was the legal owner of the building. The complications with Harte had caused the project to fall way behind schedule. The situation in Jerusalem was also deteriorating and the stock market had crashed. Viability of the project was now actually threatened. He explained how Lattof and Auburn were solid staff supported by a twenty-one-year-old Palestinian named Samy Suz. One of Heinrichs' top priorities was to hire the right type of staff to carry out the Jerusalem YMCA's mission. Not even the board could interfere in Heinrichs' hiring decisions. The role of Jerusalem YMCA secretary-general, much like Kisch's role in the Zionist Executive, was to function as the interface between the international, local, and government stakeholders. Heinrichs would be ex-officio (without voting power), but he was effectively the Association's chief executive officer. He would hire and run its staff according to the best interests of the owners, not the locals and their politics.

Smith articulated those politics in his letter, writing, "The situation in Jerusalem is....most intricate because of the Zionist Movement."[127] He explained to Heinrichs the macro political landscape with the British administration, the Mandate, and the Balfour Declaration. Then he discussed the age-old religious rivalries between and within communities. To control all of these conflicts, the British maintained a garrison in Jerusalem and a police force of "at least 200 British personnel, plus approximately double that number of British Police passing through for training."[128] Heinrichs had been selected because the IC/YMCA was convinced that "it would be a very great mistake to call a man to Jerusalem fresh from America."[129] It was Heinrichs' combination of "personal qualities, varied experience and point of view"[130] that caused the international committee to transfer "the call" to him.

Smith went on to explain[131] how Heinrichs' profile would help support the essential work of the Jerusalem YMCA and insulate it from further blows that could lead to its failure. Jerusalem was central on the world stage because of Zionism. Its ramifications extended into politics, finance, and racial questions, and had religious implications. The new building represented an enormous investment far exceeding the needs of the city. The project was unique in design and aims. Heinrichs had to operate the building in a way that justified its cost or it could hinder the entire foreign work of the YMCA Movement. The building had already been widely advertised, so it could also become an embarrassment. Thousands of people traveled to Jerusalem as tourists from all over the world and would take their opinions back home with them. If Heinrichs accepted the role, the work would be big. It would be accompanied by reputation, prestige, and pressure.

The Heinrichses considered their choice. They would not actually make their decision until their visit to the Holy City the following year. Nonetheless, Heinrichs started to correspond with Slack in New York—processing the details, implications, and more. Slack told him to converse with Harte during his visit to Palestine. Slack was very diplomatic and would not go into details. Yet clearly Harte, although terminated, was still a factor.[132] Slack also underscored how important Smith's grasp of the situation was, despite being on the other side of the Suez Canal in Cairo.

Toward the end of 1930, Smith wrote[133] to Heinrichs. He expressed his increasing hope that Heinrichs would accept the position. Heinrichs informed him that he would sail from India on March 24, 1931. Smith felt this would put Heinrichs in Jerusalem at quite a good time for his study on the ground.[134] Smith allayed some of Heinrichs' medical concerns, noting how close Europe was to Palestine and that a full medical examination would be provided to him in New York.[135] He also stressed that Harte had never really developed the program because he had not allowed junior staff to assume the required responsibilities.[136] In this regard, he ruled out any coordination with Harte, which struck Heinrichs as odd given that Slack had recently written to him suggesting that Heinrichs meet Harte while in Palestine. Who should he trust—Slack or Smith? Surely the politics of Jerusalem had already crept their way into the role before Heinrichs even accepted it and the grand building scheme was complete. On a crowded train back from Bombay, Heinrichs spent the last day of the year reading much and playing poker. And so passed the last day of the old year. The Heinrichses wondered what 1931 held in store for them.[137]

# CHAPTER 4

# The Most Thrilling
# Job on Earth

## 1.

Heinrichs had been chosen.

Since New Year's Day, senior YMCA secretaries had been in daylong sessions in Matheran, India. They decided to change pace on their fourth evening with a good game of baseball. Everyone had heard Heinrichs' news and they congratulated him. As they left their rooms to head outdoors, excited words for Heinrichs passed the lips of the Christian brotherhood.

It was a hazy and warm January day, typical winter weather for this part of India, but the evenings were much cooler. The men gathered around their makeshift baseball diamond and watched the setting sun. They marveled at the ancient mountain canvas before them. The range was lush and bright with greenery. Funnels of fog rose from flumes, which flowed with cool cascades of water. Leonard Dixon threw the first pitch. Stanchfield, who had given word to New York of the extraordinary administration of the Lahore YMCA, swung and tapped the ball down the line to first base, where Heinrichs was ready to tag him out. Heinrichs' team lagged 22–15 but eventually pulled ahead to win 25–22.[1] The brotherhood shook one another's hands at the end of the game and returned to their rooms to clean up before heading out to celebrate John Stanley's birthday. They gathered on the veranda at the Rugby Hotel.

After dinner, Dixon gave the usual closing message. He focused on some words of wisdom given to him by Dalton McClelland of the YMCA in Madras, India. He spoke of inspiration, dedication, and consecration. (McClelland would become central to the Jerusalem YMCA's crises in Jerusalem during the city's civil war and Arab-Israeli wars in the 1940s.) One of Heinrichs' colleagues approached him, saying, "It's a great compliment to India that after searching the world over they chose for Jerusalem a man India had trained."[2]

In the morning,[3] Heinrichs got up early. He bathed, shaved, and packed before getting on the 7:40 train to wind his way through the Indian countryside back to Lahore. He stopped in Bombay to begin preparations for his furlough. At American Express, he booked his passage to Honolulu by way of Port Said in Egypt. There, he planned to disembark and store his things from India, just as Wilbert Smith had advised. He would then take the train across the Sinai Peninsula to Palestine and on to Jerusalem. After assessing the situation in Jerusalem, he and his wife would travel to Haifa and finally catch a ship to Naples and onwards to the United States.

After tea time, Heinrichs hopped on the 5:15 train to Lahore. Two soldiers' wives were in the compartment with him and made it impossible for him to feel at home.[4] He really did not like senseless prattle. It was impossible to read or write with those ladies chatting, so he sat there and "thought much about Jerusalem."[5] He jotted down a few items on which to conduct his investigation into the situation in Palestine. These included "Palestine (the field), Jerusalem (immediate field), [r]elations to constituency, YMCA equipment + program, and [p]ersonal questions."[6] Each had many sub-bullets. Typically methodical. Always the executive.

Time dragged on as heavily as the train on its tracks; between six and eight o'clock, it awaited more passengers in Delhi. Heinrichs was displeased to see his female companions remain in the compartment as far as Ambala. No mercy. The train pulled into Lahore the next morning at 9:05.[7] It had been an unproductive journey. Normally during long travel, men in Heinrichs' position should be, at the very least, working through their correspondence for delivery to a stenographer upon arrival at their destination. As he got dropped off at his home, Mary, his little one, rushed out to greet him first. His wife followed, and then came Junior. It was a grand homecoming.[8] Things felt so different now that the most senior of job offers was on the table. Even though there was a need to go to the United States and be closer to home, the call of Jerusalem was strong and the position so important. It would put Heinrichs on the map.

Dorothy Heinrichs invited her husband to take a bath while she prepared breakfast. When he came to the table, Mary ran to him and hugged his leg. Heinrichs was often away and Mary was young, but he noted how she had overcome her bashfulness and finally taken to him. As always, his home mail was waiting for him on his writing desk. After breakfast, he noted in the pile the long letter from Smith in Cairo.[9] It had taken just under a month to arrive in his hands, its six pages an extremely thorough overview of the situation in Jerusalem and Palestine. The letter was "most interesting reading...a masterful presentation of the case."[10] Heinrichs realized that there was much that he did not know about the situation in Palestine. He committed to read up on it so that he and his wife could make an informed decision for the family. Then he darted off to the office at 10:30 to deposit checks, pay bills, and get official correspondence. Thereafter, he headed to Government College to see G. D. Sondhi to work on the big sports day.

University Sports was Heinrichs' favorite annual event in Lahore.[11] He had worked to support each edition as marshal-announcer, keeping the events on schedule and announcing results to the crowds that would come to see their young men perform—all promising student-athletes. As always, Heinrichs did a fantastic job, but he started to feel ill at the end of the penultimate day of the competition. A fever was coming on, and he regretfully sent a message that he would not be able to attend the finals, a great disappointment since he loved the event and this was likely to be his last.

By February, Heinrichs was feeling better and organized the 1931 edition of the Punjab Olympic Games.[12] It was satisfying to see so many records broken. At least when he left India, Heinrichs would have a record of improvement to show for it. That day, a British Tommy won the discus throw and broke the All-India record. Lieutenant Dart of the Hampshire Regiment won the half mile, setting the record at two minutes, two and two-fifths seconds (2:02.4). Heinrichs was leaving the Punjab with more All-Indian Olympic records than all the other provinces put together.

The impending departure from India caused the Heinrichses some degree of grief. With only a few days to go until their departure, the Heinrichses joined staff and members at the YMCA for its Annual Members' Dinner on March 5, 1931.[13] Chairing the dinner was G. C. Chatterji, with whom they had gone picnicking among the deodars in the Himalayas. The Heinrichs were treated as guests of honor—more than the official guest of honor himself, Dr. Datta.[14] As everyone dined at their tables, they enjoyed casual conversation with fried fish, potato chips, *pulau* and curry, mixed naan breads served piping hot from tandoori ovens, along with peach snows (a milk drink similar to a yogurt *lahsi*). Dessert and coffee followed, during which the official program began. Chairman Chatterji kicked it off with a toast to the King Emperor.[15] Then Leader Hume broke out into song. Reverend Weir gave his toast to Dr. Datta, who then spoke.[16] Heinrichs had never heard him so full of wit, humor, pathos, inspiration, and fire: it was a wonderful speech.[17] Dr. Datta's speech was followed by traditional Indian music. Then it was Heinrichs' turn to give a toast. He felt that he was not prepared and did not do well. Still, everyone knew of their departure and gave the Heinrichses beautiful parting gifts. Dorothy Heinrichs received a lovely Punjab costume, and Heinrichs got two fine paintings of the late Mughal period. There were more toasts, more singing, and Dr. Malik gave a brief speech under the title, "Save me from my educated wife."[18] After Chairman Chatterji's closing remarks, everyone went home for the night. It was hard to say goodbye to India.

Heinrichs was booked solid with sport all the way until the family left. They were feted at more dinners with friends and colleagues, including the Sondhis' home, until their departure. On March 24, they packed up their last items at eight o'clock in the morning and a taxi came to pick them up not long after. They sailed at 11:30, with Mr. and Mrs. Moses seeing them off.[19] As India slipped into the distance, the Heinrichses anticipated their arrival in the Holy City.

## 2.

The task ahead was not for the fainthearted.

While the Heinrichses sailed to Port Said, Smith wrote[20] from the Cairo YMCA to Fred W. Ramsey. He informed Ramsey that on April 6, he and Heinrichs would go up to Jerusalem—the city on a hill—for a week or ten days.

From Smith's letter,[21] one can appreciate what Heinrichs was hired to accomplish. The project was stalled. There were problems with the contractors. The athletic field was badly needed, yet not even close to completion. There were almost no staff to fill one of the largest YMCA plants in the world.[22] The Association needed customs exemptions, but its very expensive equipment had not received the normal clearances. There was so much to do. And even though Heinrichs had not yet accepted the position, Smith landed him a meeting with Sir John Chancellor, the High Commissioner, and his Chief Secretary, Edward Mills. Chancellor was in his final seven months in Palestine, having been emotionally defeated by the riots of 1929.

The Heinrichses arrived in Port Said, Egypt on April 4.[23] They disembarked, and the American Express agent met them and helped get their baggage checked off the ship and through quarantine and customs. He then took them to the American Express office to buy tickets for a side trip to Cairo. Neither of them had seen the Great Pyramids of Giza, and Mrs. Heinrichs was elated to visit one of the seven wonders of the ancient world. They took a ride around Port Said and were not very much impressed, except for some antiquities at the museum. Then they boarded their 12:15 train for Cairo. Junior and Mary slept the whole way on the uncomfortable but interesting journey. Smith met them in Cairo and put up all four of them comfortably in his flat.

Smith and Heinrichs went to a meeting at the Cairo YMCA.[24] Smith's stenographer joined them. They purchased tickets for the train trip to Jerusalem and had sixteen pieces of luggage between them. The Heinrichses left their children in Cairo and boarded their train for Kantara. The train was frightfully overcrowded and they were all jammed in like sardines. They disembarked at Kantara to board an equally overcrowded and frightening ferry boat to take them to Jaffa.

For centuries, Jaffa was the dominant economic center and port city of the central Palestine coast. At one point in its history, it had been conquered by the ancient Maccabis. By the time the Heinrichses were arriving, the city was beginning to live in the long shadow cast upon it by the modern Maccabis living in the White City just to its north.

Disembarkation was a complicated affair at Jaffa. Its harbor was an ancient one with no facility to dock boats or ships of any significant size. Large wooden boats would paddle out from its charming marina, beyond the breakwater and into the open Mediterranean. These water taxis would reach the great anchored ships waiting to unload their cargo or people. Freight, luggage, and people would be precariously lowered into them as they bobbed up and down on waves. When Heinrichs put his foot on dry land in Palestine, his first impression was that Palestinian customs were a joke because not one parcel was opened. Then the group headed for Jerusalem.

Heinrichs woke up early the next morning.[25] The preceding day, as they had journeyed from the coastal plain up to the Jerusalem mountain range, Heinrichs had been startled at the beauty of Palestine. "It was remarkably fertile and rich land we passed up to Lydda, much like home, but very new. I had expected desert."[26] But as the group traveled the long ascent into the Jerusalem mountain range by car, the landscape became rockier and dryer. His impressions of the city upon arrival were very strong. It was much newer, cleaner, and more attractive than he had expected. The trio headed to the marvelous new YMCA building on arrival. They checked into the Fast Hotel and then went off to lunch with Humphrey Bowman, chairman of the board of the Jerusalem YMCA and also the Director of the Education Department in the Palestine government. Bowman was a career colonial chap and YMCA man from England who also administered all school sport activity for the Mandate administration. After meeting Bowman, Smith and Heinrichs went to a meeting at the Jerusalem YMCA where Heinrichs was not impressed with the personnel, who he described as having long discussions with no vision.[27] That was okay, though. A key reason why Heinrichs had been hired was to fix the problem of the staff.

Heinrichs worked one morning[28] with fellow board member Richard Adamson on the plans of the building to wrap his head around just how much work was left to complete the project in the next two years. They targeted the spring of 1933 for its formal opening. A lot of work had to be done to figure out how to make the building financially viable post-Depression. Beautiful as it was, when the stock market crashed in 1929, the building became a relic of a bygone era.[29] Although stunned by the beauty of the building, Heinrichs had concerns that there had been too much emphasis on the aesthetic design. He felt that it would present problems actually functioning as an association. He kept his opinions to himself, though. That evening, following Frank Slack's December advice, the Heinrichses headed to see Harte.

The next day, Heinrichs went to see Albert Abramson,[30] a converted English Jew in charge of the Palestine Land Records Office who was also on the Jerusalem YMCA's board. He was important to the board because there was still a lot to accomplish with his office: connecting the building to the city's sewage and obtaining all of the permits necessary for the completion of the work. Land was the most complex issue in Palestine. Abramson was a good man to have on one's side. After their conversation, Richard Adamson arranged for a large Buick to take the whole group up north to Nazareth, the city in which Jesus grew up. There, they visited the house of Joseph. From Nazareth, Lattof, Smith, and the Heinrichses continued to Tiberias and the Sea of Galilee, where they enjoyed a boat ride and were put up at Hotel Tiberias six hundred feet below sea level. They gathered for a pleasant dinner as the sun set over the lake. They discussed the Jerusalem offer at length, and the Heinrichses were about ready to accept "the call".

After they returned to Jerusalem,[31] the YMCA basketball team played the American University of Beirut. After watching a depressing defeat for the Association, Heinrichs went to the installation at King Solomon Quarries Lodge (a Masonic Lodge). He very well might have seen Frederick Kisch there for the first time. He concluded his evening with a very long interview with Dr. Tawfiq Canaan, a man who would eventually become one of his primary nemeses.

Smith, Adamson, Lattof, Auburn, and the Heinrichses went over every detail of the building.[32] They discussed necessary changes to the plans. Heinrichs recorded in his diary that he thought it a tragedy that the architectural triumph should be without a perfect Association.[33] He then joined Smith for his religious work group and continued on to the home of Fakhri Bey Nashashibi, who had invited the members of the Arab Sports Club to meet with Heinrichs. The club would inherit the Jerusalem YMCA's old building. He then met with His Eminence the Mayor, who was a former Turkish artillery officer married to three women: a Muslim, Christian, and Jew. In such ways was the symbolic peace of Jerusalem maintained.

Heinrichs also had his meeting with High Commissioner Chancellor and Edward Mills, his chief secretary. Jerusalem governor Edward Keith-Roach joined them. Heinrichs found Chancellor to be a nice man, but not very forceful. Afterwards, he met Boulos Said, the treasurer of the YMCA, soon also to become one of his nemeses. After lunch, he went back up to Mount Scopus for another two-and-a-half-hour meeting with Harte.[34]

Harte was unshakable in his determination never to enter the new building. Heinrichs tried hard to win his sympathy, but Harte was a wounded, sorrowful, disappointed man, and Heinrichs felt sorry for him. Yet there was something redeeming about Harte. Heinrichs understood that Harte's conception of the new YMCA was so beautiful that he hoped to conserve as much of it as possible. Upon returning from Mount Scopus, Heinrichs and his wife ended their day with a pleasant private dinner at the home of Nicholas and Olga Lattof.

Tuesday, April 14 was Heinrichs' and Dorothy's last day in Jerusalem before they continued on to the United States. Heinrichs took a tour of the Holy Sepulcher Church, the Via Dolorosa, the Dome of the Rock, and the Wailing Wall. The latter he described as a "scene of tragedy covering over 20 centuries."[35] Adamson and Lattof saw them off. Heinrichs managed to book a first-class compartment on the train from Kantara to Cairo. It was a perfectly awful, fourteen-hour trip across the parched Sinai Peninsula.[36] They arrived at the flat in Cairo by eleven o'clock that night and were surprised to see Junior and Mary still awake, but still they were excited to see them.[37]

It was decided: Heinrichs would accept "the call". Over the next couple of days, the Heinrichses visited the British consul general in Cairo to process their Palestine immigration papers. At 11:00 p.m. on April 20, the Heinrichs family boarded the SS *President Garfield*.[38] At dawn, the engines of the ship vibrated as the transport slowly pulled out of Port Said. As the ship traveled around the Mediterranean dropping off passengers and picking up new ones, the Heinrichses took in the sights of Pompeii, Milan, Genoa, and Marseilles before the ship put out for the Atlantic. On the evening of May 11,[39] the family stayed up on deck to catch a first glimpse of America's shores. As the sun set in the bitterly cold and foggy air, they saw Nantucket Light. The blare of the fog-horn gave Junior and Mary a great fright. Mary ran at first, trying to escape it. As it blared again, she ran around in circles, collapsing on the deck in tears. Later that evening, Heinrichs recorded in his diary, "It gives me a great thrill after 5 years away to feel I am once more again within American territory."

## 3.

While the Jerusalem YMCA and Heinrichs were managing their respective leadership and career transitions, Yosef Yekutieli was hard at work. The Maccabi strategy in Palestine faced changing weather in European politics. Storm clouds were gathering. In September, the Nazi Party managed to emerge as the second largest political party in Germany. In 1931, an emerging financial crisis in Germany would give Hitler all that he needed to start moving the pieces of the checkerboard in his favor. Millions in Germany were unemployed. The disaffected ran towards the Nazi platform, which blamed the "Jew" for all of Germany's problems. President Herbert Hoover of the United States would suspend Germany's reparations payments, which it had been required to pay under the Treaty of Versailles. Only thirteen years after the war to end all wars, Germany was emerging from under the treaty's heel. And its new message was not good.

There were problems in Palestine, too (as far as the Zionist movement was concerned). In June 1931, the Palestine government published an Order of Council about the Wailing Wall in the *Palestine Gazette*, the official organ of the Mandate administration.[40] This Order of Council recognized permanent ownership of the Wall by Muslims. It was ruled *Waqf* property (this being the Islamic trust that owns and manages Muslim properties on behalf of believers). Weizmann warned the British that they were squandering the sympathies of Jews by not recognizing the moral force that Zionism enshrined.[41]

Despite these dark developments for Zionism, Yekutieli continued his Maccabi and Olympic efforts. For him, the most thrilling job on earth would be organizing his vision for the First Maccabiad.

By early February 1931, Yekutieli was already advertising the Maccabiad globally.[42] It was the year of his motorcycle tour. He described the Maccabiad as a Jewish Olympics. The Young Men's Hebrew Association on Ninety-Second Street announced the games to a meeting of New York's Jewish sport clubs, who would eventually help charter a ship to take athletes to Tel Aviv.[43]

Yekutieli targeted England as his final destination for the motorcycle tour in an effort to fortify relations between Maccabi Palestine and England. This was consistent with all other Zionist efforts. Great Britain had the Mandate power, and Herzl, the spiritual founder of Zionism, had oriented the movement toward England from the beginning (after his meeting with the Order of Ancient Maccabeans). Chaim Weizmann ran the World Zionist Organization (WZO) out of London. Lionel Shalit, eventually chairman of Maccabi Europe, wrote to Weizmann in April, shortly before Yekutieli and his motorcycle team rode for London and Manchester. He brought the Maccabiad to Weizmann's attention, describing how the international Jewish youth gathering would bring together four thousand participants, with the full intention to invite the Arab sports clubs in Palestine.[44] Shalit asked Weizmann if he would be willing to meet to discuss the event in more detail.

Shalit was connected with the Bar-Cochba Association,[45] a Maccabi Association in London's Soho Square. The association took its name after Simon Bar-Cochba, the head of the Jewish revolt against the Romans who led the stand at Massada. The board of the Bar-Cochba Association included prominent Jewish citizens like Lord Melchett (its president and British patron of the First Maccabiad) and his sister Eva, the Viscountess Erleigh (who served as a vice president).[46] Other members of the association included Sir Wyndham Deedes, who had served as Chief Secretary from 1920 to 1922 for Palestine's first High Commissioner, and James de Rothschild and Professor Selig Brodetsky. Brodetsky was a prominent mathematician who headed the mathematics department at the University of Leeds and became the second president of Hebrew University after the death of Judah Magnes. He would also become president of the Maccabi World Union when Palestine was recognized by the IOC.

Yekutieli prepared a memorandum[47] about the Maccabiad to serve as an aide mémoire to all those who would advertise it in England after he left. Upon his return, he sent it to many people and organizations that he had met in England so that they could use it to raise funds, including the Zionist office in Leeds[48] and Bar-Cochba's board members.[49] The only Maccabi organization affiliated with the Movement in England was the Bar-Cochba group.[50]

In his aide mémoire, Yekutieli described how the concept of the Maccabiad was rooted in Max Nordau's call for a new and muscular Jewry. By the time of the motorcycle tour, the Maccabi Movement was about thirty-five years old[51] and had already garnered an estimated 150,000 followers.[52] The movement had members in twenty-four countries. At the time, its headquarters were in Berlin, but with the upcoming changes in German politics, it would soon see them move to London.

Yekutieli described in his aide mémoire the Maccabi Movement as a Zionist non-partisan sports organization[53] capable of incorporating youth from all segments and levels of society. He explained how the movement had experienced significant growth when assimilated Jews were forced out of Christian clubs in Europe. This resulted in their setting up Jewish clubs. Yekutieli wanted the English to understand that the Maccabi Movement was an antidote for anti-Semitism on the Continent. Young Jews who entered its ranks experienced "its national atmosphere"[54] and "turned into good Zionists"[55]—people committed to and capable of building the Jewish national home.

For Yekutieli, the Maccabi Movement was a "bridge from assimilation to nationalism."[56] Maccabi Palestine was the pioneer of sport in the country; before the Maccabi, no one in Palestine knew anything about sports.[57] A key talking point in the aide mémoire was the Maccabis' lead in establishing the Palestine Football Association, getting it recognized by the government in Palestine, and affiliating it to FIFA.[58] This was something to talk about at the cocktail parties, when English Jews would ask other prospective Jewish donors to take out their checkbooks. In many ways, the affiliation to FIFA represented the Zionists' first entry point into the global order, a back door of sorts to the League of Nations (and, eventually, for Israel to the United Nations).

The aide mémoire explained why Palestine could not yet participate in the Olympic Games. Palestine's status as a "territory" did not align with the IOC's requirement that national Olympic committees represent a "nation".[59] Yekutieli pointed out that many Jews had distinguished themselves in the Olympic Games, but never as Maccabis. For him, the only way of getting into the Olympic Games was as "Erez-Israelians"[60] (meaning as citizens of the nation of the Land of Israel). This did not preclude the Arabs as constituents. Yekutieli would be under direct orders from Kisch and the Va'ad Leumi that the Maccabiad should remain open to non-Jews.

Yekutieli felt sport, in particular international sport, was an opportunity for enlightenment. On his way to London with the motorcycle tour, he tried to meet with Alice Milliat of FSFI in Paris. She was supportive of his efforts to affiliate Maccabi Palestine to her international federation and to develop sport among women in Palestine.[61] Yekutieli told her in their exchanges that Muslim women in Palestine still wore the veil, and that many waters would flow from the Jordan River to the Dead Sea before they uncovered their faces and allowed sport to penetrate their lives. And if that miracle ever happened, it would be thanks to Jewish women.[62]

Yekutieli stressed the economic importance of sport to building the Jewish national home. He described how municipalities invested large sums in building stadia in order to make it possible for gatherings to take place, and that this was particularly important in difficult economic times.[63] For Yekutieli, the Maccabiad would be his New Deal project for the Jewish economy in Palestine. In London, he would stress how the tourists and visitors to the Maccabiad would bring in capital, and that the building of a stadium would employ scores of workmen for at least a year. "In Tel-Aviv, the young and beautiful Hebrew town, we shall build our national stadium in which the Maccabiahs will take place."[64]

A permanent stadium was going to cost £P 50,000.[65] This was an impossible sum to raise, so he planned for the Maccabiad to take place on "an ordinary sports ground which would be temporarily arranged for the purpose."[66] His intention was to lay the cornerstone of a new national stadium during the Maccabiah. In addition, he wanted to build a gymnasium hall and a club that would serve as the school. This would be the Maccabis' "home" (*bayt* in Hebrew) "from which our doctrines will spread far and wide."[67] When one considers how small Bayt HaMaccabi actually was, it is impressive what Yekutieli accomplished from it in the interests of Jewish sport.

Finally, P.O. Box 129 would have a home. Yekutieli asked for £P 5,000.[68,69] Twenty percent was allotted to the club's construction. Forty-two percent went to work force development and employment costs. Sixteen percent went to preparation of the athletic grounds. The remaining 22 percent went to subsidize participants from abroad, to organize a Maccabi band, and for miscellaneous expenses.

The Maccabi Games were born.

When Yekutieli and his team of motorcyclists were in England, their British hosts organized an all-Jewish propaganda event in athletics at West Ham Stadium to reinforce the message that the Maccabi riders had brought forth from Tel Aviv.[70] The program commenced at three o'clock with the grand entry of Yekutieli and his Maccabi motorcyclists, commemorating the occasion of the conclusion of Maccabi Palestine's historic journey from Tel Aviv to London. Then, ten athletics events comprising seventy-eight entrants ran until 5:20 in the evening. The chairman of the British section of the Jewish Agency, Mr. Goldsmid, had previously noted how the team's crossing of the Sinai desert in just sixteen hours was evidence enough that centuries of persecution and the ghetto life had not diminished the full physical development of the Jewish people.[71] Upon his return to Tel Aviv, Yekutieli wrote to the Mayor of Stepney, Morris Davis, and invited him to lay the foundation stone for the stadium during the Maccabiad.[72]

The motorcycle ride put Maccabi Palestine on the sport map. But in Europe, the Maccabi Movement was about to enter a much more difficult period. With Hitler's takeover of Germany, things would become dangerous. The Romanian government would eventually cancel the European Maccabiad in Czernowitz when it uncovered a plot to assassinate Lord Melchett.[73] The Maccabi Movement would need to find a new home, perhaps in Palestine: its traditional heartland in central and eastern Europe was becoming increasingly unstable politically and dangerous for Jews. So, Yekutieli set about establishing the Federation of the Amateur Sports Clubs of Palestine (FASCP), anticipating the in-gathering of the Jews to their Promised Land.

Yekutieli convened the first meeting of the FASCP on December 26, 1931.[74] He was joined by Yehoshua Alouf, Shlomo Arazi, and Walter Frankl, representing the sports clubs of Tel Aviv, Jerusalem, and Jaffa, respectively. Representatives of the clubs in Rehovot, Gedera, Haifa, Tiberias, Safad, Petach Tikva, and Ekron also attended the meeting. In addition, several territorial sport governing bodies were represented: Palestine Football Association, Palestine Tennis League, Palestine Fencing Association, Tel Aviv Race Club, and the Palestine Maccabi Federation. The FASCP was certainly representative of the geography of the country, but it seemed not to be representative of the Arabs in the country. This could be a problem for international sport, as well as for the World Zionist Organization. The year 1932 would tell if there was really an intention for the Maccabis to reach out.

Yekutieli called for convening a single organization to govern sport in Palestine because sport was progressing rapidly, negotiations to join international federations had been continuing for a long time, the demands of sport clubs were increasing, and it was difficult to found a separate federation for every branch of sport. A single united federation would facilitate the application of all federations to their respective international sport governing bodies.[75]

It was a stroke of genius. Based on his experience with FIFA, the IAAF, and FSFI, Yekutieli had realized that with the curtain call coming in Europe, a much more efficient, centralized organization would have to be established in order to advocate for the needs of Jewish athletes who might need to flee Europe for Palestine.

## 4.

Back in New York, the Heinrichses disembarked the SS *President Garfield*. Slack met them at the docks with several others from the National Council of YMCAs. They cleared the enormous amount of luggage they had and then checked into the Shelton Hotel, one of New York's newest luxury hotels. Arthur Loomis Harmon, architect of the Jerusalem YMCA project and Empire State Building, had also designed the Shelton. The family went through their medical exams. In the evening the Heinrichses dined with Ramsey.[76] The following morning,[77] Heinrichs got up early, took care of the banking, and purchased tickets for Mrs. Heinrichs' and the children's return to Honolulu. He took them to Pennsylvania Station to see them off, then checked out of the Shelton. He was put up at a friend's house before starting daily meetings with YMCAs throughout the region and preparing to assume his responsibilities in Jerusalem.

Officially on furlough until the end of the year, at the end of May, Heinrichs was in Chicago. There, he was able to meet Shafeec Mansoor,[78] a young Palestinian Christian who had been sent from Jerusalem to the YMCA College in Chicago for training. Lattof had advocated for his studies in the United States and had generously made a personal financial contribution to his training.[79] Heinrichs was impressed with Mansoor and was sure that he would like to hire him for the staff in Jerusalem.

Heinrichs began to study. The Jerusalem YMCA project was a tangle of politics, administrative headaches, and unfinished construction. Slack provided him a copy of the 1930 administrative report from the Physical Department,[80] which Fred Auburn had compiled. Auburn noted how the political factor entered into every undertaking in the country, writing, "The YMCA faces this fact and endeavors to meet the situation in such a way as will not be antagonistic to any party and yet meet the common need, of all groups. Intergroup competitions, organizations of local or national committees and international competitions bring out the racial feeling before the spirit of sport."[81] From the report, Heinrichs understood that the Arab camp in Palestinian politics had split into two groups. One backed the positions of the Grand Mufti of Jerusalem, which was described as the "anti-Jewish and anti-British"[82] camp. The other camp had aligned its political positions with the mayor of Jerusalem, Ragheb Bey Nashashibi. This was considered the more moderate camp.[83] However, both camps were "united in opposition to the Jewish National Home policy in Palestine."[84]

The report further described the Jews as being "very strongly organized politically, financially and educationally."[85] Auburn reported that
they used "every means available" for propaganda and were endeavor-
ing to take over the whole country.[86] The example that Auburn provided
was the "spirit shown in the formation of the Palestine Olympic Games
Association when they demanded the majority of representatives on
the Executive Committee with the result that the organization was
postponed until such a time as the Arabs will be sufficiently organized
to counterbalance this attitude."[87]

This appears to have been the earliest, joint attempt to form a
national Olympic committee for Palestine. Although Auburn was
probably accurate in his portrayal of the Zionists' rigidity in the
meeting, his remarks about the Arab camp reveal that there was justification for the Zionist position. The Jewish community might have
been a minority in the country, but, in sport, it represented the outright majority, and one very much more advanced in its organizational
capabilities. Auburn credited the dominance of the Jewish position
in sport as being instrumental: it awakened "the Arabs to their need
of cooperation and the development of the spirit of service to their
country on the part of their leaders."[88]

As the new secretary-general of the Jerusalem YMCA, Heinrichs
was to help close the gap. He would oversee the new building, establish its programs, and get the Arab camp "sufficiently organized."[89] This
must be kept in mind in order to understand the strategic error of what
would eventually transpire between Heinrichs and the board of the
Jerusalem YMCA.

Auburn accredited the problems in the Arab camp to "the lack of
union and leadership among the Arabs in the past. However, [the Arabs
were] now alert to the disadvantages of this non-representation and
non-organization and [were] appealing to the YMCA Physical Department to take the leadership in uniting and organizing their forces for
local and nation wide development of physical education."[90]

Then Auburn continued and stressed that the desire of the Association was to help the Arabs organize themselves and promote
nationwide interest in sports. The Jerusalem YMCA began forming the
Arab Amateur Athletic Union, not to reverse the imbalance of power,

but to allow for fairer representation of the Arabs and help them work with Jews cooperatively in the field of sports. Auburn documented in his report that both camps looked to the Jerusalem YMCA for council and advice. Thus, with approval from both Jewish and Arab camps, the Jerusalem YMCA in 1930 was made the mediator for the development of national sports and an international sport initiative.

Auburn's report[91] represents the crystallization of the modern Arab Palestinian sports movement. Everything up to that point had been comparatively less organized, ad hoc, or nowhere near the level required to petition the IOC for affiliation. Despite this, the Zionist camp had approached the Association to come to some type of accommodation with the Arabs in sport. It must be understood that "physical education" is synonymous with "sport and Olympic development" during this period in history, as evidenced by the YMCA Movement's presentation to the IOC in Antwerp in 1920 and Heinrichs' activities at the Lahore YMCA to set up Olympic activity in the Punjab.

The Jerusalem YMCA began fulfilling this role by introducing more sports to Arab Palestinians in 1931, specifically cross country and basketball.[92] It also organized the tennis championship that brought together Muslims, Christians, and Jews. It invited Mayor Nashashibi to make some remarks at the formal opening of the Association's tennis courts and inaugural competition. Among the mayor's remarks was a touch of his sense of humor: "As I look at the tennis courts before me, and at the building to my left soon to be completed, I entertain the hope that our boys and young men will flock to the Young Men's Christian Association which is the greatest center for character building. When they do so, there will be fewer doctors, less crime, and fewer jails."[93] The tennis program was a microcosm of the diversity of the Holy City. Lattof reported that 134 male and female Bahais, Armenian and Greek Orthodox Christians, Jews, Muslims, Protestants, and Roman Catholics participated in it in 1931.[94]

All this explains the meetings that would begin in 1932 between Heinrichs and the Jewish camp. Heinrichs conducted these meetings with the approval of the Arab board members. Such rapprochement would not sit well with everyone, and as an emergent Nazi Germany reared its head, some in the Arab political camp would take notice for all the wrong reasons.

**5.**
___

In July 1931, Lattof wrote to Ramsey in New York.[95] He described the Association's actions following a meeting with the Zionist camp. The Jerusalem YMCA had just hosted the Second Annual YMCA Cross Country Championship for Palestine in which 107 competitors took part. It observed a notable increase in participants—47 instead of 22 the previous year. The army, police, Arab Sports Club, Hapoel, Bishop Gobat's School, Jerusalem Athletics Club, Orthodox [Christian] Sports Club, Post and Telegraph (a corporate team), and the District Police all participated. But Lattof expressed concerns to Ramsey about the attitudes of the Arab constituents. He described their enthusiasm as sporadic, and how they said a lot but did little. He acknowledged these shortcomings in light of the fact that the Jews' sport memberships ran into the thousands. Maccabi Jerusalem alone had 550 members with fair sport facilities and trained German volunteers. Both Arab clubs and Hapoel, the Jewish labor sports movement, wanted the Jerusalem YMCA to take a leading role in the Palestine Football Association to reduce the influence of Maccabi. Lattof felt that there was every reason to believe that this could be achieved.[96]

As a result of Lattof's report, Heinrichs would begin to engage Kisch, Yekutieli, and the Maccabis around football not long after his arrival in Palestine on May 8, 1932.

Toward the end of 1931, Heinrichs was traveling around the United States speaking at YMCAs on the Jerusalem project,[97] building relationships that would prove vital later. He had wrapped his head around the finances of the project in Jerusalem. There were some serious problems with the numbers, which Heinrichs put in a handwritten memorandum to Francis Harmon, the new senior secretary of the IC/YMCA, and Smith.[98]

Heinrichs was concerned about six key challenges. The financial crisis was resulting in a lower yield from the endowment, making it hard to hire foreign staff. The business plan's revenue-generating components could not cover the difference, at least for a while. The building was beautiful but extremely costly to maintain. Most of Jerusalem's residents were Muslims and Jews, not Christian, so recruiting members would be difficult. Certain Christian sects were also vocal in their opposition to the Association's work in the Holy City. Heinrichs' work seemed to be stalled out of the gates, and he asked that New York work with him to solve the problem of a serious lack of cash. It was going to be an uphill battle.

## 6.

At the end of 1931, Jerusalem was abuzz with sport activities: the finals of the Chancellor Football Cup took place at the Jerusalem Sports Club (a competition that Sir John Chancellor had started);[99] Palestine Police beat Hapoel 3–0 in the Palestine Football League;[100] Palestine Police offered good entertainment[101] at its annual Novice Boxing Championship[102] at Eden Hall;[103] the Jerusalem YMCA launched its winter session of Saturday night sport activities across football, field hockey, volleyball, fencing, cross country running, wrestling, weightlifting, and boxing;[104] the Maccabis of Ness Ziona and the Hasmoneans faced off in football;[105] British Police defeated Petach Tikva;[106] the Arab Sports Club defeated Maccabi Jerusalem 2–1 on Maccabi's home turf;[107] the semifinal of the Middle East Inter-Unit Cup was held;[108] and Arab Sports Club took on Hapoel's Reserve team.[109] Almost every day of the month, sport flowed through the veins of the Holy City. Intercultural sport was taking place in unprecedented ways, shifting the status quo, building new bridges. It was a new beginning.

Soon, Heinrichs would assume the most thrilling job on earth. And yet, with this shift in leadership at the Jerusalem YMCA, the world beyond it

# CHAPTER 5

# The Jewish Olympics

## 1.

The year 1932 would witness a seismic shift in Germany's politics and relations with the countries that, fourteen years earlier, had defeated it in the First World War. Although in March, Adolf Hitler would be defeated decisively by Paul von Hindenburg for the role of president of the Weimar Republic, by the end of July, the Nazi Party would demonstrate its emerging popularity in a landslide victory in the German parliamentary elections. The Nazi Party (NSDAP) won 230 out of 608 seats in the Reichstag elections. In June, the Lausanne Conference convened, at which Great Britain and France decided to suspend Germany's payment of war reparations. Between the global financial crisis and the economic situation in Germany, the country's treasury simply could not pay the bills.

Hitler was still one year away from seizing full control of Germany, but the long shadow of the swastika had already reached Palestine. As the Nazis took effective control in the Reichstag, a young German living in Palestine by the name of Karl Ruff received a letter from Ernst Bohle in the Overseas Organization (*Auslands-Organisation/AO*) of the German Foreign Ministry in Hamburg.[1] The AO had begun agitating for the establishment of official NSDAP party branches overseas. The German Colony at Sarona was located just north of Jaffa, not far from Tel Aviv. It had about two hundred ethnic German Palestinians residing in it who held firm to the concept of *Deutschtum*, or "Germanness."[2] There were three other such communities at Haifa, Nazareth, and Rephaim. Rephaim was just south of Jerusalem.[3] By 1930, Rephaim could be considered a suburb, connected to the New Jerusalem by the road named Julian's Way. This major artery ran right between the emerging Jerusalem YMCA and King David Hotel.

As early as 1930, Ruff thought of founding sports clubs in Haifa and Sarona.[4] There were only six NSDAP members in Palestine at the time,[5] but by the end of the year, these six would blossom well beyond the minimum number of twenty-five people to form an *Ortsgruppe*—a local Nazi group.[6] The NSDAP would begin causing significant problems at the Jerusalem YMCA. Germany had already won the hosting rights to the 1936 Summer Olympics, scheduled to take place in Berlin. The NSDAP was about to usurp those rights, and Jerusalem would become a key battleground in the Olympic boycott effort. Although Palestinian newspapers did not carry much news about the NSDAP in 1932, it would do so almost daily once Hitler took over power completely on January 30, 1933.[7]

While Karl Ruff was laying the first foundation of the NSDAP in Palestine, Waldo Heinrichs was in the United States getting ready to head to Jerusalem. One of the first orders of business for Heinrichs was to identify a small but strong team to take with him to Palestine. For Yosef Yekutieli, meanwhile, the year 1932 was all about the First Maccabiad. His dream of a "Jewish Olympics" was finally becoming a reality, and it was important to him that Jews from surrounding countries attend.

## 2.

Yekutieli had been writing to Jack Goar, the Jewish president of the Central Committee of Maccabi Egypt. For a while, Goar was also the interim president of the Union Egyptienne des Sociétés Sportives (the Federation of Egyptian Sport Clubs). Egypt was a much bigger country than Palestine, with two very large ancient cities at Cairo and Alexandria. These cities were the center of Egyptian sports, and there was also a YMCA presence in each. Although Jews did not dominate Egyptian sport in the same way that they dominated Palestinian sport, they still were an important force—as evidenced by Goar's important governance position in the national sport landscape. Yekutieli was pleased that Egypt would send a squad to the First Maccabiad (which eventually did well in track and field and diving).[8]

Much bigger Maccabi teams would come from Europe and the United States. One of Yekutieli's most important achievements was to secure an unlimited quota of athletes for the Maccabiad from the government in Jerusalem.[9] The government granted a 50 percent reduction in rail fares within the country for those attending the event, in addition to a tax waiver on sport equipment entering the country.[10] The Americans had already announced that they would send a delegation on the SS *Aquitania*—coincidentally the same ship used by Frederick Kisch three years earlier on his journey to expand the Jewish Agency and integrate American Jews into the Zionist project.[11]

Yekutieli wanted to seize the opportunity of the Maccabiad to affiliate more Palestinian sport organizations to their respective international sport governing bodies. He also needed the permission[12] of international federations to host the "Jewish Olympics". This requirement is what opened the door for Yekutieli to engage in direct consultations about affiliating Palestinian sport governing bodies while working in parallel on the planning of the Maccabiad. The process for doing so would now be easy with the establishment of a single entity to do that— the Federation of the Amateur Sports Clubs of Palestine (FASCP). In mid-January 1932, two international federations responded positively to Yekutieli's efforts. The first was the IAAF, whose president was Sigfrid Edström (and who was also on the IOC's executive commission). He informed Yekutieli that because of the great hurry to recognize Palestine in time for the Maccabiad, he had sent the members of the IAAF council a letter asking them to vote in favor of Palestine's affiliation.[13] This was a major success for Yekutieli.

The other federation was FINA, the International Swimming Federation. In the case of this federation, the response was warm, but the organization required more details. First and foremost, FINA asked Yekutieli "to give…an additional statement to the intent that any club of Palestine could become a member…irrespective of race or confession."[14] FINA assumed this to be the case because Yekutieli had already used English, Arabic, and Hebrew in his letterhead design. FINA also informed Yekutieli that its Congress would make a decision on the FASCP application when it met at the Olympic Games in Los Angeles. Palestine would eventually affiliate to FINA through the FASCP, which had been set up barely three weeks prior to FINA's correspondence. By August 1932, Yekutieli would count among his affiliations the IAAF as well as the International Boxing Federation and International Gymnastics Federation.[15] And at the VII Congress of FSFI, Milliat and her colleagues also passed the affiliation request of Palestine.[16]

The affiliations to international sport governing bodies had a maturing effect on sport governance in Palestine. The federations began holding their meetings with consistency and organizing elections according to the rules and regulations they submitted in their affiliation requests. In early February, the Palestine Football Association held its elections at its general meeting.[17] Elected to the presidency was Colonel R. G. B. Spicer, commandant of the Palestine Police. The chairman was Dr. S. Levin Epstein. Shlomo Arazi was honorary secretary. Percy Speed, also a member of the Jerusalem YMCA, filled the role of honorary treasurer and honorary secretary of League and Cup Competitions. The members of the committee included Major J. Partridge, Mr. U. Blitz, Mr. M. Ben-Dor, Mr. M. Weintraub, and Mr. E. Rubenstein. Lieutenant W. H. P. Chattay and F/O S. Z. Sheldrick assumed the roles of Service Members.

This more mature structure and the Maccabiad called for patronage. Yekutieli wanted High Commissioner Arthur Wauchope to be the patron, to which he consented. However, Wauchope insisted upon one condition—that British and Arab sport clubs from within Palestine be invited to participate.[18] This condition was reported in a private correspondence to Chaim Weizmann in London.[19] There was no concern about Arabs being allowed to participate. There was some concern expressed that this could lead to an incident because there would be so many people standing around "all on tenderhooks for an opportunity of saying 'We told you so!'"[20] The Maccabiad went off without incident in the end; however, the Jerusalem YMCA decided to boycott.

Lord Melchett, the honorary president of the Maccabi World Union (MWU), arrived in Palestine on March 22 for the event.[21] He proceeded with his sister to Migdal, the villa built by their father on the shores of the Sea of Galilee.[22] While in Palestine, Lord Melchett would attend the Maccabiad and check in on his business ventures in the country, such as his orange orchards in Tel Mond.[23] Although originally both Jewish, Melchett's son and eldest daughter, Henry and Eva, were actually practicing Christians until the rise of Hitler and Nazism, at which point they both reverted to Judaism and became strong advocates for the rebuilding of the Jewish national home.[24]

The Maccabiad was a perfect opportunity for Jewish youth to connect with their Jewish past, as Yekutieli considered it. Yekutieli truly believed that physical culture was intrinsic to Jews from the days of the Bible.[25] An ardent and unapologetic Zionist, Yekutieli sometimes wrote essays that reinforced and legitimated Jews' glorious physical past. He would cite Jacob as an "excellent athlete,"[26] noting how the son of the Patriarch Abraham had not been defeated in his all-night supernatural wrestling encounter, thereby being renamed Israel (or "[the God] El rules."[27]) To Yekutieli, Jacob's son Naphtali was a good "runner."[28] His other son Joseph was a good "target-hitter."[29] "Sampson, son of Manoach, was a standard champion."[30] King David "was distinguished for his ably taking aim."[31] Yekutieli pointed out how Josephus, the famous chronicler of the war of the Romans against the Jews, noted that "Jewish youths were engaged in gymnastics in colleges and public stadiums…and…that a great many scholars among the Pharisees, as well as the Essenes distinguished themselves in swimming and athletics."[32] Yekutieli even argued that Herod saved the ancient Olympic Games when he "built up a magnificent stadium in the city Caesaria. That stadium had been splendidly inaugurated with great pomp by him."[33] Yekutieli believed firmly that Jewish physical culture had died with the dispersal of the Jews from their ancient homeland and that Zionism, which was restoring Zion, would restore the Jewish body.[34] There could be no greater gift voluntarily given to the Jewish youth of the world. The Maccabiad was the great festival that would commemorate this restorative action.

The Maccabiad opened on March 28 with the release of 120 carrier pigeons, which were sent forth in batches of ten to symbolize the twelve tribes of Israel.[35] More than four thousand participants and members of Maccabi sport clubs paraded through the newly built stadium near the Yarkon River.[36] Mayor Meir Dizengoff of Tel Aviv led the procession through the streets of Tel Aviv.[37] "About 30,000 people lined the roads, cheering the procession as it passed."[38] The city was described as being in a brilliant holiday mood.[39] Houses, shops, and cars were decorated with Zionist flags and with Maccabean symbols.[40] Maccabi Palestine organized a torchlight procession "in honor of the thousands of visitors"[41] who had come to the city from all over the world. The stadium had been built in just seven weeks, and twenty-five thousand visitors were in town. There was not a spare accommodation in the city.[42] A huge gathering of over five thousand people at Beth Am was the site of speeches by Mayor Dizengoff, Selig Brodetsky (of the Jewish Agency Executive), Henrietta Szold (of Hadassah Hospital and the Va'ad Leumi), and Dr. Herman Lelewer (president of the MWU). Mr. Nadar, the chairman of Maccabi Palestine, declared "that by physical strength and love for Palestine all Jewish difficulties will be overcome."[43] Mrs. Ben Yehuda, who was the widow of the reviver of the modern Hebrew language, was presented with the winner's trophy in her husband's name, the cup itself having been provided to him by the American organization Young Judaea when he had traveled from the United States to Palestine in 1919.[44]

The Organization Department of the World Zionist Organization in London also supported the successful staging of the Maccabiad by coordinating a number of political actions.[45] It was actually the Zionist Executive that worked from London to secure the patronage of High Commissioner Wauchope. The Executive also ordered the Zionist Federation to arrange "lecture courses on Zionism and Palestine for the visitors to the Maccabiad"[46] and even asked that it ensure that a reliable Zionist traveled on board the ships that came to Palestine with delegations for the event "with the task of imparting suitable instruction to the visitors en route."[47] The Palestine Zionist Executive saw to a similar Zionist representative being assigned to all shipping company offices in central Europe that were selling passages to Palestine.[48]

On day three of the Maccabiad, High Commissioner Wauchope "presented a cup to be competed for in the…relay race,"[49] and an Egyptian Arab named Said Muhammed won the 500-meter event.[50] On the final day of events, American female athlete Sybil Koff won three gold medals, in the 100-meter, triathlon, and high jump.[51] The Polish football team defeated Maccabi Palestine in the football final, and the Austrian Maccabis won the swimming.[52] The tennis finals took place in Rehovot and went to the team from Czechoslovakia.[53] Polish boxers and Danish wrestlers won their respective event classes.[54] A crowd of twenty-five thousand gathered for the closing ceremonies, over which High Commissioner Wauchope presided. The closing ceremony included mass displays by scouts, gymnasts, motorcyclists, bicyclists, and equestrians.[55]

The final standing of the delegations that participated in the various events was as follows: Poland 377 points, America 285 points, Austria 254 points, Czechoslovakia 235 points, Palestine 218 points, Germany 120 points, and Egypt 120 points. Romania, Great Britain, Yugoslavia, and Greece were the next runners-up.[56]

The Maccabiad was a great propaganda success. Upon its return to the UK, the Bar-Cochba Association showed a film on the Maccabiad, including scenes from around Palestine, at the Congregational Hall in mid-September.[57] Combined with the Levant Fair of 1932 and the festivities for the Jewish holiday of Purim, the economic impact through tourism was significant. On March 28 alone, 1,650 tourists disembarked from boats at Jaffa.[58]

But the Organizing Committee itself had barely broken even. And despite the success of European teams, things were far from perfect in Europe. Palestine was successfully advertised as a destination for Jews, but this was taken by some to mean that they had somewhere else to go, even if they did not want to leave the country in which they lived. The Jewish Telegraphic Agency (JTA) reported on May 27, 1932, that the Maccabi club in Czernowitz, Romania, defeated Johann, the German football club.[59] Angry supporters of the German team then attacked the Jewish footballers, injuring several while shouting at them, "Jews go to Palestine."[60] The Romanian government also was forced to withdraw the permit to host the European Maccabiad at Czernowitz because it had discovered the plot to assassinate Lord Melchett, who was intending to patronize the event.[61] The Maccabi organization submitted a claim for compensation and the games were shifted to Prague.[62] By the end of the year, Lord Melchett traveled to Poland. En route he met with

Dr. Lelewer, and he "appealed to World Jewry to prepare for the Jewish future in Palestine."[63]

In addition to the events in Europe, Yekutieli did not get some of the traction in Palestine that he had hoped to see from the Arabs after the Maccabiad. A first blow was a letter from the private secretary of the High Commissioner.[64] Yekutieli had requested the High Commissioner's impressions for inclusion in a commemorative book that he was preparing. The private secretary respectfully declined, asking instead that "the introduction would come more suitably from someone who was more closely concerned with the 'Maccabiad.'"[65] Yekutieli also advertised in the *Palestine Bulletin* the first annual meeting of the FASCP.[66] The printed article invited all clubs to participate and identified P.O. Box 129 as the address to which to send expressions of interest to participate. But this appears not to have produced a result, perhaps because the article appeared on short notice before the actual meeting.[67] Hapoel also walked away from the FASCP, complaining that it was dominated by Maccabi (although the withdrawal was also because Hapoel espoused loyalty to its socialist leanings and to the Socialist Workers' Sport International). There remained a general problem with the Arab clubs not wanting to co-govern sport with the Jews, even though they were willing to use Jewish sport facilities and travel to the Jewish White City to participate in regional sport matches that Maccabi organized. Although it is easy to conceive of Maccabi not caring because of its ardent Zionist profile, in fact it desired the cooperation, was required by international sport to pursue it, and was waiting for someone or some type of structural link to be made that could satisfy Olympic requirements.

And then would come Heinrichs.

## 3.

After India, the Heinrichses temporarily set up in Larchmont, New York because Heinrichs had to commute into Manhattan for regular meetings with Fred Ramsey and others associated with the Jerusalem YMCA project. In early January,[68] he went into the city and met with Jan MacDonald. She was the sister of William Paton, who had been the private secretary to Prime Minister Ramsay MacDonald of Great Britain. They chatted most of the morning and Heinrichs decided that he wanted her to join him. MacDonald would be in charge of the Jerusalem YMCA library and work with the Education Department. Heinrichs felt that she would add brains, religious fervor, technique, and a great service if she were willing to come on a shoestring.

The next day, Heinrichs met with Frank Slack and Wilbert Smith to go over more details. He continued on to Enery Blum's art shop to select pictures for the Jerusalem building.[69] MacDonald joined him and was pleased with what had been selected, but Heinrichs was not so sure. He found three pictures in particular objectionable, with too much emphasis on color and not enough on subject matter. He took the layout plans home that night and shared them with his wife. She thought that the furniture was too elaborate for a Christian association. Heinrichs stayed up late doing paperwork for Jerusalem. Then he went to the Architectural Bureau of the NC/YMCA in the morning.[70] He gave them all the furniture specifications and went out to lunch. He sat down and began reading *Palestine Survey*, a review of economic and social conditions in the country.

The weekend would bring no respite. The family was moving to Palestine in early April, and there was much to do: buy things for Jerusalem, close up the house in Larchmont, and supervise the Jerusalem project from New York. Heinrichs' furlough had ended, and January, February, and March 1932 were full employment months for him in the US.

Heinrichs wrote Humphrey Bowman, the chairman of the Jerusalem YMCA's board, in mid-January. Archie Harte had always dreamed that a library containing all the books possible about the life of Jesus would be at the heart of the YMCA's building and spiritual life. It was called the Jesus Library. The day before[71] he wrote to Bowman, Heinrichs had received important news. Dorothy Heinrichs was from a well-to-do family in Honolulu. Her aunt, Margaret Hopper, had mailed Heinrichs a letter in which she promised to give a gift of $10,000 to Heinrichs for the Jesus Library.[72] She gave the money in memory of her parents, but it was also a form of support for Heinrichs as he assumed his new role. A secretary-general was not just supposed to run an efficient organization. The role was also that of fund-raiser. Aunt Margaret's considerable gift fulfilled in its entirety one of the key components of Harte's vision for the Jerusalem YMCA. Five thousand dollars was to be used to buy books in America and Europe. The other half was to be invested in an endowment fund for future purposes. Heinrichs also shared with Bowman the decision to hire MacDonald from the Palestine Section of the International YMCA to join his staff in Jerusalem. Bowman was English, so he likely appreciated that Heinrichs' first hire was from the United Kingdom.

Toward the end of January, Heinrichs discovered another unpleasant surprise in the Jerusalem financials. He had woken up early to take the train into New York to see Ramsey and complete the building budget for Jerusalem. There was supposed to be $75,000[73] available from gains in exchange on pound sterling. He discovered that it had all been used for the Jarvie Commonwealth Fund. He asked Ramsey to see the Central Hanover Bank and Trust Company about sequestering it for use in 1932. The budget was short serious cash (equivalent to the interest earned that had already been spent), and Heinrichs would have to figure out how to fill the gap.

Heinrichs continued to work on the Jesus Library and a list of technical books to support the Boys' and Physical Departments.[74] It was an enormous job. With a fat catalog of the Associated Press in hand, Heinrichs began clipping out every book on Jesus and the various phases of his life that he could find. Heinrichs sat there arranging them all, pasting them to sheets of paper, checking for duplicates, and re-lettering them to know exactly how many books there were in each class and how much they would cost. It took him an entire day. When he added up the cost,[75] 100 books on Palestine would cost $521.85[76] and 525 books about the life of Jesus would cost $1,340.[77]

Heinrichs consulted colleagues about the library project. It was suggested to expand the effort to include books on Judaism and Islam as well.[78] This could attract more people to the library and serve as a gesture consonant with the Jerusalem YMCA's mission to bring together the peoples of the three Abrahamic faiths. Some of the more liberal personnel and clergy associated with the YMCA Movement were in favor of the proposal. It was also suggested that Jews and Muslims be brought onto the board and staff. However, John Mott, president of the IC/YMCA, was against these proposals.[79] Mott was a giant in the Movement. He had put in twenty-seven years with the Movement's collegiate network and served as secretary-general of the YMCA War Work Council in the First World War. Basically, it was John Mott who had sent the YMCA secretary to Heinrichs' prison camp in Metz when the Armistice was signed. So Heinrichs could take no action on these more progressive proposals until Mott was on board with them.

In early February,[80] Heinrichs cabled Adamson in Jerusalem to secure a German nurse-girl and cook for the house. He also approved the rental of the Jamals' house for his family's use. Amin Jamal was the Senior Secretary of the Jerusalem YMCA. He and his brother were successful businessmen. Things were shaping up nicely. Shortly thereafter, Heinrichs was relieved to receive news from Jerusalem that there had been snow and rain.[81] Until the British administration began putting in a modern sewage and water system, homes in Jerusalem were reliant on cisterns to collect their drinking and washing water. Homes gathered snow and rain through drainage systems located on their roofs, and these would deposit melt and rainwater into wells on the property. Despite the British administration having begun to modernize the sewage and water system, the Jerusalem YMCA was an enormous consumer of water, and huge subterranean cisterns had been designed as part of the project to collect the water and supply the building. Checking these cisterns regularly throughout the year would be an important part of the operations cycle of such an enormous physical plant.

Heinrichs met with Rabbi Stephen Wise and Judge Julian Mack at the Woolworth Building on February 16.[82] Judge Mack had his chambers there. He was president of the American Jewish Congress and held many important philanthropic board positions in support of the Jewish national home. Rabbi Wise was one of the most important Reform rabbis and Zionist leaders in the United States and a close friend of Albert Einstein. Support of the Jewish community in Palestine was essential to the success of the Association's mission there. As the men sat by the window in the restaurant looking up at the truss structure of the Brooklyn Bridge, they talked through the delicate nature of Jewish-Christian relations. They had not been good for centuries. Only in recent times was a Protestant reform effort trying to change this trajectory. Rabbi Wise was kind and eager to help but was frank in his opinions of Jerusalem celebrities and anxious for the Association to "avoid proselytizing and religious emphases of the wrong sort."[83] The misgiving of the Va'ad Leumi in cooperating with the Jerusalem YMCA was centered on the concern that the Christian mission organization was intent on converting Jews. The Association's Arab constituents were of far less concern to Jewish leadership. Rabbi Wise committed to provide Heinrichs with many letters of introduction for his use upon arrival in Jerusalem.

A couple of days later, Heinrichs read through a letter from Ramsey about the budget constraints.[84] Ramsey advised Heinrichs to start with partial operations and occupancy of the building in mid-1932. An operations plan could be designed to ramp up activity toward full occupancy by December. The dedication would be in April 1933 when Lord Edmund Allenby would arrive from England. He warned Heinrichs that there would be a period of heavy expense and low earnings extending through the first year of operations and cautioned Heinrichs to "guard jealously every dollar."[85] He also confirmed that he had asked the Central Hanover Bank and Trust Company to reserve all the income from the endowment for 1932 for Jerusalem. Income from the endowment fund for 1933 could therefore be factored in between $22,000 to $23,000.[86]

Heinrichs then flew to Chicago to see his parents.[87] His mother had been sick, and it was time to check in. Before he left, Heinrichs had a meeting with Harmon about meeting with the IC/YMCA on April 6. Before heading to the airport, Heinrichs put in the order for the full technical library in Jerusalem to the YMCA movement's Association Press. This technical library was stocked full of books to help the Jerusalem YMCA conduct its various programs by providing literature to its staff, constituent leaders, and members. In Chicago, his mother was doing a little better. He connected with his younger brother Conrad Heinrichs, who was unemployed and looking for a job. His brother drove him to the Chicago office of the YMCA, where both met with Harmon. Conrad Heinrichs would eventually join his brother in Jerusalem.

In Washington, DC, Heinrichs met with Justice Louis Brandeis of the United States Supreme Court. Brandeis was the first and only Jewish justice on the court at the time. He described the Supreme Court justice as "an ardent Zionist and yet sympathetic with others."[88] Brandeis provided Heinrichs with the names of a number of prominent Jews to look up in Palestine who could assist him in his work. He also gave Heinrichs three more names of prominent Jews in the United States as leads for the library of Judaica that Heinrichs wanted to establish. Although Heinrichs had hoped for more out of the meeting, he recognized that Brandeis was a worthwhile contact.[89]

In a long call with Ramsey,[90] Heinrichs learned that Ramsey wanted him to take his daughter Margaret to Jerusalem. Ramsey would cover all expenses. He just wanted his daughter to develop some professional experience. Heinrichs accepted and was glad to have free services to support his work. Ramsey asked[91] if he could meet Mrs. Heinrichs so that he could assess her attitude toward his daughter joining the Heinrichses in Jerusalem. He proposed that Margaret Ramsey would join them in Jerusalem for one year as a personal secretary to Heinrichs.

On March 28, Heinrichs and Slack met with Bruno Lasker to seek his opinion on joining the staff of the Jerusalem YMCA. Lasker was very much against it, explaining that as a "non-descript Jew,"[92] he might actually complicate affairs for Heinrichs in Jerusalem. It would be very important for Heinrichs to have the support of Jewish leadership in Jerusalem if he were to deliver against the Jerusalem YMCA's stated mission. He strongly advised that the Association make it explicitly clear that it was not a proselytizing organization. Once this was understood, it would serve as a basis beyond which a nondenominational service program could attract members to the organization from the three Ambrahamic faiths.

Heinrichs took Lasker's advice to heart and would implement it in Jerusalem. It would become the foundation of the Association's service platform to the present day, but Heinrichs would face vehement protest from the board about it upon his arrival. In the meeting with Bruno, the subject of non-Christian board members was also discussed. Slack was very conservative on the question of non-Christian board members and Heinrichs equally radical.[93] The next day Heinrichs interviewed Ramsey to obtain more of his guidance on the Jerusalem project. Although Ramsey had resigned from the position of secretary-general of the National Council of YMCAs, he retained "absolute supervision of every detail"[94] on Jerusalem.

By early April, the Heinrichses were days away from their departure for Jerusalem. The stonework and plastering of the new building was almost complete, but the wood work by the carpenters was behind schedule.[95] The Physical Department had just scheduled the Jerusalem Basketball Championship for May 7 and the Palestine championship for May 19 and 20.[96] The Amateur Athletics Federation of Syria had also invited the Physical Department to select a team from Palestine for the Syrian Olympic Games.[97] Lattof reported to New York that a "Committee representing various athletic organizations of the country had been formed with the view of selecting such a representative team. The final trials would be held in Tel-Aviv on May 6. The Olympic Games…[would]…be held in Beirut on May 14."[98] Lattof hoped that some of the Jerusalem YMCA members would make the team. Clearly the YMCA was still cooperating in sport despite its boycott of the Maccabiad. If the trials for this event were held in Tel Aviv, the Association was likely cooperating with Maccabi Tel Aviv on the White City's new cinder track.

On April 6, Heinrichs met with the IC/YMCA in New York. The meeting took place at the Downtown Association at 60 Pine Street in Manhattan.[99] Heinrichs was the guest speaker. Sixteen members of the International Committee were present, including Harmon, its senior secretary. Five staff also attended, including Slack. They discussed the mandate for the work in Jerusalem, and then Heinrichs headed to the *New York Times* for an interview about the project and his upcoming departure for the Holy Land.[100] It was one of his last official tasks in New York before packing and closing up the house at Larchmont.[101] When the luggage truck arrived, the Heinrichses left Larchmont.[102] They headed into the city and had breakfast at the Shelton.[103] Then they took the children to the Bronx Zoo, had an early dinner, and enjoyed the article[104] on Heinrichs on the second page of the *New York Times*.[105]

Finally, the Heinrichs family, Jan MacDonald, and Margaret Ramsey headed to the docks to board the SS *Excalibur*.[106] It was hard to say goodbye to all the staff secretaries at the office, but everyone was supportive as well as envious of Heinrichs as he headed off to assume his strategic post.[107] Many people came to see them off, including Mott, Slack, and even representatives of the Austin Organ Company, which had outfitted the new Jerusalem YMCA building with its organ.[108] Harmon gave Heinrichs a letter of good wishes to read on board. He wrote to Heinrichs, "Both of us are ready to accept in full the implications of St. Pauls's daring assertion that 'God hath made of one blood all the nations of the earth…to dwell together on all the face of the earth.' Your own determination to bridge chasms of race and religion strikes a responsive chord in my own heart."[109] Heinrichs recorded in his diary that it was a second send-off like Lahore: the flowers, gifts, and mail jammed their cabin full.[110] Shirin, their new daughter, was exhausted but finally fell asleep in the cabin while the Heinrichses unpacked their luggage for the journey across the ocean.

The following morning was a perfectly lovely day at sea. There were no signs of sea life, but the sun was glorious and at night the moon just past the full.[111] They had a comfortable cabin with four beds and a crib for Shirin, two washrooms and a shower bath, and four hanging closets. The majority of the passengers were going to Marseilles and Naples, and from there a crew member had informed Heinrichs that there would be less than ten passengers continuing on to Haifa in Palestine.[112] (By the same time the following year, thousands would be on similar ships fleeing Germany, following Hitler's takeover of the country.) While his wife played with the children and Margaret Ramsey napped, Heinrichs opened up his file box to do some work. He felt quite important having a private secretary with a type machine, office files, and typewriters on board. He and Margaret Ramsey would work together over the course of the passage. As he worked, he thought to himself how important it would be not to "lose the human touch in the mass of administrative detail."[113]

A few days before SS *Excalibur* reached Haifa Harbor, the Jerusalem YMCA's board of directors held a meeting at the office of the Construction Executive.[114] Among a number of matters discussed, two agenda items were of particular note. The board affirmed its commitment to participate in the Syrian Olympic Games in Minute 1022.[115] This minute recorded that the board was aware that something about its participation could be construed as political. The tryouts were in Tel Aviv, which likely meant that Maccabi Tel Aviv was involved in their organization. The First Maccabiad had just concluded in Tel Aviv (which the Jerusalem YMCA had boycotted). It is curious that the board saw fit to cooperate with the Maccabis for the Syrian Olympic Games when it could not do so for its own Palestine Olympic Games.

Minute 1023[116] documents that Lattof read Heinrichs' letter to Bowman, in which he informed the Association's president of the decision in New York to recruit Jan MacDonald for the Association's community library. In the same letter, he informed Bowman of Miss Margaret Hopper's gift for the Jesus Library. The significant sum of money would have been received with great satisfaction by any board. One can assume that the Association's board had a good impression of Heinrichs upon his arrival. Yet the board would later use MacDonald's appointment to attack Heinrichs.

On May 7, the SS *Excalibur* awaited disembarkation orders outside Haifa Harbor. Heinrichs wrote, "We all were very much on the qui vive about tomorrow and wondering about the reaction…[of]…our future colleagues in Jerusalem."[117] Early the next morning,[118] everyone was up for a seven o'clock breakfast. Lattof and Adamson took the small water taxi out to the ship. The party navigated the small, rocky entrance to the port (Haifa's deep-sea harbor was still under construction) and it paid the landing fee of £P 2.60.[119,120] Heinrichs and Lattof drove up to Jerusalem together with some other men from Jerusalem. Adamson followed in a second car with Dorothy Heinrichs, Jan MacDonald, Margaret Ramsey, and the children. They arrived at the American Colony Hotel in Jerusalem and put up there for the night.

Heinrichs had finally arrived to preach his Sermon in Stone.

# CHAPTER 6

# Early Troubles

## 1.

Waldo Heinrichs arrived in Palestine on May 8, 1932, in the context of increased political turmoil. Nonetheless, the board of the Jerusalem YMCA had, only four days prior to his arrival, ratified its decision to participate against Maccabi on its new athletics track in Tel Aviv. The board noted that its decision was nonpolitical—presumably because it was linked to Olympic sport. Although the YMCA had boycotted the Maccabiad to which it was invited, it seems to have done so based only on external political pressure from the Arab press.[1] This suggests that at the outset, at least some members of the Association were serious about participating in Tel Aviv with Jewish athletes.

Heinrichs was received well and hosted with great fanfare at a reception dinner at the Fast Hotel on May 18.[2] So why did he begin encountering trouble in his professional work by July? According to Heinrichs' final assessments in his diary, it was rooted in a conflict between his insistence on carrying out the Jerusalem YMCA's mission to serve all faiths, and the opposition of a few Arab board members to this mission. Some preferred to turn the Association into an Arab nationalist entity. Eventually, a Nazi plot would lead to Heinrichs' removal. Thus, there seems to have been a strong possibility of a connection between the conflicts he began to encounter, Arab nationalism, and Nazi designs.

In 1932, the Nazi Party began its final maneuvers to use the democratic institutions of the Weimar Republic to take over the state. These external political forces might have been perceived by some at the Jerusalem YMCA as a way to advance the Arab Palestinian national cause. Indeed, a strong Arab nationalist bloc within the board and membership of the Association appears to have aligned with a Nazi bloc to scuttle Heinrichs' work. It is remarkable to witness in this story how early Nazi agitation outside of Germany could turn the tide, and to such devastating effect.

The first indicators of a possible Nazi presence in Heinrichs' work appeared in October 1932. It is not clear if the Nazi entry into the Jerusalem YMCA's affairs was coordinated with someone within the Association or if the NSDAP imposed itself on the organization. But by October, the German Colony at Sarona (north of Jaffa) responded to a YMCA tender to print a sports map of Jerusalem for the new building's dedication the following April. This map omitted the Deutscher Sportverein Jerusalem, the German sports club in the German Colony at Rephaim, that would soon be taken over by the Nazis. Very quickly after this tender, things became more turbulent for Heinrichs in Jerusalem. This turbulence increased both in intensity and tone in parallel with the rise of Adolf Hitler and Nazi propaganda.

Between May 10 and December 31, 1932, Heinrichs conducted his work transparently and in coordination with the board of the Jerusalem YMCA, to which he was accountable. Despite this, he was not employed by the local board but by the IC/YMCA in New York. His salary and correspondences to headquarters were considered confidential. Judging from the conflicts that arose, the local board was uncomfortable with this and not satisfied with Heinrichs' transparent work approach. Heinrichs' dual accountabilities seemed to undermine whatever concept of total control some members desired over the Association.

In 1932, Heinrichs recorded in his diary nineteen instances of conflict with the Jerusalem YMCA's board or staff members. He did not consider any of them to constitute a threat to him. Most of these conflicts were tinged with an intrinsic anti-Semitism. He experienced a significant deterioration in relations in August and September, and then the most significant conflict emerged over the battle to amend the Jerusalem YMCA's constitution. This conflict began on November 7 and carried well into 1933, beyond the dedication of the new building.

The battle over the constitution never should have been a conflict, and the proposed revisions could have been made within a matter of days. Someone seemed to be stirring the pot, and cooperation in sport became more polarizing.

## 2.

Samy Suz and Emile Ohan helped the Heinrichses move into temporary summer quarters.[3] Heinrichs was pleased to see the two men, having been impressed with their attitude and work on his visit to Jerusalem one year prior. They assisted him with all the particulars of his arrival. Heinrichs got his driver's license and picked up his car. Then they went to the storage facility where he had kept his things since his visit to Jerusalem the previous spring. They moved the thirty-two large cases, most of which were still intact. Jan MacDonald, Nicholas Lattof, Margaret Ramsey, and others helped them all afternoon. They spent Wednesday and Thursday unpacking the freight from Jaffa and installing the much larger items, including appliances like the fridge that they had purchased in New York. They did not have closets and storage space, and Heinrichs was bemused by how an American architect easily could have remedied this problem, thinking to himself how the Jerusalem YMCA building was better planned.[4]

Heinrichs held his first meeting with Frederick Kisch on May 14,[5] one day after Yosef Yekutieli wrote the Los Angeles Organizing Committee for the 1932 Olympic Games inquiring about press passes. Kisch was now a private Palestinian citizen leading up a number of important civic boards, including a new Palestine Olympic Association. Heinrichs did not record in his diary any discussion notes relating to Olympic matters on this occasion, but a series of follow-up conversations would transpire regarding Heinrichs' representing Arab sport interests through the Jerusalem YMCA on the boards of the Palestine Football Association and the FASCP. Heinrichs and Adamson toured the new building with Kisch, who was impressed. Adamson was careful to avoid distinctively Christian rooms, and it was agreed that cooperation would be possible as long as the Association did not proselytize. Heinrichs felt that the contact was very useful.

On May 17,[6] Heinrichs held his first staff conference and took over the financials of the new building, removing the Imprest Fund from Lattof's authority. He then called upon the Armenian Patriarch's business manager to see about the rental terms for the YMCA hut in Jerusalem, which had been the center of many of the Jerusalem YMCA's past activities. He released the athletic field for use, his first major administrative action contributing to the establishment of an Arab Palestinian sport history in the city of Jerusalem. He would later give instructions for further work on it so that it could be compliant with Amateur Athletic Union requirements and be used for international sport competition.[7] The athletic field of the Jerusalem YMCA remained for decades a center of sport life for the city.

Because the building was in final phases of construction, Heinrichs and Dr. Tawfiq Canaan met about the bids for the furniture.[8] Heinrichs noted in his diary after the meeting that Canaan had "an anti-Jewish complex,"[9] but Heinrichs thought that he would come around.

At the King David Hotel, across the street from the Jerusalem YMCA, Heinrichs saw the Tannous brothers' auto show and then worked with Anton Halaby and Boulos Said on the Association's finances. He found "both very strong and well respected men locally."[10] That evening, the Heinrichses were the guests of honor at a reception dinner at the Fast Hotel.[11] Heinrichs announced that Lord Allenby had accepted to be the keynote speaker at the dedication, and the guests received this news well. Canaan was an expert at maneuvering the Heinrichses around the tables to meet all the Arab and European couples present.

Avraham Fast had opened the Fast Hotel in 1907. He was a member of the German Colony and a German Templer. The Temple Society was a Germanic Protestant fraternal order. In the 1930s, it served as the source for all but two of Palestine's Nazi Party leadership.[12] It had a community hall in Rephaim and a sports ground that the Nazi Party would use to celebrate major Nazi festivals from 1933 onwards. Unbeknownst to the Heinrichses, when they were the guests of honor at the Fast Hotel, the recruitment process for these Nazi leaders had already begun.

There was another Fast, born in 1911, by the name of Waldemar.[13] He would eventually apply to the Nazi Party in 1933 and join it in the spring of 1934,[14] at the height of Heinrichs' troubles. He escaped Palestine just before the Second World War. He was suspected by the British of being a spy, and joined the Reich Central Security Office,[15] serving in Heinrich Himmler's SS. He allegedly served in a killing unit in Russia in the early part of the war.[16] These were early Nazi death squads that executed en masse, by firing squad, Jews and other perceived Nazi enemies or undesirables. The Nazis deployed these mobile groups before they developed more efficient methods of gassing those they would intern in the concentration camps. The killing squads were replaced because they were too slow and the work was too difficult on the men. Shooting hundreds of people a day at close range caused severe psychological distress. Eventually, Waldemar Fast would be involved in prisoner exchanges between German Palestinians from internment camps in Palestine and Jews in concentration camps in Europe.[17]

These were some of the people who welcomed the Heinrichses to Jerusalem in early 1932. A few appear to have had the ears of key board members at the Jerusalem YMCA. For decades, scholarship has referenced a Nazi newspaper incident at the Jerusalem YMCA's library that resulted in the resignation of the secretary-general. The story of the "file" includes the fullest explanation and context of this incident to date, which seems related to the Berlin Games and the mysterious appearance of an alleged Palestinian delegation at them.

By the time Heinrichs arrived in Jerusalem, he was in way over his head. A review of the archival record indicates that Heinrichs was never really accepted in Jerusalem. A murky coalition of Nazis and Arab sympathizers influenced the Association's board and, early on, poisoned the relationship between the new secretary-general and his board and staff. Heinrichs was constantly provoked, perhaps for an intentional political purpose. The goal might have been to create a leadership vacuum at the Association, paralyze the oversight of Jerusalem by New York, and pull together a Palestinian Olympic team for the Berlin Games that would be devoid of Jewish athletes. However, there is no explicit documentation confirming this theory. But it is curious that Heinrichs' troubles emerged quickly and occurred in parallel with efforts to form a representative Olympic sport organization. At the same time, the International Olympic Committee was discussing Palestine's affiliation and the growing campaign to boycott the Berlin Games.

## 3.

Two days after the dinner reception at the Fast Hotel, Heinrichs met with the Building Committee. This committee oversaw the construction of the new building, was independent of the National and International Committee in New York as well as the local YMCA board, and was chaired by Canaan (reporting exclusively to Fred Ramsey).[18] The meeting discussed the tenders for the building's furnishings.[19] Albert Abramson, the Mandate Commissioner of Lands, was Jewish. He had not been convinced that all qualified firms had been receiving tenders for projects associated with the building. His insistence had led to a subcommittee, which reported back to the Building Committee when it would meet.[20] In observing the subcommittee's interactions, Heinrichs realized that all decisions about which firms got tenders seemed to be in the hands of Canaan. Heinrichs challenged this, and Canaan threatened to resign if most of the contracts went to Jews instead of Christians.[21] Heinrichs was able to convince him that the Arab Christians could not tender in some respects, that their prices were high in other respects, and that conflict of interest rules forbade other Christian bids. This conflict was the first of the nineteen that Heinrichs encountered in 1932, and it happened only thirteen days after his arrival. Arab board members would continuously reject the involvement of Jews in the project.

The following day, Heinrichs wrote to Ramsey in New York to update him on the general situation.[22] He informed him that he had released the athletic field because they badly needed it to generate some income and close the gap in the budget. While on the SS *Excalibur* to Palestine, Heinrichs had written to Lord Allenby in London to request his patronage at the new building's dedication. He informed Ramsey of Allenby's acceptance. It required an additional $1,200[23] of expenses. Heinrichs had spoken with High Commissioner Wauchope and confirmed that Government House would provide for Allenby's entertainment while the Association would provide his car.[24]

The High Commissioner then attended the Palestine Cross-Country Championship, which was over a five-mile course that concluded "at the enclosure at the foot of Talbiyeh."[25] Heinrichs presented to him the building and the athletic field. They got along well as former soldiers, and Heinrichs found him very pleasant. A couple of days later, Heinrichs attended his first meeting of the board of directors of the Jerusalem YMCA at the Construction Executive (on the building site).[26] The chairman that evening was Canaan. He was joined by Albert Abramson, J. Gordon Boutagy, Mr. Clark, Mr. Freidj, Mr. Jamal, Mr. Hannoush, George Khadder, Mr. Mantoura, Boulos Said, Mr. Salameh, Mr. B. Shiber, Nick Lattof (the acting secretary-general), and the Construction Executive. In addition, Jan MacDonald and Margaret Ramsey attended as invited guests.

Canaan welcomed Heinrichs, MacDonald, and Ramsey. At this meeting, Heinrichs formally took over as secretary-general and Lattof was elected associate (vice or deputy) general-secretary.[27] The board appointed a subcommittee to prepare for the dedication that included Abramson, Canaan, Campbell, and Salameh. Heinrichs also reported to the board the progress of the Jesus Library and the anticipated arrival of its books. He shared his desire to secure similar libraries on Islam and Judaism, and the board assigned the Education Committee the task of collaborating with MacDonald "in connection with the establishment of a Communal Library."[28]

After the meeting, everyone gathered for dinner at a restaurant and then proceeded to Adamson's office for another three hours of work on the furnishings. The tenders had to be ready by the next day so that the subcommittee could get them out to the contractors.[29] The next evening, Heinrichs worked for another three hours with the subcommittee from 8:30 to 11:30 at night and, once again, Canaan expressed "leading objections about Jewish contractors."[30]

Especially attentive to relations with the Jews, at the end of May, Heinrichs met with Dr. Bergman of the Hebrew University Library.[31] Bergman offered to loan a significant portion of their collection to the Jerusalem YMCA to anchor its Judaica collection. Heinrichs accepted at once. In the afternoon, he drove north with Lattof, Dorothy Heinrichs, and Junior to Tiberias to see Archie Harte and try to bring him back into the fold.[32] After dinner together, Heinrichs and Harte spoke for three hours. Heinrichs found him most congenial. Harte advised Heinrichs' "slow acceptance of Hebrew University Library" so as not to alienate the Arabs.[33] Heinrichs did not have an intuition for such sensitivities. When Heinrichs told Harte of Lord Allenby, he was surprised to hear Harte suggest other keynote speakers, including King Faisal of Iraq. Heinrichs told him off for listening to gossip. Despite the tension, Harte was still "surprised to see how many of the things he wanted in the Jerusalem YMCA...[would]...be retained."[34] In the morning, Dorothy Heinrichs and Junior stayed at the hotel in Tiberias while Heinrichs and Lattof went off to the YMCA campsite with Harte to better understand his vision.[35] They met with the mayor, a Bahai, who promised them that the Jerusalem YMCA could plant as many trees as it would like. Heinrichs was committed to spend all that he could to fulfill Harte's vision for the campsite because he felt that this would be a way to win him back.[36] Surely this would go over well with the Arabs and Canaan, who trusted and liked Harte.

Back in Jerusalem, Heinrichs worked with Fred Auburn and Lattof on the organizational chart and required salary cuts.[37] Because of the lingering effects of the Depression, a 15 percent cut was due to both Auburn and Lattof, which Heinrichs agreed to take out of their dollar portion underwritten from the United States rather than their Palestine pounds, which came from the operating budget. At the time, the Palestine pound was tied to British pound sterling on a one-to-one ratio, and this made it the dominant currency.

On the king's birthday, Heinrichs went to the parade at the Talavera Barracks near Talpiot and Government House.[38] He was the only person not in frock coat and silk hat. Then he and his wife went home to change for the formal garden party at Government House (the residence of High Commissioner Sir Arthur Wauchope), where he met all the notables of Palestine, including the Grand Mufti.[39]

Over the weekend,[40] he received Norman Bentwich and a number of other senior Zionists at the Jerusalem YMCA. He gave them a tour of the building and learned that the inscription over the building's north wing was too sacred even for use on a synagogue. He considered dismantling it. The incident highlighted the disconnect between the Jerusalem YMCA project and the city's different religious communities. After the Zionists left, Heinrichs and Auburn then went to Hapoel's Jerusalem football ground to watch the Jewish team take on an Egyptian Arsenal team. He subsequently learned at a meeting of the Physical

Department Standing Committee that its Chair, Mantoura, was having difficulties because of "the maneuvering of the members and Physical Director [Auburn] in rather dubious political methods."[41] It is not clear what these methods were. Heinrichs might have been observing the fallout from an increasing tendency in Arab circles to politicize sport, especially in tennis.

## 4.

When the board met[42] to discuss the operating budget and the offer of Hebrew University to contribute a portion of its collection as a Judaica library for the Association, Heinrichs was surprised that the university's offer raised a storm. Mantoura told him that he was having his leg pulled. Heinrichs insisted that the authority delegated to standing committees must bind the board to a committee's decision or no work would be achieved. Heinrichs did not realize it, but it was in this meeting that he gave committees the ability to attack him. He had assigned MacDonald to work with the Education Committee on establishing the communal library, and it is through that committee, whose actions would now be binding on the board, that the Nazi attack against Heinrichs would come.

The next day, Heinrichs wrote a long letter to colleagues back in New York.[43] One of the subjects that had come up in the board meeting was the request of the board that it scrutinize the expenses of the three American secretaries: Heinrichs, Lattof, and Auburn. This would require disclosure of their salaries, which Heinrichs refused. In doing so, he created additional tension with Canaan.[44]

Heinrichs had to revise what Wilbert Smith (from Cairo) had prepared in order to obscure the figures. Smith had included the operating expenditure from the old YMCA hut in the balance sheet for the new building. This amounted to £P 1,200.[45] Heinrichs was aghast and insisted to New York that US salaries in this line item not be accessible to the local board. By insisting that Smith's line items be removed, Heinrichs inflated considerably the deficit on the balance sheet. He informed New York that £P 3,677.50 in 1932 and £P 5,983 in 1933 would be required to cover the anticipated deficits. Heinrichs already had permission to draw on some funds from London in 1932 to cover the deficit, but these were only £P 2,000.[46] That figure still left him missing £P 1,677.50[47] for 1932. He stressed that there was no way he could move forward with the work in Jerusalem until New York could confirm how much money would be available from the endowment. These numbers are important because, as the board continued to clash with Heinrichs over all things Jewish, he would be shocked by its prioritization of those matters over fiduciary responsibility.

The deficit was of great concern to Heinrichs because he was beginning to recruit the local staff. Hundreds would apply. On the same day as commencing interviews, Heinrichs called on Kisch again. Perhaps he wanted to understand from Kisch the best Arab profiles for working with the Jewish members. Many of the candidates were not worth the time. Other interviews were tough to handle, like the one with Levi Anishka. He was a young Russian whose salary was only £P 3 per month,[48] whose parents were completely dependent on him, and who broke down and cried in front of Heinrichs during the interview.[49] Heinrichs left to meet with Gershon Agronsky, who was setting up the *Palestine Post* newspaper. Kisch, who served as chairman of the newspaper's board of directors, probably referred Heinrichs to Agronsky to ensure that he had allies within the Jewish press in Jerusalem.

## 5.

Lattof and Heinrichs drove back to Tiberias for more meetings with Harte.[50] Harte showed them his private collection of Arabica in a special room that he called the Arab Room of the house. The room was decorated with paneling partway up the walls, with a low divan around the perimeter. Beautifully woven pillows provided color, form, and function for propping oneself up. The closets were paneled in old colored glass, and he had a thousand-year-old rug from Dagestan on display on the floor. The men gathered for tea and sipped out of traditional thin glasses. The tables were covered in traditional blue and white ceramic bowls filled with rose water and floating flower pedals. It was sublime. Heinrichs described Harte as "an artist to his finger tips."[51] In the afternoon, Heinrichs enjoyed, for the first time in six weeks, his first hot bath, and then the trio drove north to Damascus and Beirut, enjoying lunch at the Omayad Hotel in Damascus. They returned to Jerusalem the next afternoon, where Heinrichs attended a meeting of the Physical Department at which fees were discussed further. The November move-in date for the building was also fixed.[52]

At the end of June, Heinrichs met with Henrietta Szold. She impressed him as "the leading Jewess in Palestine, quite the finest character, the keenest mind and most clear thinker"[53] that he had met in the country. She expressed doubts about Arab-Jew concord and the Jerusalem YMCA's ability to be a place of reconciliation, and was concerned that it could threaten Jewish culture. She made it clear that all Jews were afraid of proselytizing. Afterward, Heinrichs met with the Physical Department Committee and finally established the membership fees.[54] The first tour of the building for members then took place to show them what they were getting for their money.[55]

On June 30, Heinrichs met with District Commissioner Campbell of Jerusalem to finalize plans for the dedication.[56] They set the dedication celebrations for one week following Easter, and Heinrichs prepared a budget of £P 800[57] to cover everything. That evening, he and his wife finally had the chance to meet Chaim and Mrs. Arlosoroff, with whom they dined at the Scottish Hospice. As mentioned previously, Arlosoroff was now head of the Jewish Agency (after the departure of Kisch). Heinrichs found Arlosoroff charming and brilliant, and the Heinrichses drove them home after dinner.

The next day, Heinrichs joined Canaan for a delightful tea in the German Colony and was introduced to the Colony's leading residents.[58] Heinrichs attended the tennis matches between the Jewish tennis team from Degania colony near Tel Aviv and the Jerusalem YMCA's team.[59] The matches were all close, with the eventual tally 7–4 in favor of the Association's players. Heinrichs then gave a tour of the new building to the Jewish teams, once again taking care to avoid the more conspicuously Christian rooms so as not to raise Jewish suspicions.

Heinrichs then convened a difficult meeting on the question of the organizational chart. Changes needed to be made, but they needed to be done in a way that did not hurt feelings.[60] The staff seemed satisfied and decided to raise the recommended changes to Humphrey Bowman, the Executive Committee, and eventually the full board for approval.[61] Then,

Heinrichs hosted a large tea at the Jerusalem YMCA for the leading Jews of Jerusalem,[62] including Henrietta Szold and Emmanuel Mohl. Mohl would become Heinrichs' go-between with the Va'ad Leumi in the coming months. Relations with the Jews seemed to be warming within two months of his arrival. Miss Szold was so important in the Jewish community in Palestine that her attendance was a statement to her community that the Jerusalem YMCA deserved its attention.

On July 9, a meeting convened at the Jerusalem Sports Club about founding the Palestine Tennis Association.[63] The Jerusalem YMCA and club wanted to form the new federation with representation in governance according to equal numbers of playing members at each of the Big Three clubs. In addition to the Association and Jerusalem Sports Club, the third member of the Big Three was probably Maccabi Rehavia's tennis club. Heinrichs invited the chair of the Association's Physical Department Committee to dinner, presumably to discuss the scheme.[64] A. F. Nathan worked in the Mandate administration's Department of Agriculture. Heinrichs "found him very charming but bitterly anti-Jewish and anti-Palestinian"[65] and marvelled at how past antipathies made it so difficult to function.

On July 26, Heinrichs' efforts to expand sport cooperation with Jews in tennis met its first major roadblock. He went to the Tennis Club meeting and found "the hatred and unwillingness to cooperate with the Jews, most depressing and hard to meet."[66] Feeling depressed, Heinrichs felt that sentiments and attitudes would ruin the Association's work, and he committed to working against them. He wondered why Jews were so universally hated and decided to play some more tennis with the Arab members of the Association to improve relations. Percy Speed, a member of the board of Yekutieli's Palestine Football Association, came to speak with Heinrichs about these problems within the Physical Department, and he told him that Heinrichs could "only win these fellows one by one."[67]

## 6.

August marked the beginning of the first major decline in Heinrichs' relations with the board. This was as much a result of the Arab members' perceptions about what the new building should mean for them as it was with Heinrichs' warming relations with the Jews. At this stage, the IC/YMCA and the local Arab Christian Board of the YMCA were never really on the same page about what the new project meant.

Heinrichs met with the Committee for the Tennis Championship for Palestinians. He and two others had a conflict with George Khadder over his emphasis on petty details.[68] Such encounters, although seemingly insignificant to Heinrichs, could come off as severe slights in Arab culture. Heinrichs should have been more sensitive to these matters. Heinrichs was overworked. He was also distracted by his fifth edit of a sizable brochure on the Association that Ramsey had suggested he produce for the dedication.[69]

As the people discussed the tennis championship, the *Palestine Bulletin*[70] fired a shot over the bow of the YMCA. The Association had published its tennis announcement in the paper.[71] The *Palestine Bulletin* decided to resurrect the Association's withdrawal from the Maccabiad. The author pointed out that when the Jerusalem YMCA withdrew, it had already registered and paid for its entrants, this despite non-Jewish clubs being invited from Palestine, Syria, and Egypt. Heinrichs, in his diary, had previously attributed the withdrawal to pressure from the Arab press. The letter stated that "this step was taken as a result of pressure which was brought to bear by certain influential Arab members."[72] The author referenced Daniel Prenn's suspension from tennis in Germany. Prenn was considered one of the best tennis players in the world in 1932. He was Jewish. In 1931, accusations that Prenn had turned professional and sought sponsorship led to his being stripped of his titles and suspended from the sport. Many pointed to an increase in anti-Semitism in Germany from the growing influence of the Nazi Party as a causal factor in the case. The *Palestine Bulletin* drew a parallel between this type of politicization in sport in Germany and an increasing trend in Palestinian sport of the same nature.[73] The letter in the paper continued: "There is every indication that Jewish clubs and Jewish members of any club will refrain from entering the competition unless the [YMCA] committee is able to clear up the 'Maccabead' mystery."[74]

Heinrichs was concerned about the appearance of the article. He prepared a letter of explanation[75] to the newspaper and took it to

Auburn, Khadder (who was on a temporary committee charged with organizing the Association's tennis championship), and Canaan to receive their feedback. All of them advised Heinrichs not to send it and instead to go see the *Bulletin*'s editor, Peretz Cornfeld. Heinrichs complied. He and the editor prepared a statement together for publication the following day. Heinrichs hoped that it would be printed as they had agreed. If it was, he felt that it would lift the Association's work to a higher level of appreciation. The next day the article appeared as prepared.[76] The Jews commended it, and it was as unpopular with the Arabs. Heinrichs did not perceive that, by this time, he was probably considered an enemy to many Arabs.

It is at about this time that Yekutieli published in the *Palestine Bulletin* his announcement of the general meeting of the FASCP, inviting all clubs in the country to join it. No Arab club seems to have appeared at that meeting, but two days later, on August 15, Maccabi sent a representative to the YMCA for meetings. The meeting took place at three o'clock and Heinrichs noted in his diary that it was about the FASCP.[77] Heinrichs insisted that politics be kept out of the federation. He felt that the Jerusalem YMCA had a degree of power in the discussions and that the Jews were all keen to have the YMCA in the federation.

The Second Annual Tennis Tournament for Palestinians finally began on August 22.[78] There were more entrants than the previous year, despite the boycott of the event by the Jewish team from Rehavia (which had hosted the tennis tournaments for the Maccabiad and felt entitled to boycott the Jerusalem YMCA in return). Heinrichs felt that the boycott of the Maccabiad had been a mistake and that he would have prevented it had he been in the country. He understood why the Jews took offense at it and that the Association was paying the price.

After the tournament, Hapoel approached Heinrichs to request his involvement in Yekutieli's Palestine Football Association (PFA).[79] Hapoel wanted to back Heinrichs' candidacy as president of the organization against the Maccabi nominee, Percy Speed. Speed was associated with the Jerusalem YMCA and the Palestine Police. Auburn and Heinrichs subsequently attended an all-day meeting[80] of the board of the Palestine Football Association, where they witnessed the dynamics of intra-Zionist infighting. Hapoel withdrew from the league and the PFA elected Heinrichs one of six members of its Executive.

In the presence of Auburn, a trusted employee of the Jerusalem YMCA who preceded Heinrichs' tenure with the organization, the Maccabi Movement made good on its commitments to international sport to integrate representation for Arab clubs into the leadership structure. Hapoel walked away from the table over its own internal disputes with Maccabi (citing Maccabi's domineering attitude against the Jewish labor sports movement). Maccabi's fulfillment of its commitment to keep the door open to the Arabs is important. Heinrichs was not a representative of the government. He was not a Percy Speed or a James Pollock (the British officer who would join the Palestine Olympic Association). Heinrichs was the chief executive of the most important sport organization in the country; the Association was representing, by invitation of the Arabs, the Arab stake in Palestinian sport. A main reason Heinrichs had been brought to Palestine was specifically to formalize Arab sport governance and close the skill gap with Jewish sport clubs.

## 7.

On September 5, there was another conflict at the board meeting. This came as a shock to Heinrichs because he had already met with board member Anis Jamal[81] and was under the impression that everything was fine going into the meeting. But Jamal was one of the persons who attacked him. It appeared to be a setup. The attack centered on appointments being made without the board's sanction, the budget not being approved, the failure to make regular reports to the board as per the constitution, and Heinrichs' alleged failure to report on the amount of the endowment in New York.[82]

With regards to appointments, these were exclusively under Heinrichs' authority. On the subject of the budget, this was a matter for New York and foreign staff. The Board's concern about lack of approval likely stemmed from its realization that it did not fully control the finances of the organization. The same can be said about the complaint about the endowment fund, over which constitutionally and legally the board had no authority whatsoever. With regards to the complaint about not reporting to the board, there might have been some validity to this point. But the board also seems to have amplified its complaint: Heinrichs had been in regular board meetings with the members, and minutes were being distributed, which constituted a form of official report. The reason behind the board's complaints might ultimately have been rooted in individual members' concerns about cooperating in any way with Jews. If so, these concerns were hypocritical because sport cooperation had been occurring prior to Heinrichs' arrival and was ongoing at the time of this specific conflict.

Heinrichs had to make his way around the city the next day with Jamal to calm things down.[83] He saw George Khadder and Boutagy first, who he was fast considering his archenemies (because of their constant antagonism in meetings). Then he met with Halaby and Mantoura. After pacifying them fairly well, he went to a Physical Department Committee meeting in which they debated joining the FASCP. Heinrichs kept the committee's "wheels on track better than the board".[84]

Although meeting minutes are not available from the board meeting of September 5, one wonders if Heinrichs' maneuvers with the PFA and FASCP—which were completely transparent and conducted at the initiative of the Physical Department Committee—were a main contributing factor to the conflict. It is important to note that the subject of affiliating to the FASCP and PFA came up in the Physical Department Committee, because this documents that the Jerusalem YMCA was considering officially joining forces with Jewish sport—not at the executive level, but at the operational (staff) level. Affiliation was not merely a personal endeavor of any one committee member or of Heinrichs.

On September 13, Heinrichs finally got the board to approve the budget and his staff selections.[85] The board wanted no English staff and only Palestinians, but Heinrichs resisted. Heinrichs wrote to Ramsey in New York and reported that although it had been his most difficult barrier to pass, the board had told him that his chief difficulties were over. He included the cryptic sentence, "What I have passed through with the Board in the last six weeks I can only tell you personally when I next see you."[86]

# 8.

The Latin Patriarch, Louis Parlisina, was the official representative of the Roman Catholic Church in Jerusalem. He reminded his flock of an edict against the YMCA Movement.[87] The edict had already caused one member to resign from the Association. Heinrichs contrasted the Catholic attitude with that of the World Zionist Organization, who he considered very friendly. Many Jews were requesting information on the official attitude of the Zionist organization toward the Association. Because of the meetings that Heinrichs had held with Zionists, there was no official attitude. Consequently, the Association had "enlisted some very strong Jews, in fact very top men in all departments, as members of one or another"[88] of its sixteen standing committees.

In contrast, the Latin Patriarch referred to the YMCA as "a deadly poison to the true faith"[89] which was "doing a great harm to the true Christian principles."[90] He reminded his flock how the Holy Council had issued an edict in 1920 against the YMCA Movement because it aimed to subvert the spiritual life of men through alluring means.[91] Clearly, Zionist suspicions of the Jerusalem YMCA's alleged proselytizing intentions were not unique, and yet the Jewish attitude was more pragmatic than that of the Latin Patriarch.

Sensitivities were ubiquitous in Jerusalem. On September 16, Heinrichs was involved in another long meeting about the FASCP that revealed to him that the YMCA ideal would "be crushed between the forces of Arab and Jewish nationalism."[92] He wrote in his diary that organizations were rendered meaningless in such circumstances. The Jerusalem YMCA had not yet decided against affiliating to the FASCP, but clearly there was growing opposition to the concept. What he felt to be a lack of support for meaningful work would have been reinforced by his preference to associate with moderate Arabs like Hassan Bey Dajani[93] and Fakhri Bey Nashashibi. Both individuals' political positions ran afoul of the Grand Mufti and both would eventually be murdered (Hassan Bey in 1938 during the Arab Revolt and Fakhri Bey in 1941 in Baghdad).

In late October,[94] Heinrichs went to Jaffa to get the quotation from Sarona for the sports map. The Germans underbid, thereby reducing the cost of printing significantly. The map was eventually printed at the Syrian Orphanage Press in northwest Jerusalem, which was affiliated with the Germany Colonies in Palestine. It became a favored press for the Nazi Party in Palestine and offered members a discount of 10 percent for the use of its printing services.[95] When the monthly board meeting convened, there was another significant battle. This time it was over the constitution. Canaan had participated in the Constitution Committee meeting at Lattof's house and everything should have been ready, but the board decided to strike out Heinrichs' inclusion of the term "non-proselytizing". This edit was a nonnegotiable for the board, but Heinrichs' inclusion of the term was also nonnegotiable. He knew that without the term "non-proselytizing," Jews and Muslims would forever avoid the Association and prevent it becoming "the agency for mutual advancement and cooperation among the races"[96] that it hoped to be.

Heinrichs felt that the board was narrow, nationalistic, and petty in some matters. It would have been nice to believe in the sincerity of the Arabs' Christian convictions; however, the Arab Christians were in no position to proselytize to Jews and certainly not to their Muslim compatriots. Heinrichs' assessment was that the board's insistence to strike the term "non-proselytizing" from the constitution was 100 percent about halting cooperation with the Jews. In their position, the board had as their ally the Anglican Bishop. After the board meeting, the Harrises (who had only just arrived as employees of the Association) went to dinner with the Bishop and his wife. They reported to Heinrichs that they found the Bishop "offensive, bitter and altogether antagonistic to the YMCA"[97] and that the Bishop's wife was "very much against…[Heinrichs]…personally."[98] Heinrichs considered it to be her anti-American bias and noted that the staff and president Bowman would resign if the Association declared itself a proselytizing organization. The Harrises told Heinrichs that the Bishop had informed them that Chaim Arlosoroff "was going to do all he could against the YMCA."[99] Heinrichs called up Arlosoroff and joined him for dinner. Arlosoroff stated emphatically that the Bishop had lied.

Heinrichs had no intention of caving and asked the Constitution Committee to prepare the amendment to the constitution with the "non-proselytizing" terminology.[100] The board approved it with eleven "ayes" and one "nay."[101] Heinrichs sent out copies to all board members for the upcoming board meeting on November 21. At that meeting, the constitution was finally approved and the Association finally had a constitutional mandate with which to work.[102] Henceforth, everything should have been smooth sailing.

But the next day, a long list of people came to Heinrichs with further complaints. Basil Shiber was concerned that the board would "lose control of the members and association" because of non-Christian members.[103] Khadder and Boutagy expressed concerns of a "Greek Orthodox 'putsch.'"[104] Jamal felt insulted at the departure of young members from the vote and hated "Salaman for fear of his rivalry in business."[105] Isa Hazon wanted to know where Heinrichs stood after his younger group had walked out of the meeting.[106] Heinrichs sat back "hugely enjoying the signs of life in the [A]ssociation"[107] but not appreciating fully the boiling cauldron on which he was sitting.

## 9.

With the passage of the constitution, the Association hosted its first major tea for the press.[108] It was not as well attended as Heinrichs had hoped it would be, yet there were still members of the Jewish and Arab press there. The Association provided a tour of the building, and Bowman gave a fifteen-minute speech with no hint of proselytizing.[109] Heinrichs felt the spirit was excellent. He ordered £P 100[110] of gym equipment and took his first ride up the elevator in the building's Jesus Tower that day.[111]

The *Palestine Bulletin* printed a positive article about the press tea and the new building,[112] stressing its nonsectarian and inter-racial character. Perhaps feeling accomplished, Heinrichs wrote what appears to be his only letter to the International Olympic Committee's secretary-general Berdez. He inquired about setting up an Olympic committee for Palestine and asked specifically about the status of the FASCP in Tel Aviv.[113] Heinrichs did not reference this letter in his diary. He appears to have decided to look into the matter of affiliating a Palestine Olympic Association to the IOC and how the FASCP might factor into those plans. Perhaps the Jerusalem YMCA's Physical Department Committee had commenced an effort to lead the Olympic initiative for the country?

Unfortunately for Arab Palestinians, Heinrichs was distracted from his Olympic inquiry by more constitutional troubles, even though the latter was supposed to be settled. Six members came to Heinrichs with more complaints, including the elimination of the Paris Basis.[114] Heinrichs rejected the extraordinary request. The Paris Basis—in effect since 1855—was the foundation upon which the World Alliance of YMCAs governed relations between associations around the world. The basis had two key themes. The first was respect for local association autonomy. No single administrative model could work for the entire global movement. Adaptations were inherent to cultural differences. The second tenet of the Paris Basis was recognizing the unified Christian identity of the global Christian community, irrespective of doctrinal differences. Therefore, for Arab Palestinian members of the Jerusalem YMCA to do away with the Paris Basis for fear of Muslim pressure, while also insisting on proselytizing, was both insincere and hypocritical. Such a recommendation belied the apparent intention to turn the Association into a microcosm of the Muslim-Christian Associations, avowedly anti-Zionist clubs that formed the basis for the Palestine Arab Congresses and Palestinian organized political resistance to Zionism.

These political problems began impacting negatively the membership campaign. By early December,[115] only 105 out of a targeted 500 new members had signed up to join. There was ample criticism from the press, too. Heinrichs was sure more trouble was brewing with the board and, sure enough, at its next meeting members attacked Heinrichs, who began to boil when they criticized him for the membership campaign. He blew up at Canaan as no one had ever dared. Heinrichs felt relieved, but depressed that he had lost control. He walked home with Major Nathan, who told him that such encounters were a daily occurrence in government circles. Harris and Lattof visited for a long chat and were less worked up over the incident.

Heinrichs barely slept that night. He subsequently asked the US consul to join the board and learned that Emmanuel Mohl was pushing for Jewish action against the Association because it did not grant Muslims or Jews either seats on the board or voting membership.[116]

Heinrichs went to the office feeling that with Catholics, Muslims, Jews, and the Anglican clergy against the Association for opposite reasons, the work would be very difficult. He asked himself, "Is the middle course the less courageous?"[117]

So the next day, Heinrichs and Lattof met with the Grand Mufti, Haj Amin Al Husscini,[118] about the critical news coverage in the Arab press. The Mufti asked them if Bowman, the Association's president, was the Director of Education or a missionary. They were able to calm the Mufti down, but Heinrichs was suspicious of him on political and religious matters. Then they met with Mohl, who told Heinrichs frankly that the conservative element in the Jerusalem YMCA had the upper hand.

Heinrichs attended his first cabinet meeting of the Va'ad Leumi.[119] He presented the Association's case. Henrietta Szold, Yitzhak Ben Zvie (who would eventually reject Adolf Eichmann's clemency appeal, allowing his execution to proceed in 1961), Dr. Arlosoroff, and others were in attendance. They remained suspicious on the matter of prose-lytizing and explained to Heinrichs that he was a staff liberal doomed by a reactionary board. Still, Heinrichs was satisfied with the meeting's progress and asked the Va'ad Leumi not to take any action, pro or con. They agreed. That evening, Heinrichs and his wife dined at the Arloso-roffs' with the Bentwiches and Van Vrieslands. Mr. Van Vriesland was the treasurer of the Palestine Zionist Executive.[120]

Although he had calmed the front with the Va'ad Leumi, Hein-richs' own house at the Association continued to be out of order. At the board meeting on December 19, there was more trouble. Hannoush was upset because his name had not been included by Heinrichs on a list of men of high character submitted to the Nominating Commit-tee.[121] Said was angry because Heinrichs had not gotten his approval for expenses to pay for the cook's passage. Khadder grumbled about Hein-richs not having chosen a Palestinian for a staff position. There was also more pressure on the question of the Paris Basis, and Abramson told Heinrichs that he would resign if it was changed. Heinrichs went home discouraged and feeling extremely frustrated with "Boutagy's stinking tactics of criticism."[122]

The next day, Heinrichs anticipated more trouble over the award of the insurance contract for the building and property.[123] He made sure to get agreement from the Insurance Committee that the names of the list of companies would not be shared with the financial tenders. Heinrichs kept the key to the locked file to himself, with the agreement of the decision makers. Heinrichs wrote that during the meeting,[124] members asked again for the names of the companies, "and at once the fat was in the fire. George Shiber was out for the elimination of all companies below best rates (since his brother's company was included), Halaby was out to eliminate the Jewish agent and include his friend Albina whose rate was higher! *Non-discrimination!*"[125] Heinrichs also recorded in his diary that board members Halaby and Shiber nearly came to blows in the meeting. The latter threatened to resign and Jamal actually did resign because he was afraid that he would not be reelected.

"What a sweet little job I chose when I came to Jerusalem."[126] And with that, Heinrichs concluded 1932.

# CHAPTER 7

# Rise of the Reich

## 1.

There are many pivotal years in history, and 1933 is one of them. It is impossible to overstate the impact of Adolf Hitler's takeover of Germany on January 30. Nearly every global policy we live with today (and which is under pressure) finds its origins in a system designed after the Second World War to prevent a recurrence of the policy decisions that led to the Nazis' rise to power.[1]

The Nazi takeover of Germany ricocheted beyond Europe and into Palestine. What began in November 1931 as one letter of interest to form a local Nazi group (Ortsgruppe) written by a zealous Palestinian German[2] became a movement to form one of the more active overseas Nazi groups in the world. Whereas most overseas Nazi groups comprised "barely five percent of all German citizens abroad,"[3] in Palestine the number of ethnically German Palestinians who joined the NSDAP was "almost 19 percent."[4] These numbers indicate great Nazi interest in the fate of Palestine.

To understand the potential negative influence that this group of Nazis had on the psychology of many of the Arabs in Palestine, one need only consider how the Arabic-language newspaper *Falastin* would eventually describe the global political environment: according to the paper's reporting in December 1935, the Arabs considered Hitler "the most powerful head of state whose orders could not be stopped by any party or law; Germany would be turned into a huge…arms cache which would terrify the rest of Europe."[5] Heinrichs felt the effect of Nazi influence immediately. What began in August 1932 as minor differences of opinion about the role of Jews at the Jerusalem YMCA became an ugly fight with international consequences. Only a few days after his arrival in the country, Heinrichs' meeting with Frederick Kisch appears to have immediately captured the attention of some of the Jerusalem YMCA's more anti-Zionist board members. They warned Heinrichs to be careful in dealing with the Jews and privately discussed how they would not be treated like Indians by Heinrichs.[6] However, their Arab nationalist sentiments might not have been the only fuel for their anti-Zionist attitudes. Perhaps the Nazi Ortsgruppe that had been established in 1932 was active enough in Jerusalem by mid-1933 to influence high-profile citizens at the Jerusalem YMCA.

Hitler's rise to power also affected Kisch and Yosef Yekutieli. They ramped up their sport and Olympic organizing. The fate of German Jewish athletes hung in the balance. In 1933, there was a major spike in Jewish emigration from Germany to Palestine. Some of these immigrants were athletes from Germany's Maccabi Movement. Within this context, Kisch and Yekutieli worked toward the formation of a Palestine Olympic Association. Yekutieli also began laying the foundation for Mandate Palestine's first entry into international sport governance by supporting the co-founding of the Western Asiatic Games Confederation with G. D. Sondhi—Heinrichs' former colleague from Lahore.

When the Olympic Games came under Nazi control, this laid the groundwork for the emergence of a strong boycott campaign against Germany's right to host them. The macro-environmental factors converged in 1933 with significant impact on the "file". The Law for the Restoration of the Professional Civil Service purged Jewish and communist employees from the civil service right before Heinrichs was finalizing his arrangements for the dedication of the new Jerusalem YMCA. Shortly after the dedication in April 1933, Hermann Göring formed the Nazi secret police (Gestapo) and Hitler banned all other political parties.[7] It is understandable that, under such circumstances, so many Germans began looking for ways to leave Germany. Many of the Jews looked to Palestine for a way out.

In late September,[8] Joseph Goebbels took over the Reich Chamber of Culture and began to dominate the cultural landscape of Germans, both domestically and overseas. On October 14,[9] Germany walked out of the League of Nations, effectively declaring to the world that its new Führer, or leader, was going to carve his own path. On November 12,[10] the Nazis won 95.2 percent of the Reichstag: Germany became a single-party state. On November 15, the Gestapo received authority over all of Germany. A few days later, a propaganda emissary from Goebbels' ministry arrived in Palestine[11]—a man by the name of Dr. Iven. Within three and a half months of Dr. Iven's arrival, the Nazis would exert influence at the Jerusalem YMCA to such an extent that Heinrichs would have to withdraw to New York.

All these changes in Germany occurred in the lead-up to the Berlin Games and the ongoing efforts in Palestine (since 1930) to form a fully representative Olympic committee (of Jews, Muslims, and Christians) with the facilitation and mediation of the Jerusalem YMCA. Germany had been awarded the Games on May 13, 1931, when the country was still a federalist system under the Weimar Republic.[12] After Hitler came to power, individuals and institutions started to question whether Germany should be permitted to keep the Games, including the *New York Times*.[13] Shortly after the critical press coverage, a boycott of Jewish businesses in Germany began.[14]

## 2.

The two architects of Germany's successful bid for the Games were Dr. Theodor Lewald and Carl Diem. Lewald was Jewish and had been president of the German Olympic Committee since 1924.[15] Diem had been captain of the German team in the Stockholm Olympics in 1912.[16] Both men had attempted to bring the Games to Berlin in 1916 but were "grief-stricken when their preparatory work in 1913 and 1914 had been wrecked by the [First World W]ar."[17] German athletes were barred from competing in Antwerp in 1920 and in Paris in 1924.

In 1929, during the lead-up to the Los Angeles Games of 1932, Lewald and Diem toured America as they prepared Berlin for its next Olympic bid.[18] When the bid emerged victorious, it symbolized the German republic's full return to the fold of the Olympic family.[19] But after the *New York Times*' critical article, Lewald and Diem were removed from their posts in the German Olympic Committee and sport university, respectively.[20] IOC president Count Baillet-Latour had to intervene to enable Lewald to retain his post in the Organizing Committee for the 1936 Games.[21] Diem was also allowed to stay in the Organizing Committee as secretary.[22]

Goebbels participated in the meeting during which Lewald was removed from the national Olympic committee of Germany.[23] He "had realized that the [G]ames were a splendid opportunity to demonstrate German organizational talent and physical prowess."[24] Goebbels would take time to monitor the Palestine Olympic file and ensure that it did not muddy his Olympic waters.

By June 1933, the new Reich Ministry of Science, Education, and Culture banned Jews from all sport clubs.[25] This gave rise to concerns that Jews would not be eligible to compete for slots on Germany's Olympic team. Such a situation would have represented a clear violation of Olympic rules. The IOC was scheduled to discuss the German situation in Vienna at its Session on June 7. The German representatives committed to allowing German Jewish athletes to be a part of the German Olympic team.[26]

But the Nazis had no intention of complying. In fact, although Jews were permitted for a period to use public clubs, their expulsion from private clubs—which represented the real base of German sport—was upheld.[27] Charles Sherrill is often remembered as the US member of the IOC who took the stance of appeasement in the boycott debate. And yet despite his soft stance, it was Sherrill who "had to persuade his British colleague on the Executive Board, Lord Aberdare, that the I.O.C. was indeed within its rights to demand that the makeup of the German team conform to the rule."[28] In fact, Lord Aberdare would become the most vocal opponent of affiliating a Palestine Olympic Association to the IOC based on his claim that the association was not in conformance with IOC rules. In Aberdare's confidential correspondence on the subject to Baillet-Latour, he argued strongly against affiliating Palestine,[29] this despite the reported suicide in July of Fritz Rosenfelder, a German Jewish athlete, following expulsion from his sport club[30] and the dissolution of the Maccabi branch in Bavaria.[31]

In October, Hitler toured the construction site of the Olympic stadium. Ultimately he committed 20,000,000 reichsmarks[32] to the project, much to the astonishment of Lewald and Diem.[33] Reichsminister Goebbels now had all he wanted to use the 1936 Olympic Games to whitewash the Nazi doctrine. Would Palestine play a role in his plans?

Reports of religious discrimination continued to flow from Germany through those who managed to escape and bring out news to the press in other countries. On November 22, Gustavus Kirby of the Amateur Athletic Union (AAU) decided to table a resolution threatening to boycott the Games at the convention of the American Olympic Association.[34] By December 1, the *New York Times* reported his colleague Sherrill's opposition to the boycott.[35] The next day, a Jewish-owned newspaper called *Westland* published its first in a series of pieces on the boycott debate.[36] It was operating out of the Saar region. In 1933, the Saar was still under French control from the Treaty of Versailles. But the region's population comprised a vast majority of ethnic Germans. One of Hitler's key objectives was to get the Saar returned to Germany. The population of the Saar region eventually voted overwhelmingly in a plebiscite to return to German control. After the plebiscite, the owner of *Westland* lost control of the paper, and its reporting on the Olympic boycott ceased.[37]

*Westland* ran a front-page article under the headline "*Olympisches Ehrenwort*" [Olympic Word of Honor]. The paper claimed to be one of two in Germany reporting on the boycott from a non-Nazi perspective. The article claimed that the American threat to boycott the Games put Germany in a frenzy.[38] Throughout the article, it is possible that the term "Germany" is synonymous with "Goebbels": *Westland* referenced him several times in the series of boycott articles. These articles implied that a conversation between senior Nazis, Maccabi Germany, Maccabi Palestine, and the Palestine Olympic Association (through Kisch) was ongoing. The implication was so severe that Yekutieli was compelled to correspond with the editors of *Westland* and rebut its claims (perhaps after other Zionists scrutinized Kisch and his handling of the Olympic invitation). Indeed, between 1933 and 1934, *Westland* became a critical Jewish voice of alleged Nazi and Zionist interactions in the boycott debate.

*Westland*'s coverage of the boycott debate exhibited suspicions of all parties involved. Perhaps the suspicion was warranted. IOC member Sigfrid Edström was a central actor in the negotiations around the "file" during the boycott debate. Only two days after *Westland*'s first article in December 1933, Edström was expressing privately his more intimate feelings on the Jewish question in German sport to Avery Brundage, which included his opinion that even in the United States, the day would come where the activities of the Jews would have to be stopped.[39] It is not clear to which activities of the Jews Edström was referring in his correspondence to Brundage, although he referred to Jews as "intelligent and unscrupulous" and that "they must be kept within certain limits."[40]

*Westland* was not the only Jewish voice suspicious of the IOC and concerned about Germany keeping the hosting rights to the Games. The *Jewish Daily Bulletin* reported that the acts of the Nazis mocked their pledge of fair play to Jewish athletes and noted that Jews were forbidden from working on the construction projects associated with the Games.[41] Under another article titled *"Kommt Amerika zur Olympiade!"* [Come America to the Olympiad!],[42] *Westland* argued that the Nazi leadership was not informing the German public about the potential threat of an American boycott. It noted how Hitler had given a solemn authorization to start building for the Games, which was reported in all German newspapers. But it also pointed out that three other papers under Nazi influence had used soft language to obscure the expectation that Germany would treat its Jewish athletes the same as all its others. *Westland* argued that the right-wing (i.e., Nazi) media did not report on any of this and that the German public was only privy to the preparations for the Games in the Nazi press—not the authentic pressure that was actually emerging against the Games. In contrast, *Westland* implied that the American boycott would actually go ahead and that other European countries would follow suit.

As things continued to heat up, a large anti-Nazi rally was held on March 6, 1934, at Madison Square Garden in New York City.[43] This was only three days before Heinrichs had to leave Jerusalem because of Nazi agitation. AAU member Kirby spoke at this rally and kept the American sport position solidly on the undecided track with regards to accepting the German invitation to the Games. Back in Jerusalem, Waldo Heinrichs was days away from fleeing Jerusalem because of the Nazis. By May 15, 1934, the IOC met again at an important Session in Athens, Greece, to decide the fate of the German Games for the first time. Ultimately, the IOC was satisfied by German explanations and ruled in Germany's favor.

It is generally remembered that influential American sport leaders were not convinced by the IOC's position at this May meeting, and the boycott issue raged well into late 1935. But what is generally forgotten—although it was reported to the world at the time—is that a Palestine Olympic Association was formally affiliated to the IOC at the same Session. This association should have included representation of Arab sport interests through Heinrichs and the Jerusalem YMCA, but it did not. Heinrichs' exclusion probably had more to do with the Nazis than it did with Aberdare's claims that Maccabi Palestine was the root cause of lack of representation in Palestinian sport. This is because, in 1933, the Nazi Party became very active in Palestine, especially in Jerusalem.

## 3.

On March 19, 1933,[44] the German swastika banner was hoisted for the first time on the Fast Hotel, which housed the German Consulate for Jerusalem. The hotel was owned by German Templers and was one of the more prominent hotels in the city. The consulate within it would deal with the inevitable influx of German Jews fleeing Germany. Only ten months before the hoisting of the Nazi banner, the Fast Hotel had hosted the Jerusalem YMCA's reception dinner for the Heinrichs to celebrate their arrival in Palestine. One month after the swastika was raised, the Jerusalem YMCA would dedicate its new building.

By August, German consul Heinrich Wolff officially supported the Haavara (Transfer) Agreement. The agreement was a financial mechanism worked out with the Nazi government that allowed for the transfer of a limited amount of Jewish financial assets to Palestine.[45] It operated for six years, ceasing operations on the eve of the Second World War.[46] Between 1933 and 1935, it operated outside the authority of the Jewish Agency (in Jerusalem) and the World Zionist Organization's Zionist

Executive.[47] After 1935, the agreement came under the authority of the Zionist Executive. Nonetheless, Chaim Arlosoroff had been central to the negotiations with the Nazis. For this reason, the agreement might have been a factor in Arlosoroff's assassination on June 16, 1933, which occurred as he strolled down the Tel Aviv seaside at night with his wife. Shot twice in the abdomen by assailants who asked him the time in perfect Hebrew, Arlosoroff died shortly thereafter. Over one hundred thousand people attended his funeral.

To this day it is not known who killed Arlosoroff. His demise might certainly be linked to the increasing Nazi agitation in Palestine during this period. One of the more recent theories suggests that Goebbels himself might have played the decisive role.[48] During his university years, Arlosoroff had been friends with Goebbels' new wife, Magda, and was aware of her Jewish upbringing. This theory suggests that Goebbels wanted Arlosoroff dead to hide her heritage, because 1933 was the pivotal year of the Nazis' transition of Germany from a democracy to a dictatorship. Given the Nazis' racial policies, the Jewish ancestry of the wife of the persecutor-in-chief of the Jews was incriminating. Recently, it has even been claimed that Magda Goebbels' father was actually a German Jew who died in 1939 in the Buchenwald concentration camp.[49]

By Heinrichs' accounts, he and his wife's relationship with the Arlosoroffs was warm. On occasion, the Heinrichses dined with Chaim and Sima. Heinrichs relied upon Chaim in his negotiations with members of the Va'ad Leumi to work against the more radical elements within the Zionist movement who were opposed to Jewish cooperation with the Jerusalem YMCA. He shared Arlosoroff's role in this regard with the Reverend Everett Clinchy in a letter, which Clinchy subsequently circulated in the United States without Heinrichs' approval. At a soirée at the French Consulate in Jerusalem on March 23, one week after the swastika was raised in Jerusalem, Chaim spoke to Heinrichs to express his concern about the leak.[50] Although this incident was likely not a contributing factor in Arlosoroff's death, the incident highlights much about the context in which Heinrichs was working. Competing European powers, a disempowered German consul, the complexities of factional Zionist fighting, and the interfaith dynamics of the Jerusalem

YMCA's work, all made for a complex political landscape. Indeed, by August, the German consul himself would be under secret investigation by the German Palestinian Nazis Walter Ruff, Ludwig Buchalter, and Cornelius Schwarz: Consul Wolff was married to a Jewish convert to Protestantism and was distrusted accordingly by the Nazis.[51]

In September, Heinrichs took a tour of the Syrian Orphanage Press[52] with Ernst Schneller.[53] The Nominating Committee of the Jerusalem YMCA recommended Schneller as one of the sixteen persons to be considered by New York for appointment to the board of the YMCA.[54] What Heinrichs and New York did not know is that Schneller, like other Palestinian Germans at the Jerusalem YMCA, applied to the Nazi Party at about the same time.[55] Schneller and other members became formal party members on February 1, 1934[56]  exactly at the height of the Nazi agitation at the Jerusalem YMCA.

By October, enough Nazi activity was taking place in Palestine for it to be reported in the world press by the *Jewish Daily Bulletin*.[57] Sourced from a Jewish Telegraphic Agency (JTA) special correspondence of September 16, an article stated that "Eissa Bendak, editor of the radical Christian-Arab bi-weekly 'Sowt Es-Shaab' published in Bethlehem, has left for Paris where he will receive instructions from a group of Germans and Arabs on 'conducting Nazi propaganda' in Palestine. Bendak was recently instrumental in organizing the Arab Fascist Party at Bethlehem whose object is to harass the Jews."[58] This pro-German, anti-Jewish pot also bubbled in Jerusalem cafés. Heinrichs would overhear pro-German, anti-Jewish conversations at places like Haddad's, a confectionary shop close to his residence.[59]

At the end of October, a new wave of riots broke out in Jerusalem, in part as a response to the increase in the number of Jews fleeing to Palestine from Germany. Heinrichs recorded in his diary that "two… ships were passed on from Jaffa to Haifa, as the boatmen refused to unload the 1600 - 1800 Jewish immigrants."[60] As the situation escalated, Heinrichs noticed two planes heading north.[61] He heard from German radio news that they were flying to pacify Tul Karem, but regular Palestine radio did not report on it. Heinrichs probably heard these reports on the "'people's receiver' (*Volksempfänger*),"[62] small radios that the Nazi Party introduced in 1933 and started shipping to foreign Nazi groups to give ethnic Germans overseas the ability to remain in touch with the news of the Reich.[63] It was around this receiver that NSDAP members in Palestine would gather to hear the news about the Saar being returned to German sovereignty.[64]

On November 16, 1933, Dr. Iven arrived.[65] The Jerusalem Nazi Party membership at the time of Dr. Iven's arrival included Buchalter, who by January 1936 would be listed on the stationery of the German Sports Club in Jerusalem.[66] The club also had branches at Sarona and Haifa, but the Jerusalem branch was located in the German Colony at Rephaim, just down the road from the Jerusalem YMCA. There was a flurry of Nazi activity as a result of Dr. Iven's trip. The Nazi Overseas Department (*Auslands-Abteilgung*) nominated Ruff as undercover National Socialist Agent for Palestine.[67] On December 4, the first compulsory meeting (*Pflichtabend*) for NSDAP members took place in Jerusalem (two days before the Nazi newspaper incident started).[68] By the end of 1933, NSDAP membership in Jerusalem numbered forty-two adults and four Hitler Youth.[69] This number is approximately equivalent to the forty members of the YMCA who would demand from Heinrichs that the YMCA Education Committee subscribe to and include in its Reading Room the Nazi Party's leading newspaper, the *Völkischer Beobachter*.

## 4.

The rapidly evolving situation in Europe put Kisch and Yekutieli in overdrive. The years 1933 and 1934 are the two most pivotal years in the history of sport in Mandate Palestine. The strategic maneuvers of the competing camps reverberated for decades. It can almost be argued that the Nazi agitation at the Jerusalem YMCA and the consequent affiliation of a Zionist-led (rather than fully representative) Palestine Olympic Association to the IOC in 1934 cemented the irreconcilability on the world stage of emergent Israeli and fledgling Arab Palestinian states. The events of 1933 and 1934 are some of the historical anteced-ents of the Munich Massacre.

Most likely because of the exclusion of Jews from German sport, the spike in Jewish immigrants from Germany, and the need to absorb and benefit from arriving Jewish refugees, Yekutieli continued to affiliate the Federation of the Amateur Sports Clubs of Palestine to more international sport governing bodies. He also took three bold moves. First, he began to work with G. D. Sondhi to found the Western Asiatic Games Confederation and send a delegation from Palestine to participate in Sondhi's First Western Asiatic Games. The Jerusalem YMCA—through Heinrichs' personal connections to Sondhi—should have been involved in these discussions. Instead, Christian Palestinians at the Jerusalem YMCA, embroiled in infighting and attacking Heinrichs, damaged their sports cause through dissent rather than constructive, forward-thinking actions. Furthermore, the Nazi involvement appears to have destroyed cooperation between Arabs and Jews during this period of critical importance. In the sport domain, the world has forever paid the price for this Nazi agitation.

Second, Yekutieli and Kisch pushed forward with great intensity their attempt to affiliate a Palestine Olympic Association to the IOC. They made a sincere effort to engage the Jerusalem YMCA, which appeared to withdraw from those efforts under the growing cloud of acrimony that finds its roots in the Arabs' anti-Zionist and anti-Jewish attitudes, as well as a growing, sinister NSDAP presence among the membership. Any hope for including the Arabs in the Palestine Olympic Association (through the Jerusalem YMCA) was lost in March 1934 when Heinrichs abruptly left Jerusalem.

Third, following Yekutieli's success in affiliating FASCP to Alice Milliat's FSFI, and with the subsequent affiliation of a Zionist-led Palestine Olympic Association to the IOC in May 1934, Yekutieli was able to send a fully Jewish team of female athletes to the Women's World Games in London in August—a significant nod to emerging freedoms and acknowledgement of the role of Zionist women on the international stage. The team included the likes of Susannah Borstein, Zelda Solek, and Leah Lederman.

In addition to the situation in Palestine, in 1933, the Maccabi World Union (MWU) in Germany realized that it needed to terminate the operations of its headquarters in Berlin and move them to London. The movement was comparatively weak in London, despite Yekutieli having concluded his 1931 motorcycle trip there. So, Yekutieli started to use the planning for the upcoming Second Maccabiad (scheduled for 1935) to strengthen the financial and organizational footprint of the Maccabi Movement in England. Lord Melchett's sister, the Viscountess Erleigh, became central to this work and the hosting of the Second Maccabiad in Tel Aviv.

Running in parallel to Kisch and Yekutieli's Olympic and Maccabi activity on the ground were the Mandate administration's sport activities in schools. These activities demonstrate how deeply invested the Zionist sports movement was at all levels of sport in Mandate Palestine. Humphrey Bowman was chairman of the board of directors of the Jerusalem YMCA. He was also the director of the Mandate administration's Education Department. This department organized an annual Jerusalem Inter-School Sports Program each May in which many YMCA, Maccabi, and Hapoel personnel cooperated as organizers and officials. These sport activities would go off without a hitch each year, but cooperation on national and international sport governance matters had difficulty getting off the ground.

Why might the Nazis have targeted cooperation in sports at the Jerusalem YMCA and not the Education Department? Perhaps it is because the latter was a government entity in which Jews and Arabs worked to toe the official line. It would have been difficult for the Nazis to penetrate such cooperation unnoticed by the British. In addition, the Education Department would not be involved in selecting athletes for an Olympic team from Palestine for the 1936 Games because its constituents were secondary students or younger. The Jerusalem YMCA, on the other hand, was a private organization with national and international clout. It was an ideal target because its ongoing negotiations with Zionists regarding the affiliation to the FASCP were not yet concluded and could potentially influence German actions around the Olympics. Because Heinrichs' discussions were not secret, the Jerusalem YMCA likely made itself a target. The stature of Heinrichs and the YMCA were sufficient to bring about a representative Olympic committee for Palestine with the Zionists. To stop those discussions would mean taking out Heinrichs, who was very committed—arguably religiously committed—to the YMCA's mission in the Holy City.

## 5.

Sondhi was the honorary secretary of the Indian Olympic Association. He wrote to the private secretary of the High Commissioner for Palestine about a proposal to host an inaugural Western Asiatic Games.[70] It took some time for the High Commissioner's office to respond. When it did so, a letter from Julius Jacobs to Yekutieli, dated May 16, said that the Chief Secretary's office had informed Sondhi that it had forwarded the invitation to local organizations that would be in touch directly with him, if they so chose.[71] Julius Jacobs signed his note to Maccabi "for Acting Chief Secretary."[72]

Jacobs was not a nobody. When Kisch had been the chairman of the Palestine Zionist Executive, Jacobs served as secretary of the organization. Why did Jacobs sign this letter instead of the British administration's Chief Secretary, Edward Mills? The *Palestine Gazette* reported that the High Commissioner had departed Palestine for the United Kingdom.[73] Edward Mills, who was Acting Chief Secretary, became the Acting High Commissioner. Perhaps to fill the role that Mills normally held, Julius Jacobs stepped in, even though Mills was signing other official documents as Chief Secretary on May 16.[74] Jacobs seems to have sent Sondhi's inquiry only to Yekutieli.[75] Jacobs, through Kisch, would have known exactly to whom it should go.

Jacobs' reply was a stroke of luck for Maccabi Palestine. Kisch and Yekutieli were well prepared to receive it. Three days prior, they had held the first meeting of the Palestine Olympic Association.[76,77] Yekutieli had opened the meeting with the objective that the POA be formed so that "Palestine should be able to take part in the Olympic Games as all other countries."[78] The regulations Yekutieli had typed up at the end of 1932 were circulated and approved. The meeting elected an executive committee that included Kisch and Yekutieli, as well as James Huey Hamill (J. H. H.) Pollock, a British officer and Assistant District Commissioner of the Southern District, Alex Epstein, Shlomo Arazi, Zvi Nishri, and Yehoshuah Alouf.[79] Minutes of the meeting stated that "[t]he Association should be registered by the authorities and should be affiliated to the International Olympic Committee."[80]

Yekutieli was ready to get things rolling at the international level. At the end of May, he wrote to the IOC's secretary Colonel A. C. Berdez, to inform him of the meeting and constitution of the new committee.[81] Yekutieli was sure to point out that the committee comprised the representatives of national governing bodies associated with their international equivalents, as has been directed by Berdez. Yekutieli then asked Berdez that Palestine be allowed to participate in the Olympic Games as an independent nation. Yekutieli was already receiving the *Bulletin Officiel* of the IOC and was surely eager to see Palestine's name registered between New Zealand and Peru in the directory of IOC-recognized national Olympic committees.[82]

After writing to the IOC, Yekutieli then addressed Sondhi to tell him that he was doing his best to get a team to India.[83] Sondhi wrote Yekutieli two letters. The first[84] concerned the eligibility of national representation and posed a potential problem for German Jewish athletes who were fleeing to Palestine. Many were not Palestinian citizens yet. Even if they were naturalized, Olympic rules did not allow them to compete for Palestine if they had already competed for another country in the Olympic Games. The second letter[85] asked Yekutieli if the FASCP approved of the idea of organizing a Western Asiatic Games, whether it was willing to join the Western Asiatic Games Confederation, and if Yekutieli would provide the name of Palestine's representative member. Yekutieli responded in the affirmative[86] and said that Zvi Nishri would be Palestine's representative to the new confederation. Although Yekutieli knew that he could not turn down the offer, he had concerns about the cost.[87]

At the same time, Baillet-Latour was in Vienna at the IOC Session discussing the German situation. He took time to write Yekutieli to tell him that his affiliation request had been passed on to the IOC's Executive Committee.[88] But Aberdare had not been pleased in Vienna. Having been pushed by Sherrill to accept that the IOC had a right to force the German team to comply with the Olympic rules regarding its fully representative composition,[89] and following Baillet-Latour's letter[90] to Yekutieli, Aberdare wrote a confidential letter on his private stationery to the IOC president. Upon return to England, he had taken up the question of Palestine with the Colonial Office. He could not advise supporting acceptance. He told Baillet-Latour that it would only bring embarrassment, if not harm, to the IOC. He explained how the self-styled committee was not fully representative, only comprising Maccabi members, and did not include Muslims and Christians. He said that the Palestine government would deprecate recognition of the committee in the way that it was currently constituted, although he also told Baillet-Latour that the IOC could count on the likes of Kisch and Yekutieli if they could incorporate all of Palestine sport.

Based on Aberdare's letter, Baillet-Latour decided that the POA could not be recognized by the IOC. Nonetheless, in his reply[91] to Aberdare, he remained open to acceptance if Palestine incorporated Muslims and Christians. He seemed to be unaware of the historical and ongoing negotiations between the Jerusalem YMCA and FASCP. But perhaps Palestine could facilitate resolution of the IOC's emerging problem with Germany? Baillet-Latour presumptuously concluded his correspondence by saying, "In the meantime I will see that they are not invited by Hitler to the Berlin Games!!!"[92] It was a remarkable way to end the correspondence given that only one day earlier, Germany's Jewish athletes had been forbidden to attend the Prague Maccabiad.[93]

In early September, the IOC sent Kisch a letter implying that the POA had been duly recognized. Kisch replied to Baillet-Latour requesting confirmation.[94] The IOC sent out a contradictory note the next day to Yekutieli expressing how anxious it was that a committee for Palestine had been formed, but that it could not grant an affiliation request until "the whole of modern Palestine"[95] were represented on it.

By October, the direction that the new Germany was taking was clear to all. Germany's actions made the Jewish sports movement appear more important: previously less engaged, the Viscountess Erleigh (Lord Melchett's sister Eva Violet Mond), became "deeply interested in the Maccabee movement because she [felt] that it [was] one of deepest importance to Jewry; a movement destined to grow, and to play a great and worthy part in the history of the Jewish people."[96]

Later that month, Sondhi replied to Yekutieli to express his pleasure that Palestine had agreed to the concept of the Western Asiatic Games Confederation and communicated that it would participate in the Games.[97] He requested from Yekutieli a sketch of Palestine's flag so that he could have them made in India for display around the stadium.[98] Such a request presented a problem. Which flag to send: the Union Jack or the Zionist colors?

As Yekutieli was planning for India, Kisch wrote[99] to Baillet-Latour to explain how efforts had been made to get non-Jewish clubs into the FASCP, even though they constituted less than 10 percent of clubs in Palestine. He specifically referenced the Jerusalem YMCA and correctly informed Baillet-Latour that the YMCA had refused to cooperate, "apparently on the grounds that it could not obtain a measure of control to which neither its members nor the standard of its sports activities entitle it."[100] But he committed to keep the door open and maintain an official position of nondiscrimination.

Perhaps to emphasize the point of the POA's openness and transparency, the FASCP provided the JTA in Jerusalem with notice of its invitation to the Western Asiatic Games on December 3, 1933. The article appeared under the title "Jew, Arab Athletes to Compete in India: Palestine Maccabi Unit Invited to Send Team to Western Asiatic Olympics."[101] The same article noted the invitation to Yekutieli for the Maccabi organization to participate in the Women's World Games scheduled to take place in London in 1934, saying, "Both invitations will probably be accepted with the approval of the Maccabee [sic] Alliance...While the London games are considered important as a sports event, much significance is attached to the invitation to the New Delhi Olympiad since a number of important Arab sports associations will be represented there. The invitation of the Palestine Maccabee [sic] group to compete in the events there is thus taken to be an indication of the contribution of sports to international amity."[102]

It was only two days prior that the New York Times had reported Sherrill's stance that the United States should not boycott Berlin. The next day, Westland ran its first article on the potential success of the Olympic boycott effort. And on December 3, exactly the same day as the JTA wire about the Western Asiatic Games, Edström was privately expressing to Brundage that, with regards to the situation for Jews in Germany, he fully understood that "an alteration had to take place," even if he was in disagreement.[103] The debate was raging, the Nazis were agitating severely at exactly this moment at the Jerusalem YMCA, and Aberdare took the time to write to IOC Baillet-Latour on Christmas Eve. He informed the IOC president that he would consult the Colonial Office semi-officially before preparing a draft reply to the second request from Palestine.[104] Aberdare included with his letter a six-page report titled "Jewry and the Next Olympiad."[105]

Aberdare's report shed some light on the potential solutions to the boycott issue. He acknowledged that it was within the IOC's right to re-allot the Berlin Games to another country[106] and felt "the whole thing turns upon that one sentence, 'the true spirit of the Olympic [M] ovement.'"[107] He proposed a "bene geste"[108] from Germany in which some Jewish sportsmen would be allowed on the German Olympic team, which "would certainly establish the good faith expressed in the Vienna resolutions."[109] Such a solution was constructed in part on Aberdare's consideration of "the feelings of Jewish sportsmen of British nationality… We must not place ourselves in the ungracious position of sending our teams to take part in a festival which could not, even on purely sentimental grounds, be attended by those of our Jewish comrades in sport who are British."[110] Prima facie, Aberdare's attitude seemed a "bene geste" in itself, but it was laced with a suspicion of Jews: Aberdare stated, "Jewry is unique, in that it is wide-spread throughout the world, and the fact remains that every Jew has two loyalties. The one is an intense patriotism which binds him to the country of his birth, or adoption…the other is a subtle but nevertheless equally intense racial loyalty, which unites the Jews of all the earth."[111]

Given the situation in Germany and looking at various IOC members' attitudes, one can understand the sense of surprise that Kisch expressed in his letter to Baillet-Latour. In that letter, Kisch made an unusually frank and undiplomatic reference to the Jerusalem YMCA. Why? What had happened in 1933 in the negotiations to bring Jewish and Arab sport together? The year should have been the one in which Jewish and Arab sport united in Jerusalem under a representative Palestine Olympic Association. Heinrichs was at the helm of the Jerusalem YMCA and was positioned and empowered to help this transpire.

## 6.

The year started out at the Jerusalem YMCA with a meeting focused on the revision of the Jerusalem YMCA's constitution. What happened at this meeting set the stage for a lot of Heinrichs' later problems. A number of issues were at stake, including representative governance, leadership, the power of committees, financial transparency, and membership with other organizations, including sport organizations.

Heinrichs knew that the Paris Basis would split the membership in half if it was not changed to prevent the perception of the Association being a proselytizing association. There was also growing pressure to remove president Bowman. At the meeting, the membership put forward a motion to vote in the president direct from the membership, but this was lost.[112] The cap of one-third non-Palestinians and one-third church groups on the board was also defeated in the meeting.[113] The proposal that chairmen of standing committees be voted in by the members of their committees was won.[114] Unfortunately, this victory strengthened the ability of the Jerusalem YMCA's committees to act independently of the board and would empower the Nazis later in the year. Still, Section 18 of the new constitution empowered the board to "overrule any decision of standing committees inconsistent with the spirit of the Constitution and where the standing committees, in the opinion of the Board, have exceeded their power."[115] Heinrichs also successfully blocked Anis Khadder, a board member, from auditing the accounts in order to comply with Section 27, which barred anyone from the board auditing the Association's accounts.[116] Section 28[117] gave the board the power to terminate Heinrichs' negotiations with the FASCP and Zionist sport organizations, and Section 29 specified that either Bowman or Heinrichs would be the members of such organizations, restricting them to nonvoting status. In this regard, Heinrichs' negotiations with Zionist sport organizations were constitutionally compliant, and any lack of voting rights within the FASCP (which were guaranteed by the FASCP regulations) was applied by the Jerusalem YMCA, not the Zionists. Although the meeting was tough, Heinrichs felt that he had finally succeeded and put most of the constitutional issues behind him, expecting only to lose reactionaries.[118]

But the ideological sympathies of some reactionaries would cause his troubles to continue.

The Va'ad Leumi seemed unconvinced by the constitutional changes. Mohl told Heinrichs to anticipate their opposition.[119] So Heinrichs decided finally to write to Wilbert Smith in New York to explain how the constitution had become so divisive.[120] He explained to Smith how fifty members had requested the changes. Historically, the Association had been using a constitution prepared between 1910 and 1920 by Archie Harte, referred to as the White constitution. This had been revised in early 1931, before Heinrichs arrived, because it was unworkable with the new building. It was replaced by the Blue constitution, which also didn't work. Heinrichs told Smith that he was practically assassinated for suggesting the Blue constitution be changed. After five months of inefficiencies, the board finally realized that it could not control every aspect of the building and allowed for the creation of fourteen standing committees and two special committees with the ability to make decisions on behalf of the board. This was a perfectly reasonable management solution, just not in Jerusalem. The problem that Heinrichs did not foresee was that certain persons in those committees might not share the values of the YMCA Movement. He went on to explain to Smith how a Constitution Revision Committee was formed in late 1932 and over three sessions prepared a draft constitution that was presented to the full membership on November 21.[121] Heinrichs had wanted a discussion at that meeting, but he was overruled by Bowman.[122] A group of younger Bolshevik[123] members stormed out of that meeting and put forward an additional list of forty revisions, which Heinrichs summarized in five points for Smith.[124] Heinrichs and his staff considered numerous proposals for how to accommodate the suggested changes by the Bolsheviks, including a switch to the Latvian Basis.[125] But none of these placated the competing camps and the more religiously fundamentalist members. The Anglican camp was particularly opposed to the changes referencing Christ.[126] Nonetheless, Heinrichs was able to move the parties toward a revised constitution and assured Smith that Jerusalem had moved beyond dogmatic interpretations.[127]

Heinrichs also expressed his concerns to Smith about the dynamic between the board and the role of secretary-general. Keeping in mind that he was unaware of what Nicholas Lattof had overheard said about him by the board after its first meeting with Heinrichs in May 1932, Heinrichs told[128] Smith that under Harte, the board was just a rubber stamp for the secretary-general. When Lattof arrived, the pendulum swung the other way and the secretary-general lost all his power. He explained that one of his main tasks was to bring back balance, but that to remove power from "an inexperienced Board afflicted with a very rabid type of nationalism"[129] was very difficult for a new secretary-general and that many of the Palestinians were out for his scalp.

Heinrichs' assessment was probably accurate. Despite board members like Dr. Tawfiq Canaan having a long-time family connection to the Jerusalem YMCA,[130] this did not mean that the board members' skills in running the new facility—one of the largest, most modern sport facilities in the world—were commensurate with the task. Since Heinrichs knew that the board had the power to hold him responsible for the work of the Association, he insisted that he, not the board, hire the staff.[131] The board refused, wanting to have a say on even the lowest paid employees, and 350 applications piled up.[132] Eventually the board, not wanting to deal with the selection process, asked Heinrichs for recommendations, but still the board refused European candidates, even if the Palestinian ones were not as competent.[133]

Heinrichs also brought to Smith's attention what he considered to be the board's poor trusteeship. The effects of the 1929 stock market crash were still being felt, and the foreign senior staff was already earning less in Jerusalem than they could be paid in other places around the world.[134] The board seemed obsessed with minor expenditures and knowing the salaries of foreign staff.[135] In a postscript to his letter, Heinrichs noted to Smith how the long delay in moving in to the new building was negatively affecting the membership and, consequently, the Association's projected income. Instead of 500 projected new members, the Association only acquired 188. In addition, there was tension with Albert Abramson (of the Building Committee) because of the failure to set a definite end date for the construction, which had cost the Jerusalem YMCA a lot of money for overages.[136] He concluded by saying, "[t]o coordinate the activities of the staff comprising, Palestinians, Syrians, Turks, Armenians, Russians, Germans,

English, Americans, Scotch, Kurds, and Jews, makes the situation very comparable to August 1914."[137] Such a lack of unity of purpose was not present in the Zionist movement.

At the end of January, Heinrichs was still facing some residual Jewish skepticism towards attempts at cooperation. He met at Mohl's house with the Zionist leadership. It was agreed with Arlosoroff that the Palestine Zionist Executive would not "boycott, in personal ways to be friendly, but not to participate officially or personally in the YMCA."[138] This is important because even though the Executive was monitoring the situation closely, it was open to the idea of friendly relations while preserving the Maccabi Movement's apolitical nature. Ensuing conversations between Heinrichs and the FASCP would not be interpreted as an extension of Zionist political activity. Indeed, the Maccabi World Union, although Zionist in nature, was "a non-party organization since its creation…Only after acceptance of the Jerusalem Program by the Zionist Organization in the early 1970s did the Maccabi Union join the Zionist Movement."[139] Still, Dr. Leon Roth expressed his concerns that the "YMCA, by mixing all types, will continue to create a Levantine culture as opposed to our aim of a Jewish culture." Mohl advised Heinrichs, "Participate in any way possible, and make the YMCA the common meeting ground of all communities. The separatist ideal is impossible and creates friction and trouble and riots."[140]

## 7.

In early February, Heinrichs hosted the Jerusalem YMCA's open house to try and increase the membership to the organization.[141] Between six and seven hundred visitors came, with fifteen to twenty-five new prospects showing interest. The High Commissioner and his staff played squash, adding additional prestige to the event. Two days later, the Physical Department appointed Nathan and Khadder to meet with the Palestine Lawn Tennis Association.[142] Here was an example of the autonomy of the standing committees exercising their constitutional right to make their own decisions. This is important because it shows that Heinrichs was not imposing his choices about sport cooperation on the Palestinians. Tennis was a major area of cooperation in sport between all the faiths, and the Jerusalem YMCA's Tennis Club included twenty-six Jews.[143]

But because problems continued in the lead-up to the building dedication, Heinrichs gave Dr. John Mott notice.[144] Mott was due in Jerusalem for the dedication. Heinrichs wrote to him that the stiffest resistance was actually from within the Christian community, primarily the Greek Orthodox (who constituted 30 percent of the members) and the Latin Catholics, whose Patriarch in 1932 had reinforced the Vatican's fiat against the Association.[145] Heinrichs enclosed the new constitution for Mott to review and pointed out the clear stance against proselytizing in Section 8.[146] Rabbi Stephen Wise in New York also had concerns based on an article in the *Jewish Daily Bulletin*.[147] In a private correspondence,[148] Heinrichs assured Wise that there had been progress on the proselytizing issue. He told him how he felt that the success of the Jews was dependent on the goodwill of all the communities in Palestine. He spoke of growing religious and political antagonism toward the Jews and wrote that he was himself being accused of being a pro-Jewish, anti-Arab agent to perpetuate British domination of Palestine. He urged Wise to consider that the Jews in Palestine would lose a valuable ally if they did not cooperate with the Association.

As the dedication approached, Heinrichs was still mired in trying to employ staff to fill the building. On March 4, he conducted "interview after interview for hours,"[149] but the next day President Franklin D. Roosevelt closed US banks to prevent a run. Heinrichs was concerned that America was about to go off the gold standard, wreaking havoc on his budgets.[150] This would result in a further reduction of pay for the foreign staff of 50 percent, and they would have to give up their homes and move into the YMCA building.[151] Heinrichs could not get a break.

Still, the Association continued its activities. It hosted the Inter-Service Boxing Tournament[152] to show off its new gymnasium to the six hundred who were in attendance for the bouts.[153] Fred Ramsey, the representative of the building's owner and the father of Heinrichs' personal secretary, also had arrived from New York to support final preparations for the dedication.[154] Lattof and Heinrichs worked closely on the budget with Ramsey because of the enduring economic turmoil and in order to get it ready for the Finance Committee for approval before the event.[155]

Once they had finalized the local budget, they turned it over to Ramsey.[156] There were still challenges with the building completion and its contractors, Katinke, Dounie, and Albina.[157] The discovery of antiquities on the construction site had delayed and increased the cost of the work.[158] In addition, the depreciation of the Palestine pound from the time of tender to the year 1933 had gutted the project's profitability for the contractors,[159] and there had also been possible corruption on the project.[160, 161]

As the Track and Field Committee prepared the program for the dedication, Heinrichs began avoiding dinners at the Fast Hotel, which had just hoisted the swastika for the first time.[162] To alleviate the pressure from the board about the ongoing constitutional issues, Heinrichs had begun a conversation with Mott and Ramsey about affiliating the Jerusalem YMCA to the YMCA World Committee.[163] It was hoped that Walter Gethman, the World Committee's secretary-general, would join Mott in Jerusalem for the dedication.[164] Ramsey and Mott were well aware that Jerusalem had a problem percolating because of the attitudes in the local board.

On April 1, just a few days before the dedication, Heinrichs worked with Matson Photography to shoot the press photos of the building.[165] He received the official permission-to-occupy letter from Ramsey. This letter had a number of stipulations. First, it identified the donors—as a reminder that the building's operating ability rested in investment funds that existed outside the reach of the local board. Included in the list of donors were Margaret Hopper, Dorothy Heinrichs' aunt.[166] As a gesture of confidence in Heinrichs, or at least the role of the secretary-general (and to shield the project from the issues within the board), a number of safeguards were put in place as conditions to occupy the building. These included the requirement that "not less than one-third of the membership of the Board...be appointed annually by the International Committee,"[167] that "Section 15 of the By-Laws be amended to provide that the General Secretary [sic] shall be appointed by the Board of Directors on the nomination of the International Committee,"[168] that "it be provided in the Constitution that no amendments be made therein without the concurrence of the International Committee,"[169] "that the work be carried on...in harmony with the purposes and ideals of the...[YMCA]...Movement,"[170] and "that the Christian character of the enterprise be maintained."[171] These stipulations are important because the coming actions of the Nazis in Jerusalem and the actions of the board to remove Heinrichs would be in violation of all these conditions. Clearly Ramsey and Mott were of the opinion that the issues within the YMCA were not only the result of Heinrichs.

At the time that Heinrichs received permission to occupy the building, the board comprised twenty individuals.[172] Ramsey wrote, "To avoid disturbing the elective status of the present twenty, the International Committee would select four of its eight appointive members from the present membership of the Board, selecting others in due course from the community."[173] One of those community members, unbeknownst to the International Committee, would be applying for membership in the Nazi Party in 1933.

The ongoing tension was expressed beyond the discussions between Heinrichs, Ramsey, and Mott. Emile Khadder,[174] a dentist who was one of the board members, wrote to Ramsey directly. Ramsey had met with the board in contentious meetings ahead of the dedication to smooth things over. In the letter, he told Ramsey of the nationalistic bias "which was shown so very clearly in the [board] meeting"[175] that Ramsey had attended. He assured Ramsey that he would always uphold the principles of the YMCA, especially with regards to nondiscrimination. Yet for Heinrichs, many on the board treated him as a friend of the Jews and a spy for the English. And clearly, no one from the International Committee or foreign staff seemed to understand that there might be a possible Nazi connection to all of Heinrichs' troubles.

At the same time, Heinrichs noted that a strong offensive was being mounted against the YMCA playing Hapoel Tel Aviv because the Arabs did not want a Jewish team to play at the dedication in front of Lord Allenby. Heinrichs wrote in his diary on April 1, "They are using every excuse to mask their real intent & purpose. I am determined to resist."[176] Perhaps in defiance, Heinrichs went to a meeting with the Maccabi leaders of the FASCP who seemed ready to incorporate the Jerusalem YMCA as a member club.[177] He also went to the Menorah Club as a guest of the Arlosoroffs in honor of Dr. and Mrs. Chaim Weizmann.[178] These actions probably did not make Heinrichs additional friends among his already nationalistic board.

Heinrichs' next days would be consumed by the final preparations for "elaborate dedication exercises for the period beginning April 9 and ending April 24."[179] These included religious exercises, musical events, lectures and educational tours, social events, dramatics, physical department activities, and the formal dedication exercises.[180] Canaan would provide one of the lectures, on "Folk Lore in the Holy Land."[181] The sports program included the Open Squash Tournament for Palestine and Trans-Jordan, open to all amateurs from both territories; the Fourth Annual Cross-Country Championship; and the Track and Field Championships according to Olympic standards on the new cinder track and athletic field.[182] Gymnastics, boxing, and basketball would also be on the program, the latter against the American University of Beirut team.[183]

## 8.

The program of events commenced on April 9. Heinrichs got off early to the coast to meet Mr. and Mrs. Perry and Miss Jarvie, the representative of the donor's family and the Jarvie Commonwealth Fund. Once he reached the port, Heinrichs noted 1,200 passengers from the MS *Vulcania*, many of them immigrants from Germany fleeing Hitler's anti-Jewish campaign.[184] How much the conditions in Europe had changed since his arrival to Palestine one year prior on a ship that carried only ten other passengers from Naples to Haifa. The Dachau concentration camp had just been opened, and Hermann Göring was about to establish the Gestapo. Heinrichs returned to Jerusalem for the board meeting to approve the budget before the dedication so that the building could be fully operable. Incredibly, even though Ramsey was in attendance, it did not go as expected. The nationalistic bias dominated the meeting and exhausted Ramsey, who began to understand the difficulties facing Heinrichs.[185]

And to think that Lord Allenby and his wife were arriving on April 12.[186] Heinrichs went to meet them quayside and took a day's rest by the coast. He then joined the dignitaries in their train coach to Jerusalem to discuss their program.[187] The train arrived to a flag-bedecked station with a red carpet and "a mere handful of government officials who had been pulled together at a moments notice."[188] It all felt a little last minute.

Finally, the day of the dedication came: April 18, 1933. Heinrichs recorded the event in his diary.[189] He was able to get only four hours' sleep. He had the building beautifully decorated with flags and flowers. The religious heads, consular corps, government, officials, and general public jammed the terrace full. At 2:30 there was a carillon concert. Loudspeakers took care of the overflow audience in the boys' rooms, lecture hall, gymnasium, and social rooms. Heinrichs estimated two thousand attendees. He gathered the speakers in the board room, and at 3:15 the main events went off like clockwork. Heinrichs thought that the Anglican Bishop's invocation was selfish, provocative, and tactless, a rather asinine talk to God for fifteen minutes while people stood uncomfortably to listen. In contrast, he thought that Rabbi Silver's Twenty-Third Psalm ("The Lord is my shepherd..."[190]) was the most impressive thing on the program. Mott spoke well but too long, and in a manner that was too much like an International Missionary Council address. Heinrichs was mortified for the sake of Muslims and Jews.

The International Committee of YMCAs put out a press bulletin addressed to the presidents and general secretaries in North America, noting that NBC would cover the event in the first international broadcast from Jerusalem.[191] It noted the importance of the occasion within the context of the fresh waves of racial hatred and religious intolerance that were shocking the world.[192] Allenby's speech, the keynote and final address of the dedication, reinforced the message:

> Here is a spot whose atmosphere is peace; where political and religious jealousies can be forgotten, and international unity be fostered and developed.
>
> We are all aware of a strongly-rooted prejudice, in many minds, against the cult of internationalism. Nationalism is generally accepted as high virtue, while [i]nternationalism is often regarded as almost criminal.
>
> Why should this be? There is no sane reason for so narrow a view.
>
> We have to live together. We are prisoners on this planet; we cannot escape. For thousands of years to come, human beings

may continue to inhabit the Earth; and they will, perforce, have to endure the companionship of their fellows.

Is the Human Race to exist in harmony: or is Nation evermore to war against Nation?

Change is a law of nature; and, as the centuries roll by, mankind must advance or recede, grow better or worse; but…"The New World" cannot rest on mutual distrust and jealousy; cooperation alone can make it a habitable abode for men.

Happily, the tendency of Evolution is advancement; and there are good grounds for courageous hope. Human nature contains more good than evil; is, on the whole, well-intentioned and generous. It can compel to savage fight; in defense of family, tribal or national right; but, when battle is over, old hatreds are soon forgotten.[193]

The *Palestine Post* covered the ceremony, describing Allenby's words as "an exhortation for peace among nations and understanding among peoples, an exhortation that extolled all instruments for the outlawing of war and denounced all engines making for war."[194]

The dedication of the Jerusalem YMCA was one of the highlights of Jerusalem's history during the British Mandate for Palestine. Yet on his way home from Palestine, Mott wrote to Ramsey from Alexandria. Although he expressed "large confidence in the Board,"[195] he also made clear the point that the International Committee would "*appoint* not *nominate*"[196] eight members of the board.[197] Shortly after the dedication, Ramsey also wrote to Jerusalem YMCA board member Albert Abramson, who was Commissioner of Lands for Jerusalem in the Mandate administration. He requested a copy of the deed of sale in the Land Registry Office in Jerusalem for the IC/YMCA's vault in New York.[198] Clearly there were some concerns after the discussions in Jerusalem. These concerns appear to relate to New York being able to influence the board's actions and protect its ownership of the new building.

The concerns were warranted. Heinrichs continued to have trouble as soon as all the guests and dignitaries had departed. Some of these troubles were linked to the ongoing financial issues facing the Association because of the US decision to go off the gold standard. Staff had to be let go. The first was Harris, the Religious Works Director.[199] Heinrichs also had to visit the mayor of Jerusalem, Ragheb Bey Nashashibi, to negotiate a reduction in municipal taxes.[200] Then Boulos Said resigned his position in the Finance Committee and as treasurer of the Association without explanation. Heinrichs met with him on May 16 to convince him to withdraw the resignation[201] and also met with Mantoura, only to learn, much to his surprise, that Mantoura had criticized Heinrichs' administration to Ramsey.[202]

Heinrichs probably felt that he needed more allies in the building. He had nominated two Arab employees for YMCA scholarships to continue their studies in the United States. This meant that the Physical Department would be temporarily short an Associate Physical Director. Heinrichs decided to nominate his brother Conrad Heinrichs to the role.[203] This probably contributed to more trouble for Heinrichs (although his brother would prove important in March 1934 when Heinrichs had to leave).

Heinrichs' brother had been unemployed in the United States since the market crash. Heinrichs' parents were coming to Jerusalem for a visit, and he asked that they bring his brother with them. Heinrichs was aware of the potential trouble this could cause, but he pushed ahead. He needed help in the Physical Department, and sport continued to be an area of friction. The subject was important enough for Heinrichs to include in his annual report to New York.[204] He informed New York that he had been elected to the Palestine Football Association and had also been asked to cooperate with the Palestine Amateur Football Federation, the Arab equivalent of Yekutieli's FIFA-recognized body. He explained how the Jerusalem YMCA was being crushed between powerful Jewish sport organizations and an extremely nationalistic Arab sports club (probably Arab Sports Club) that would not cooperate with the Jews on forming any federations. Heinrichs' position was for the Jerusalem YMCA to remain neutral. He noted that during the sport activities during dedication week, the Maccabi and Hapoel teams walked away with 90 percent of the awards and were offensive to Muslims and Christians over their cockiness, but that participation was better than boycott.

Heinrichs' situation got worse in June with the departure of Abramson from his post in the Lands Office for leave.[205] Heinrichs took him to Jaffa to meet the SS *Vienna* and lost an ally on the board for several months. The same day a cable from Springfield College came, approving one of the two staff scholarships. That evening at a meeting with the board, Heinrichs allowed Dr. Tannous to bring up the subject of replacing the Arab employee temporarily with Conrad Heinrichs. "I told them 1) that he was my brother and so a cause for embarrassment and 2) That he had been divorced for lack of support during his unemployment."[206] Yet the board accepted Heinrichs' brother as a replacement unanimously, with the exception of J. Gordon Boutagy, who would soon prove to be quite the thorn in Heinrichs' side.

## 9.

On the evening of June 16, Chaim Arlosoroff was assassinated in Tel Aviv. The Heinrichs felt a great sense of personal loss.[207] A board meeting was called two days later to decide on Harris' replacement as Religious Work Director. Well into the meeting, Heinrichs asked leave so that he could express his condolences to Mrs. Arlosoroff. The board refused and Heinrichs found it "[o]ne of the most disgusting evidences of petty nationalism"[208] that he had seen. This incident would not have eased Heinrichs' concerns that new trouble was brewing. Judge Cresall, a board member, was making extensive changes to the constitution[209] (following the meetings with Mott during the dedication). The extensiveness of the changes worried Heinrichs. He knew circulating them would create more challenges and that it would be difficult to get them passed by the board and members.[210] Sure enough, there was a large block of opposition for the meeting with the membership on July 15. But Heinrichs, Lattof, and Emile Ohan worked on three lists of active members on whom they knew they could count to back up the changes. Lattof got sixty, Ohan got twenty, and Heinrichs got forty-two members from the air force and fifteen others. The meeting started at 5:30 p.m. with 90 members present, but soon there were 136 in attendance and every single item for which he had fought for eight months was passed without dissenting vote. Heinrichs recorded in his diary that the enemy was mad.[211] He wired New York the good news: "ENTIRE CONSTITUTION PASSED APPOINTIVE PROCESS ACCEPTED = HEINRICHS."[212] This should have put everything to rest.

Once again, it did not. The board found other things at which to pick. By August, Said was back as treasurer and refused to sign a £P 2,000[213] to settle the Herbert E. Clark Antiquities Collection on display in the building.[214] It is not clear why Said refused to sign the check, but it was the beginning of a series of conflicts that would ultimately place Said in Heinrichs' "triumvirate" of opposition within the Jerusalem YMCA.[215] Another distraction erupted at home: the same day Said refused to sign the check for the collection, Heinrichs had to fire his house boy Minwar. He had "committed fornication"[216] with the Heinrichs' German cook Martha, who was married. Five weeks later, Minwar attempted to murder Martha's husband while she walked with him in Jerusalem by shooting him.[217] The case created quite a stir, and Heinrichs had to follow the trial and serve as a witness.

At a subcommittee meeting on contracts and appointments, Boutagy attacked Heinrichs.[218] He would be antagonistic again at the end of the month, this time at the board meeting where he asked if Conrad Heinrichs was the private secretary to his brother, there to conduct private work.[219] The next day Heinrichs felt a sense of hatred of Boutagy for what he perceived to be his obstructionist tactics.[220]

In the first week of October, Heinrichs met with Hapoel to negotiate use of the YMCA's athletic fields.[221] The board's Executive Committee also convened to select the sixteen names that would be sent to New York, from which eight would be appointed from America.[222] Heinrichs felt that the Arabs did not like him because he had befriended the Jews and played "an absolutely neutral part in all their rivalries and hatreds."[223] He cited three board members who he characterized as particularly problematic: Boutagy, Said, and Canaan.[224] Nonetheless, he remained optimistic about the sports work.[225] Auburn was doing a good job in the Physical Department. A year before, the Jews had boycotted the tennis championship. Now they were back in full cooperation and had even won the majority of prizes at the dedication week. Arab Sports Club had recently moved into the YMCA's old quarters and would be using the football field regularly. Even though the Association had to work on the principle of cooperation with them, the Physical Department was a great asset, and Heinrichs believed if they could achieve cooperation in sport, other areas would follow.

But two days later, riots broke out.[226] Heinrichs was focused on the installation of the Clark Collection of Antiquities while "the dire prediction by the Arabs of what was going to happen"[227] swirled around Jerusalem with people saying, "This is the beginning."[228] The day the riots broke out, Hapoel played at the YMCA.[229] Heinrichs probably appeared detached from reality to some of the Arab board and general members, and he was beginning to make it easy for himself to be targeted again. The riots intensified, spreading to Jaffa on October 27 and Nablus the next day. Jerusalem's streets were deserted and the King David Hotel across the street was barricaded.[230] The Jerusalem YMCA was scheduled to have a social, which the Arabs wanted cancelled. Heinrichs refused but eventually had to back down because the performers themselves backed out.[231] Still, Heinrichs tried to be sensitive to certain Arab concerns. He upset the Englishmen resident at the YMCA's hostel by asking them not to dress in uniforms and carry rifles. A delegation of Muslims and two Arab Christians had complained to him about this English behavior.[232] Heinrichs also donated money anonymously to a fund for people killed in the riots.[233] Although the riots subsided, they foreshadowed the Great Arab Revolt of April 1936, which would consume Palestine until the beginning of the Second World War.

## 10.

The November board meeting[234] occurred during the month of Dr. Iven's Nazi propaganda visit to Jerusalem. On the agenda was the auditor's report and the employment of Miss Shapiro, a Jewess. She was the cataloguer, and some of the Arab board members wanted to use her observance of the Sabbath to fire her. The Jamals and Said had two other candidates with whom they wanted to replace her. Heinrichs opposed them and the board opposed Heinrichs, who began experiencing his first real inclination to resign.

The case of Miss Shapiro caused Heinrichs to wake the next morning before dawn "with a heavy sense of oppression."[235] He wrote a long letter to the IC/YMCA in New York. He went over everything with them from the time he had accepted the post to the confrontation about Miss Shapiro. He asked for their backing against the Arab board members' effort to turn the Jerusalem YMCA into a nationalist association. Lattof asked Heinrichs not to send the letter, arguing that the situation would calm down. Auburn said the storm was growing and that two private board meetings had already been held. The next day[236] Heinrichs learned what the board had discussed. The Arab board members wanted Bowman to table two proposals: the first that the Christian Sabbath had to be observed and the second that every employee had to work six days a week. Assuming that every Jew was observant, surely the adoption of this policy would guarantee for the Christian Palestinian leadership of the Association that no Jew could work in its building. Heinrichs felt that the second proposal was a clear violation of the Association's principles and that the Arab board was out to get rid of him, Lattof, and Auburn.

Heinrichs called a staff conference to get back to basics and build support for his position among the staff.[237] In the meantime, Canaan, Jamal, and Said met with Bowman and tried unsuccessfully to get his approval of the two proposals. Bowman told Heinrichs that he was being pigheaded,[238] but Heinrichs would not relent on principles. He told Bowman, "We will never yield if they wish to get Miss Shapiro out because she is a Jewess."[239] Five days later, the cable arrived from New York with the appointments to the board. New York chose five Europeans and only three Arabs,[240] a boost to Heinrichs and an apparent lack of confidence in the emerging political climate in the board. Heinrichs was also relieved to have Abramson return from overseas (who had left in June) and to have an ally back on the board after feeling that a fortress had closed in around him in his absence.[241] The two attended the "long insisted upon and much dreaded meeting of the Board"[242] on November 20 to discuss Miss Shapiro. Heinrichs did not speak unless they asked him for data, which he would only then give. Abramson "stood off the entire gang of Palestinians," and they worked out a resolution on Sabbath observance.

On November 25, Heinrichs and his wife decided finally to move into the YMCA for their accommodation. Because of the pay cuts

**Figure 1.** *Military portrait of Frederick Hermann Kisch, circa Second World War. Kisch was chairman of the Palestine Zionist Executive from 1923 until 1931 and the founding president of the POC, which the International Olympic Committee (IOC) recognized on May 16, 1934. On November 4, 1934 Kisch and Yekutieli formally communicated Palestine's boycott of the 1936 Berlin Olympic Games to the IOC. Mysteriously, a Palestinian delegation with possible Nazi connections appeared at the Berlin Games anyway, captained by a Palestinian staff member of the Jerusalem Young Men's Christian Association (YMCA). To this day, the Palestinian delegation to the Berlin Olympics, which seems connected to a Nazi cell in Jerusalem, remains shrouded in mystery. Kisch, through Yekutieli, denied in writing any dealings with Nazi officials around the Berlin Games.*

*Source:* Abraham Malavsky, KKL-JNF Photo Archive.

**Figure 2.** *First World War military portrait of Waldo Huntley Heinrichs Sr., circa 1917. "First to the Front" with the United States' 95th Aero Squadron in the war. This portrait was taken prior to Heinrichs' being shot down on September 17, 1918 by a German Fokker D.VII of the Red Baron's squadron. Shot and severely injured, he almost died in a German prison hospital in Metz, France. After surgeries and convalescence, he dedicated his life to the YMCA's foreign work, first in India, where he helped establish the Punjab Olympic Association with Guru Dutt (G. D.) Sondhi. The International Committee of YMCAs selected Heinrichs from a pool of candidates to be the secretary-general of the new Jerusalem International YMCA, at the time one of the largest association and sport projects in the world.*

**Figure 3.** *Kisch (left of center, behind fence panels and wearing a hat) and Yekutieli (right of Kisch and wearing white suit, peaked cap, and spectacles) at the First Maccabi Games in Tel Aviv on March 31, 1932.*

Source: PHO\1354010, reproduced with permission of the Central Zionist Archives. Original held at the Central Zionist Archives 558/16.

**Figure 4.** *Maccabi House* (Bayt HaMaccabi), *from which Yekutieli and other Zionists built Mandate Palestine's international sport connections. The building was one of the key legacies of the First Maccabiad. Circa early 1930s, Tel Aviv, Mandate Palestine/Eretz Israel.*

**Figure 5.** *A portrait of the board members of the Jerusalem YMCA. This photo was published on December 31, 1931 on page six of In the Heart of the Holy City, the Jerusalem YMCA's annual report on the occasion of its twelfth anniversary (after its reconstitution after the First World War). The Association announced the appointment of Heinrichs to the post of secretary-general in the same publication, referring to it as one of the year's "outstanding events." At left in the back row is Lattof (wearing the bow tie) and at center in the back row (the tallest individual) is Dr. Canaan. Others identified in the publication as board members at the time (but whose exact location in the photo was not discerned), include I. Gordon Doulagy, Boulos Said, and George Khadder, all of whom (along with Canaan) Heinrichs referenced in his diaries as presenting a serious impediment to the realization of the Jerusalem YMCA's interfaith and interracial work.*

*Source:* University of Minnesota Libraries' Department of Archives and Special Collections, Kautz Family YMCA Archives, Records of YMCA international work in Palestine and Israel. Reproduced with the permission of the Office of the General Counsel of the YMCA of the USA.

**Figure 6.** *The Jesus Tower and main entrance of the Jerusalem International YMCA, designed by Arthur Loomis Harmon of Shreve, Lamb & Harmon, the architectural firm that designed the Empire State Building during the same period. Photo by Matson Photo Services for Jerusalem YMCA, possibly taken on April 1, 1933, as recorded in the diary of Waldo Huntley Heinrichs Sr.*

**Figure 7.** *Field Marshal Edmund Henry Hynman Allenby, 1st Viscount Allenby (left), reviewing matters relating to the dedication of the Jerusalem YMCA with Heinrichs (right). Lord Allenby arrived in Jerusalem for the dedication exercises on April 13, 1933 and gave the keynote address at the formal opening on April 18, 1933. The memorable event was a highlight of Mandate Palestine's history. The radio broadcast of the dedication was the first international broadcast from Jerusalem.*

**Figure 8.** *Hotel Fast, a center of Nazi activity in Jerusalem, was where the German Third Reich's consular office for the city was located. In the lower left of the photo is the travel office of Waldemar Fast, who, in the spring of 1934, joined the Nazi Party at the height of the newspaper incident at the Jerusalem YMCA (see Wawrzyn, 2013, pp. 160-161). Fast's travel office became the agency responsible for providing "all particulars" in Mandate Palestine regarding the 1936 Olympic Games in Berlin, Germany. During the Second World War, Fast eventually joined the SS, served in a killing unit in Russia, and was posted to Ankara as the assistant to Ludwig Moyzisch, the head of the Gestapo in Turkey and handler of Cicero, one of the most effective spies for the Nazis during the Second World War. In 1941, 1942, and 1944, Fast facilitated three prisoner exchanges between interned Germans in Palestine and Jews in concentrations camps in Europe. During 1942, Fast's senior SS colleague Walter Rauff, who had conceived of the gas vans to kill Jews as an extermination method during an early phase of the Nazi holocaust, was assigned to lead a SS killing unit for Palestine to accompany the advance of Rommel's army into the territory. Kisch, the president of the Palestine Olympic Committee and chief engineer of the Allies' Eighth Army, died helping to turn back Axis forces in the Battle of Wadi Akarıt on April 7, 1943. After the war, the remainder of the German population in Palestine was deported to Australia and Chile. Rauff settled in Santiago. It is not clear what became of Fast after the war.*

**Figure 9.** *The Jerusalem YMCA Reading Room, center of the Nazi newspaper incident and controversy over the subscription to the* Völkischer Beobachter. *The Reading Room is now the Harte YMCA Restaurant at the Three Arches Hotel, named after Archie Harte, who was the secretary-general succeeded by Heinrichs. Ironically, it was Heinrichs who conceived and oversaw the planting of the fruit and vegetable gardens that first supplied the Jerusalem YMCA cafeteria with fresh produce.*

**Figure 10.** *Mandate Palestine's delegation to the First Western Asiatic Games, circa February – March, 1934 in India (either at Patiala or New Delhi). At far left, the Olympic Flag and Symbol and the flag of the Western Asiatic Games Confederation, co-founded by Palestine. At right, the Shield of David flag, now the flag of Israel. From left to right: Yaacov Goddard, Dov Rabinowitz, Shlomo Marantz, David Almagor (team manager), Walter Frankl, Theodor Levy, and Alfred Gutt. Frankl, Palestine's long-distance runner, had fled Vienna, where he had been an active athlete at Hakoah Wien, the same club that had won the European football championship in 1924.*

Source: Reproduced with permission of the Joseph Yekutieli Maccabi Sport Archives, Kfar Maccabiah, Ramat Gan, Israel.

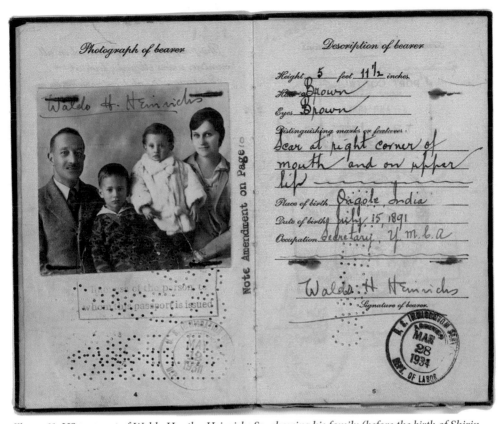

**Figure 11.** *US passport of Waldo Huntley Heinrichs Sr., showing his family (before the birth of Shirin, who arrived during the interval in Larchmont, NY between Lahore and Jerusalem). From left to right are Heinrichs Sr., Waldo Huntley Heinrichs Jr. ("Huntley" or "Junior"), Mary Heinrichs (in white coat), and Dorothy Peterson Heinrichs. "Junior" was an early competitor in the swimming pool of the Jerusalem YMCA, once defeating the son of Henry Mond (Lord Melchett, Honorary President of the World Maccabi Union). In one of the many photos taken of the Jerusalem YMCA's dedication, "Junior" can be seen scaling one of the columns of the new building. Dorothy remained in Jerusalem with Heinrichs' brother to inform on developments with the Nazis. The passport bears two stamps. The one on the left from May 12, 1931 documents the family's return to the US after years of service in India and after the Heinrichses had toured Jerusalem in the spring of 1931, before accepting the "call" to be the Association's secretary-general. The stamp on the right documents Heinrichs' return to the US on March 28, 1934, after being forced to flee Jerusalem by the Nazis.*

*Source:* Bequest of Waldo Huntley Heinrichs Jr. and reproduced with permission of the Department of Special Collections and University Archives, W. E. B. Du Bois Library, University of Massachusetts Amherst.

NICHOLAS M. LATTOF
*Acting General Secretary*

B.A.S., The Y.M.C.A. College, Chicago;
Ph. B., The University of Chicago;
Member, National Honor Society of
the Y.M.C.A. Colleges of America.

FREDERICK W. AUBURN
*Physical Director*

B.S., Robert College, Constantinople;
B.P.E., International Y.M.C.A. College,
Springfield, Mass., U.S.A.

SAMI I. SUZ
*Office and Accounts*

B.B.A., American University of
Beirut, Syria.

EMILE OHAN
*Membership*

Graduate of St. George's, Jerusalem.

**Figure 12.** *Key employees of the Jerusalem YMCA during the Nazi newspaper incident. Clockwise, from top left: Nicholas Lattof, assistant secretary-general to Heinrichs, Frederick Auburn, director of the YMCA Physical Department, Sami Suz, in charge of Heinrichs' office and accounts, and Emile Ohan(ian), in charge of membership. Suz and Ohan backed Heinrichs' position against the Nazis. Lattof was subsequently forced to fire them in dubious circumstances and had to flee Jerusalem hurriedly with his family in the spring of 1936 in the lead-up to the 1936 Berlin Olympic Games. Neither Lattof nor Auburn were permitted to return to Jerusalem, with the circumstances surrounding their departure shrouded in mystery.*

Source: University of Minnesota Libraries' Department of Archives and Special Collections, Kautz Family YMCA Archives, Records of YMCA International Work in Palestine and Israel. Reproduced with the permission of the Office of the General Counsel of the YMCA of the USA.

**Figure 13.** *German (swastika) and Olympic flags fly in Berlin during the Olympic Games. Berlin, Germany, August 1936.*

Source: PHOTOGRAPHS 77805, United States Holocaust Memorial Museum, as incorporated in the museum's online Holocaust Encyclopedia, from National Archives photo no. 242-HB-22037-2, National Archives and Records Administration, College Park, MD.

**Figure 14.** *Much like the Jewish Displaced Persons in Europe after the Second World War, Palestinian refugees found respite in sport. Here, a group of women play basketball at Kalandia Refugee Camp in 1951. After the collapse of Palestinian and Arab forces in the 1948-49 war, the evacuated Arab staff of the Jerusalem YMCA reestablished services in the Jordan Valley and East Jerusalem (when those areas were under the control of the Hashemite Kingdom of Jordan). The United Nations Relief and Works Agency for Palestine Refugees (UNRWA) in the Near East was also an important provider of sport and vocational training (among other) services.*

Source: UNRWA photo No. WW/Kalandia/1A.

**Figure 15.** *The Munich 11. Top row, left to right: Mark Slavin (wrestler), Eliezer Halfin (wrestler), Moshe Weinberg (wrestling coach), Yossef Gutfreund (wrestling referee), and David Berger (weightlifter, and also an American). Second row, left to right: Amitzur Shapira (track coach), Andre Spitzer (fencing coach), Kehat Shorr (shooting coach), Yossef Romano (weightlifter), and Ze'ev Friedman (weightlifter). Third row, far right: Yakov Springer (weightlifting judge).*

Source: Private collection. Reproduced with permission of KKL-JNF.

**Figure 16.** *The signing of the Declaration of Principles on Interim Self-Government Arrangements (Oslo I Accord) between the government of Israel and the Palestine Liberation Organization (PLO) on 13 September, 1993. Moments after the signing, a reconstituted (in name) Palestine Olympic Committee, which had been founded only two months before the Munich Massacre took place, sent its request for affiliation to the International Olympic Committee to IOC president Juan Antonio Samaranch. A few days later, the POC was granted provisional recognition by the IOC at its 101st Session, held in Monaco from September 17-24, 1993.*

*Source:* William J. Clinton Presidential Library.

from America, they selected six rooms on the second floor to save £P 23 per month,[243] which Heinrichs described as "the difference between a balanced budget and disaster."[244] Perhaps an uncomfortable shift, the decision would present some dividends in the coming months when Heinrichs would leave Jerusalem. His wife and brother would remain behind, close to the action inside the YMCA, and would keep him informed.

## 11.

On December 6, the situation at the Association finally reached its tipping point. MacDonald wrote to Heinrichs to inform him of a matter that had been brought to her attention. Two days after Dr. Iven's visit from Goebbels' Reich Ministry to Jerusalem's German Colony, a Palestinian German YMCA member named Herbert Liebmann had written a letter to the Educational Department of the Jerusalem YMCA. In this letter, he asked the Library Committee to remove the *Frankfurter Zeitung* from the Reading Room and to replace it with the *Völkischer Beobachter*, the official paper of the Nazi Party. Whereas Heinrichs and the Jerusalem YMCA could have been responding to Maccabi Palestine's December 3 press announcement about Jewish and Arab athletes preparing to compete in India, Heinrichs was instead consumed by a scandal.

In the period of greatest potential for cooperation between the Association and FASCP, Heinrichs had to deal instead with a Nazi cell that only weeks later would force his departure from the Jerusalem YMCA. With certainty, if Heinrichs had been permitted to remain focused on integrating sport initiatives, Mandate Palestine's sport history might have taken a different trajectory. Unfortunately, in Heinrichs' absence, the Arabs could not leverage Heinrichs' historical relations with Sondhi and how that could factor into sending a fully representative team to the First Western Asiatic Games. Filed under the heading "German newspaper controversy" in the Kautz Family YMCA archives, the ripple effect of the "Newspaper Incident" would spread into the future of global politics for decades.

# CHAPTER 8

# Palestine's Olympic Moment

## 1.

In 1934, Germany became a complete dictatorship. In April, Adolf Hitler convinced key army and navy officials to back his bid to succeed President Hindenburg, and he transferred the Gestapo from Hermann Göring to Heinrich Himmler and Reinhard Heydrich.[1] They integrated it into the SS, the Nazi Party's elite security apparatus. The SS would ultimately be responsible for the most serious Nazi war crimes during the Second World War, including the attempt to exterminate all those deemed by the Nazis as either undesirable to German society or enemies of the Nazi state. This included targeting eleven million Jews within and beyond the boundaries of Europe.

Between June 20 and July 2, the SS purged Hitler's rivals who led the SA, the Nazi militia that numbered over one million members.[2] Many of Hitler's political enemies (going all the way back to the early 1920s) were also killed in what became known as the Night of the Long Knives. (Rabbi Stephen Wise would later recount this bloodbath in personal correspondence to Heinrichs following the latter's experience with Nazi agents in Jerusalem.) Hitler defended the purge of his enemies on the basis that he had "the right to act unilaterally as 'supreme judge' without resort to courts."[3] When President Hindenburg died in August, Hitler became Führer und Reichskanzler (Leader and Reich Chancellor)[4] and Germany's transformation to a total dictatorship was complete.

The rapidly changing situation in Germany was felt in Mandate Palestine. On January 30, the Nazis who began agitating against Heinrichs celebrated the first anniversary of Hitler's rise to power,[5] this despite Ludwig Buchalter, Hans Kirchner, and Erich Herrmann only seven months earlier forming their Jerusalem branch of the NSDAP (in June 1933).[6] Initially blocked from expanding by Germany,[7] the ban on their new members was removed in October or November 1933,[8] right around the time of Dr. Iven's trip to Palestine and their subsequent agitation against Heinrichs. By February, the NSDAP in Germany also restructured the Overseas Department (*Auslands-Abteilung*) and renamed it the Overseas Organization (*Auslands-Organisation*) with the purpose of "supporting the Nazis' efforts abroad and encouraging the formation of NS groups. Its propaganda, training program, and political agitation were aimed at increasing the number of Landesgruppen (country groups), expanding Germany's influence in foreign countries and building a strong Pan-German movement in each country."[9] Almost everyone involved in the attack against Heinrichs became a formal Nazi Party member during this month.[10] Heinrichs called it out, but no one would listen, not even the IC/YMCAs of North America and Canada (despite acknowledging behind closed doors that Hitler was crushing the YMCA Movement within Germany itself).

The Nazi activity in Palestine was not restricted to Jerusalem. There was activity organized in Haifa led by Gottlieb Ruff, "the…training officer…[who] was responsible for the program of historical topics from the National Socialist viewpoint, such as 'Austria in German History,' 'The Second Reich,' and 'International Jewry.'"[11] The network of German sport clubs (Deutscher Sportverein) across Palestine would become central staging grounds for these often compulsory Nazi activities.[12] On February 28, the Auslands-Organisation in Germany officially upgraded the local NS groups that attacked Heinrichs.[13] These groups had achieved the critical mass for recognition and support required by Germany of at least twenty-five members.[14] Perhaps the Jerusalem group in particular had proven its mettle and ardent Nazi agenda at the Jerusalem YMCA?

By April, new Hitler Youth were being sworn in at the German Consulate in Jaffa[15] and more propagandists from Germany were arriving to speak at Deutscher Sportverein Jerusalem on subjects like "The Ideological Basis of National Socialism."[16] Over the years, Joseph

Goebbels himself sent "specially trained agents to Palestine to recruit new members…[These included]…Hans Dunkel, Erich Arens, Walter Mehrer, Richard Groehl, and Paul Gregor in Jerusalem."[17] Throughout 1934, regular propaganda events occurred, including the celebration of Hitler's birthday (organized by Ludwig Buchalter),[18] a lecture on the positive effects of the State Labor Service on the German economy and morality,[19] Labor Day celebrations,[20] the celebration of the Solstice Festival by Hitler Youth,[21] and the Hindenburg Sportsfest (which included German Palestinian Nazis sending telegrams addressed to the Führer himself).[22] By November, Ludwig Buchalter reported to Germany the takeover of the Deutscher Sportverein Jerusalem by a completely Nazi board and "expressed his hope that from now on the cooperation between the sports club and the party would improve 'for the sake of Deuschtum' [Germanness]."[23] Would this cooperation lead to a secret Palestinian delegation at the 1936 Berlin Olympics, sourced from the Jerusalem YMCA Physical Department?

## 2.

In the midst of this Nazi activity, Heinrichs was left to confront, alone, the consequences of Herbert Liebmann's letter requesting the subscription to *Völkischer Beobachter*, the Nazi Party's official newspaper. His time would have been better spent mediating between Jewish and Arab sport organizations to send a representative team to India to participate in the First Western Asiatic Games, organized by his former colleague and friend G. D. Sondhi. Instead, unbeknownst to him, he was only weeks away from leaving Jerusalem forever.

With thousands of Jews fleeing Germany for Palestine, Frederick Kisch and Yosef Yekutieli could not afford to wait for the Jerusalem YMCA to sort out its problems. As Jews arrived in the territory, they were forcibly denaturalized at the Nazi consulates,[24] including the one at the Fast Hotel. Sport provided a way for Maccabi to integrate some of these Jews—who were effectively stateless because it would take time for them to become citizens—into Palestine. So Kisch and Yekutieli continued their efforts to affiliate Palestine to the IOC, and Yekutieli, in particular, took advantage of the window of opportunity that had opened regarding the First Western Asiatic Games.

## 3.

On January 5, Yekutieli confirmed to Sondhi that the FASCP had authorized the "Maccabee [sic] Sports Club, the best Athletic Club of our country, to represent Palestine, and to send a Team."[25] He expressed concerns about the cost of the voyage and inquired about support, indicating that he would only send five to ten athletes.

Back in London, his counterparts from Bar Cochba and British Maccabi were also exploring the possibility of Palestine's participation in the British Empire Games. Lord Melchett wrote a personal letter to Chaim Weizmann regarding the inclusion of Arab athletes as part of the proposed team.[26] Although Lord Melchett's letter exhibited the same concerns held by the IOC regarding the Maccabi dominance of Palestinian sport, it also showed that far from Palestine and as late as 1934, there remained a dialog among Zionists regarding the importance of engaging Arabs in sport activity. Indeed, the newspaper article in the *Jewish Daily Bulletin* on December 3, 1933, which had announced Arabs and Jews competing in India, was published one month before Yekutieli wrote to Sondhi (finally confirming his intention to send only athletes from Maccabi). Liebmann wrote his letter to Jan MacDonald requesting the *Völkischer Beobachter* only three days after the *Jewish Daily Bulletin* announcement. The crisis at the Jerusalem YMCA erupted almost immediately, becoming the talk of the town. Whatever window existed for a conversation to engage the Arabs about joining the team closed: as Jewish board members of the Jerusalem YMCA threatened to resign, many of the Arabs on the board backed the Nazi position and tried to eject Heinrichs from his job, and the newspaper incident engulfed the building for the remainder of 1934, well after Heinrichs' departure for the United States.

By mid-January, Sondhi replied to Yekutieli.[27] Palestine had been the second country (after Afghanistan) to accept Sondhi's invitation.[28] Having written many of his contacts unofficially, Sondhi was eager for Yekutieli to confirm whether Alfred Gutt would be part of the Palestine delegation.[29] In December 1932, Sondhi had reached deep into his list of constituents and corresponded personally with them before he sent the formal invitation (in April 1933) to the High Commissioner. Heinrichs was on that list. Heinrichs promised his friend and colleague from Lahore "help without, however, lending out much hopes…[Palestine]…being, in his own words, 'the most remote of all the countries invited and, probably, economically one of the poorest.'"[30] This means that before the decision of the Jerusalem YMCA's Physical Department not to cooperate with the FASCP, it is quite likely that the Western Asiatic Games were actually discussed between the parties, although it is not clear to what extent from the official correspondence record or from Heinrichs' diaries. Because Heinrichs had received notice from Sondhi as early as December 1932 and the Jerusalem YMCA's Physical Department did not decide against cooperation until September 11, 1933, that would imply that Maccabi Palestine and the Jerusalem YMCA could have been collaborating around the subject of the delegation to India. After Julius Jacobs forwarded the official invitation to Maccabi Palestine, it appears that Yekutieli waited to decide on who should go to India as conversations continued with the Jerusalem YMCA (between May and September of 1933). With the Nazi newspaper incident erupting at the Jerusalem YMCA in full force by December 1933, Yekutieli probably decided to take the helm.

When Sondhi replied to Yekutieli, he asked him to join Zvi Nishri and send "five large size actual flags of Palestine…[to be]…flown round the stadium and for the March Past."[31] He included for Yekutieli the agenda of the inaugural meeting of the Western Asiatic Games Federation, set to take place on March 3, 1934.[32] In a letter the next day, he asked Yekutieli to either send a color sketch of the flag instead, in the event it was too difficult to ship, and offered to sew the flags in India, or to bring five full flags.[33] Sondhi also asked Yekutieli to provide "your national anthem."[34]

Twelve days later, the German Maccabi organization announced through the *Jewish Daily Bulletin* that negotiations had started with German authorities to admit Palestine to the 1936 Olympiad.[35] Consequently, the Western Asiatic Games took on an increased level of importance. The games were organized by a man who had been to three

Olympics[36] and who was extremely well connected in international sport. He was also a close friend of Heinrichs. The Arabs could have leveraged his relationship with Sondhi in the same ways the Maccabis were about to.

But they didn't.

Yekutieli could not go to India because of other commitments.[37] He wrote[38] to Sondhi and explained the various constraints facing the delegation. The Jewish athletes were not wealthy and had to take time off from their jobs. They needed to keep expenses to a minimum and agreed to travel on deck. Only the Italian ship *Conte Verde* offered deck passage within the required time frame and was leaving Port Said on February 17. It was scheduled to arrive in Bombay ten days later. Consequently, Maccabi was unable to send its best swimmers. Yekutieli explained that he was still trying to raise funds and that they could only afford to send a delegation of four persons. Zvi Nishri, who was supposed to lead the delegation and represent Palestine in the new confederation's first congress, could not go because he was a physical education teacher and could not get time off in the middle of the school year.

Incredibly, only ten days prior to departure, Maccabi Palestine was still trying to figure out a way to get its team to India in time for the games.[39] That same day, the first marathon was organized between Tel Aviv and Ness Ziona, in which Walter Frankl, who would join the team in India, finished first: he ran the twenty-five miles in three hours and fifteen minutes.[40] A day before the team departed, Yekutieli wrote to Sondhi to inform him how pleased he was to be able to send even the small team of four, headed by David Almagor. Almagor would serve as team manager and a judge to help officiate the competitions.[41]

The importance for the Jewish sport movement of the delegation's participation cannot be overstated. It can almost be said that Israel was born as a modern country at the First Western Asiatic Games in India. In the absence of official correspondence, one can only wonder if Maccabi's participation—along with the recognition of a Maccabi-dominated Palestine Olympic Association two months later—informed the Palestine Liberation Organization's decision to attack both the IOC—by targeting the 1972 Munich Olympic Games—and the Israeli Olympic delegation participating in them. When the Munich Massacre occurred, the events of the 1930s were well within the bounds of personal memory, and many of the people associated with the nascent Olympic Movement in Mandate Palestine, as well as the IOC officials who had engaged it, were still alive.

Sondhi was an important person in the Olympic world. He had attended Paris 1924, Amsterdam 1928, and Los Angeles 1932, and had poured his heart and soul into creating an Asian event modeled on the Olympic Games themselves. For the Maccabi athletes from Palestine, these games would be the first opportunity to perform and be recognized on the world stage at an event endorsed by the founder of the modern Olympic Movement and the presidents of the IOC, IAAF, and others from the international sport world. Fifty years after their participation, a single typed sheet now stored at the Joseph Yekutieli Maccabi Sport Archives recalled the landmark participation. This document notes how the blue and white colors were raised and used in the march past, and that it was the first time national Jewish sports participated outside *Eretz Yisrael*.[42]

That's right. Yekutieli had sent Sondhi a sketch of the blue and white Zionist flag for use at the event,[43] and only fourteen years later it would become the official flag of Israel.

But which other flag could the Maccabis have brought with them to India? The government of Palestine did not regularly endorse sport events (beyond occasional patronage within the territory through the presence of the High Commissioner). Wauchope would certainly not authorize the use of the Union Jack, the official flag of Palestine at the time, in another country without a British official at the head of the delegation. Britain also only had a Mandate for Palestine: the territory was not analogous to other territories under British rule. While Mandate Palestine used a red ensign flag as an administrative solution on ships registered to Palestinian ports,[44] it could not use the blue ensign flag typical of most other British-ruled territories.[45] The Arab Palestinians could have prevented the remarkable use of the Zionist blue and white flag and Shield of David in India, but they had walked away from the negotiating table with the FASCP on September 11, 1933. As the Magen David was flying over the Irwin Amphitheater in Delhi, these Arab Christian leaders who had walked away were embroiled in an apparent poisonous Nazi-instigated plot that would remove Heinrichs from the Jerusalem YMCA only six days after the games closed in Delhi.

What a wonderful occasion it could have been for Heinrichs to return to India and share with his friend Sondhi a representative team of Muslims, Jews, and Christians. That would have been front-page news.

Instead, it was only the Maccabis who went to India. On April 26, 1984, during the run-up to the Los Angeles Olympics, the *Jerusalem Post* ran an article[46] that claimed that the High Commissioner asked all sport bodies (Jewish, Arab, and British) to try out at the Jerusalem YMCA for the right to compete for Palestine. According to this narrative, Maccabi won all eleven events and received a letter of congratulations and appointment from High Commissioner Wauchope himself. The article correctly identified the four athletes selected by Yekutieli and noted that each had to contribute £P 20[47] from his own pocket to travel. The delegation comprised David Almagor, Dov Rabinowitz, and Walter Frankl. Two sprinters had to try out for the fourth : Shlomo Marantz, who was Palestine champion, and Theo Levy, who had just fled from Germany. The organizers of the delegation held a race on the beach in Tel Aviv, which Marantz won by a nose. Levy protested because he had to run on the softer sand, farthest from the water. The organizers rejected his protest and Levy was furious, crying out, "You'll see that I'll take part!"[48]

The article recounted how the team received uniforms of blue blazers and white trousers. On the breast pocket was the Magen David and "Palestine" in English and "*Eretz Yisrael*" in Hebrew. They traveled from Kantara and onward to Alexandria by train, where they picked up the Lloyd steamer *Conte Verde* and then traveled to Bombay.[49] Frankl recalled years later that Levy forcibly boarded the train as it was pulling out of Tel Aviv station to head south towards Egypt.[50] With no transit papers for Egypt on him, the team had to rely on some elbow grease with customs officials to get Levy all the way to Alexandria.[51]

According to the *Jerusalem Post*,[52] on the *Conte Verde* the delegation traveled steerage, sliding through a trap door into the hold of the ship. For the first three days, they shared the space with families from China, Korea, and Japan. They would illegally enter third class and hide among a pile of sacks while the ship's Italian cook smuggled them macaroni, salad, and tea twice a day. On the fourth day, they were discovered and brought to the captain for punishment, but a Jewish millionaire in first class heard about their situation and paid for them all to continue passage in third class. This finally enabled the team to have mattresses, three meals a day, and use of the deck for their training. When the team arrived in Bombay, it had no one to receive it. The athletes picked a Jewish name out of the phone book: Haskell.

S. H. Haskell was an Iraqi Jew who was also the president of the Bombay Zionist Association. The article's version of events is backed up by two letters that Haskell sent to Mayor Dizengoff of Tel Aviv. Haskell wrote the first letter[53] on personal stationery, one day after the Maccabi team departed Bombay for New Delhi. He told Dizengoff of the pleasant surprise in meeting the team and that Almagor had gifted him a souvenir signed by the mayor. Haskell's second letter to Dizengoff (after the games ended) used the official stationery of the Bombay Zionist Association and pointed out the total lack of preparation for the team. The team had arrived without notice from Dizengoff or the Palestine Zionist Executive. Haskell was dismayed that the delegation had to travel third class, at its own expense, and with limited food. He felt that it reflected poorly on the country to send out athletes so unprepared, and noted how other countries' delegations had arrived a month earlier at the expense of their governments.

Still, Haskell noted for Dizengoff the great impact of the team for Zionism in India and globally. The team impressed Indians with how many medals it won, and many were intrigued by the Zionist flag, which flew next to the Union Jack and the flags of the other participating countries. He congratulated Dizengoff for making Palestine famous in the world of sport.

Haskell had the team picked up with three cars and threw a banquet for them that was fit for royals at the Taj Mahal Hotel.[54] He gave them "Palestinian cakes, jams, marmalade, sweets, dried fruit and bottles of lemon juice"[55] that the team could distribute as gifts to other delegations. In Delhi, the team was "astonished to find what purported to be the flag of Palestine, but what was the Zionist flag…flying high among the flags of all the nations."[56] They were also surprised in the Olympic Village when Yaacov Goddard arrived, a seventeen-year-old swimmer who had been denied the trip because of lack of his ability to pay.[57] He brought clothes and food in a rucksack and hid in one of the overnight mail trucks that traversed the desert between Jerusalem and Baghdad.[58] He presented a letter of recommendation he had brought with him to the Orient Lloyd line and managed to get money to travel to Basra with an additional letter requesting a job on a ship sailing to India.[59] Thus, Goddard managed to work his way across the Indian Ocean to Karachi, whence he travelled by *tanga* to Delhi.[60] The original team of four had grown to six, and then they were joined by Gutt, Sondhi's Austrian Jewish friend who was a swimmer. He had been in the United States and decided to travel at his own expense to join the team. Unfortunately, the team had only four blazers!

The games were a "clarion call to the youth of Western Asia…advocating a sporting fraternity…an attempt at a synthesis of the ideals of physical and mental fitness of Ancient Greece and of the ideal of Brotherhood and unity of the East."[61] They were an ideal platform for Maccabis to express their sporting prowess, since they perceived themselves as bringing Jewish identity back to its roots in the East[62] and reclaiming their pre-classical physical culture. In the East, Jews could connect comfortably with Sondhi's perceptions of the comparatively more authentic "Aryan" sport ancestors of India, "who participated in horse races and chariot races…for the sake of keeping their horses and themselves fit and strong…[and where] even the problems of vital importance were settled by means of challenge-tournaments."[63] Such historic Aryans were distinct from the growing SS cult and racial fictions that were blending Teutonic legend with pagan rituals in the Nazi Party.

## 4.

Sondhi first announced the concept of the Western Asiatic Games Federation in October 1931. This was shortly after Heinrichs had left India for his post in Jerusalem. Sondhi invited a number of countries to form the organization, including Palestine and Syria.[64] At first, none of the countries responded officially, but Sondhi's personal correspondences to his colleagues had produced some results and given hope.[65] Eventually, there were five founding members: Afghanistan, Ceylon, Palestine,

Persia, and India.[66] They were represented in the organization's logo by five interlocked rings, which Sondhi placed in the lower right of a shield, underneath the rays of a midday sun (located in the opposite, upper left).[67] Sondhi chose Delhi because "only at Delhi could one legitimately expect His Excellency the Viceroy, the representative of His Majesty the King-Emperor, personally to open the Games according to the Olympic custom."[68] Sondhi wanted the games to be an official Olympic event. He sought in vain to get the government to declare the day of the opening ceremony a half holiday.[69] There was little support, even for the arrival of teams from Ceylon and Palestine, and Sondhi had to thank H. C. Buck, the principal of the YMCA National College of Physical Education in Madras (and another of Heinrichs' colleagues), for the critical support he provided to Ceylon.[70]

On the day of the opening ceremony, the Viceroy and his spouse the Countess of Willingdon made their way from Viceroy Lodge "with the customary ceremonials…with his bodyguard"[71] to the Irwin Amphitheater. He provided his band to enhance the ceremony.[72] The official report noted, "To make the reminiscence of the ancient Hellenic trials complete, pigeons, as of old, were provided. Trumpeters were requisitioned to add to the dignity of the moment."[73] Sondhi had many of the flags around the stadium made in Lahore: "These flags flying in the air in their variegated hues were to present a beautiful panorama all along the Amphitheatre [sic] and were to be a symbol of mutual goodwill of the Nations taking part in the trials."[74] The sky was "azure blue,"[75] the sun shone "brightly,"[76] and the air was "pleasant and bracing."[77] At ten minutes to three, "[a] number of Indian Princes, the Members of the Executive Council, of His Excellency the Viceroy, other high dignitaries of State and the Indian nobility…[took]…their seats in the reserved boxes, while a large crowd…[was]…seated in the stadium."[78] A hush blanketed the stadium as the Viceroy and Countess of Willingdon entered the gates of the amphitheater, escorted by a bodyguard "in full dress."[79] Their "State Coach [was] pulled by six magnificently caparisoned white horses,"[80] which stopped in front of the Royal Box. Cheers rang out as the bodyguard lined up in front of the Royal Box.[81] His Highness the Maharaja of Patiala met them at the steps to the Royal Box, they ascended, and the Royal Salute was given.[82]

The march past began. The teams entered the stadium in alphabetical order, with India last as host (according to Olympic custom).[83] When Palestine's Maccabi athletes entered the stadium to the march music being played by the Viceregal band,[84] "Dov Rabinowitz was the flag-bearer, in a blazer, then came Almagor, Marantz and Frankl, dressed in full regalia, followed by Levy, Goddard and...[Gutt]...in light blue shirts, bearing a Shield of David emblem in white. They all wore long white trousers. They got a tremendous ovation."[85] As they passed the Tribune of Honor, the team's "Escutcheon-bearer gave a half turn"[86] so that the occupants could read the name "Palestine" written on it. Rabinowitz dipped the Zionist flag while the other Maccabis saluted the patron and dignitaries.[87] They took their places on the field of play facing the stand and behind their escutcheon.[88] Sondhi had installed a microphone in the amphitheater, and the Maharaja of Patiala approached it to address the assembled delegations. He spoke of the history of national gatherings in India to test the prowess of the body, their connections to the modern Olympic Movement, and the fact that the Western Asiatic Games were the first time that Ceylon, Afghanistan, Palestine, and India were meeting "to decide by friendly and honourable [sic] competition the country to which the laurels of sport should go."[89]

Then Sondhi stepped forward to read the messages from world sport officials. He started with the message from Coubertin, who expressed his thanks for the support of his global Olympic effort as represented in the Western Asiatic Games.[90] Sondhi then read the message from IOC president Count Baillet-Latour, with whom Palestine was in close negotiations to affiliate to the IOC. Baillet-Latour hoped the games would be as successful as the Far Eastern Games and looked forward to seeing the best athletes from the participating countries at the upcoming Olympic Games in Berlin.[91] Sigfrid Edström sent a message from cold dark Sweden. He sent all the delegates greetings from the IAAF, stressing that the Western Asiatic Games were a step in the right direction of practicing sport without prejudice against race or religion.[92] Dr. du Coteau, president of the International Hockey Federation, made special mention of Palestine, offering their sportsmen "the cordial salute of all the Hockeyers affiliated to the International

Federation."[93] Then the Viceroy declared the games open and the flag of the games was hoisted to the fanfare of trumpets, "showing the sun in its mid-noon splendour [sic]…and the five interlinked circles of different colours [sic] symbolizing the five member countries of the Western Asiatic Federation."[94]

Following the release of the pigeons, the Maccabis and other athletes formed a semicircle around Dhyan Chand, who took the Athletes' Oath on behalf of all the competitors: "We swear that we will take part in the Western Asiatic Games in loyal competitions respecting the regulations which govern them and desirous of participating in them in the true spirit of sportsmanship for the honour [sic] of our country and for the glory of sport."[95]

## 5.

Maccabi Palestine faired quite well at the games. They competed using the Hebraic versions of their names, a practice that would become a hallmark of Jews who made *aliyah* (who emigrated) to Mandate Palestine (and later, Israel). Frankl entered as Ze'ev, Gutt as Gutt-Alfred, Almagor as David (already a Hebrew name), Levy as Matatjahu, and Rabinowitz as Rabinah. The events started with swimming (before the opening ceremony) in Patiala because Delhi had no swimming tank.[96] The Maharaja of Patiala made available his personal tank at the Moti Bagh Palace, one of his numerous residences, for the event.[97] Gutt was Palestine's swimmer. He had real competition against the only other team that had entered swimmers: India.[98] His rival N. C. Mallik was a Calcuttan who had already competed in the Los Angeles Olympics in 1932 and held the All-India record in the one-mile freestyle.[99] He finished fifty yards ahead of Gutt, who completed the race in 28 minutes 14 $^4/_5$.[100] Strong winds blew across the estate and hampered the race, which was neck and neck for the first lap of the 440-yard freestyle. Gutt eventually conceded first place to his rival, N. C. Mallik.[101] Gutt also took the bronze in the 110-yard freestyle behind Sushil Bose (silver) and Raja Ram Shawoo[102] (gold). The final rankings placed India first after six events with six gold, four silver, and five bronze, and Palestine in second with two silver and one bronze.

In track and field, Almagor served as a track judge along with D. C. Lal, who was a field judge.[103, 104] The official report of the committee tallied the results: "Thirty-seven men representing four Nations took part in the seventeen events comprising the Athletic Programme [*sic*] of the First Series of the Western Asiatic Games. When the event concluded, one British Empire record had been equalled and four Indian records had been lowered."[105]Athletics began after the opening ceremony. Palestine competed in both heats of the 100-yard sprint. In the first heat, Palestine lined up against India and Afghanistan, and in the second, India and Ceylon.[106] Palestine finished a close second in each to Vernieus and Whiteside of India.[107] Vernieus' win in that heat established a new All-India record at nine seconds, and eight-tenths of a second (0:09.8). Ceylon won the mile race and shot put and India took the gold in high jump.[108] The winners would each ascend a small podium located behind potted juvenile palms. A flag pole was located behind the winner, who would stand on the highest step as his flag fluttered behind him and his anthem played.[109] Frankl competed against Gujar Singh in the six-mile race. Singh was ahead the whole race and finished 600 yards ahead of Rabu Ram of India and 1,200 yards ahead of Frankl of Palestine, setting a new All-India record.[110] In the three-mile race, there was a little more excitement for Palestine: "Kishen Singh, the All-India Record Holder...led the other two entrants right through. After seven-eighth of the distance had been covered...Frankl...who was occupying third position in the race overtook Gujar Singh and finished second, a distance of about a hundred yards separated the first and the second."[111] According to the final report,[112] the relay race was the most thrilling event. India was ahead of Ceylon and Palestine, but one of its runners dropped the baton. Ceylon was then able to maintain its slight lead, with India coming second, Afghanistan third, and Palestine fourth.

## 6.

Off the field of play, life in the Olympic Village was a sight to behold. The Organizing Committee considered housing the athletes in bungalows at a number of locations.[113] Instead, cost constraints required that the visiting delegations be housed in tents on the Patiala estate (adjacent to the Irwin Amphitheater).[114] The Maharaja provided twelve EP tents, each accommodating twenty people, and eight Swiss Cottage tents.[115] Furniture for the Village was provided by the Public Works Department. The report notes, "It was here that the contingents of the Four Nations lived for nearly a week. A spirit of perfect harmony and comradeship prevailed…[i]n spite of the difference in language and customs."[116]

It was unusually cold during the period of the games. Unfortunately, Sondhi had informed everyone prior to arrival of the Indian custom not to provide beddings, but Swiss Hotel saved the day by providing the necessary coverings to spare the athletes from the unusual nighttime chill.[117] To warm the contestants after sunset, organizers lit a large bonfire each evening opposite the entrance of the Village's Durbar Hall. The Durbar was a large covered gathering spot constructed of shamiana tents.[118] The municipality piped in water and provided electricity to allow the use of the hall throughout the games. Pathways to the Olympic Village from the main road were illuminated with temporary light posts. Athletes received laundry, valet, medical, and first-aid service in the camp, too.[119] Traditional Indian food was on offer, with accommodations made to the menu when visitors requested it. Contestants, officials, and guests would congregate in the Durbar Hall, which became a "rendezvous of the sporting world where the spirit of sportsmanship transcended that of nationality, caste, colour or creed and the stalwart Olympians met each other with a feeling of fraternal goodwill and affection."[120] The hall also included writing tables and daily newspapers for all the athletes to correspond and read the news.[121] The Village was a huge success and "[t]he whole establishment shone forth at night informing the passersby that something new in the annals of sport in India had been set up—a home for athletes belonging to divers[e] nations, yet breathing the same air, taking the same food, occupying the same lodgings and participating in the same sports."[122]

At the closing ceremony, "Mr. David Almagor, the Manager of the Palestine Team, after thanking the Municipality for their hospitality, announced, amidst cheers invitations from the Lord Mayor of Tel Aviv for holding of the next Championships of the Games in Palestine. In the end he paid a glowing tribute to Mr. G. D. Sondhi for having so successfully organised [*sic*] the Games."[123] The teams then toured Old Delhi and enjoyed in particular the Kutb Minar and the Badshahi Mosque.[124]

The official report noted[125] how, after the games were over, everyone was invited to Patiala to enjoy the splendor of the oriental court. From Patiala, the delegation traveled to Lahore upon the invitation of the Punjab Olympic Association, which Heinrichs had help establish. Raj Bahadur Ram Saran Das lent them a bus to tour the city. The sportsmen of Lahore hosted a luncheon for them. They competed in a swim meet with teams from Punjab at Government College, and Mrs. Sondhi received them at the Sondhi residence and provided them with a souvenir trophy for their trip.

If only Heinrichs had been allowed to do the work for which he was hired, Palestine's first international participation in what was understood at the time as an Olympic sporting event could have included the unified team of Jews, Muslims, and Christians that had been so evasive since the 1929 riots.

## 7.

After the First Western Asiatic Games, suddenly Mandate Palestine's sport profile was enhanced on the international stage. But now the profile was synonymous with Jewish sport and the Jewish national home. The Maccabi team wrote a letter[126] to Yekutieli from the boat while traveling home to Palestine. Almagor remarked on the value of the trip, despite its very rushed nature. The trip had been a tremendous success and exceeded everyone's expectations. He lamented how all of Maccabi's close friends, except for Yekutieli and Kurland, had mocked the delegation and was glad that it had now proven them all wrong. He acknowledged the propaganda value for Palestine, the Jewish nation, and Palestine's agricultural produce, which the team had distributed as gifts to other delegations (courtesy of Haskell). He also expressed pride in the sport results. Palestine had won twelve gold, twelve silver, and eleven bronze medals, and picked up three trophies. The Magen David flag was omnipresent and newspapers covered the delegation and printed its photos. Indian Jews were particularly proud and promised to send a delegation to the Second Maccabiad in the spring of 1935. Almagor told Yekutieli that he had never been honored as he had been honored in India. He asked Yekutieli to arrange a reception for the team's return.

Clearly, Maccabi Palestine had not conspired regarding its participation in the games. In fact, it appears there was disregard or outright opposition from many Maccabis regarding participating at all. According to Almagor, Yekutieli was one of only two believers who had understood the importance of the India delegation in relation to the ongoing correspondences with the IOC. In addition to the broad exposure Palestine received, Maccabi Palestine had co-formed a regional international sport federation in the first meeting of the Western Asiatic Games Confederation (held at the Persian Consulate in Delhi on the last day of the games).[127] In India, Maccabi Palestine officially became part of international sport governance.

What a massive miscalculation on the part of those busy attacking Heinrichs at the Jerusalem YMCA. On the same day that Maccabi Palestine entered international sport, Lattof and Auburn took Heinrichs to the George Williams Room inside the Jerusalem YMCA and told him that "Dr. Canaan, Mantoura, Salameh, Major Stubbs, even Nathan and of course the irreconcilables Boutagy and Said"[128] would resign if Heinrichs did not leave the post of secretary-general of the organization. Instead of receiving letters of gratitude and congratulations from the Maharaja,[129] Sondhi,[130] and others regarding a representative delegation, the accolades went only to the Maccabis. To this day, Arab Palestinians have paid a price for the Nazi interference in its Olympic affairs and the lack of foresight of those within the board of the Jerusalem YMCA who opposed Heinrichs.

## 8.

After the games and as always, Yekutieli just kept on working. He continued to organize athletics, fencing, gymnastics, boxing, wrestling, and football events for the Levant Fair, writing to consulates in Jerusalem to coordinate the arrival of international sport teams.[131] As part of these efforts, a most important Olympic guest would arrive in Palestine to assess the real sporting situation on the ground: Theodor Schmidt, member of the IOC.[132] Schmidt was central to the sensitive negotiations regarding Palestine's participation in the Berlin Games (with Palestine's intentions already being reported in the Jewish Telegraphic Agency at the end of January).[133]

Only a few days after the JTA article appeared, *Westland* published an article on February 3 that might have influenced Schmidt's visit to Palestine.[134] Titled "*Göbbels und die Makkabäer*" [Goebbels and the Maccabi], the article recapped the events of 1933: the exclusion of Jewish athletes; the position of the Americans; how the reassurances by the Germans had failed to sway the American camp. The article explained that in response, Reichssportführer Hans von Tschammer und Osten had asked Goebbels for help. Goebbels then started to work behind the scenes. *Westland* claimed that Goebbels' work resulted in the announcement of a German Maccabi Circle, which included the majority of Jewish sports clubs, that a Palestine Olympic Committee had been formed, and that this committee was expected to finish the paperwork for participation in the 1936 Olympic Games in Berlin soon. The paper pointed out that such an agreement would eliminate the basis for America's boycott and warned that if Jewish athletes from Palestine were to participate in Berlin, it would not do anything for the actual situation of German Jewish athletes. *Westland* accused the German Maccabi Circle of not having any idea of the role the Nazis had plotted for them to play, and that the Maccabi athletes were perhaps being led to believe that they could compete for Palestine instead of Germany. *Westland* was doubtful that Palestine's Jews were in a position to match Goebbels' scheming. The paper pointed out that if Jews in Palestine did not insist on fair treatment of German Jews, certainly America would not either. *Westland* raised the question that Goebbels understood these matters clearly, but did Maccabi Germany?

This was the political context in which Schmidt arrived in Palestine. He was owner of the well-known Viennese chocolate factory Victor Schmidt & Sons and was also president of the Austrian Olympic Committee.[135] Assuming there is truth to *Westland*'s claims, perhaps the Austrian was serving as a German-speaking interlocutor between the IOC, FASCP, Maccabi Germany, and the Nazi German government regarding Palestine's affiliation request within the broader context of the raging boycott debate. Schmidt would prove himself an important ally to the Jewish cause. On Saturday night, March 17, at nine o'clock, he spoke at Kadima Hall on Nahlat Benjamin Street in Tel Aviv on the subject of the Olympic Games.[136] He had been invited by the FASCP. The event was open to the public and free.

Unfortunately, on the same evening that Schmidt was presenting, Heinrichs was in London watching *My Beloved* at the Capitol Theatre while in transit to the United States. He was on his journey home to try and keep his job after being squeezed out by the Nazis at the Jerusalem YMCA.[137] Heinrichs' absence from the board of a Palestine Olympic Association presented a real problem for Maccabi Palestine's bid to affiliate the territory to the Olympic Movement. The negotiations were complicated and on the day of Schmidt's presentation in Tel Aviv, *Westland* continued to apply pressure from the Saar region, this time directly on Kisch in Palestine. The paper alleged in mid-March that Kisch had held negotiations with senior Nazis about Palestine's participation in Berlin.[138]

Lord Aberdare also monitored the situation, previously having contacted the Colonial Office in London for more information on Kisch's letter to Baillet-Latour (of November 27, 1933). On April 12, 1934, the Colonial Office in England replied, having heard finally from the government of Palestine.[139] Although it noted how the Olympic association was comprised of all sport associations in Palestine affiliated to their corresponding international federations, the Colonial Office pointed out that these associations comprised only Jewish clubs. At the same time, it acknowledged that the FASCP had done all that was required of it to form a fully representative federation. "Nevertheless, the fact remains that, whatever the reason, the Federation is not fully representative of Palestine, although it does appear to be fully representative of the sports of the Jewish National Home [sic] in Palestine."[140]

The Nazi Party's agitation against Heinrichs now appears to have been the reason for the lack of full representation.

The Colonial Office then suggested that the IOC simply draw its own conclusions but that it would be reasonable to defend the position of Baillet-Latour that the Palestine Olympic Association was not yet completely representative.[141]

But on April 24, Yekutieli received a letter of congratulations regarding Palestine's participation in the First Western Asiatic Games from Edström. The letter implied a warming disposition toward the Palestine Olympic Association. The track and field events in India had been an important footprint for the IAAF in Western Asia, and Yekutieli had helped to create it.

A few days later, Kisch formally denied *Westland*'s claims about negotiations with the Nazis. He issued the following statement for publication: "As regards Colonel Kisch personally, the statement that he had come to some arrangement with General Goering [*sic*] in this matter [Palestinian participation in the Berlin Games] is as false as it is ridiculous. Colonel Kisch has had no contact of any kind, direct or indirect, with the Minister in question, in regard to this or any other subjects."[142] In fact, the *Westland* article had not referenced Göring at all. Instead, it pointed out the central role of *Reichminister* for Propaganda Joseph Goebbels in the Palestine Olympic file. What was the puppeteer really up to? Was Goebbels talking to another Palestine Olympic Committee? Did his scheming involve directing (through intermediaries) the actions of the Nazis who were agitating at the Jerusalem YMCA?

On May 2, Yekutieli responded to *Westland*'s charges directly. He accused its editorial staff of raising serious suspicions about Kisch and the Jewish sports movement in Palestine.[143] Yekutieli suggested that the paper had fallen victim to a deception.[144] He noted that Palestine was not yet even recognized by the IOC and therefore any discussion of its participation in Berlin was premature.[145] Was the Nazi Party in Germany spreading misinformation to derail Palestine's warming negotiations with the IOC? Were the Nazis concerned that Palestine's Olympic Movement might interfere in Germany's domestic policies towards its Jewish athletes? Yekutieli took particular umbrage with *Westland*'s claim that "Eretz Israel" was pursuing a policy in sport that disregarded the fate of Jews outside of Palestine.[146] He reminded *Westland* that Palestinian Jewish sport had been working for fifteen years[147] (since as early as 1919) to try and affiliate to the IOC.

*Westland*'s March article accusing Kisch directly seemed to threaten the Olympic negotiations at their most sensitive juncture. All efforts to form a representative committee had failed, and the best chance to achieve it—Heinrichs—was gone. In order to affiliate, Yekutieli needed to find a substitute. Candidates from the Jerusalem YMCA were not an option because of the ongoing Nazi agitation. There was also no clear or easy path to an Arab Palestinian competent in sport matters to help solve the long-term challenge of closing the skill gap between Jewish and Arab sport (as had been a primary objective of both Lattof and Heinrichs since 1930 and 1932, respectively).

Yekutieli found his substitute in Ali Bey Mustakim, a prominent Muslim of Jaffa. By March 1934, the ancient port city located on the central coastline just south of Tel Aviv was beginning to live in the shadow of the White City. It is not clear exactly how Yekutieli knew Mustakim. Yekutieli wrote to him asking that he join the Palestine Olympic Committee as vice president. A week later, Mustakim accepted.[148]

Yekutieli forwarded Mustakim's acceptance letter to IOC honorary secretary Colonel Berdez on May 3, 1934. In his cover letter, he described Mustakim as "one of the most prominent personalities of the Moslem Community of Palestine"[149] and argued that because he had accepted the vice presidency of the association, "the present Palestine Olympic Committee is the representative body of all creeds that make up the population of Palestine. The formation of the said Committee, we hope, would not leave any question as to the possibilities of our final affiliation to the I.O.C. My wish is to draw your utmost attention to our case, so that it should be put on the agenda of the forthcoming convention of the I.O.C. which is to be held in Athens, in the month of May, 1934."[150] Yekutieli also dispatched a similar letter to Schmidt in Vienna.[151]

On May 10, 1934, as delegates were on their way to Athens for the crucial IOC Session that would debate Germany and Palestine, the Jerusalem Inter-School Sports Programme convened its tenth gathering.[152] In a twist of irony, Boutagy Stores advertised[153] its HMV radios in the event's brochure, and Shlomo Arazi, a member of the FASCP, was one of the recorders (along with Amin Jamal of the Jerusalem YMCA's board). Once again able to cooperate on the field of play in Jerusalem, but unable to do so on international matters, the Palestine file to be decided six days later in Athens could and should have included the Arabs. Unfortunately, a handful of Jerusalem YMCA board members prevented that from happening.

On May 14, two days before the IOC vote, *Westland* replied to Yekutieli's letter of May 2 and underscored that it had been the only newspaper to call out the Nazis' attempt to play off the Jewish athletes of Palestine against the Jewish athletes of America at the expense of the Jewish athletes of Germany. It insisted that Kisch had been implicated by the German Maccabi and refused to recant or publish a correction, although it did consent to inform its readers of Yekutieli's letter, according to his request.[154]

The IOC Session convened. On May 16, the IOC finally admitted Palestine to the International Olympic Committee. The *New York Times* carried the news on May 18.[155,156] On May 19, 1934, the IOC sent out its long-awaited confirmation letter to Kisch.[157]

Kisch and Yekutieli had done it.

## 9.

In its June bulletin, the IOC finally listed Palestine as a member (between New Zealand and Paraguay).[158] An additional note clarified the IOC's decision by explaining that "[t]he Palestine Olympic Committee, whose admission had been postponed at Vienna [in 1933] because it did not represent the entire population of Palestine, expanded its activities outside the Jewish organizations by admitting the Christian and Muslim organizations, of which a representative, Ali Bey Mustakim, is now its Vice-President. The IOC has recognized the Palestine Olympic Committee."[159] Of course, the association had actually always been open, but the IOC was not fully informed.

There was no mention of Heinrichs. Had he been allowed to assume his role within the FASCP, Arab Palestinian sport during the Mandate might have had a very different trajectory. Instead, Ali Bey Mustakim attended the first meeting of the newly recognized committee on June 20, 1934.[160] The minutes of the meeting noted the importance of IOC member Schmidt's visit, during which he was able to see "the activities of the various Pal. Federations on the spot and reported accordingly to the Olympic Congress in Athens in May 1934."[161] In addition, the minutes recorded Mustakim's formal assumption of duties as vice president, the requirement that all federations affiliated to the POA be informed of the IOC's recognition, that explorations begin regarding the formation of the Palestine Lawn Tennis Association (which Heinrichs had started with Maccabi Palestine and the Jerusalem Sports Club), and that the committee examine the possibility for British servicemen to represent Palestine in Berlin (as had been established by precedent in the case of India in 1912 with a British serviceman at the Stockholm Olympics).[162]

The Organizing Committee of the XI Olympiad in Berlin sent its formal invitation to Palestine on June 22, 1934.[163] The invitation had not arrived in Palestine by June 26 when Yekutieli publicized the news of the first meeting of the newly recognized Olympic committee to the editor of the *Palestine Post*.[164] The article appeared, and on June 28 Kisch included it as a clipping in his correspondence to Baillet-Latour.[165]

Four months later, Palestine officially boycotted the Berlin Games. On November 4, 1934, Kisch replied to correspondence No. 2374/34 L/M, of June 22 from the president of the Organizing Committee. He explained that Palestine's Olympic committee was too young and sent his regrets that participation in Berlin could not be considered for that reason.[166] The news of Palestine's boycott was carried by the *New York Times* on November 21 along with the convenient excuse that Kisch had provided to the Organizing Committee.[167] The IOC was not pleased. Edström wrote to Yekutieli in early January 1935, questioning the wisdom of the decision and stating, "I write this letter on my own behalf and simply because I am interested in the general welfare of mankind regardless of religion."[168] Subsequently, Aberdare declined the invitation to attend the Second Maccabiad, writing to Yekutieli on March 7, 1935, that he could not accept the invitation "owing to engagements in England."[169] In the same handwritten note, he inquired with Yekutieli if there was any chance to "see some of your athletes perform in Berlin in August 1936."[170]

Yekutieli replied to Edström with an undiplomatic frankness not typical of the Olympic Movement. He acknowledged that Kisch's reason for not participating was an excuse, but in this private letter, he proposed a solution, suggesting that Palestine might compete if all Jewish athletes in the world were permitted to register to compete for Palestine as the birthplace of the Jewish nation. Yekutieli felt that if the IOC passed such a resolution at its next Session, this would represent an appropriate Jewish answer to the attitude of the Germans, delivered directly to them in their capital city.[171]

Eleven days later the *New York Times* ran another article announcing Palestine's boycott of the Berlin Games.[172] In September, following the passage of the Nuremberg Laws, the Reich Maccabi then withdrew from the Berlin Games.[173] The announcement specified that "since Jews are no longer citizens in Germany they cannot represent the German nation, in sports as well as in other fields...Jewish nationals can represent Jews only."[174] In December 1935, the IOC published in its official bulletin its official opinion on the boycott effort, along with an exchange of two letters between Maccabi World Union president Selig Brodetsky and Baillet-Latour. (Brodetsky in England had recently replaced the German Dr. Herman Lelewer at the top of the Jewish sports organization.) Baillet-Latour argued that the boycott campaign did not originate from national Olympic committees; rather, its origins were external to the Olympic Movement and purely political in its origins.[175] Brodetsky informed Baillet-Latour of the MWU's wish "to urge all Jewish sportsmen, for their own self-respect, to refrain from competing in a country where they are discriminated against as a race."[176] Baillet-Latour replied, thanking Brodetsky for the MWU's decision not to question the IOC's decision regarding Berlin as the venue for the Olympic Games. It appeared as though an entente had been reached between the parties and that for its part, the IOC would not object to the personal choice of those who chose not to attend the Games. Baillet-Latour took the position he had shared privately with Brundage—that the IOC respected the individual liberty of athletes and had no intention of coercing anyone to go to Germany, although it was also against people being blocked from going.[177]

Clearly the respective boundaries of the two organizations had been drawn. Then in early February 1936, Kisch wrote to Yekutieli and approved the draft of another letter to Schmidt.[178] The origins of the draft are unclear, but it is possible that its purpose was to obtain another concession from the IOC for Jewish sport as the situation for Jews in Germany worsened in the lead-up to the Berlin Olympic Games. In his letter to Schmidt, Yekutieli described how, at a gathering of "Sport lovers, sport fans and promoters your name was highly praised as the man

responsible for the acceptance of Palestine as a member of the…[IOC]…
thereby enabling us to partake in future Olympic games."[179] Yekutieli
described how Palestine had no representative in the IOC. He continued,
"We propose to appoint our President Lt. Colonel F. H. Kisch as an official representative on the…[IOC]…and hope that your assistance and
advice will put us right."[180] In his reply of March 7,[181] Schmidt was warm
to the idea and explained that he had already discussed the matter with
Baillet-Latour. Nonetheless, Olympic convention regarding such matters
did not allow for the Executive Committee to make the decision without
the entire board. Furthermore, members could not be nominated and
countries that had not yet participated in the Olympic Games were ineligible to join the Executive Committee. Kisch expressed satisfaction with
Schmidt's position to Yekutieli: "I think that the conditions which Dr.
Schmidt has communicated to us are entirely reasonable."[182]

In the lead-up to the IAAF Congress that was held in Germany and
coincided with the Berlin Games, Kisch and Yekutieli sent Edström their
apologies for not being able to attend. In their letter, they included a more
honest explanation than the one that they had used in their withdrawal
letter to the Organizing Committee of the Olympic Games. They cited
specifically "the prevalent spirit in Nazi Germany, which provides for
racial differences between peoples, with particular expression towards
the old and noble Jewish Nation, which differences are in absolute and
strict contradiction to the spirit of modern sportsmanship, which aims
at, and longs for complete equality between nations and race."[183]

However, Palestine's boycott embittered Edström for years. In
January 1939, he wrote to Yekutieli and told him, "I much regret that
your country did not participate in the Olympic Games in Berlin
because in not doing so you mixed politics in the Olympic Games
which is a sin hard to forgive."[184]

But Palestine was at the Games. And Heinrichs was there too,
seated not far from the Nazi leadership using special tickets provided
to him by Sondhi.

What had happened to Heinrichs in 1934? And how on earth did an
alleged Palestinian delegation—presumably Arab and German in composition—get to the Berlin Games if Kisch and Yekutieli had boycotted?

# CHAPTER 9

# The Newspaper Incident

## 1.

While Yosef Yekutieli was preparing to send athletes to India, Waldo Heinrichs was instead dealing with the nefarious Nazi presence at the Jerusalem YMCA. On January 16, 1934, Heinrichs met with the German group advocating for the subscription to the *Völkischer Beobachter* and the paper's inclusion in the Jerusalem YMCA Reading Room. Dr. Gruelin agreed to see Dr. Rohrer and Liebmann about it that night.[1] Dr. Herbert Rohrer was a thirty-one-year-old teacher in Jerusalem.[2] Heinrichs was unaware that he had formally applied to the Nazi Party in 1933 and was two weeks away from being admitted as a formal member.[3] He lived in the German Colony and became the Vice-Ortsgruppe Leader in Jerusalem. Liebmann, who had written the original letter requesting the Nazi paper, was another teacher who allegedly became a party member in the spring of 1934, although his membership number is unknown.[4]

Heinrichs had been dreading the next meeting of the Library Committee because of the intense and bitter feeling created by the Nazi paper.[5] Heinrichs felt the Jews were right to object and knew that it would make it impossible for them to cooperate with the Association. But the Germans considered it a point of honor that Jews would not force them into the position of giving way by a threat of resignation. The Germans, in turn, threatened to resign if they did not get their way. In the meeting, Heinrichs said that International Committee in New York wanted goodwill and for no action to work against this goal. Dr. Tawfiq

Canaan felt that his honor was affected, resigned from the committee, and abruptly left the room. Heinrichs was sure there had been a misunderstanding. The meeting ended without any decision. MacDonald felt that Canaan had jumped off the deep end and added deliberately to the trouble.[6] Heinrichs went to see Canaan but was unable to reconcile him.

The deterioration with the Germans seemed to extend beyond the newspaper issue. Theodor Fast,[7] owner of the Fast Hotel, was also upset that the Jerusalem YMCA's hostel was cutting him out of his share of hotel guests in the city. He objected to the YMCA taking women and tourists unrelated to their business. Heinrichs simply gave him his viewpoint on the matter and moved on to the other German members of the Association. They were meeting to discuss the newspaper question. Heinrichs asked Friedrich Lorenz, an employee of the Syrian Orphanage,[8] to get him invited to their meeting so that he could share the YMCA point of view.[9] He did not know that Lorenz had also applied to the Nazi Party and was about to become an official member.[10] Lorenz was supposed to call Heinrichs at a quarter past eight in the evening but he never called. Dorothy Heinrichs felt that the German group was afraid. Oh, how she was wrong. Within five weeks, her husband would be on a boat back to New York.

The following morning, Lorenz came back to Heinrichs with an ultimatum.[11] Twenty-five Germans had met the night before and decided that either the Association take the *Völkischer Beobachter* or else it had to cancel all political papers. If the Association did not choose one of these courses of action, all German members would resign. The benchmark of twenty-five was key: this was the minimum number of Germans required to form a Nazi Ortsgruppe overseas.

Heinrichs returned home for lunch. As if an omen, Cleopatra, the family puppy, started coughing and groaning and suddenly died. At the next staff conference, Shafeec Mansoor brought up the paper issue in the context of Boutagy and Said.[12] Heinrichs asked him sarcastically if Boutagy and Said could even read German, and he informed everyone at the meeting of the details of the emerging situation. After meeting with Agronsky, the editor of the *Palestine Post*, regarding the publication of the Association's annual report, he wrote to Frank Slack[13] in New York about the emerging problem.

Heinrichs told Slack that the Germans in question had only recently joined the Association after many years of no engagement. They protested the *Frankfurter Zeitung* as a Jewish-dominated paper and argued that the *Völkischer Beobachter* was the only paper truly representative of the new Germany's point of view. He warned Slack that to accept the paper would mean the withdrawal from the Association of the Jewish members. Heinrichs preferred not to lose either group of members, but he told Slack that the trouble was being whipped up by two or three Nazi agents who had joined the Association, and that the Arabs would use any excuse to take a crack at the Jews and align themselves with the Nazi position. Heinrichs felt that anything running counter to goodwill should not be tolerated and that the Association had to be prepared to pay whatever the cost might be.

In a bid to shore up support locally, Heinrichs met with the Anglican Bishop Graham Brown for lunch.[14] After the Bishop, he went to see Rohrer to pick up a letter from the Germans (addressed to the Library Committee) so that the matter could be formally discussed in its meeting in time to make formal recommendations to the board.[15] Rohrer was not available as agreed, having left Jerusalem to go on an-all day picnic—a seemingly convenient absence.

## 2.

When *Westland* was reporting on Goebbels and the German Maccabi Circle, Heinrichs began working on a memo summarizing the German newspaper issue for the Jerusalem YMCA's board. The purpose of the memo was to present a summary of how the issue arose, share the demands of the Germans with the board, and request the board to provide guidance on how to select newspapers consonant with the policy of the YMCA.[16] After developing the first draft with MacDonald, Heinrichs took it to Humphrey Bowman, who added several corrections.[17] Heinrichs then had the stencil cut (to make copies) and sent it to each board member. He knew that it was the most difficult problem yet faced and could set back for years rapprochement with the Jews.

At the next Board meeting on February 5, the newspaper question was on the agenda.[18] The whole city awaited the decision. Jews wanted to see if the Association was genuinely friendly. Germans wanted to see if it would back Nazi nationalism. Arabs wanted to know if the Jerusalem YMCA was pro-Jewish. Heinrichs described the three groups' attitudes toward one another as cordial hatred.

Judge Cressall put forward a motion that a controlled press was not suitable and was defeated. Abramson proposed that only a subscription to Reuters be allowed and was also defeated. Board member Saba then put forward the German proposal: any group of twenty-five would be entitled to get their newspaper provided, as long as it was not anti-Christian or agnostic. This passed and the Arabs and Germans were jubilant. Heinrichs felt that he had been licked.

The solution used by the Arabs and Germans to squeeze in the *Völkischer Beobachter* was to set a minimum requirement of persons equal in number to that required to form a Nazi Ortsgruppe. The minutes of the meeting recorded the decision and added the provision that each group be provided no more than one paper,[19] thereby guaranteeing the Nazi publication would be ordered.

After confronting Canaan about his behavior in the meeting,[20] Heinrichs went into damage control mode. He met with Hebrew University[21] to review the memo on the newspaper question with Dr. Bergman and Dr. Mayer, then met with the Anglican Bishop to get his opinion, too. He then decided to get a higher ruling and travelled to Beirut to see Dr. Archie Harte and Dr. Bayard Dodge.[22] Heinrichs got permission from Fred Auburn, the Physical Director, to release his brother so that he could drive him north. They left just as Yosef Yekutieli and the Maccabis were making their final preparations for India. On the drive, they discussed how a trip to New York might help, but Heinrichs was unconvinced that such a trip would prevent a split in the Association.

In Beirut, they checked into the German hotel Metropole[23,24] and went to watch the new movie *King Kong*. In the morning,[25] Heinrichs met Dodge, president of the American University of Beirut, for advice on the memo and then proceeded to Damascus for meetings with Harte.[26] He and his brother returned to Jerusalem late the same evening.

Heinrichs called his staff together.[27] They reviewed the memo for an hour and a half, and Heinrichs presented to them all the facts of the case. Nicholas Lattof felt hurt that Heinrichs had not first consulted him. He volunteered to meet with the Germans privately and confidentially. Auburn was opposed to this and recommended meeting with the board first. Bowman was out of town, so Heinrichs called Canaan to his house to review the memo. He was the most influential Arab leader with the Germans at the Association because he was married to one. They went over the whole memo, and Canaan expressed his dissatisfaction with Heinrichs' meeting with the three elders.

Heinrichs then sent a long letter to Slack in New York outlining the "exceedingly difficult situation."[28] He copied John Mott, Fred Ramsey, Francis Harmon, and Walter Gethman. In this letter, he made it clear that "German Nazi agents are at work here whipping up the German feeling, and they have found very strong allies in the Arabs, both Christian and Moslem members and the press."[29] He told Slack, "I have repeatedly said it is better to sacrifice a few newspapers than to have a split in the membership. If I am overruled in this I want you to understand that I have taken every possible step to avoid a crisis, and to settle it in a friendly manner."[30] Clearly aware that he was being spied upon, Heinrichs warned Slack that everything in his letter and all the attachments were to be kept strictly confidential. He kept numbered copies locked up in his desk, and under no conditions were Dr. Dodge's letter or the memorandum from the Bishop, Harte, and Dodge to be published.[31]

## 3.

The "Memo on the German Newspaper Question in the Library Committee" summarized the time line of events. Heinrichs attached to it copies of the contributions from each of the three elders and the various correspondences that had triggered the controversy.[32]

On November 19, 1933, Liebmann had sent the original letter requesting the Nazi paper. The Library Committee then met on December 2. The Jewish members of the committee objected and it instead chose the *Neue Freie Presse* of Vienna. This resulted in Canaan approaching MacDonald directly to point out that the committee's decision would create ill feeling. She then sent out a circular letter on December 6, which brought the matter to Heinrichs' attention. It then took three weeks until Dr. Rohrer replied on December 29. Was this because the Nazi cell was coordinating its actions directly with Germany?

The Library Committee convened on January 18—immediately after new members were chosen for the year—out of a sense of urgency. No decision could be reached and then the Germans met privately as a group, declining to include Bowman and Heinrichs. The group then sent a new letter on February 1 reaffirming their desire for the Nazi paper and presenting their demands to avoid their resignation en masse. The Library Committee then met on February 3 and ruled that the board needed to provide guidance to the committee on how to select papers in accordance with the policies of the YMCA Movement as a whole.

The copies of letters that Heinrichs attached included his own to the three elders. He explained to them the reasons for accepting "the call" to Jerusalem, pointing out that the objective of the Association was to create a common meeting ground for all communities in a friendly spirit of cooperation.[33] In their resulting memorandum,[34] the three elders stressed some essential points to guide the resolution of the issue. They did not want the Jewish members to leave. They also wanted to emphasize YMCA values. Harte noted that the word "National" in "National Association" did not mean that the YMCA Movement sought to direct its work from the standpoint of national groups.

The three elders stressed that, without a change in course,[35] they would prove the Jewish members wrong in the eyes of their own community. The Jewish members had joined the Association on the belief that it worked to foster an atmosphere of goodwill among members of different faiths. They had done so despite widespread opposition from their coreligionists. The elders stressed that no Christian had a right to evade the command "[s]o let your light shine before men that they may see your good works and glorify your Father which is in heaven." They wanted the Germans to exhibit Christian conduct and self-denial. It would be a tragedy if, within a year of the dedication, the newspaper incident set back for many years the Association's work. Dodge warned in his personal letter to the board on the matter, "Who knows what trials may still be in store for the people of Palestine? During this period of comparative calm, when the questions of literature is before your board, let me urge that the members think not only of the moment, but also of the future. Prevention is always better than cure."[36]

Things calmed down until the next board meeting[37] to discuss the memo. Boutagy forced Heinrichs to share the letter he had written to Dodge and argued that Heinrichs had embarrassed the case in favor of the Jews. The other board members disagreed and Boutagy went wild. When the matter went to vote, the board approved of its February 5 decision but also approved the memo. They appointed Stubbs, Jamal, Canaan, and Heinrichs to see Hermann Schneller, Rohrer, Gruelin, Liebmann, and Rhein so that these individuals could then present the memo to the German members. Heinrichs felt he had won a partial victory.

## 4.

But Heinrichs was not being left alone to settle the affair. The Arab newspaper *Meraat Elsherk* began publishing a series of highly provocative articles about his administration. He received a translation of one,[38] which accused Heinrichs of living in luxury at the expense of the Arabs and diverting money for his personal use. Samy Suz, Emile Ohan, and Mansoor were upset by its publication. Heinrichs informed Slack in New York and copied Mott, Ramsey, Harmon, and Gethman.[39] He updated them on the formation of the subcommittee and the *Meraat Elsherk* newspaper articles, noting that his triumvirate on the board was behind them, along with "a tourist guide who is trying to blackmail the Association for the benefit of the work he may secure."[40]

So while Alfred Gutt was charging down the swimming tank at the Maharaja's palace in India, Heinrichs was meeting with the subcommittee to arrange its first meeting with the representatives of the German group that had imposed the *Völkischer Beobachter* affair on the Jerusalem YMCA: Hermann Schneller, Herbert Rohrer, Ernst Rhein (who never joined the Nazi Party, despite demonstrating sympathies for it), and Herbert Liebmann.[41] Rhein met with the Anglican Bishop for lunch the next day. The Bishop had been upset by the violent attacks on Heinrichs in *Meraat Elsherk*.[42] Anis Jamal informed Heinrichs that the Germans would meet with the subcommittee at four o'clock and that things were hopeful. In reality the Germans were in a terrible mood. Canaan, Stubbs, and Anis Jamal managed to prevent their resignation while Heinrichs worked to get the *Meraat Elsherk* newspaper articles translated.[43, 44]

And while the Maccabis were getting ready to enter the Irwin Amphitheater in Delhi, Heinrichs was discussing a defamation lawsuit with Judge Cressall against *Meraat Elsherk*.[45] He also met with Stubbs to be briefed on the preceding day's meeting with the Germans. The news was nasty. Some of the Germans accused Heinrichs of being a Jew, others that he was pro-Jew. All believed him to be un-Christian. Schneller and several others threatened to resign. He then went to the Bishop's home, where he and the Bishop met with Boulos Shehadeh, the editor of *Meraat Elsherk*. Shehadeh said that the Jerusalem YMCA was all wrong because it was not an Arab YMCA. Heinrichs told him that that policy would never change and drilled him on his numerous mis-statements in the paper. Shehadeh could not answer. After the meeting, Heinrichs finally had to instruct his Library Committee to meet on Tuesday and order the Nazi newspaper.

Instead of cofounding the Western Asiatic Games Confederation at its inaugural meeting at the Persian Consulate in Delhi with Almagor, on that day, Heinrichs learned instead that he might have to leave Jerusalem. Lattof and Auburn took Heinrichs to the George Williams Room and told him that the Jamal brothers, Canaan, Mantoura, Salameh, Stubbs, Nathan, Boutagy, and Said would resign if Heinrichs did not surrender the role of secretary-general. Both men told Heinrichs that if he were forced out, they would refuse to work under Adamson or Wilbert Smith, who they expected to be his replacements, and would also leave. They proposed to Heinrichs that he withdraw for three to six months on a call from New York so that things could calm down. They guaranteed Heinrichs that a memo forcing his resignation would not come up in his absence, that there would be no conflict or board meetings, and that Arabs did not talk in someone's absence. They told Heinrichs that they would go north to see Harte and get his input and return by Vespers Service the next day.[46]

The series of articles that had attacked the Jerusalem YMCA and Heinrichs raises the question of whether *Meraat Elsherk* was producing them on the instigation of the Nazi Party members. Heinrichs wrote to New York, updating it on the situation. He attached copies of all the articles from the paper. He said that the Germans were obdurate and refused to consider the YMCA's principle. The Germans were planning on meeting again that night, before reconnecting with the subcommittee. Heinrichs was not sure what they had up their sleeve. He told Slack that the articles from *Meraat Elsherk* "have very carefully been incited, as I definitely know, by the two Jamal brothers, Mr. Boutagy and Boulos Said, and are gaining an increasing feeling."[47] He also told Slack that he had met with the editor and warned him that he was carried away by Arab nationalism. Although his paper had a small circulation, it could still do immense damage. He told Slack that Shehadeh had won all the malcontents in the Association.

Unfortunately, the articles in *Meraat Elsherk* had been vicious and already achieved their objective. From the translated copies sent to Slack, the full scale of the damage they caused in the politically charged and socially conservative community of Jerusalem is apparent. The first article (from February 14)[48] accused Jews of bossing around Christians and telling Germans what they should read. It implied that Jews should go to Jewish institutions and keep out of Christian ones. The February 20 article that had attacked Heinrichs for living rich also accused him of mocking and despising the Arabs. It cited the case of his refusal to lower the Association flag to half-staff on the death of King Faisal, and contrasted this action to his lowering the flag for the death of the apostolic delegate.[49] There were two other articles in the same issue. One complained about allowing laborers to work on Sunday.[50] The other alleged that Heinrichs ranked Christianity on the same level as Buddhism.[51]

On February 26, the paper's article made a veiled reference to the emerging competition between hotel rooms in the city between the Fast Hotel and the Jerusalem YMCA. It accused the Association of eating into the livelihood of Arab hotel owners and critiqued it as a commercial center with a restaurant, barber shop, and place for exhibiting antiquities.[52] And on the day of the opening ceremony of the First Western Asiatic Games, the last article appeared, titled "The YMCA and the German Newspaper: The Hotel Heinrichs."[53] This accused Heinrichs of weakness and cowardice in front of the Jews and suggested he resign for failure to implement the board's decision to allow the Germans to have their paper. It argued that the Association was not his hotel but if it was, that the board should step aside and rename the building "The Heinrichs Hotel".

Clearly, this last article is what spurred Auburn and Lattof to speak to Heinrichs in the George Williams Room on March 3 and suggest that he withdraw to New York. Heinrichs, Lattof, and Auburn then cabled New York asking that it send an urgent cable requiring the secretary-general for three months of finance work in America, and that his absence from Palestine was essential without replacement.[54]

## 5.

Heinrichs began clearing out his files so that nothing could be used against him by a traitor.[55] He began to wonder if Lattof had exaggerated the generality of opposition to him but was still convinced that the paper incident could split the Association. He went to the office early the next day expecting a cable from New York. None came. He was anxious that no one know before the Library Committee meeting, which met at five o'clock.[56] There was barely a quorum there. Heinrichs suggested that the Germans still needed to make their request as a group of twenty-five. Thirty-eight had actually requested the paper, and Theodor Fast went to collect their signatures. Heinrichs was sure that one day's delay would result in his being kicked out. He immediately ordered Suz to subscribe to the *Völkischer Beobachter* and sent Lattof out to buy current copies from the newsstand. The Germans were placated, but Heinrichs was sad that the Jewish members would certainly leave. Boutagy told Auburn that he did not want Heinrichs to leave, which Heinrichs considered a lie. Auburn wanted Heinrichs to stay, but Heinrichs had already decided that if the cable from New York came, he would go.

Another day passed. Heinrichs waited. A dark, black day. But the cable did not come and Heinrichs could not sleep until one in the morning. He thought about how only a divided staff or disloyal direc tors could block the work. He was concerned for Lattof, who he felt was blind to numerous enemies. He felt that Lattof could only count on Mansoor and that the rest of the Arab staff were opposed to him.[57]

On March 8, two cables finally arrived.[58] Ohan handed them to Heinrichs. The first was from Slack and Harmon recalling him for three months of finance work in New York. The other was only from Slack, asking Heinrichs to meet with Mott in London en route to the United States. Heinrichs went to see Bowman, who was suspicious that cables had gone out from Jerusalem to New York. Heinrichs then booked passage on the mail ship MS *Maloja* from Port Said to Marseille, with transit in London between March 17 and 21. He was due to arrive in New York's waters on March 27. He saw the Bishop, who was being pressured by his clergy to resign from the Association's board because it had rejected the advice that Heinrichs had given to it. Last, he met with Halaby, Blatchford, and Boutagy. Heinrichs' demise was evident.

## 6.

The next day,[59] the board granted Heinrichs leave. Heinrichs was concerned that, in his absence, historic problems between Lattof and Auburn would reemerge. He received Lattof and Auburn to mediate their long-running dispute. They prayed, gripping hands, and made a promise to be loyal to one another. Lattof, tired and nervous, broke down and cried in Heinrichs' office after lunch, and he tried to prevent Heinrichs from seeing Mott in London. Heinrichs then received Bowman in his office and met with every member, even Boutagy. In the evening, Heinrichs' family had a long conversation at dinner and they agreed that the quicker he escaped from Jerusalem, the better. Dorothy Heinrichs would remain in Jerusalem with the children.

In New York, Slack wrote to Ramsey[60] to tell him that he had consulted Mott before he sailed to London and also talked to Harmon. They agreed that for Heinrichs' own sake, New York had better bring him back. Slack told Ramsey that Mott was experiencing repercussions of the Nazi situation among German missionary groups and others. Clearly, the Jerusalem YMCA was not the only Christian mission activity targeted by the Nazis, and the IC/YMCA leadership knew it.

Heinrichs was set to leave Palestine.[61] He packed his things, ate breakfast, and kissed his little girls goodbye. At Lydda, the Jaffa train was one hour late, so he asked his wife, brother, and son to leave him and be spared the wait. He ate lunch on board the diner car at Gaza. The train arrived in Kantara on time but was an hour late into Port Said. There, he boarded the MS *Maloja*, which was crowded with civilians and officers returning from India. He entered his cabin above the propellers. Smooth seas were expected. But the turbulent waters of Jerusalem were not behind him.

## 7.

On board the MS *Maloja* Heinrichs got straight to work. He wrote to Lattof and Auburn "trying further to bind the links of their new found friendship"[62] and also to Canaan "in an effort to mitigate the antagonism."[63] He worked for two hours compiling the events that led up to the Nazi newspaper incident for Mott in London and the IC/YMCA in New York.[64] While drafting the list in chronological order, Heinrichs realized that there were fourteen points that might substantiate a desire to kick him out. However, he still felt that he had stood for a principle in each case.

Once the ship docked in France, Heinrichs took some time to disembark and retrace his steps from August 1917. He recalled the first time he saw the wounded during the First World War.[65] Bayard Dodge, in the meantime, was writing from Beirut to the IC/YMCA[66] with his concerns about the impracticality of the scale of the YMCA project in Jerusalem. He thought that Heinrichs was an unusually fine man, but that he was not a superman. He warned the IC/YMCA not to allow Jerusalem to become an international scandal.

In London, Heinrichs had lunch with Lord Allenby and then met Mott at the Victoria Hotel.[67] Mott agreed to sign the memo of the three elders and also endorsed Dodge's letter. Mott assured Heinrichs of his support, saying, "I'll go to the end of the road with you, old man. God bless you." They met again two days later to discuss the letter from the Bishop of Jerusalem in order to prepare Mott before his meeting with the Archbishop the next day.[68]

As Mott met with the Archbishop, Heinrichs boarded the RMS *Olympic* at Cherbourg, headed for the United States. He gave the ship's stenographer some work for Mott and air mailed it to him from the ship so that it would reach him before he left London for South Africa.[69] Heinrichs also received a radiogram confirming that he had been booked to be broadcast on NBC about the economic and political situation in Palestine.[70] As Heinrichs was pulling out of Cherbourg, Slack was hard at work doing damage control. One of his first moves was to write to Ramsey inquiring whether it would be possible to withdraw the powers of attorney granted to Canaan.[71]

The journey across the Atlantic was quiet. Heinrichs noted that no messages were arriving for him on board. He wondered if anyone in New York was aware that the secretary-general of Jerusalem was coming home.[72] But others were writing about him. Canaan wrote a letter to Slack.[73] The letter was designed to put the nail in Heinrichs' coffin. In particular, Canaan said that Heinrichs' war injuries had rendered him unfit for the work. If he returned to Jerusalem, it would destroy his nervous system and general health. Francis Harmon, senior secretary of the IC/YMCA, also wrote to Slack and backed Heinrichs' position on principles. Harmon doubted seriously whether the IC/YMCA should allow the Nazi newspaper, especially considering the fact that Hitler was crushing the YMCA Movement and the type of Christianity in which it believed.[74]

## 8.

Heinrichs arrived in New York and was met at the docks by Slack.[75] They had lunch together and Heinrichs explained everything, including how the board had arrived at wanting his resignation. The men went to New Haven[76] so that Heinrichs could meet with Harmon. Heinrichs found Harmon to be rabidly anti-Nazi and anti-Hitler. At this meeting, the men discussed the subject of how to ensure the continued involvement of Bergman and Mayer with the Jerusalem Association. After all, Heinrichs had only been recalled to New York and was still, in theory, the Jerusalem YMCA's secretary-general. So he continued to function in that capacity, interviewing Arthur Rugh to be the Religious Works

Director[77] and giving his fifteen-minute NBC broadcast about Palestine on April 4.[78] Heinrichs also prepared a summary of the German newspaper incident for the IC/YMCA convention in May, provided it to Slack, and cabled to Lattof about the arrival in Jerusalem of T. G. Smith, vice president of the Central Hanover Bank and Trust Company.[79] There would be complete silence from Lattof's end.

In early April, Heinrichs received, by way of his parents in Canton, Ohio, a strange cable[80] from his wife in Jerusalem. It said that things were quieting down, that any action by the International Committee would be unwise, and that the paper question would have to be settled in Jerusalem. Heinrichs wondered why she had cabled his parents instead of him directly at the office in New York.

At about the same time, Harmon started collecting opinions on the newspaper incident from the various members of the IC/YMCA. He met with Harmon and Slack to rehash the Jerusalem situation further and then filled in his wife by post. He began to travel extensively across the Midwest and east coast to speak at YMCAs and shore up his case. Heinrichs would wake up early, grab breakfast and a paper, and note how the *New York Times* was beginning to carry a lot of news on Hitler that he felt was not too discouraging. He wondered if the editorial tone represented appeasement of the Nazis.[81]

Heinrichs arrived at his parents' home in Canton. Letters from Conrad and Züssmann, a part-time office clerk he had hired, were waiting "stating that the staff situation was bad, that the Jews were organizing to boycott the YMCA from a nationalist point of view and that Bergmann [sic], Mayer & Hyamson had resigned."[82] Heinrichs recorded in his diary that Lattof had not sent a word to him and that this made him feel resentful: "Certainly if what Conrad says is true, things have gone completely to pot as far as staff unity is concerned."[83] Then another letter from his wife arrived confirming Canaan's opposition to Heinrichs, which worried Heinrichs more than he wanted to admit.[84]

Heinrichs continued on to Chicago. While there, Heinrichs' father forwarded to him a pivotal cable from Dorothy Heinrichs in Jerusalem: "Board written asking resignation. Send investigator. Situation without investigation intolerable."[85] Heinrichs was shocked. He called Slack immediately and telegraphed it to Ramsey. He knew it would mean a long, drawn-out fight.

Ramsey telegrammed Heinrichs back, asking him to come immediately to his residence in Cleveland. Heinrichs caught a flight and was met by Margaret, who had since returned to the United States from Jerusalem.[86] She drove him to their home, and Heinrichs and her father stayed up until 1:30 a.m. going over everything. Although Heinrichs felt that Ramsey was unconvinced of his efforts to win over Canaan, Boutagy, and others, he stressed to Ramsey that he had kept his temper "in the strictest control and often in the face of severe provocation."[87] Heinrichs was unaware that Ramsey had already made up his mind— Nazis or no Nazis. That same day, Ramsey had written Slack a letter (after learning of Dorothy Heinrichs' cable referring to the resignation request) in which he acknowledged that reconciliation was unlikely and that the IC/YMCA immediately had to consider a successor for Heinrichs.[88]

While on a long train ride back to Chicago with Grover Little, Heinrichs agreed to resign[89] from the position of secretary-general. He was beginning to accept Mott and Slack's position that the IC/YMCA had to stick to its principles. It would be better to close the building than to give in. Heinrichs would sacrifice his position as long as a Nazi newspaper was not allowed in and the local Arab board members were overruled. The next day, mail from New York arrived with letters from Heinrichs' wife and brother.[90] They suggested that Lattof was opposed to an investigation because in its absence, it would leave the Heinrichses in the cold. His wife explained that she had sent her cable about things quieting down because she had been urged to do so by Lattof, and perhaps Auburn. Heinrichs was suspicious.

## 9.

On April 24, the board convened to take action on the recommendation of a secret Executive Committee decision. Auburn explained, "I did not know this meeting was being held until it was over and no information of any nature was given to me concerning the agenda and outcome of this meeting…[I]f I had any intimation of the intention of the Board of

Directors and a concerted effort had been made by Lattof and myself we could have prevented the Board taking this step at this time."[91]

Auburn called for an investigation: "This situation in Jerusalem is not a recent development but is the climax of slow accumulation over a period of years. I feel that Heinrichs is reaping the whirlwind. He has stood on his principles and has dealt fairly and squarely with his staff. He has always stood for the principle he believed right and for what was good for the Association."[92]

New York agreed to send Ramsey and Slack as investigators almost immediately.[93] Heinrichs traveled to Cleveland to see Ramsey and was met by him and Margaret. He and Slack wanted Heinrichs to stay on in the United States and have his wife return to Honolulu to rest. Heinrichs did not like the way things were turning.[94] He then traveled to Washington and obtained the support of Justice Brandeis.[95] Bowman cabled Heinrichs from Palestine and advised him to remain in the United States.[96] Heinrichs cabled back giving him the news that Slack and Ramsey were coming out to Jerusalem. Heinrichs shared his bitterness with Slack as they ate their lunch.

Finally a letter[97] from Lattof arrived explaining Boutagy and Said's reactions to Heinrichs' administration. The men had agreed to keep Heinrichs' fate out of the board meeting, where he would have enough Westerners to defend him. Boutagy and Said agreed to discuss Heinrichs' fate only at the level of the Executive Committee. This included Jamal, Canaan, Said, and other Arabs who were opposed to Heinrichs. He did not stand a chance.

Heinrichs was scheduled to meet with the IC/YMCA at its meeting in New York on May 9. Their agenda item was the situation in Jerusalem. Heinrichs was pleased to hear from Fakhri Bey Nashashibi by cable.[98] Nashashibi told him that a majority of the membership of the Association was opposed to the decision to remove Heinrichs. Nashashibi had demanded an investigation to protect the Association's prestige. Heinrichs let Harmon and Slack know, and it definitely caught their attention. Heinrichs spoke on Jerusalem at the meeting for ten minutes. He rang the bell as he had seldom rung it, thinking of it as his swan song yet feeling good to know that he was right.

In an ironic twist, the very next day, the leading antagonists at the Jerusalem YMCA were once again cooperating with Jewish sport organizers to put on the Tenth Jerusalem Inter-School Sports Programme.[99] Although the majority of schools participating were Arab, Jewish teams were present from Alliance, an important Jewish trade school, as were Jewish technical officials, including one from the FASCP.[100] Prior to his resignation, Heinrichs and the YMCA's Physical Department had been working toward interfaith sport governance and programming, with early success. Many on the Executive Committee[101] of the Inter-School Sports—Bowman, Hannoush, Auburn, Mantura, Totah, and Tannous, all associated with the Jerusalem YMCA—had attacked Heinrichs (or did not support him adequately) in his fight against the Nazis and for promoting an open platform inclusive of Jews. Why attack Heinrichs for advocating cooperation in sports with the Jews yet work with the Jews on the field of play? This begs the question, "Why did Heinrichs have to go?" Cui bono? The answer to the latter question is not entirely clear, but the answer to the former is probably that Heinrichs was the one person who could actually succeed in bringing the parties together through sport. His pedigree was of too high a quality, his connections and experience in international sport development too strong. As early as January 1930, he had met Edström on his visit to the Punjab.[102] He was a known entity. If someone did not want a unified Olympic committee for Palestine, Heinrichs would need to be out of the picture. The proximity of the Berlin Games raises a number of unanswered questions.

## 10.

While Arabs and Jews were cooperating on interschool sports, Heinrichs was back in New York meeting[103] with Rabbi Wise, Judge Julian Mack, and Emmanuel Mohl as part of his campaign to spread the word about Nazis in Jerusalem. They were amazed at the board's bigotry and that of the Germans, thought Heinrichs was absolutely right, and felt that the bigger issue than the Nazi paper was the need for the IC/YMCA to stick by Heinrichs. Heinrichs thought it was funny to observe Muslims and Jews running to his aid and to have all the Christians aligned against him.

But the IC/YMCA was not going to stick by Heinrichs. He started getting signals after its committee meeting of May 9. Harmon sounded him out for new finance positions in New York.[104] It appears that the committee was looking for an exit strategy that would solve the problem of Heinrichs being too principled in Jerusalem.

The IC/YMCA meeting in New York empowered "Ramsey and Slack to represent the Committee in negotiating with the Board of Directors of the Jerusalem [YMCA] regarding all pending problems having to do with the work…in Jerusalem and…its relation…thereto."[105] A strictly confidential correspondence from Mott and Harmon to Bowman pointed out the hypocrisy of the same Library Committee, which in November 1933 (the time of Dr. Iven's trip) had cancelled "a subscription to a Hebrew newspaper, the organ of an extreme political group…for the perfectly valid reason that…[the]…paper was provocative of ill-will in an Association which is dedicated unreservedly to the development of good-will in the true spirit of Christian brotherhood."[106] The letter also rejected the board's decision that twenty-five members constituted justification for a specific group's action within the Association.[107] Mott and Harmon included a veiled reference to the fact that Nazis were not allowed to make decisions for the Jerusalem YMCA.[108]

Mott and Harmon demanded that the board rescind its decision of February 5, 1934—the one whereby any group of twenty-five was entitled to decide matters on behalf of the Association. They provided an aide mémoire to Ramsey and Slack to guide them in their investigation. They noted the second article of the Jerusalem YMCA's constitution, which stated clearly that "the Association shall maintain a strictly non-political character and shall make no distinction of race, nationality, or faith in its service."[109] They noted how "[t]here is much controversy in these times of racial animosity and religious dissension"[110] and that the work should emphasize "points of agreement and striv[e]…constantly to remove points of friction."[111]

Although Liebmann had written the original request for the newspaper, Mott and Harmon's memo identified "Dr. Rohrer, principal of the German School in Jerusalem, and German member of the Library Committee"[112] as the person who "appealed to the principle that every national group should have the right to select its own paper."[113] Rohrer, of course, was a full-fledged Nazi Party member by this time.[114] He accused the Jewish members of the Association of taking away the German group's rights, "possibly out of hatred."[115] The Jewish members, on the other hand, wrote to Heinrichs at the time and argued that the Reading Room of an Association working towards inter-racial cooperation was not the place for a Nazi paper. They suggested alternatives that were rejected. The Jews determined—probably correctly—that the incident was a test case "used to throw open the gates of the [YMCA] to anti-Jewish propaganda."[116] Perhaps it was also a strategic step on the road to forming a Palestinian delegation to the Berlin Olympic Games, sourced from the YMCA and German sport club just down the road. The latter's board would soon be taken over by Nazis.

Mott and Harmon's memo also noted how the articles from *Meraat Elsherk* newspaper "further inflamed the feelings of the national and religious groups involved in this unfortunate controversy and have tended to widen the zone of conflict."[117] Were the *Meraat Elsherk* articles deliberately placed according to a Nazi plan? Was the test case identified because of Heinrichs and the Jerusalem YMCA's historic roles in working to bring together the various communities through sport? Why did no one make the link to the fact that the Nazi Party had suddenly inherited the hosting rights to the Berlin Games?

Mott and Harmon seemed sufficiently concerned about the Nazi sympathies of some of the Arab board members and other Jerusalem YMCA committee members that among the alternatives they considered for applying pressure was leveraging their Title to Property and permission-to-occupy powers.[118] If invoked, it would represent an extremely public rebuke of some of the leading Arab Christian citizens of Jerusalem.

## 11.

Dorothy Heinrichs, in a sudden reversal, decided to remain in Jerusalem on the same day that Slack set sail to investigate. She cabled her husband, "Feeling fine. State objections to my remaining in Jerusalem until June 17. Local situation demands my presence during investigation.

Cable money. Dorothy."[119] Mohl agreed with Heinrichs that she should stay.[120] Heinrichs met with Harmon for two and a half hours over lunch to discuss his future. Lattof clearly came up because Harmon told Heinrichs that he thought Lattof needed to go.[121] Later, in Cleveland, Heinrichs bluntly gave his position on Lattof becoming secretary-general in Jerusalem by stating that he was inadequate.[122] However, Ramsey reserved judgement and felt that the Jerusalem board had to decide. Heinrichs thought that Ramsey erred and saw the situation only from the point of view of Jerusalem.[123]

On the same day that the International Olympic Committee recognized the Palestine Olympic Committee, Heinrichs went back to Canton to see his parents. They were in agreement that Heinrichs stay in the United States and for his wife to remain in Jerusalem.[124] He wrote to Ramsey to prepare him for his journey to Jerusalem, suggesting that he keep notes of all interviews because people in Jerusalem were inclined to forget what they say.[125] He also suggested that Ramsey stay at the Fast Hotel to placate its German owners. Heinrichs then quietly mailed copies of the aide mémoire and decision of the IC/YMCA meeting of May 9 to his wife and brother in Jerusalem.[126]

Heinrichs had been given information by his wife and Auburn[127] suggesting that Lattof was the reason for the board's demand that Heinrichs resign. He was very upset, but also relieved. He felt that Lattof's alleged actions explained everything. However, Heinrichs might have misread the situation regarding Lattof. Ramsey was only willing to consider Auburn's letter "evidence, but that judgement must be reserved."[128] On the same day that he received Auburn's letter about Lattof, the *New York Times* printed an article that reported the IOC's decision to recognize a Palestine Olympic Committee.[129] While Heinrichs was contemplating Lattof's alleged treachery,[130] the IOC sent out its official recognition letter to Kisch.[131] *Westland* also published another article about the boycott debate titled "*Sie kommen – Sie kommen nicht!*" (They come - they do not come!).[132] Something else might have been going on. Someone might have been trying to influence the Jerusalem YMCA's Physical Department—which, after all, was perceived to represent Arab Olympic sporting interests—in the broader boycott debate.

On June 7, Heinrichs gave his seventy-fifth speech on the Jerusalem situation, this time at Prospect Temple in Brooklyn.[133] He took time thereafter to visit the graves of his brother Edgar and sister Doris in Newark.[134] On June 11, he received news from Jerusalem that his wife was pretty tired and that Slack and Ramsey had advised her to "benefit of Hilda's company [her house help] at least to Boston."[135] At a speech in Canton, Heinrichs "thanked the crowd for coming out to witness…[his]…'public execution'"[136] and gave a twenty-three-minute radio broadcast.

## 12.

On June 25, Slack finally offered the secretary-general position in Jerusalem to Smith.[137] Then Slack quietly sent a radiogram to Harmon: "AFTER THOROUGH CONSULTATION BELIEVE HEINRICHS RETURN INADVISABLE FOR IMPORTANT REASONS NOT IDENTIFIED WITH NEWSPAPER ISSUE DESPITE GREAT SERVICE RENDERED…PROPOSE IMMEDIATE REESTABLISHMENT PERMANENT BASIS WILBERT SMITH."[138] Heinrichs, who had not heard from Harmon in some time, decided to call him on June 28. He learned that Harmon wanted him for "a long and unhurried conference on Saturday morning"[139] but did not realize that a decision had already been made against his return to Jerusalem.

At the meeting,[140] Grover Little broke the news that Slack and Ramsey had found Heinrichs' return inadvisable. Then Heinrichs met with Harmon and they discussed Ramsey and Slack's cablegram. Heinrichs kept his feelings to himself, but they ran the gamut from mild rebellion to wanting to smash the hell out of his enemies. He felt that Ramsey and Slack had sidelined the newspaper issue, merely hoping it would be resolved. Harmon was in agreement with Heinrichs that Ramsey and Slack were hedging. Heinrichs threatened a series of press articles and circular letters if they did. Harmon told Heinrichs that he backed him but that he could not convene the IC/YMCA until September. Things would have to wait until then. Then Harmon and Heinrichs cabled Slack and Ramsey that no compromise on the Nazi paper was possible. The investigators had to stick to their guns on that issue.

However, Harmon only waited a day to approve Heinrichs' transfer[141] and confirmed in a separate cable to Ramsey and Slack that he secured Heinrichs' promise not to do anything rash.[142]

Meanwhile, various newspapers heralded Heinrichs' ousting. The JTA ran its front-page article under the title "Jerusalem 'Y' Official Quits in Nazi Clash: Had Banned Anti-Semitic Berlin Paper After Jews' Objections."[143] It reported how Ramsey and Slack's investigation deferred the decision on the newspaper question to the local board upon their own departure back to the United States the preceding day.[144] Another *Jewish Daily Bulletin* article appeared under the title "Jerusalem Official Upheld By Secretary: Harmon Concurs in Resolve to Ban Nazi Papers." The *Bulletin* had approached Heinrichs, and he referred the reporter to Harmon so as not to embarrass the IC/YMCA. However, "when asked for comment on the Jewish Telegraphic Agency dispatch stating that he had resigned because the Board of Directors had insisted on keeping the Hitler-controlled newspaper in the files of the "Y," [Heinrichs] voiced bitter condemnation of Hitler's anti-Jewish decrees and said that the J.T.A. dispatch was 'substantially correct.'"[145]

On July 9, Dorothy Heinrichs arrived in Boston. She and her husband drove out to Wellesley together, her alma mater, and passed a wonderful afternoon alone.[146] They spoke of Jerusalem and how Slack and Ramsey had missed their great opportunity for the YMCA, undergirded a hopeless board, and tried to soften the blow by flattery. The most thrilling job on earth had come at a high cost, indeed.

## 13.

Heinrichs found it was hard to extinguish his bitterness. In July, as he was preparing to go west to San Francisco and onward to Honolulu, he got to work writing his life history for President Paul Moody of Middlebury College as an informal application for a job.[147] While waiting for their medical approval to proceed from San Francisco to Honolulu on the SS *Mololo*, the Heinrichs received Mrs. Taylor for lunch. She had donated the funds for the sport equipment at the Jerusalem YMCA, and they discussed how the Arabs on the board had blocked Heinrichs' administration.[148] On board the SS *Mololo* to Hawaii, he thought very

much about Jerusalem and how he had lost the best and most important job he had ever had or would hope to hold.[149] The Heinrichs were
willing to feel better if the IC/YMCA cleared him at its September meeting.[150] But it was hard to wait until September and Heinrichs struggled
to conquer his hatred of those he felt had betrayed him.

While in Hawaii, Heinrichs received a cable from Moody of Middlebury College with a definite job offer.[151] Finally a break! He had a
weapon to wield in his discussions with New York in September. Heinrichs replied confirming that he would be in Middlebury on September
13. He also wrote to Harmon saying that he would be in New York on
September 10 to receive the final report of the investigation.[152] At Middlebury, he would begin teaching Contemporary Civilizations to first-year
students; men in the fall and women in the spring.[153] Heinrichs received
a check in the amount of $628[154] for the sale of the car in Jerusalem.[155]
The Holy City began to slip into the background. As he drove up the
"Pacific Heights and Round Top over the Hog's back to Tantalus and
Makiki, then into Punchbowl and home,"[156] the rain "raised memories
of Darjeeling, Hong Kong and Bengal...The verdure, the rain, the iso-
lation all appealed to...[him]...after the barren dryness and nosiness
of Jerusalem."[157] A more positive tone set in, and Heinrichs purchased
forty of "the most beautiful"[158] postcards he could find of Honolulu to
send to Jerusalemites. Conrad, too, put Jerusalem behind him, arriving
at their parents' home in Canton toward the end of August.[159]

On September 1, Heinrichs set out from Honolulu for New York
to receive the investigation's final conclusions.[160] It was not easy to say
goodbye, but it was much easier than when he had left Jerusalem. The
future was clearer. On his first day at sea, Heinrichs played three sets
of deck tennis, winning all of them, and enjoyed watching *The Chase
for Beauty* in the ship's cinema.[161] The next day, he did his first trap-
shooting since his war days, hitting thirteen out of twenty-five with
his one arm.[162] The ship pulled into San Francisco on September 5,
where Heinrichs received advice not to take any drastic action if the
newspaper issue was not settled.[163] He continued on to Chicago and
Canton, where his brother briefed him for one and a half hours.[164] All
that Heinrichs could think about was his meeting with the International Committee in New York on September 11.[165] He had dinner[166]

with his parents and brother and then the family did a final reading of the last letters from Ramsey, Auburn, and Lattof. His family took him to the train station, where he boarded the 7:28 evening train to New York for Judgment Day.

## 14.

Heinrichs arrived[167] in New York at 8:00 a.m. and went directly to the Shelton. A message was waiting for him from Slack, who called on him at 10:00 a.m. Harmon was out of town. Ramsey was upset with Heinrichs. He learned formally from Slack that the investigators met with his wife first, then worked through the board. The investigators started with Bowman and in each instance Ramsey started with a statement about their intention to reconcile the board and secretary-general. Canaan felt that the IC/YMCA was going to force Heinrichs on them and that they felt the newspaper issue was settled. Slack and Ramsey assured them that it was not and forced them to rescind their February 5 decision to take the Nazi paper. The two men felt that the board was fairly representative of Jerusalem and sincere in its desire for work, unless they were liars. They gave eleven reasons asking for Heinrichs' resignation: (1) no misdemeanor or crime, (2) anti-Arab bias, (3) incompatibility, (4) verbal explosions, (5) fighting complex, (6) his brother's engagement, (7) the appeal to the three elders, (8) health, (9) letter to Canaan, (10) provocative attitude of Jerusalem, and (11) staff most divided on earth.

The next day, the International Committee sewed up the affair with a formal memorandum under the title "REPORT ON SETTLEMENT OF NEWSPAPER CONTROVERSY IN JERUSALEM Y.M.C.A."[168] It confirmed that the board had reversed its February 5 decision and cancelled the *Völkischer Beobachter*. The document concluded with its expression of deep obligation to Slack, Ramsey, and the board for their loyalty to the fundamental principles of the Association and for making possible closer and more intimate fellowship in pursuance of the common task in Jerusalem.[169]

The memo made no reference to Heinrichs. He was written out of its history. Even until today, the book *History of the Y.M.C.A. in*

*North America* by C. Howard Hopkins, published first in 1951 and considered an authoritative history of the YMCA Movement through the
mid-twentieth century, ignored Heinrichs' contribution. More than
that, it implied that Ramsey was the secretary-general who had extended
the invitations to the dedication. Hopkins referenced the architectural
and artistic triumph of the building and the world-class facilities for
the time, including the library—which included the Jesus Library, the
heart of the building and spiritual life of the Association, that Dorothy
Heinrichs' aunt, Margaret Hopper, had funded. But there is no mention
of the Hopper, Peterson, or Heinrichs families at all. Perhaps after the
Second World War, some people just preferred to forget the warnings
that Heinrichs had given about the Nazis in Jerusalem.

Heinrichs wrote a six-page letter on the Shelton's stationery to his
wife the same day that the report was released. The bulk of the information he provided came from the private meeting he had held with Slack
the night of September 11, after the International Committee had made
its decision. Hebrew University president Judah Magnes, who had
cooperated well with Heinrichs, refused to have anything further to do
with the Jerusalem YMCA "until Jews were accorded a voting power."[170]
Heinrichs explained how the investigation had proceeded.[171] Slack and
Ramsey had spoken very highly of Mike Haddad[172] in particular,[173] who
had backed Heinrichs. The investigation found "the great majority [of
the board] good, and three or four nasty"[174]—perhaps Heinrichs' triumvirate. The International Committee acknowledged that the board's
responsibility had been put under extreme strain "with the million and
half dollar plant which had been thrown into the lap of…[Jerusalem]…
without their consent…They felt that the Board was committed to an
inter-racial work *unless the Board were liars*."[175] Heinrichs implied that
the nasty minority of the board were liars by reminding Slack that seven
of the board members had pledged never to be satisfied until every for-
eigner was out of the Association.

None of the members of the IC/YMCA believed Heinrichs that
the whole affair was deliberately forced into a major issue by paid Nazi
agents.[176] They proposed that the Germans felt that they were being
deprived of their rights, which had been granted to all other groups,
and that the handling of this issue by the administration had allowed

things to escalate emotionally. The Arabs had simply sided with the Germans against the Jews and had found a new political ally.

We now know that the entire incident did, in fact, erupt immediately after the arrival of Dr. Iven, Joseph Goebbels' Nazi propagandist. What we don't know—although it seems quite possible, indeed probable—is the extent to which the affair arose because of a Nazi reaction to the Jerusalem YMCA's efforts to bring Jewish, Muslim, and Christians together in sport governance, and Heinrichs' early success in working toward that goal—as evidenced in his election to the Palestine Football Association. The sudden decision of the Physical Department Committee not to cooperate with the FASCP in September 1933 might have been the first Nazi nail in that coffin. The eruption of the newspaper incident a few weeks later, after the arrival of a Nazi propagandist sent from Goebbels' Reich Ministry of Public Enlightenment and Propaganda, raises even more eyebrows.

Heinrichs told his wife in the letter that the Arabs believed him to be pro-Jewish because of his stand on the newspaper issue[177] and that they felt he was "possessed of an anti-Arab bias."[178] Conrad Heinrichs was also an issue. Slack characterized Heinrichs' decision to bring him to Jerusalem as an error in judgement.[179] Heinrichs had, in fact, received the board's approval formally. He reminded Slack that it was a temporary arrangement while the two Arabs were being trained in Chicago and Springfield, that his brother had come for half the salary of an American, and that the family had paid his passage and half of his board bills. Heinrichs felt that if his brother had not been present in Jerusalem the preceding three months, he would probably have been made a widower.[180] With regards to the matter of his health, Heinrichs felt content that Middlebury College had used his war injuries as a reason for employing him while the Jerusalem board used it as a reason for his discharge.[181] On the subject of staff, Slack and Ramsey "had never seen in all their experience a staff so divided; such a veritable cesspool of charges, collusion and intrigue. This applied to the entire group."[182]

Heinrichs concluded his letter[183] by saying he had felt it to be a distinct personal compliment to be hated by such men and that Jerusalem had many historic precedents of such hatred. He was upset that Slack and Ramsey had let his family down very badly on a personal level and that he had counted upon friendship, even to the death, as he had known in the 95th Aero Squadron. Apparently, Slack was at the point of tears when he left Heinrichs' hotel room at the Shelton. He came back from the elevator and begged Heinrichs not to let the situation alter their personal friendship. Heinrichs responded by expressing his gratification in the successful outcome of the newspaper issue, which had been well handled and a complete victory.

Heinrichs added the following postscript in his handwriting: "P.S. Slack and Lattof felt most deeply the loss of friendship as evidenced by your having thrown their flowers out the window, or port hole. I fear Conrad let this be known, but I'm glad it is known."[184]

## 15.

Slack eventually apologized by letter to Heinrichs toward the end of the month.[185] Heinrichs broke his silence with Lattof and MacDonald and wrote[186] both calmly, coldly, and cruelly that they had completely forfeited his confidence. Then he wrote to Judge Cressall to fill him in so that he could have an informal advocate in the inner circle of the board to guard his reputation.

In early October, Heinrichs received a letter from Gil Winant, the governor of New Hampshire, likening his discharge from Jerusalem to Christ's Victory in Defeat.[187] He also began working with Slack on a circular to be sent to his seven hundred constituents to tie up the loose ends regarding his departure.[188] Emile Ohan wrote[189] to him that he, Suz, and Haddad were being fired on excuse of non-cooperation and inefficiency but really due to loyalty to Heinrichs. Heinrichs wired the news right to Slack and wrote a letter of protest. Two days later, Harmon sent out the letter to Heinrichs' seven hundred constituents under his own signature, noting that the final settlement of the newspaper incident "was in harmony with Mr. Heinrichs' convictions."[190]

Supportive responses to Harmon's letter began pouring in to Heinrichs from his constituents at the end of the month.[191] Rabbi Stephen Wise wrote one of them.[192] He felt it a great moral victory for Heinrichs to have succeeded in removing the *Völkischer Beobachter* from the Reading Room at the Jerusalem YMCA, and that he should have been rejoicingly and proudly sustained by the IC/YMCA. Wise explained how he was unhappy with much of present-day Christianity, which somehow seemed unable to see the Christlessness of the Nazi attitude toward the Jews. He lamented how people remained silent as long as it was only Jews being murdered, wronged, and degraded in Germany.

Heinrichs responded by saying, "I do not object and rather glory in becoming a casualty in that conflict."[193] The same day, he received word[194] in Middlebury that Lattof was experiencing trouble for dismissing Ohan, Suz, and Haddad. *Falastin* had taken up their case and accused Lattof of revenge on Heinrichs' friends, aided by Canaan and Said.[195] Five days later, Heinrichs recorded in his diary his decision to clear out his last things from Jerusalem and sort and file what he wanted to keep. He then burned the rest in a full basket of rubbish.

Smith visited Jerusalem from Cairo and concurred, in a letter to Slack,[196] that the situation was a mess. A special committee had been formed to deal with staff issues. This committee authorized Lattof to fire the three employees before the year's end, and at his discretion. But one of the men went to the employees and told them of the decision, and so Lattof had to give them notice. He told Slack that Lattof's hand had been forced. Two of the employees started a petition and forced two of the subcommittee members to reverse their decision, which made Canaan and two or three other members of the subcommittee furious. Smith believed that the pressure of people or groups with vested interests would continue to be a factor in the work in Jerusalem.

Clearly, Smith felt that there were still external elements at work in the Jerusalem YMCA. Lattof's actions appear not to have been his own, but forced. Perhaps this was the case at the height of the newspaper controversy, too. Lattof was not immediately removed from the YMCA. In fact, he did not leave until April 1936, just shy of the Berlin Games and only a few weeks after the start of the Great Arab Revolt in Mandate Palestine. This revolt was a general strike that very quickly took on an armed uprising as one of its components. It was not completely subdued by the British until the outbreak of the Second World War. The Nazi role in militarizing this revolt has been debated over the years.[197]

According to conversations with a descendant of Lattof and to family documents that they provided, Nicholas Lattof and his family had to leave Jerusalem suddenly. They went to Harte's house near the Sea of Galilee and laid low for many days before boarding the SS *Excalibur* on May 16, the same ship that had brought the Heinrichses to Jerusalem four years earlier. As the Lattofs departed by car to the port, they apparently hid their children in trunks, perhaps to conceal the fact that they were departing permanently. The Lattofs arrived in New York on May 27, 1936.[198] The precarious situation, concern, and sudden departure of the Lattofs is supported by official YMCA correspondence.[199]

There was increased Nazi activity in Palestine focused on the Olympic Games at the time of the Lattofs' sudden departure. This activity involved Waldemar Fast, who during the Second World War joined the SS and ultimately was appointed to serve under the head of the Gestapo in Turkey.[200] It appears that Heinrichs might not have fully understood the factors influencing Lattof's actions. Perhaps he was simply a young staff member trying to stay neutral in what he recognized as a dangerous war of spooks. As someone who had grown up in the region, he was certainly more astute than Heinrichs when it came to the local Arab politics, and he could monitor the conversations in Arabic without appearing remotely suspicious.

Lattof's departure coincides exactly with the period in which an alleged Palestinian delegation to the 1936 Olympics would have formed. The alleged delegation comprised a football team that included at least one staff member—who claimed to captain the team—from the Jerusalem YMCA. It is certainly possible that Lattof became aware of these Olympic plans and had always been just a man stuck in the middle of forces much stronger than him.

Heinrichs ended 1934 in Middlebury, Vermont, reflecting[201] on the great tragedy of his lifework, the debacle in Jerusalem. He could not forget it and blamed it on his personality. He stopped communicating with Slack towards the end of November,[202] but heard through the grapevine that Mott was wishing that he were back in Jerusalem.[203] He gifted a rug that had been given to him by Lattof to Moody, the president of Middlebury College. He was cutting his ties to all things Jerusalem, taking solace in some final words he received from Judge Cressall in Palestine: "[I]t did not require any of Sherlock Holmes' propensity to discover that the main idea in the minds of the Christian

Arabs, who flooded around you when the new buildings were opened, was to secure control of the whole show, by fair means or foul. We both saw their true attitude over the 'Constitution' question, and, believe me, Mr. Heinrichs, the difficulties of 'control' are not yet over."[204]

Despite the newspaper incident, the Va'ad Leumi took up the question of cooperating with the YMCA once again.[205] Lattof continued Heinrichs' work. Perhaps he was eventually targeted for this, too. It was an ironic twist. Lattof wrote, "Jewish athletic organizations had refused for a while to participate in our activities and accused us of conducting anti-Zionist propaganda. We informed them that the German newspaper no longer appeared in our [R]eading [R]oom. The matter…went up before the 'Vaad Leumi' [sic]…The decision was given in favor of participation. We have had Jewish teams recently taking part in our track and field and swimming championships and basketball matches. Old relationships are being restored."[206]

Heinrichs decided to get in the last word to Slack on December 21, forwarding him the letter from Judge Cressall (a district judge in Palestine and member of the board of the Jerusalem YMCA who eventually died in a Japanese internment camp in Hong Kong during the Second World War). In forwarding the letter, Heinrichs told Slack that "[c]ontrary to your belief, I have embarrassed the International Committee in no way…It is considerable satisfaction to me personally to see that he [Cressall] verifies what you have been unable to agree to, that Arab intrigue was the cause of my ejection…I repeat my warning thrice sounded before, that until the cancer there is completely cut out, there can be no permanent cure…The organization is unsound at the core…This is a day of strong arm methods and we can take a leaf out of Europe's notebook in such times of crisis. Suit your action to the great urgency of your most strategic post."[207]

Heinrichs read until 11:15 p.m. on New Year's Eve.[208] Then he talked the year out with his mother. He called it one of the major crises of his life, and yet if he had to do it over again, he would not have done it any differently.

"I'd rather lose everything and be able to live with my self respect unimpaired."[209]

# CHAPTER 10

# From Berlin to Helsinki

## 1.

Waldo Heinrichs' removal from the Jerusalem YMCA certainly involved a clash of character, but it appears that there was also a subversive agenda. The actions for which Heinrichs was targeted—efforts to bring the interfaith community together, especially through sport—were oddly no longer an issue after his departure. Something must have been achieved in someone's interest.

Nicholas Lattof's monthly report to the board of directors for February 1935, only one year after Heinrichs' ouster, demonstrates an increase in attendance at the Physical Department of 3,226 persons.[1] The Maccabis were back at the Jerusalem YMCA using the swimming pools every Saturday.[2] Even the FASCP held its Second Annual Open Swimming Championship at the Jerusalem YMCA pool.[3] Of all organizations, this one should have created more of a stir. Yet Auburn was listed as a timekeeper at the event alongside FASCP personnel like Arazi, Alouf, and Almagor.[4]

Despite the relative calm, Arab sport was beginning to activate its own national sport bodies. At the Second Annual YMCA Open Track and Field Championships in November 1934, a team registered for the first time from the Arab Palestine Sports Federation (APSF).[5] This federation was the Arab nationalist equivalent to the FASCP. It had been founded after the 1929 riots[6] and possibly grew out of Lattof and Auburn's earliest efforts to form a Palestine Olympic Committee. Author Issam Khalidi points out that in April of 1931 the federation sent invitations to all clubs in Palestine, the newspaper *Falastin* advocated for the clubs' participation in the meeting, and two months later it was constituted from ten clubs.[7] The federation focused on football but was reluctant to call itself the Palestine Football Association because that had already been established and was dominated by Jews.[8]

The APSF became more active in athletic competitions at the Jerusalem YMCA at exactly the time that Frederick Kisch and Yosef Yekutieli boycotted the Berlin Games. The Organizing Committee for the Berlin Games, the Reich Ministry of Public Enlightenment and Propaganda, and the German Consulate in Jerusalem had monitored the creation of the Palestine Olympic Committee. The Organizing Committee notified Consul Wolff in Jerusalem about the recognition[9] and felt that the acceptance of an invitation to the Games by Palestine would subdue the English and American pressure to boycott.[10] It requested from Jerusalem intelligence on the personality of Kisch and the composition of the new committee.[11] Jerusalem provided a report and also assessed that although the Maccabi might not be 100 percent opposed to rejecting the invitation to Berlin, it was likely that most within the Maccabi Movement would be opposed to its attending.[12] The Organizing Committee replied to Wolff that it felt that the Palestine Olympic Association would wait to make a decision until the Americans and English made theirs.[13]

Of course, Kisch and Yekutieli did not wait. They declined Palestine's participation on November 4, 1934. Subsequently, the Organizing Committee informed the consulate in Jerusalem on November 14.[14] It is not unreasonable to question whether Nazi spies at the Jerusalem YMCA were passing this information around to whoever might be their local points of contact in the Arab camp.

At the time, Yekutieli was focused on preparations for the Second Maccabiad, which were scheduled to take place in April 1935. The German Consulate in Jerusalem exchanged correspondence with the Nazi government about the Second Maccabiad. It seems that Goebbels himself might have consented to the decision of the Reichssportführer to allow Maccabi Germany to send a delegation to Tel Aviv: it was the Reich Ministry of Public Enlightenment and Propaganda that sent a correspondence to this effect to Wolff in Jerusalem.[15] Perhaps Goebbels wanted to rise above the boycott behavior exhibited by the Palestine Olympic Committee towards his own Olympic Games?

## 2.

In the lead-up to the Berlin Games, Heinrichs was traveling Europe with a group organized by Sherwood Eddy,[16] assessing the situation on the Continent. Heinrichs followed the lead-up to the Games as almost everyone did, including the boxing match between Joe Louis and Max Schmeling.[17] On his way to Europe aboard the RMS *Queen Mary*, Heinrichs attended the lectures organized by Eddy for the group. He noted that Eddy's choice of speakers on Palestine and Zionism left the Arab point of view untouched.[18] Upon arrival in England, Heinrichs ran into Abramson by chance[19] and they went to Wimbledon for supper and talked much about the Jerusalem YMCA.[20]

While in France, Heinrichs wrote to General Hermann Göring in Germany to try and set up a meeting for the Eddy group.[21] He failed. The group arrived in Berlin one week ahead of the opening ceremony of the Berlin Games. Heinrichs described[22] a massing of humanity on the sidewalks like he had never seen before. The swastika was everywhere and the Unter den Linden, the main boulevard in front of the Brandenburg Gate, was a Via Triumphalis of the Nazi Party. Heinrichs appears to have met with Carl Diem, referring to him only as "the man who has charge of the fire from Olympia to Berlin."[23]

On July 28, Heinrichs called G. D. Sondhi to get tickets to the opening ceremony.[24] He went to the Adler Hotel where Sondhi gave him two passes for the opening of the Olympic Games. They were *Ehrenpass* (honorary passes) for seats in the stand beside the Reichsfürer Himmler, head of the SS.[25] Heinrichs saw the Eddy party off for Warsaw and stayed one extra day to watch the opening ceremony. He noted how the Nazi propaganda was very evident, and very effective.[26]

On the day of the opening ceremony, Heinrichs watched the march past of athletes, but did not record any reference to Palestine in his diary. Strange. One would expect that if Palestine had attended the Games and walked in the march past, Heinrichs would have mentioned it. But he did not.

Very little is known about the alleged Palestinian delegation to the 1936 Olympic Games. So little is known that one must be cautious to draw the conclusion that it existed at all.

There was a lot of Nazi activity at the Jerusalem YMCA. Several of the alleged delegation's members came from the Jerusalem YMCA because in 1947, there was interest at the Association in forming *another* Olympic team for the 1948 Games in London.[27] The alleged delegation comprised a football team captained by a staff member from the Jerusalem YMCA. When this individual moved to the United States after the Second World War, the curriculum vitae on record at his place of employment listed him as Captain, Palestine Soccer Team, Olympics, Berlin 1936.[28] In 1965, an article identified this individual as "the secretary and the technical advisor of the Palestine Sports Federation from 1935 - 1947."[29] Khalidi notes that he was part of the first Arab Palestinian national football team to compete against the American University of Beirut in 1931.[30] *Falastin* wrote about this team, saying, "[I]f this team will be formed, it will be [one of] the strongest teams in Palestine among the Jewish and the British...It will refute the Jewish claims and the Zionist propaganda that the Palestinians are ignorant and have no relation with sports."[31]

Palestine was not listed as an entrant in the football section of the official report that the Organizing Committee published after the 1936 Berlin Games. The only Arab entrant in the Olympic football competition in 1936 was Egypt, which was eliminated by Austria in the first round. But in December 1961, the *Springfield Sunday Republican* reported a claim that a Palestinian soccer team participated in the 1936 Olympic Games and was eliminated in the third round.[32] What appear to be the interview notes associated with this article do not include the same claim.[33] The only reference to Palestine in the official report of the Games is the notice of the invitation sent to Kisch and Yekutieli on June 22, 1934. Perhaps the delegation was not there after all—at least in an official capacity.

In 1954, another article claimed that the alleged delegation's members were housed in the Athletes' Village: "They placed us in separate villages...and the only time we met was on the field of competition."[34] This article identified the captain as a "one-time soccer player

214

on the team representing Egypt in the 1936 Olympics at Berlin, Germany."[35] But the official report of the 1936 Olympic Games identified the Egyptian team members, and none of the names or photos of athletes associated with the Egyptian team appears to be any Palestinians from the Jerusalem YMCA.

It is curious that the financials of the Jerusalem YMCA for 1936 were not identified alongside adjacent years in the Kautz Family YMCA archives in Minnesota. There is a memorandum to Frank Slack[36] documenting his receipt of a copy of the proposed budget for 1936 on March 6. There is also a copy of a letter to the Central Hanover Bank and Trust Company of the same date,[37] referencing the attached 1936 budget. But in both cases, the budget that is supposed to be attached is missing from the archive.

There is some documentation in the Israel State Archives to question the possible involvement of Waldemar Fast, the person who joined the SS.[38] His German Travel Office, located at the Fast Hotel, was responsible for providing "all particulars"[39] regarding the Berlin Games for those interested in traveling to see them. Given his profession in Jerusalem and promotion of the Games, Fast was probably also responsible for the display of posters that advertised the Olympics and Germany in eighteen locations around Mandate Palestine, including at Jerusalem locations like his family's Fast Hotel and the Tempelbank.[40] In early 1934, Heinrichs had informed Slack about a "tourist guide"[41] who was "trying to blackmail"[42] the Jerusalem YMCA as part of the Nazi newspaper incident. Was this Waldemar Fast?

What about other German Palestinians? Although no archival evidence was found to connect them directly to an alleged Palestinian delegation to the Berlin Games, such persons were citizens of Palestine and would have been eligible to join a team if one had been formed. We know that Nazis were serving on the board of the Deutscher Sportverein Jerusalem[43] before the Olympic Games and that this club was just down the road from the Jerusalem YMCA. Nothing in the archival material about the settlement of the Nazi newspaper incident suggests that the German Palestinian Nazis terminated their connection to the Jerusalem YMCA.

For the period between the 1948–1949 Arab-Israeli War and before the 1972 Munich Massacre, there were only two published references to this alleged Palestinian delegation that were identified in archival records. One claimed that the delegation was Egyptian[44] and the other that it was Palestinian.[45] After the Munich Massacre, one article from 1979 referred to the same captain, but this time he was referred to as captain "of the Middle East Soccer Team on which he played during the 1936 Olympics."[46]

A couple of final clues to the origins of the alleged Palestinian delegation to Berlin can be found in Dylan Baun's research on Lebanon's connections to the 1936 Berlin Games.[47] Baun states that "the best available option to experience the games within an official capacity was to fund and organize a non-participating delegation. Pierre Gemayel formed a mission for this purpose under the banner of the Lebanese Football Federation."[48] Baun also notes that the Nazis hosted a number of events in parallel with the Games.[49] One of these included an international football conference organized by someone called Herr Schreker.[50] The conference took place between August 13 and 14.[51] Lebanon was able to affiliate to the IAAF and FIFA at this conference.[52] The Games ended on August 16. Did the alleged Palestinian delegation to Berlin attend Schreker's international football conference? Was the delegation trying to be admitted to the IAAF and FIFA like the Lebanese, but under the banner of the Arab Palestine Sports Federation?

Despite Lebanon's affiliation to FIFA at this conference, the origins of the Lebanese delegation remain shrouded in secrecy (and the Palestinian delegation even more so). How would the Lebanese and Palestinian delegations to Berlin be remembered and interpreted if fascism had been victorious in the Second World War? It is worth imagining these alternate trajectories. For an indication of what might have happened, we need only look north to Lebanon after Gemayel returned from the Games. In his book *Pity the Nation* about the Lebanese civil war, Robert Fisk relates how Gemayel's participation in the Nazi spectacle inspired his founding of the Phalange Party, a political movement with fascist leanings.[53] The Phalange's military wing was called the Forces Libanaises. In 1982, these forces eventually perpetrated the Sabra and Shatila massacre of Palestinian refugees, one of the war's most atrocious acts. In a meeting with Gemayel, Fisk was unable to get the Phalange leader to discuss much more than his role as captain of the football team and president of the Lebanese Football Federation.[54] In a subsequent meeting with Gemayel, Fisk noted that the former football player did "not wish to talk further about his visit to Berlin in 1936."[55]

If the alleged Palestinian delegation participated in this Nazi football conference, it would increase the likelihood of direct engagement between the Nazis and Palestinian delegation members. Many people looked differently at the Berlin Games after the Second World War, but those who in hindsight had misgivings about attending them always had the viable excuse that they had been engaged in an official Olympic (rather than Nazi) activity. For those who attended the Games in the more personal way described by Baun, such an excuse would be less credible.

The alleged Palestinian delegation to the Berlin Games—if it existed at all—is one of the great unsolved sport mysteries of the last century, perhaps even its greatest secret.

## 3.

In 1937, Yekutieli received notification from Sondhi that Ceylon had withdrawn from hosting the Second Western Asiatic Games.[56] Sondhi asked Palestine to take on the responsibility of organizing them. It took some time to decide. Ultimately, Palestine had to cancel the games because of the instability caused by the Great Arab Revolt.[57] The Third Maccabiad, also scheduled for the spring of 1938,[58] had to be postponed indefinitely (and did not take place until 1951—after the creation of the State of Israel). Nevertheless, local sport activity with the Jerusalem YMCA continued throughout the disturbances. The finals of its tennis championship took place the day after a bombing in which Arabs had died.[59] The finalists were Jews and Arabs. Despite pressure to cancel, the Association held the event and the majority of winners were Jews. Everyone still stayed for the tea that followed, and there was no indication of the political problems facing the country.

Despite the political difficulties and deterioration in public safety, Kisch made plans to attend the IOC Session in Egypt in 1938.[60] He and

Yekutieli even discussed inviting Count Baillet-Latour to Palestine, despite the political unrest.[61] Participation at the 1940 Olympic Games was a condition for Kisch to be eligible for membership on the IOC board. Kisch asked Schmidt to arrange the meeting with Baillet-Latour.[62] Cooperation with Arab sport clubs was on the agenda. The Jewish position[63] stressed that it had always been looking for sport cooperation with the Arabs. Because of the Arab Revolt, it was nearly impossible to cooperate with them at the time, but it was hoped that cooperation could be achieved in the near future.

The *New York Times* carried news of the meeting between Kisch and Baillet-Latour.[64] Kisch also convened a meeting of the Palestine Olympic Committee at the San Remo Hotel in Tel Aviv to brief them on the meeting and begin preparations for the 1940 Olympic Games.[65] At this meeting, Yekutieli became the vice president of the Palestine Olympic Association, Nahum Heth took his place as honorary secretary, and Kisch moved the organization's headquarters to his home in Haifa,[66] informing Lausanne accordingly.[67]

By 1939, the clouds of the Second World War were looming on the horizon. Once again, Heinrichs was touring Europe for a second time with a Sherwood Eddy group to assess the political situation. He managed to see Humphrey Bowman in London. They patched fences over lunch at the United University Club.[68] By August 22, Heinrichs arrived in Rome where he stayed at the YMCA at Piazza Indipendenza.[69] He wrote to his parents that he had initially scheduled to leave Europe on September 9, had bumped it up to September 2, and with the war scare, wished he had scheduled to leave Europe on August 26.[70] The Second World War broke out five days after he wrote the letter. In describing the scene of a young mother (who had twin girls of two and a half years) being dumped on a train platform at 3:00 a.m. by passport officials, Heinrichs wrote, "I hope God will bring justice on the men that create physical and mental suffering on millions of…innocents."[71]

Heinrichs got out on one of the last ships to leave Europe. On September 9,[72] safely across the Atlantic on the St. Lawrence River in Quebec, he wrote to his family a gripping account of his voyage. He described how the cables, radio, and telephone had been taken over by the French three days prior to his departure. He left Cherbourg on

September 2 only two hours after the SS *Athenia* sailed from Glasgow. They were just two hundred miles south of her location when German torpedoes struck her. On board his ship, all radios were confiscated, but a few passengers hid theirs and word of the *Athenia* spread. They zigzagged across the Atlantic in four days. Everyone had to wear life preservers at all times, even in the bathrooms. Many women did not change their clothes for the entire journey. Portholes were painted over, smoking banned on deck. It was very tense, with many of the passengers on board having had friends or family on the *Athenia*.

## 4.

The British subdued the Great Arab Revolt in Palestine just before the war. Waldemar Fast escaped to Germany and joined the SS. He facilitated prisoner exchanges in 1941, 1943, and 1944 between German Palestinians (who had been interned by the British in camps in Palestine) and Jews in concentration camps in Europe (who had relatives in Palestine).[73] The British arrested Dr. Tawfiq Canaan on September 3, the day that Great Britain declared war against Germany.[74] They interned Canaan for nine weeks[75] for his "friendly connections to the Germans."[76] He, his wife, and her sister were accused of propaganda for Adolf Hitler's Germany.[77] According to Khaled Nashef, writing in the *Jerusalem Quarterly*, "It is not known whether this was the official charge, nor do we know the type of court in which they were tried."[78]

Prior to his arrest, Canaan had become president of the Jerusalem YMCA sometime in the late 1930s. Dimitri Salameh had replaced him by 1939.[79] Canaan's name remained on the letterhead of the organization through 1942, when it was replaced by that of Stubbs.[80] Maccabi ramped up its sport cooperation with British military teams, organizing events in aid of the War Comforts Fund.[81] Kisch reenlisted and became the Chief Engineer of the Allied Eighth Army in North Africa. Yekutieli tried to enlist with the British army, but the British turned him down and suggested that he serve in a Palestinian unit where he could obtain a non-commissioned rank.[82]

The Jerusalem YMCA, mindful that America might enter the war, began to think about its American staff.[83] There was a chance that the Germans would reach Palestine, and in such case, Miller (the secretary-general who replaced Heinrichs and would eventually be considered for the position of mayor of Jerusalem as a neutral respected resident of the city) appointed Jamal, Gelat, Atalla, Canaan, Krikorian, and Fisher to represent Slack and look after the equipment.[84] Throughout the war, the Jerusalem YMCA's Physical Department remained active, particularly with Hapoel, and the war years witnessed a comparatively peaceful engagement between Jewish and Arab sport organizations. The Jerusalem YMCA was also extensively involved in supporting the war effort with three hostels for soldiers in operation, facilities shared with American troops and the Red Cross, and services provided to prisoners of war and Polish refugees.[85]

## 5.

In 1941, Heinrichs visited his wife's family in Hawaii. He stopped by Pearl Harbor and spoke at the University of Hawaii on the situation in Palestine.[86] At an August lecture at the Rotary Club, he incorrectly argued that Japan was in no position to take on the United States in war.[87] On December 7, 1941, the Japanese proved him wrong when they attacked Pearl Harbor.[88] Heinrichs immediately began actions towards reenlistment, even though he was disabled from his injuries in the First World War. He reported to Fort Ethan Allen on January 6, 1942, for his comprehensive medical.[89] As a result of a minor hernia, his aspirations to join the Air Corps faded.[90] Then he received word that Air Corps Intelligence might be able to use him.[91] On April 23, his orders came in. He gave his last class at Middlebury on May 13, and students broke out in cheers as he entered the room in his new uniform.[92] Heinrichs shipped off to serve in Combat Intelligence.[93]

From time to time during his war service, Heinrichs would think about Palestine. In a letter to his wife, he confessed to a serious case of nostalgia, not for the YMCA but for the country and its climate.[94] On September 1, 1943, Heinrichs was promoted to the rank of lieutenant colonel[95] and he put on his silver leaves for the first time.[96] In October, his son Junior, the once-young boy who had scaled the Jerusalem YMCA's pillars during its dedication and triumphed over Lord

Melchett's son in its pool, went before the draft board in the United States for the war.[97] Upon selection, Heinrichs wrote to him, "Dearest Soldier Son…I am very proud of you, as any father should be and especially a father who is seeing service in his Second World War."[98]

Waldo "Fish" Heinrichs was eventually relieved of duty in October 1944 after serving overseas in Great Britain.[99] He died suddenly at Middlebury College on June 15, 1959. The college's newsletter published an announcement, remembering him as a man who was honest and forthright in his beliefs in a better world, deeply religious by nature, one who held the highest ideals of patriotism and served his country with distinction and self-sacrifice in two great wars, vigorous and uncompromising toward error and sham, but modest and gracious in all social relations. Waldo Heinrichs was generous, understanding, and sympathetic toward his fellow men.[100]

On April 7, 1943, Fred Kisch was killed in action. He died on the same day that Claus von Stauffenberg sustained the injuries—depicted in the opening scene of the film *Valkyrie*—that ultimately impaired the German's ability to carry out the assassination of Hitler in the July 20 plot. The *New York Times* carried news of Kisch's death[101] and his commemoration by Field Marshal Bernard Law Montgomery.[102] Fred Kisch was posthumously promoted to brigadier general, and the Federation of the Amateur Sports Clubs of Palestine organized an annual Brigadier Kisch Memorial Track and Field Championship in his name.[103] Gad Frumkin, the first Jewish judge on Palestine's Supreme Court (who had worked with Kisch to try to buy the Wailing Wall in the 1920s) took over as president of the Palestine Olympic Committee.[104]

## 6.

The comparatively peaceful relations during the war between Jews and Arabs in Mandate Palestine did not last long after its conclusion. The APSF reconstituted and began a new campaign to join the international sport governing bodies, only to be directed to the Federation of the Amateur Sports Clubs of Palestine because only one organization in each country could represent a nation.[105] The battle in FIFA was particularly sharp, with the APSF and Palestine Football Association applying significant pressure in support of their cases in the lead-up to the FIFA Congress in the summer of 1946.[106]

On July 22, 1946, a beautiful and sunny day in Jerusalem, the chirp of the Holy City's birds suddenly ceased and it seemed as though its pealing church bells and the calls of the *muezzin* were drowned out forever. A massive bomb planted by Jewish operatives of Lehi, an extreme Zionist faction, obliterated the Secretariat of the Government of Palestine and the headquarters of the British Armed Forces in Palestine in the southwest wing of the King David Hotel, immediately across Julian's Way from the Jerusalem YMCA. The seismic tremor of the blast reverberated across the golden walls and the roofs of the Old City and through its surrounding valleys. Plaster fell down from the Jerusalem YMCA's beautiful, Bezalel-frescoed ceilings, its windows shattered.

Julius Jacobs and many members and staff of the Jerusalem YMCA died, their lives ended in a smoldering, dusty pile of pancaked floors, concrete, twisted metal, and office furniture. As papers blew around the more than eighty corpses of lost souls buried in the rubble, Jerusalem had entered a new age: the first spark of a grinding civil war in the city had been struck and its neighborhoods would be barricaded. The area surrounding the Jerusalem YMCA was sealed behind barbed wire, and the work of the Physical Department was greatly affected.

No one had ever seen anything like it before in Jerusalem. Although the city had been besieged over forty-six times since 1500 BCE,[107] there was always an awareness of an approaching conquering army, a long siege, and the mercy—or lack thereof—of the eventual victor over the vanquished. Not in modern warfare.

Al Miller wrote to Dalton F. McClelland in New York[108] and explained how the premises had been taken over by the military. No one could enter without presenting Association membership and identity cards. The athletic field was covered with tents and occupied by troops. There was only one approach to the building, guarded by machine gun towers. When Mildred and Alvah Miller sent out their annual holiday letter for 1946, they shared the sad news engulfing Jerusalem. For them, the YMCA had become an example of the armed camp into which Palestine had unfortunately been turned: "It calls for a stretch of the imagination to think of Palestine as the Land of Peace and of Jerusalem as the Holy City."[109]

## 7.

In late 1946, Paul Hartman came to join the Jerusalem YMCA's Physical Department. Its Physical Director was leaving to the United States. By early 1947, Hartman was considering organizing a *second* Jerusalem YMCA delegation to the Olympic Games, this time to London in 1948. He noted in a correspondence to Harold T. Friermood, a member of the US Olympic Committee, that "I think it should be possible as…a group went in 1936 and they are still talking about it."[110] In a subsequent correspondence[111] to Friermood, he wrote that the *Palestine Post* had published about Palestine entering teams in the Olympics. Hartman was new and had little background in the "file". He was unaware of a national governing body for Olympic sports in the country. The paper had carried a story about Palestine Hockey preparing for the Games. He had also received a call from Tom Moffatt, a sports broadcaster, inquiring about it. He asked Friermood to consult with Avery Brundage or Gustavos Kirby about it and get more information. He termed the Olympic proposal "a Zionist hope phrased in terms of fact."[112]

Hartman then wrote to the Chief Secretary of the Palestine government to ask for the name of the committee that might be in charge of organizing such a delegation.[113] Before he got a reply, United Nations delegates trying to figure out a solution to the problems in Palestine began "descending upon…[the Jerusalem YMCA]…in hordes."[114] Miller wrote that practically all of the YMCA had been taken over by them[115] These meetings interfered in Hartman's ability to follow up on the Olympic delegation to London. He wrote[116] to Friermood and told him that he had reached out to the government but was not sure what committee could be in charge of the Olympic planning, unless FASCP had been recognized by an international body. He acknowledged that in that case, Arabs interested in going to the Games would be eliminated from consideration because they were not part of the FASCP. He did not say that this was on the basis of the Arabs' own refusal to join.

A few days later, Hartman received the reply to his inquiry to the government from the office of the Chief Secretary, which confirmed that the Palestine Olympic Committee had been recognized in 1934 by the International Olympic Committee.[117] The reply included the current names of the members (including Judge Frumkin, who had replaced Kisch) and the postal address in Haifa.

Hartman was obviously too new in Palestine to understand the complex history of the "file" or the history of Jewish-Arab sport relations through the Association. Perhaps after the Second World War, the role of the Nazis in destroying the Jerusalem YMCA's work toward a unified representational Olympic body for Palestine was purposely forgotten by all sides.

Still, Hartman's relative ignorance did not prevent his writing directly to Brundage, who by this time was on the Executive Committee of the IOC (and would soon become the IOC president). In the IOC archives, there has been filed for decades an anonymous report, dated September 13, 1947, on the situation of sport in Palestine. The report appears to have been distributed among IOC members to discuss the "file" and used to inform its discussions about the Palestine Olympic Committee's request to participate in both the St. Moritz Winter and the London Summer Games in 1948. This report was critical in determining that Palestine/Israel would not participate.

In fact, this anonymous report was lifted verbatim from Hartman's letter to Brundage of the same day.[118] Hartman had sent a copy to Friermood, and this copy, which documents the origins of the report used by the IOC in its decision-making, survived in the Kautz Family YMCA Archives in Minnesota. In a bitter irony for Jewish national sport, the Jerusalem YMCA unknowingly gave Brundage his second opportunity to stifle Jewish sport aspirations. After all, it was Brundage who had frustrated the American boycott effort against the Nazi Olympics in the 1930s.[119]

Hartman's report was biased against the Jewish sport interests and sympathetic to the Arab position, declaring that "[t]he Federation of [the] Amateur Sports Clubs of Palestine is the apparent recognized organization in International Sports. It is 100% Jewish and was organized at a time when Jewish power was on the rise and the Arabs had not been awakened as to what was going on. I believe they had a small representation before the difficulties of 1935, but had no say in administration of the Federation."[120] All that Hartman could see was the sport situation's terminus, not its origins. And yet in expressing his fervent belief, Hartman appears to have unknowingly made a vague reference to Heinrichs' brief stint representing Arab sport interests on the Palestine Football Association and the Physical Department's discussions to join the FASCP between 1930 and 1933. In a handwritten note on the reverse of Friermood's copy of the letter, Hartman noted that he did not even write to Nahum Heth, the honorary secretary of the Palestine Olympic Committee, until three days after the date of the report.[121] This means that he had drawn his conclusions without even speaking to the Jewish side of the equation.

Hartman's assessment of the APSF also included some inaccuracies. He wrote, "They have a good group of officers and the Federation includes all Arab clubs in the country, including both Moslem and Christian. They hold a number of championships each year and conduct leagues in Football and Basketball. They are primarily a young organization as Sports are new to Arabs. They have come a long way in fifteen or twenty years without any outside help to speak of."[122] This statement could not have been further from the truth. Arab sport had strengthened tremendously because of the Jerusalem YMCA's involvement and because of the Arab teams' constant encounters on the field of play with the Jewish teams. In a typed note that he included, Hartman deviated from the historical mission of the Association: "Contrary to what we would like to believe, sports competition between Arabs and Jews would stimulate trouble between the two peoples rather than make the situation better, although I feel that the participants themselves would benefit from a more mutual understanding between individuals, but not in the political situation."[123]

Hartman was present in Jerusalem for the bombing of Ben Yehuda Street, a massive attack by Arab operatives against the heart of New Jerusalem's Jewish business district. In scale, it rivaled the attack against the King David Hotel. He wrote to Friermood about it. "The bombing of the Jewish Business section the other morning was terrific. They say that it is many times worse than you can picture in your mind. We have made no attempt to see it, but several from the [American] Consulate were up and say it is just unbelievable. It broke windows more than a mile away."[124] The bombing killed fifty-eight and injured one hundred and twenty-three people.

As the country slid into total civil war at the end of 1947 and early 1948, the *New York Times* reported that Elo Katz, the coach of the Palestine Olympic team preparing for London, was murdered in Magazi camp near Gaza.[125] Yekutieli also experienced tragedy. The saddest day of his life was in April when one of his six children, a son named Amnon, was killed in battle as a member of the Palmach, the elite fighting force of the Haganah (which eventually became the Israel Defence Forces). The Palestine Olympic Committee attempted to take part in the Winter Olympic Games in St. Moritz, Switzerland, but this was rejected by the office of the Chief Secretary, citing financial technicalities.[126] As things got worse, the UN considered Miller to serve as the neutral mayor of Jerusalem in the conflict.[127] He wrote to McClelland in New York about the imminent collapse of the Arab resistance.[128] On May 11, the Jerusalem YMCA became a neutral relief center for refugees.[129] David Ben Gurion declared the establishment of the State of Israel on May 14, 1948. The next day, the Jerusalem YMCA went under the flag of the International Red Cross[130] to protect it from being taken over by either side in the conflict and as Arab armies invaded Mandate Palestine—now Israel.

As the war intensified, it was difficult for the YMCA to avoid the associated risks. On June 2, 1948, an armored car associated with the Stern faction claimed that it was sniped from the area of the Jerusalem YMCA, injuring three of the vehicle's occupants.[131] The Stern group was formally called Lohamei Herut Israel, or Lehi, and was constituted by some of the more militant Zionists associated with Betar. Lehi sent a letter to the International Red Cross threatening that all Arab employees had to be removed from the Jerusalem YMCA by midday or the Stern group would cease to regard the Geneva area comprising the Jerusalem YMCA and King David Hotel as neutral.[132] The Haganah came to inspect the property. In a letter to McClelland in New York, Miller described the visit: "Friday morning, we were visited by some thirty Haganah, under the leadership of a personal friend of mine, a former tennis player of the [YMCA]. They were extremely courteous, but said that, to allay this constant difficulty, they wanted to make a complete search...Naturally, we welcomed this, and they were most thorough and completely satisfied."[133]

In this respect, the Jerusalem YMCA's reconciliation efforts through sport over the years had borne some fruit. An individual action based on relationships built through sport led to the YMCA being protected by Jews against some of their own, more extreme Zionist factions. A Haganah seal was placed on the door of the Jerusalem YMCA's tower to vouch for the security of the building, proof that the Jesus Tower was not being used as a sniper's nest.[134]

Nonetheless, Hartman's predictions that sport would not make a significant impact on the broader political situation also rang true in the sniping incident. Miller told McClelland[135] that after the search, he was informed that since the area was behind Jewish lines, command would not permit any Arab of military age to remain. Twenty-five staff needed to be evacuated to behind the Arab lines in exchange for their not being taken prisoners of war. The order was put into effect and the last Arab staff of the Jerusalem YMCA were evacuated to behind Arab lines on June 26.[136] It was the end of an era.

## 8.

Shortly thereafter, the Organizing Committee for the 1948 London Olympics sent the Palestine Olympic Committee notification that it would not be permitted to participate in the Olympic Games. The POC sent a strong telegram of protest[137] to Sigfrid Edström, who by now had assumed the presidency of the IOC. Arab states had rejected the notion that Israel be allowed to participate in the Games,[138] and on July 23, the JTA reported that the IOC rejected Israel's appeal against barring its delegation.[139]

The IOC, however, discussed the matter again on July 27. Yehoshuah Alouf wrote[140] to Edström from the Prince of Wales Hotel, where he was waiting for the IOC decision. Alouf reminded Edström of their consultations in Paris in 1924 and that the Jewish sports movement had followed his advice on how to organize sports in Palestine. Jewish Palestinian sport clubs had always been open to all in Palestine, without distinction to race or creed. He reminded him of how they were affiliated to international federations and the IOC between 1932 and 1934, how they had participated in the First Western Asiatic Games and the

Women's World Games, and organized numerous sports meetings with neighboring countries, also traveling with football teams to Europe, America, and Australia. By 1948, the same organization had received the invitation to London, only to receive a subsequent message citing Edström specifically for barring them from the Games on the grounds that Palestine no longer existed as a country. He asked to appear personally before the IOC and appeal Israel's case.

Edström replied: "The Committee has considered the question and while we also regret that this matter has been raised so late, we must inform you that the question is so involved at present, that the Committee cannot reach a decision at this time."[141]

The JTA reported the criticism of Edström's action in his home country of Sweden.[142] The Palestine Olympic Committee replied to him by telling him that they had changed the name of the committee from the Palestine Olympic Committee to the Israel Olympic Committee without any change whatsoever to the constitution of the affiliated sport bodies.[143] Still, the IOC would not concede. Four days later, the JTA reported that the IAAF voted to defer discussions on the subject: "The International Amateur Athletic Association, by a vote of 32 to 14, decided today not to continue discussions on whether it should recognize the Sports Federation Israel, thus leaving the question as to whether the Israeli delegation to the Olympics is eligible for participation in the international sports gathering in abeyance. Joshua Alouf, Israeli representative to the Olympics, walked out on the meeting after his appeal for recognition was turned down."[144]

Nine months later, in April 1949, the renamed Olympic Committee of Israel wrote to the IOC in Lausanne. It used Kisch's old letterhead from the Palestine Olympic Committee, still bearing Kisch's name. Typing dashes over the two words "PALESTINE OLYMPIC" to cross out the old name, the Committee typed in all caps above them "OLYMPIC COMMITTEE OF ISRAEL."[145] By this point in time, armistice lines had been agreed between most of the belligerents, and the Green Line was nearly established.[146] It was clear that Israel as a state was not going to be wiped out in the way the invading Arab armies had hoped. Heth wrote that since the UN Security Council had recommended that Israel be recognized, there was no reason whatsoever for the IOC not to recognize its Olympic committee.[147]

The IOC replied in January 1950, informing the Olympic Committee of Israel that it would take a decision at its Session in Copenhagen in May 1950.[148] Edström insisted that Israel comply with IOC regulations regarding the nondiscrimination-in-sport clause.[149] Heth replied in writing in March. "I am instructed by our committee to submit herewith our assurance that our committee - as it did in the past - will also in the future - always and in all respects - adhere solemnly to the olympic [sic] principle of religious and racial indiscrimination between athletes and others, and that accordingly - all athletes in our country without distinction of religion or race will be admitted by the national federations of Israel and also recognized by our authority."[150]

But once again, the IOC did not make a decision. Daniel Ferris of the Amateur Athletic Union traveled to Israel and sent a report on the situation to Brundage, informing him that the Arabs in Israel had been admitted to citizenship and were competing in sports in Israel.[151] His visit seemed to influence positively the IOC's perception. In March 1951, Edström met with Minister Abraham Nissan of Israel in Sweden. He explained to him that the IOC would recognize the Olympic Committee of Israel if it guaranteed that Arabs could compete for Israel and if Israel committed not to take part in the Mediterranean Games.[152] Subsequently, the two men agreed that the Olympic Committee of Israel could be "sleeping members" for the remainder of 1951 and that effective January 1952, a full valid membership would be granted.[153] Maccabi and Hapoel, overcoming their historic rivalry, agreed to cooperate to form the new committee: each had petitioned the IOC separately to be recognized as the Olympic Committee of Israel.[154]

In the lead-up to the 1952 Helsinki Summer Games, Betar (the more militant Zionist faction) also put forward its own application to the IOC.[155] Minister Nissan intervened, informing Edström that Betar was a political organization and that the IOC "need not take any consideration about"[156] its application.

Finally, on December 31, 1951, the IOC recognized the Olympic Committee of Israel, and it asked the Organizing Committee of the 1952 Games at Oslo and Helsinki to send out their invitations to the

Jewish State. The IOC wished the Olympic Committee of Israel the best of success and said that it was trusting it "to develop the Olympic ideal in your country."[157]

## 9.

Yosef Yekutieli entered the stadium at the opening ceremony of the 1952 Helsinki Games. He was not Israel's flag bearer but was nonetheless proud. The Maccabi soldier was the last man standing, with Kisch dead and Heinrichs long gone. His accreditation card[158] from the Helsinki Games can be found in the Joseph Yekutieli Maccabi Sport Archives, documenting his long journey from Bresa in the late nineteenth century to Ottoman Palestine, British Mandate Palestine, and eventually *Medinat Yisrael*—the State of Israel. Eventually a recipient of Israel's highest civilian honor, the Israel Prize, his family asked that I stress one thing about his life to readers: that all that he did for sport was as a volunteer. Yekutieli died in 1984.

# CHAPTER 11

# From Munich to Atlanta: Palestine's New Olympic Moment

## 1.

The official report of the XX Olympiad that took place in 1972 in Munich, Germany, included an unusual second chapter. Titled "September 5, 1972," it presented an eerily cold treatment of the barbarity that occurred at the Munich Olympic Games. Beginning with a description of the security procedures that clearly failed, it then provided a time line of the events that led to the deaths of eleven members of Israel's delegation, one German police officer, and the majority of the Palestinian attackers. Many books have been written about what happened in Munich. This book is not an effort to be another one. Yet it is important to convey in brief to a new generation what transpired.

At 4:55 a.m., the first shots were heard in the Olympic Village coming from the direction of Connollystrasse. The Israeli delegation was housed in number 31 Connollystrasse. Police responded but were blocked by men with machine guns. At 5:30 a.m., the first demands were made from the balcony of the apartment where the Israeli hostages were being held. For nearly twelve hours, the Israelis and their captors were inside the apartment in the Athletes' Village. Then the first demand was made to transport them to another location. Two helicopters eventually arrived and took the men to Fürstenfeldbruck

Air Base. The botched rescue attempt at the air base resulted in all the hostages dying.

Two of the hostages died in the Olympic Village, one of them castrated in front of the others to terrorize them. The other nine hostages died in the shoot-out, tied to their seats in the two helicopters, one of which caught fire from an exploding hand grenade, burning those inside.

## 2.

September 13, 1993 was a sunny day on the White House lawn. Hundreds were gathered across its green expanse, gathered with hopes, history, and memories of past pain and bygone bloodshed. As the master of ceremonies called out the names of dignitaries to their front-row seats and stage, the crowd applauded. Television cameras beamed unbelievable images around the world. Israeli and Palestinian leaders were about to sign a historic agreement.

Assembled on the stage were Shimon Peres,[1] Mahmoud Abbas,[2] Andrei Kozyrev,[3] Warren Christopher,[4] Yasser Arafat,[5] Yitzhak Rabin,[6] and William Jefferson Clinton.[7] They congregated around the same wooden table upon which US president Jimmy Carter, Egyptian president Anwar Sadat, and Israeli prime minister Menachem Begin had signed the Camp David Accords in 1978. The desk was about to witness another historic agreement: the Oslo I Accord. Known formally as the Declaration of Principles on Interim Self-Government Arrangements (between the Israeli and Palestinian parties to the Arab-Israeli conflict), all parties were hopeful, but each warned that the agreement was only the first step down the long road of healing.

At the same time, Ahmed Al Qudwa, known within the Palestine Liberation Organization (PLO) as Haj Mutlaq, and Omar Hussein Ali Shuweikeh, known as Abu Hussein, were ready to coordinate their moves from their small and humble office in Tunis and write to the IOC in Lausanne. Since July 1972 (only two months before the Munich Massacre), Haj Mutlaq had been president of a reconstituted (at least in name) Palestine Olympic Committee.[8] Abu Hussein had been its secretary-general. By the time of the Oslo I Accord, they had been working behind the scenes with the IOC through Tunisian and Kuwaiti intermediaries toward Palestine's new Olympic moment.

At the time of the Accord, Tunisia was hosting the PLO leadership, which Israel had ejected from Lebanon in its 1982 invasion of the country. Thus, Tunisian sport officials served as intermediaries.[9] In the case of Kuwaiti mediation, the Palestine Olympic Committee was able to rely on the fact that it had maintained headquarters there in the 1980s. But Kuwait still had a bone to pick with the Palestinians, and the mediation had to be handled carefully: although Chairman Arafat had denounced the invasion of Kuwait by Iraq, he proposed a conditional Iraqi withdrawal in which Israel would also withdraw from the West Bank and Gaza Strip. For this reason, Kuwait's Olympic advocacy for the Palestine file actually occurred through the Kuwaiti president of the Olympic Council of Asia (OCA), Sheikh Ahmed Al Sabah, but not the national Olympic committee of Kuwait. Sheikh Ahmed's father was Sheikh Fahad. He had chaired the OCA before Iraqi soldiers murdered him in the 1990 invasion. In the 1980s, Sheikh Fahad had been a champion of Palestinian Olympic rights in Asia.[10] He helped carve out Palestine's position on the Continent. Given Sheikh Fahad's background of Palestinian advocacy, it was perfectly logical that his son Sheikh Ahmed would carry this on by supporting the Palestinians' historic affiliation to the IOC through the OCA—despite the lingering bad blood between the State of Kuwait and the PLO.

As soon as the Oslo I Accord was concluded, Abu Hussein signed his letter to IOC president Juan Antonio Samaranch. He reached for the POC's official stamp. The stamp had traveled the Middle East, from Beirut to Kuwait City to Tunis. Since 1972, it had witnessed all of the Palestinians' hopes as well as their string of strategic failures. Abu Hussein stamped the letter with a thud reminiscent of the artillery shells of the Palestinian resistance. Everyone hoped this would be the last thud.

In the center of Palestine's Olympic stamp was a map of the territory of Mandate Palestine,[11] ensconced in two ears of wheat. Above the map were the Olympic rings. The map's ink shimmered like blood spilled on the land from generations of potential athletes who had instead become fighters. Now their blood was drying. A new page was being turned.

In his letter, Abu Hussein informed President Samaranch that "[s]ince 1979, we have submitted an application to the International Olympic Committee."[12] He recounted how the organization had contacted President Samaranch many times in Morocco, Moscow, and Kuwait to discuss Palestine's affiliation to the IOC. Now Abu Hussein felt that the Palestine Olympic Committee had fulfilled "all the terms wanted to this affiliation."[13] Specifically, Abu Hussein cited that the PLO had finally acquired, through the Oslo I Accord, the physical territory upon which to set up operations. He also reminded Samaranch that Palestine had already been working for twenty-two years with its sport federations to participate in Asian and international sport competition "in full sport spirit."[14] Of course, he omitted that this occurred at the expense of Israel's place in Asia, despite Yekutieli's role in establishing the Western Asiatic Games Confederation during the British Mandate.

It probably did not matter. This page needed turning, yet for nearly seventy years the "file" just would not go away.

Abu Hussein testified that "[a]ll we seek is to develop Palestinian sport in accordance with the Olympic soul [spirit] and cooperate with all nations in seek of love and peace."[15] Most important, Abu Hussein pointed out to President Samaranch that the Palestine Olympic Committee had been affiliated to the IOC since May 16, 1934,[16] having been recognized in Athens[17] at the same IOC Session in which Germany was initially allowed to keep the Games of the XI Olympiad. Abu Hussein's inclusion of this history in the official record proves that a memory of the events of the 1930s was still alive in the corridors of Palestinian Olympic power, probably in the 1970s when Munich occurred as well as on the day that the Oslo I Accord was signed.

But the PLO account of history had a twist: the Palestinian narrative implied that the first Palestinian Olympic body had been an Arab organization. It had never been so. Except for the faint hopes of a temporary dialog between the Va'ad Leumi, Frederick Kisch, Yosef Yekutieli, and Waldo Heinrichs Sr. (pro the Jerusalem YMCA's board, its Physical Department Committee, and Arab Palestinian sport clubs), Palestinian Jews, Christians, and Muslims were able to cooperate in sport successfully at the national level, but could not agree on the matter of who would control an Olympic committee in the international domain. They appear to have come very close to an agreement, but the long reach of the Nazi swastika interfered and ruined years of effort and trust-building measures to do so.

In Atlanta in 1996, Majid Abu Maraheel was the sole Arab Palestinian athlete who led the Palestinian delegation into the Olympic stadium. Carrying the Palestinian flag into the stadium for the first time, it is hard to describe the sense of redemption and hope that filled the hearts of many Israelis and Palestinians, respectively. Although the Palestinians' presence was extremely controversial to some, comfort could be found in some of the stories that emerged. These narratives point to the potential for healing that came out of the 1996 Atlanta Games.

In the ABC Sports documentary *Our Greatest Hopes, Our Worst Fears*, Anouk Spitzer, the daughter of slain Israeli Olympic fencer Andre Spitzer, shared her memories about the emotions experienced by the fourteen children of the Israeli Olympians who died in Munich. As they stood to watch Majid enter the Olympic stadium: "We wanted to show the world that things can be different and this is how it should be. The Olympic Games…should not [be] about people sitting tied up in a room and being terrified and horrified and coming home in coffins. This [act of people coming together] is the Olympic idea and we [children of the Munich 11] can move on and give respect to these people who are athletes, and after that they are also Palestinians, but first of all they are athletes and we have respect for them."[18]

At a memorial service hosted by the Jewish community in Atlanta, the Palestinian delegation met with the families of those who died in Munich. Oshrat Romano-Kandel, the daughter of slain Israeli weightlifter Yossef Romano, recalled how Palestine's *chef de mission* approached her: "I gave a speech at the reception and the head of the Palestinian delegation came and kissed me on the forehead. It was a very emotional moment."[19] Abu Hussein recounted to me this story in person. For the documentary, he recalled (as translated): "The Israelis invited us to attend the reception in Atlanta and we all wanted to attend. We wanted to find a way to put Munich behind us. We want[ed] a fresh understanding as athletes. We believe we can find a way if we try…It's time for people to become sane and think about the future".[20]

# Final Words

I asked the descendants of Waldo Huntley Heinrichs Sr. to provide the last words for this book. One member provided the following:

*When I was a child around the house of my grandparents, Waldo (Sr.) and Dorothy Heinrichs, I heard often about the years in India, about two World Wars in which Waldo served, and about his years teaching freshmen at Middlebury College a required course in Contemporary Civilization. I do not remember hearing a word about the years in Jerusalem from Waldo or Dorothy. The pieces I garnered from family lore, amplified now by Mr. Haddad's research, tell a disheartening story—but not an unfamiliar one. There was once, in the early 1930s, a not impossible dream of a joint Olympic Committee representing the three great faith communities under the British Mandate in Palestine. Waldo came to the Jerusalem YMCA with that dream in mind, and with years of YMCA-based Olympic organizing experience behind him in India.*

*The dream died from attack without and institutional weaknesses within. In retrospect the dream may appear distant and perhaps naïve. Yet I remember wandering through stacks of Waldo's books years after his death. I was struck then by the power the dream had had for him. Among his books were copies of the Koran and Islamic poetry in translation, Christian biblical and social commentaries, Jewish and Zionist narratives longing for a homeland, an anthology of Hindu religious literature, and early works by Mahatma Gandhi (about whom Waldo was skeptical but fascinated). Waldo was not a scholar. He simply lived and breathed worlds alive with conflict and possibility.*

*In the years after Jerusalem and before the US entry into WWII, Waldo criss-crossed the northeastern United States speaking broadly on the dangers of Nazism and then later in support of President Roosevelt's Lend Lease program, America's first tentative outreach into the European conflict. In the face of rising America-first and isolationist sentiment, Waldo sounded to some like a war-monger. Yet he knew personally of the totalitarian threat about which he spoke. And today, in another rising tide of nationalism and religious tribalism, his argument for cooperation among enemies through sport begins to sound less like a dream, more like necessary truth-telling, and a place to begin again."*

# Postscript and Acknowledgments

*The File* is particularly pertinent in light of the political landscape facing today's world. Many people and organizations are asked to take a stand on the Israel-Palestine conflict in sport and should have as much context as possible. This requires looking at the sport history of the "file," an important part of which I reveal in the main chapters of this book. It also requires a better understanding of the values of Olympism and the governance model used by the Olympic Movement. These factors influenced how I constructed the book and why I selected the three main characters.

That said, the history in this book needed to be revealed on its own merits. It seems to be of a highly sensitive nature. Perhaps for this reason I faced many challenges in completing the picture. I caution readers not to overinterpret the history. I lay out facts and raise questions for others to examine and for which I could not find answers. These outstanding questions are relevant, of public concern, based on archival evidence, and indicate that our understanding of the Nazi Olympics has been missing a few pieces of the puzzle for quite some time.

It will be tempting for some readers to pass judgment on the characters. But the creation of history is dynamic. The key actors, many of whom were quite young, were making decisions in real time and often without complete information. They were also making decisions based on what they perceived to be in the best interests of their respective communities, organizations, or constituents. Of course, I cannot change the fact that people's perspectives might be different from mine, but I consider these points to be an important factor to keep in mind.

The writing challenges were primarily fourfold. First, much of the history was forgotten or obscured, perhaps purposely. Revealing it within the highly charged context of the Israel-Palestine conflict can disrupt personal perspectives and entrenched positions in an uncomfortable way. I have tried to emphasize the fundamental message of the three key actors as they related to an Olympic and organizational mission: (1) that organizational structures exist to moderate the individual agendas of their actors, and (2) that organizational missions, when benevolently inclined and made the focus of the actors' actions, have the power to mediate positively between competing personal interests. To the extent one accepts the stated goal of the global Olympic Movement to practice sport without discrimination as a benevolent intention, I approached the actions of the three key protagonists—Frederick Kisch, Yosef Yekutieli, and Waldo Heinrichs—as supporting that fundamental message. In doing so, I do not mean to obfuscate the more complex factors or agendas of the times.

The second challenge was that I know the history to be incomplete. The core of this story is still shrouded in mystery and buried somewhere, with someone. I can only say that it was not my intention to cast the die and that I tried hard to learn as much as I could over many years of research. I was not successful in all avenues. That said, I believe that the story that I have told in these pages is sound in most of its foundation. I will leave it to other researchers to dig deeper to discover that which I could not. I believe that the fundamental message that I wanted to emphasize endures in relevance today.

The third challenge was a personal one. I wanted to write the story from the perspectives of the key actors. Their experiences triggered emotional reactions in me vis-à-vis my historical interactions with the Olympic Movement, the Israel-Palestine conflict, and my father's Palestinian history. I was impressed by the way in which attributes of each character spoke to me, whether he was Zionist (Kisch or Yekutieli), Internationalist (Heinrichs), or Arab Nationalist. Embedded within those silent exchanges with long-deceased people in the archives, and through the experience of sport, was our commonality as people. Thus, I did not write exclusively as a historian, but I consulted with several academics and each agreed that the story brings interesting history to light.

The fourth challenge was the glaring limitation of this book: the absence of a positive role model from the Arab political camp. I selected one, wanting very much to present four heroes who could serve as connection points for readers from across the spectrum. My failure to gain access to more information about the fourth character, coupled with a letter from a lawyer, caused me to exclude him. I can only apologize to readers in advance for my failure and state here that I had found his character quite inspiring, despite one instance in his history requiring clarification that I could not obtain.

The book is based on a review of over ten thousand documents selected from archives. From these I selected over 1,800 primary archival sources to tell a story that paints a fairly comprehensive but still incomplete picture of the first Palestine Olympic Committee. I selected over 300 pictures from a review of thousands, all of which relate to the narrative. Yet, for the purpose of publication, I was obliged to select only sixteen. I had to cut about 35 percent of the selected archival material, leaving it for a second book. Even after these cuts, I ended up with over 156,000 words that I needed to cut to approximately 90,000, which I assumed would be reduced further by an editor. This process eliminated the book's Epilogue, in which I had laid out eight steps that could be taken to pave a positive pathway forward, learning lessons from the history of the "file." Not everyone will be satisfied with the final approach that I took, but I believe that most people who read *The File* will focus on the novel story and its messages. Readers of literary nonfiction and academics should find value in turning its pages.

A number of clarifications are therefore required about what I included and what I did not include to construct the narrative of the story.

The research drew upon primary sources from nearly twenty archives. The book is not peer-reviewed or a dissertation. I excluded dozens of journal articles and sources of secondary literature. Only in a few instances did I cite such material and when I did (in the case of articles), it was usually from within an edited volume. My reasons for doing so (among many) include that I wanted to target the mass market, for which academic content is often not well suited.

I did not make extensive use of the Hebrew content from many of the archives, having screened out most of it. For example, for sources from the Joseph Yekutieli Maccabi Sport Archives, when Hebrew documentation was relevant, it was used. But the Olympic Movement has communicated officially in English and French for decades. Thus, most of the relevant sources from these archives (as they relate directly to the events in this book) are in these two languages.

Two major Jewish sport movements in Palestine are not central to this story, even if they were pivotal in a few key instances: Hapoel and Betar. Referencing the pivot point as it relates to this narrative was sufficient from within the Maccabi records. This does not mean that the other organizations were not a major part of the sport landscape: during the period of the mid-1930s (and depending on the source), Hapoel claimed as many as ten thousand registered members within its sporting ranks in Palestine. Betar, the more militant Jewish sports movement, comprised seventy thousand global members during the same period.

In the case of non-Jewish Palestinian sport during the British Mandate, meaning Arab, Armenian, Greek, British, Armed Forces, private corporations, and so on, most of these files are not in accessible archives, are in private collections, and/or have been lost to history. From what is available, the majority of Arab sport activity seems to have been centered in the three cities of Jerusalem, Jaffa, and Haifa. There was activity in other cities and even in some of the smaller towns. Some of this activity was of a significant quality and consistency. But there is no way to equate the scale of this activity with that of the Jewish sports movement, especially on a transnational level. The only real competitor institution on the ground in Palestine to that of Jewish sport was the Jerusalem YMCA. That is why the FASCP had to engage with it around the Olympic file, as well as the Arabs. When I use the term "competitor institution," I mean that the Jerusalem YMCA had the physical plant, financial capital, and global connections to compete for the right to organize the representation of Palestine in the Olympic Movement. In reality, it saw itself as a facilitator of this Olympic effort and was happy to use its strength for the benefit of all Palestinians of the period—Jewish and non-Jewish.

Which is why the story is so tragic for Arabs.

Any perceived lack of discussion of the full range of organizations in my book (Jewish or non-Jewish) does not represent in any way an attempt by me to deny their existence, revise history, or downplay their role. An entire field of academia has already documented numbers and capabilities within the Jewish sports movement in Palestine that demonstrate that it was the dominant force in sport in Mandate Palestine. For this reason and because of the Nazi Olympics, Jewish sport had significant leverage with the International Olympic Committee in its negotiations. The strategic actions of the Arab Palestinians contributed to forestalling their Olympic recognition for nearly sixty years.

One of my key objectives was to focus on the interactions and decisions of principal actors in the Olympic file, the value camps that they represented, and the decisions they took together or behind one another's backs. More importantly, I was interested in the consequences of these decisions as they related to the prospects of recognition of either (or both) parties (Jews and non-Jews) by the IOC. Those consequences had real impact on people at the time and until today. A simple case in point is how the massive security expenditures of an Olympic Games today finds its roots in the actions of the Palestinians at Munich in 1972.

Secondary sources included biographies, edited (published) diaries, and edited volumes of collected works. For more minor characters, organizations, events, and ideologies, and to connect the protagonists' reactions (documented in the archival record) to major historical events, I relied heavily on compendia like the *New Encyclopedia of Zionism and Israel* and the Jewish Virtual Library (for Zionist and Israeli history) or Wikipedia (for general world history). If I quoted or consciously paraphrased any of these sources, I provided citations. Otherwise, dates, names, organizational affiliations, events of minor importance, and other such details are not referenced back to a source in the endnotes.

This book is not a story about the organizations that made up the Palestine Olympic Committee, nor is it a comprehensive history of any of them. I emphasized two movements (Maccabi and the YMCA) because they served as the pivot points in this shared sport history. This book is also not a history of Arab Palestinian sport, although it includes an important part of that history. I opine that Israeli and Palestinian sport history is shared—especially during the Mandate. Consequently, I believe that *The File* represents an important part of

Arab Palestinians' lost history while rightfully attributing to the Israelis their own accomplishments. This shared, complicated history—like everyone's history—has its highs and lows, from which we all need to learn how to adapt constructively.

Finally, this is a story about a representative Palestine Olympic Committee that never came to be, and the people, movements, and ideologies who were instrumental in its demise. It is a look at the Israel-Palestine conflict through the lens of sport, one that actually allows us to experience the thrill of victory and the disappointment of defeat at a level to which most of us can relate, and in a manner (hopefully) more efficacious than academic discussion. I hope that I have created a story through which the reader can identify with his/her own heroes and antiheroes while also humanizing everyone. The characters presented in the book led complex, multifaceted lives that extended well beyond the realm of sport. No summative assessment of their character—even those I excluded from the book—should be made by the reader or is advanced by me as an author.

Some remarks on the style versus history in the book.

There are clearly a few dramatic scenes in the book, especially in presenting Yosef Yekutieli's interactions with Frederick Kisch and the way in which they handled the invitation to the Berlin Games. I also enhanced some details of the motorcycle tour for literary impact. This was done to engage the reader early in the book's pages. It should not be taken as pure history; however, where there is a source, there is a historical fact. For example, Kisch and Yekutieli did receive the invitation to the Berlin Games. Yekutieli did captain the motorcycle tour between Tel Aviv and London.

The diaries of Waldo Heinrichs (used extensively in his character introduction in chapter 1, "Soldier Sons," and from chapter 3 onward) are so rich that the scenes constructed are almost always as they were presented in the source. In fact, in the vast majority of cases, I did not change the language too much (even if I did not use quotation marks) because I wanted Heinrichs' voice and story to come through after decades of being silenced.

The character of Kisch was built largely around his published administrative journal, *Palestine Diary*, as well as the biography about him written by Norman Bentwich and Kisch's son Michael, and Kisch's own Olympic correspondence. I did not use his unpublished diaries because of the length and nature of this book. This is what accounts for my less colorful presentation of Kisch, who is a fascinating historical figure in his own right.

A few acknowledgements are in order.

The Palestinian-American Research Center made this research possible by providing, in 2004, my first grant to begin the research. Fifteen years later, I remain exceedingly grateful to PARC. Over the years, the list of people who engaged me in discussions on the archival record is endless. I am grateful to each one. A special thank-you is in order to all archivists and staff at centers of study, but especially those at the Historical Archives Olympic Studies Centre in Lausanne, Joseph Yekutieli Maccabi Sports Archives in Tel Aviv, Zvi Nishri Archive for Sports and Physical Education in the Wingate Institute in Netanya, the Weizmann Archives in Rehovot, the Kautz Family YMCA Archives in Minneapolis, Springfield College Archives and Special Collections in Springfield, Special Collections and University Archives in Amherst, Yale Divinity Library Archives and Manuscripts in New Haven, and the Library of Congress in Washington, DC.

And of course, a few key individuals—not listed in any specific order—deserve special attention for their vital role in bringing the book to fruition in its final stages. My agent, Lynne Rabinoff, with whom I enjoyed immensely our collaboration, and my publisher, Post Hill Press, both of whom exhibited the patience of Job at each of my delays in delivering the manuscript. My parents, who have been an example to me of enduring through hardship and provided support through feedback and other means. My wife, Rachel, who put her aspirations on hold and consented to the sacrifice of significant resources, shared time, and my parenting, thereby taking on the burden of raising our children by herself for months at a time. Rachel's edits and reflections were also valuable. Elizabeth and Ross, for all the support while in town. Tanya for her work on restoring the YMCA sports map of Jerusalem. Jenny and Theo, for their feedback, conversation, and input. Two generations of my in-laws (parents- and grandparents-in-law) who altered their schedules to support my wife in my absence and provided seclusion while on family holidays. Tamara, whose endless emotional support, critical mind, and investment in my own growth enabled me to tackle this project. Ken, who housed me for ten months at no cost and provided weekly coffee breaks so that I could focus on finishing the book. Sherman, for his belief in serendipity and positive influence on me (and generations of students) as an educator. Allen, who engaged me in conversation and shared his expertise. John and Annegret, who supported the analysis of the NSDAP, *Westland*, and other archival material in German. Corinne, who helped compile the appendices. The families and direct descendents of Waldo Huntley Heinrichs Sr., Nicholas Lattof, and Yosef Yekutieli, who engaged with me on the book's content to varying degrees and provided personal details about their ancestors (many of which I was able to include), thereby helping me to craft a message that might resonate some of the shared values for which their ancestors stood.

To all those who I may have omitted through error, I apologize. Please do not think for a moment that I have not appreciated your contributions in real time, or reflected on them at length in my own.

# APPENDIX 1
## Archives Consulted

**Historical Archives Olympic Studies Center (Lausanne, Switzerland). Various IOC, Israel, and Palestine papers.**

Notice 0074965 CIO FI ATHLE CORR OU MO 01 14 33 ATHLETISME [1916-1966]

Notice 0074967 CIO FI ATHLE CORR OU MO 01 14 33 ATHLETISME [1976-1977]

Notice 0074968 CIO FI ATHLE CORR OU MO 01 14 33 ATHLETISME [1978-1980]

Notice 0074969 CIO FI ATHLE CORR OU MO 01 14 33 ATHLETISME [1981-1982]

Notice 0090961 CIO FI VOLLE FIVB OU MO 01 14 33 VOLLEYBALL [1947-1982]

Notice 0090965 CIO FI VOLLE FIVB OU MO 01 14 33 VOLLEYBALL [1970-1985]

Notice 0090968 CIO FI VOLLE FIVB OU MO 01 14 33 VOLLEYBALL [1946-1973]

Notice 0090983 CIO FI VOLLE FIVB OU MO 01 14 33 VOLLEYBALL [1974-1979]

Notice 0090986 CIO FI VOLLE FIVB OU MO 01 14 33 VOLLEYBALL [1980-1982]

ID Chemise 6529 CIO MBR-ABERD-CORR Correspondance de Clarence Aberdare [1930 a 1957]

Notice 0077504 CIO CNO ISR RECON OU MO 01 14 36 ISRAEL RECONNAISSANCE [1934-1952]

Notice 0077558 CIO CNO ISR STATU OU MO 014 14 36 ISRAEL STATUTS [1951-1984]

Notice 0077562 CIO CNO ISR BUREX ISRAEL BUREAU EXECUTIF [1951-1984]

Notice 0077564 CIO CNO ISR PUBLI OU MO 01 14 36 ISRAEL PUBLICATIONS [1975-1983]

Notice 0077643 CIO CNO ISR CORR OU MO 01 14 36 ISRAEL Correspondance [1930-1948]

Notice 0099378 CIO CNO PALES RECON OU MO 01 14 36 PALESTINE RECONNAIS-SANCE [1976-1984]

D42/004-30G. 4333 CIO CNO-PALES-RECON [PALESTINE/RECONNAISSANCE 1933 à 1995.

**Israel State Archives (Jerusalem, Israel). Online. Various folders on sport and the NSDAP in Mandate Palestine.**

פ-317/172

מ-5148/16 ,2-120-9-5-9

מ-5220/11 ,2-120-4-9-7

מ-5216/15 ,2-120-4-9-6

מ-5734/16 ,2-120-4-11-3

מ-354/11 ,2-112-8-5-3

מ-342/8 ,2-112-8-5-1

מ-228/41 ,2-112-8-3-2

מ-736/32 ,2-112-5-6-1

מ-707/26 ,2-112-5-5-6

מ-653/24 ,2-112-5-4-7

מ-318/56 ,2-112-4-9-1

מ-316/8 ,2-112-4-9-1

מ-304/18 ,2-112-4-8-9

מ-303/22 ,2-112-4-8-9

מ-299/19 ,2-112-4-8-8

מ-242/40 ,2-112-4-7-8

הפמ-5226/1 ,2-112-11-1-12

2-112-05-03-01, 556/16-מ

2-108-9-6-6, 6359/32-מ

2-108-6-10, 4347/61-מ

2-108-5-11-3, 4247/9-מ

2-108-3-9-5, 2685/8-מ

2-108-3-9-5, 2684/47-מ

2-108-3-9-5, 2684/43-מ

2-108-3-9-5, 2684/36-מ

2-108-3-9-5, 2683/33-מ

2-108-3-9-5, 2683/17-מ

2-108-3-9-5, 2681/24-מ

2-108-3-9-4, 2680/25-מ

2-108-3-9-4, 2677/22-מ

2-108-3-9-4, 2677/20-מ

2-108-3-9-4, 2677-20-מ

2-108-11-34, 5000/11-מ

2-108-11-3-4, 5000/17-מ

2-108-11-3-4, 5000/14-מ

2-108-11-12, 4961/1-מ

2-108-11-11-07, 4897/27-מ

2-108-11-10, 4850/8-מ

2-108-11-10, 4850/14-מ

2-108-11-10-9, 4850/11-מ

2-108-1-8-9, 1328/9-מ

2-108-1-8-9, 1328/8-מ

2-108-1-8-9, 1328/7-מ

2-108-1-8-9, 1328/12-מ

2-108-1-8-9, 1328/11-מ

2-108-1-8-9, 1328/10-מ

2-108-1-1-3, 853/36-מ

02-120-05-05-10, 4/5-מ

02-113-03-06-02, 16650/10-לג

02-113-03-05-05, 16634/4-לג

02-113-03-05-05, 16610/6-לג

02-113-03-05-05, 16610/11-לג

02-113-03-05-03, 16612/2-לג

02-112-08-08-02, 526/12-מ

02-112-08-04-10, 335/28-מ

02-112-07-07-09, 823/17-מ

02-112-07-07-09, 823/16-מ

02-112-07-07-09, 822/15-מ

02-112-07-07-09, 821/7-מ

02-112-07-03-06, 1046/13-מ

02-112-05-03-02, 564/1-מ

02-112-05-03-02, 561/7-מ

02-112-05-03-02, 561/33-מ

02-112-05-03-02, 561/27-מ

02-112-05-03-02, 561/11-מ

02-112-05-03-01, 560/2-מ

02-112-05-03-01, 560/1-מ

02-112-05-02-02, 506/65-מ

02-112-05-01-10, 491/54-מ

02-112-04-94-04, 335/12-מ

02-112-04-10-02, 383/34-מ

02-112-04-10-02, 381/46-מ

02-112-04-09-10, 370/7-מ

02-112-04-09-10, 370/6-מ

02-112-04-09-05, 343/46-מ

02-112-04-09-05, 342/50-מ

02-112-04-09-04, 337/41-מ

02-112-04-07-04, 218/44-מ

02-112-04-07-03, 212/22-מ

02-112-04-07-02, 202/54-מ

02-112-04-06-09, 188/22-מ

02-112-04-06-04, 157/43-מ

02-112-04-05-08, 119/19-מ

02-112-04-05-08, 117/44-מ

02-112-04-05-04, 97/50-מ

02-112-04-05-03, 91/42-מ

02-112-04-05-01, 79/10-מ

02-112-04-04-06, 49/11-מ

02-112-04-04-03, 28/20-מ

02-112-04-04-02, 25/5-מ

02-112-04-01-03, 3218/14-מ

02-110-07-06-02, 3067/1-מ

02-108-11-12-09, 4974/53-מ

02-108-11-12-09, 4974/39-מ

02-108-11-12-09, 4974/30-מ

02-108-11-12-09, 4974/23-מ

02-108-11-12-09, 4974/15-מ

02-108-11-11-07, 4900/14-מ

02-108-11-11-07, 4897/25-מ

02-108-11-11-07, 4897/24-מ

02-108-11-11-07, 4897/1-מ

02-108-11-03-10, 5039/13-מ

02-108-11-03-07, 5017/11-מ

02-108-11-03-06, 5005/11-מ

02-108-11-03-04, 5000/19-מ

02-108-11-03-02, 4989-30-מ

02-108-10-08-05, 6585/14-מ

02-108-06-01-09, 4342/9-מ

02-108-06-01-09, 4341/1-מ

02-108-06-01-08, 4333/24-מ

02-108-06-01-07, 4329/19-מ

02-108-06-01-05, 4316/21-מ

## Joseph Yekutieli Maccabi Sports Archives (Ramat Gan, Tel Aviv, Israel).

**Kautz Family YMCA Archives (University of Minnesota, Minneapolis, MN, USA). Records of YMCA International Work in Palestine and Israel: Y.USA.9-2-2.**

Box 3: Folders 09, 10, 11, 12, and 13

Box 04: Folders 01, 02, 03, 04, 05, 06, 07, 08, and10

Box 05: Folders 01, 02, 03, 04, 05, 06, 07, 08, and 09

Box 06: Folders 01, 02, 03, 04, 05, 06, 07, and 08

Box 18: Folders 02, 04, 05, 07, and 08

Box 20: Folders 01 and 02

Box 21: Folders 01 and 16

Box 36: Folder 06

Box 43: Folder 03

**Lattof Family Private Papers. By email.**

Miscellaneous personal writings of Nicholas Lattof.

**Library of Congress (Washington, DC, USA).**

*Newspaper and Current Periodical Reading Room:*
- Germany 19th and 20th Century Newspapers in Original Format (Bound Volumes).
- Westland 1933–1935.

*Prints & Photographs Reading Room:*
- Library of Congress Prints and Photographs Division Washington, D.C. 20540 USA.
- Miscellaneous Olympic photographs, numerous collections.
- Matson (G. Eric and Edith) Photograph Collection.

**Middlebury College Special Collections & Archives (Middlebury, VT, USA). By email. Faculty Files.**

Box H-He: Folder Heinrichs, Waldo.

**National Archives and Records Administration (College Park, MD, USA). Various 1936 Olympic and NSDAP files, including in Mandate Palestine.**

Declassified NND 61695 RG 319 ENTRY ZZ-6 Box 11 NSDAP Members PLE D115610.

Declassified NND 61695 RG 319 ENTRY ZZ-6 Box 14 Palestine Political D137501.

Declassified NND 61695 RG 319 ENTRY ZZ-6 Box 14 Palestine Underground D195970.

T120 Index German Foreign Ministry 1920–1945, Bound Volume, Volumes 01, 02, and 03.

A3340, 242, Berlin Documents.

A3341, 242, Berlin Documents.

A3343, 242, Berlin Documents. Membership Applications to the NS.

A3344A, 242, Frauenschaft/Deutches Frauenwerk. Rolls A1-A200. Membership applications to the NS.

National Library of Israel (Jerusalem, Israel). Online. Arabic Newspaper Archive of Ottoman and Mandatory Palestine and Historical Jewish Press.
*Falastin* and *Meraat Elsherk* and *Palestine Bulletin* and *Palestine Post.*

*New York Times* Article Archive (New York, NY). Online. 1851–PRESENT.
Keyword searches (and their variants) for: Berlin Olympics, Frederick Kisch, Joseph Yekutieli, Munich Olympics, Palestine Olympic, Waldo Heinrichs.

Personal Archives of Omar Hussein Shuweikeh (destroyed in the Gaza Strip in 2007). Palestine Olympic Committee.
Palestine Olympic Committee Stationery.

The Pinchas Lavon Institute for Labour Movement Research (Tel Aviv, Israel).

| | | |
|---|---|---|
| IV-112-2 | IV-244-140 | IV 244-383 |
| IV-112-10 | IV-244-289 | IV-244-477 |
| IV-112-A1 | IV-244-290 | IV-244-492 |
| IV-112-D | IV-244-296 | IV-244-505 |
| IV-244-95 | IV-244-297 | IV-244-534 |
| IV-244-99 | IV-244-298 | IV-244-602 |
| IV-244-115 | IV-244-299 | IV-244-610 |
| IV-244-119 | IV-244-311 | IV-244-611 |
| IV-244-123 | IV-244-346 | IV-244-692 |
| IV-244-124 | IV-244-349 | IV-244-698 |
| IV-244-135 | IV-244-352 | IV-244-877 |

The Springfield College Archives and Special Collections (Springfield, MA, USA). MS528 Attalah A. Kidess Collection.
Box 01: All folders     Box 02: Folders 01, 15, and 16     Box 03: All folders

UMass Amherst Special Collections & University Archives (Amherst, MA, USA). Waldo H. Heinrichs, Jr. Papers.
This collection had recently been received and was not sorted into boxes or folders at the time of consultation. The archive permitted publication without standard archival references to a collection number, boxes, and folders.

UNRWA Photo and Film Archive for Palestine Refugees (Gaza City, Gaza Strip). Photos.
Sport.

## The Weizmann Archives (Rehovot, Israel).

429-742 JCT to Kisch, Individual Correspondences

742-407-742 Kisch KKL Kisch, Individual Correspondences

742-740 Kisch to Ruppin, Individual Correspondences

742-787, Individual Correspondences

742-846 Kisch to Samuel

742-859 Keren HaYesod

742-885-742 Kisch Stors Kisch, Individual Correspondences

742-891-742 Kisch May Kisch, Individual Correspondences

742-1018-742 Kisch ZO London Kisch, 742-1018, Individual Correspondences and 1018-742, Individual Correspondences

742-1022-742 Kisch PZE Kisch

742-1022, Individual Correspondences

742-1041-742 Kisch to Entwich to Kisch, Individual Correspondences

742-1075-742 Kisch to Government House to Kisch, 742-1075, Individual Correspondences and 1075-742

742-1341 Kisch ZE to London, Individual Correspondences

742-1922 Kisch to Treasury Department

742-1960 Kisch to Va'ad Leumi, Individual Correspondences

742-3048-742 Kisch to Naamani Sec. PSE to Kisch, Individual Correspondences

742-3243 Kisch to Palestine Government, Individual Correspondences

742-3399 Kisch to Abou Ramadan, Individual Correspondences

742-3627-742 Kisch to Chancellor to Kisch, Individual Correspondences

742-3639 Kisch to Sir Harry Luke Chief Secretary, Individual Correspondences

742-3701 Kisch to Mabel Maas

742-3836 Kisch to Jewish Agency Executive, Individual Correspondences

1341-742 ZE London to Kisch, Individual Correspondences

4237-British Maccabi-Olympic, Individual Correspondences

742-47 Kisch to Cowen, Individual Correspondences

742-217-742 Kisch to Weizman to Kisch, 217-742, Individual Correspondences and 742-217, Individual Correspondences

742-818 Kisch to Deedes, Individual Correspondences

742-824-831-63-848-782 Tisch to Soloveichik, Neidisch, Cohen, Feile and Lipsky, Individual Correspondences

742-862 Kisch to Dr. Goldstein

742-1198 Kisch to Bramley

Kisch-Clayton Sir Gen Gibert F Secr Palestine Govt, Individual Correspondences

Kisch-Janet Lieberman, Individual Correspondences

Kisch-Stein Leonard J., Individual Correspondences

Maccabi, Individual Correspondences

Stein Leonard J.-Kisch, Individual Correspondences

The History of the Maccabi Organisation

742-102

742-106

742-364-1495-872-2307-1306-1689-401-1826-210

742-865

742-885-1084-93-1321-825-1566-342-1771-1461

742-889

742-922-1222-1532-869-1561-1265-962-899-1589-1078-930

742-988-1589-1436-3765-3694-3675-767

742-1035-1871-1473-782-1133-1000-750-3711-2327-2043-4975-1586

742-1126

742-1203-1313-1327-2325-1708-3346-3182-3655-3390-5

742-1213

742-2327

742-3362

742-3694-771-290-913-818-1433-978

742-3741

## Yale Divinity Library Archives and Manuscripts (New Haven, CT, USA). Waldo Huntley Heinrichs Papers (115).

Box 1: Folders 01, 02, 03, 04, 05, 06, 07, 08, 09, 10, 11, and 12
Box 2: Folders 21, 23, 24, and 26
Box 3: Folders 33, 38, 39, 41, 42, 45, 46, and 47
Box 4: Folders 49, 50, 54, and 55
Box 7: Folder 64
Box 8: Folders 65, 66, 68, and 69
Box 9: Folders 09, 15, 17, and 27

## Zvi Nishri Archive for the History of Physical Education and Sport in Israel (Netanya, Israel).

1.02_39 in 21 [1940-48]
1.2_111_252 Correspondence
1.19_61 in 284 HaVoad HaO-limpi [1924-56]
5.01 53 Joseph Yekutieli
AR 33 (News Clippings)
AR_15 Falastin (Newspaper)
HaPoel Chronology (Wingate Archives)
HaPoel Report 1940-1942 (Wingate Archives)
HaPoel Report February 1944 (Wingate Archives)
Loose Publications from Wingate Archives 1939-1948
Maccabi Tel Aviv Report 1938 (Wingate Archives)
Maccabi Tel Aviv Report of Operations 1939-1940 (Wingate Archives)
Maccabi Tel Aviv Report of Operations 1940-1941 (Wingate Archives)
Maccabi World Union Eretz Israel Report 20.01.1944 (Wingate Archives)

Orde Wingate A Zionist British Soldier
Personal Collections
Publications, Student Writings and Bibliographies from the Wingate Archives
SYNSO 0001556 IN ADI.29 0002 FASCP
SYNSO 0001557 IN ADI.29 0001 FASCP [1936-1941]
SYSNO 0000704 IN AD 1.19 0007 Vo'ad HaOlimpi HaYishraeli [1952-1960]
SYSNO 0000724 IN AD 1.19 0003 Vo'ad HaOlimpi HaYishraeli
SYSNO 0001539 IN ADI.29 0007 FASCP
SYSNO 0001540 IN ADI.29 0006 FASCP
SYSNO 0001541 IN ADI.29 0005 FASCP
SYSNO 0001542 IN ADI.29 0004 FASCP
SYSNO 0001555 IN ADI.29 0003 FASCP

SYSNO 0001771 IN AD 1.10 0023 Maccabi-HaPoel
SYSNO 0002096 IN AD 2.001 0002 Maccabi 'Olami Tik 2
SYSNO 0002155 IN AD 1.19 0062 Olimpi Tikim
SYSNO 0002577 IN AD 5.16 0003 Tikim
SYSNO 0045044 IN AR 0001 Select News Clippings [1950-1951]
SYSNO 0045118 IN AD 1.09 0136 Tikim HaPoel
SYSNO 0052466 IN AD 5.27 0002 Shlomo Arazi
Vaad Leumi Department of Physical Training Summary 1944-1945
Vaad Leumi Reports 1942-1943 (Wingate Archives)
Zionist Sport Between 1895 and 1998

# APPENDIX 2

| Date | Event |
| --- | --- |
| 1792 | Daniel Mendoza is the first Jewish boxer to claim the title of English boxing champion, holding it through 1795. |
| 1858 | Jews granted legal emancipation in England. |
| 1892 | First Aliyah (wave of Jewish immigration to Palestine) begins. |
| 1895 | German Jewish academics establish in Constantinople (Ottoman Empire) the first Jewish sport association, *Israelitischer Turnverein Constantinopel*, in January in the Ottoman Empire. |
| 1896 | Jews win six gold medals at the first modern Olympic Games in Athens. |
| 1897 | Fabius Schach from Cologne attempts to convince other delegates at the First Zionist Congress in Basel, Switzerland of the need for pro-Zionist sport associations. |
| 1898 | Max Nordau coins the term "Muscular Judaism" and the first Jewish sports club in Europe is founded. |
| 1901 | Thirteen Jewish sport clubs are in existence in Central Europe and Martin Buber appeals for a Jewish renaissance. |
| 1903 | First Aliyah ends. Approximately 35,000 Jews arrived in Palestine during this wave of immigration. |
| 1903 | Maccabi movement established. |
| 1903 | League of Jewish Gymnasts in Germany calls for a national Judaism. |
| 1904 | Second Aliyah begins. |
| 1907 | Jewish women start participating in the Imperial German national exposition (*Festschrift*). |
| 1912 | Jewish football team plays visiting team from Beirut in Palestine. |
| March 13, 1912 | League of Jewish Gymnasts travels to Palestine, returning April 27, 1912. |
| July 6, 1912 | Olympic Games open in Stockholm, inspiring Yosef Yekutieli (only fifteen years old and in Palestine) to conceive of a Jewish Olympics (the Maccabiad). Pierre de Coubertin, Henri de Baillet-Latour, Sigfrid Edström, and Avery Brundage, are all in attendance. Theodor Lewald and Carl Diem are also present. |
| 1914 | Second Aliyah ends. Approximately 40,000 Jews arrived in Palestine during this wave of immigration, Yosef Yekutieli's family among them. |
| July 28, 1914 | First World War begins. |
| November 2, 1917 | Balfour Declaration. |
| December 9, 1917 | Surrender of Jerusalem to Allenby's forces. Martial law declared. |

| Date | Event |
|---|---|
| 1918 | Occupied Enemy Territory Administration (OETA) established in Palestine (military administration). |
| November 11, 1918 | First World War's hostilities cease with the Armistice Agreement. |
| 1919 | Third Aliyah begins. |
| 1919 | Formation of the German Circle (the confederation of national Jewish gymnastics associations), precursor to the Maccabi World Association (MWA, now Maccabi World Union or MWU). |
| 1919 | 1st Maccabi meeting convenes in Palestine with eleven sport associations in attendance from Palestine and one from Syria (perhaps now located in Lebanon). |
| June 28, 1919 | Treaty of Versailles concluded, formally ending the First World War. |
| 1920 | Global sport begins to boom after the First World War as a central concern of nations. |
| 1920 | Presentation of Young Men's Christian Association (YMCA) to the IOC in Antwerp, Belgium at the Summer Olympic Games. |
| July, 1920 | Mandate for Palestine passed to Great Britain. |
| August, 1920 | OETA disestablished. |
| 1921 | MWA established at the Twelfth Zionist Congress in Carlsbad, Czechoslovakia. |
| 1921 | Palestine Maccabi territorial organization setup. |
| November, 1922 | Frederick Kisch arrives in Palestine. |
| 1923 | Third Aliyah ends. Approximately 40,000 Jews arrived in Palestine during this wave of immigration. |
| January, 1923 | Kisch takes up his duties as Chairman of the Palestine Zionist Executive in Palestine. |
| July 19, 1923 | Correspondence from Kisch's secretary to Yekutieli requesting that sport meets in Palestine not take on a political tone. |
| 1924 | Fourth Aliyah begins. |
| 1924 | German Jewish sports leader, Lewald, becomes an IOC member. |
| 1924 | Hakoah Wien (Vienna) wins European football championship. |
| 1924 | First discussion between Maccabi Palestine and International Amateur Athletic Federation (IAAF, with Edström) about Palestine affiliating to the international federation (at the Olympic Games in Paris). |
| June 9, 1924 | Correspondence from Kisch to IOC in Paris, introducing a delegation from Palestine Athletics Federation "L'Organisation Maccabi", signed as President of Maccabi Palestine. |
| 1925 | Mandate administration begins using English, Arabic, and Hebrew on official government artifacts. Palestinian citizenship introduced. |
| April 26, 1925 | Eleven Jewish sport clubs gather in Essen, Weimar Republic (Germany) to form the neutral Jewish sports group Vintus (to unite Zionist, liberal, and neutral Jews in Germany). |
| 1926 | Re-internment of Max Nordau's remains in Jerusalem. US tour of Hakoah Wien. |

| Date | Event |
| --- | --- |
| May 1, 1926 | Maccabi club Hakoah Wien plays against a select US team in New York in front of 46,000 fans. |
| December 13, 1926 | Z. Weizmann writes to Jerusalem Liaison Commission regarding exchanges between Egyptian and Palestinian sport teams, including in football. |
| 1927 | Zionists begin electrifying Palestine. |
| 1927 | A Jewish team wins the Palestine Football Competition Cup. |
| 1927 | Jewish football in Palestine begins efforts to organize matches with Egyptian teams. |
| 1927 | Yekutieli, Grasowsky, and Abulafia begin surveying sport clubs that are practicing organized football in Palestine. Jewish football clubs in Palestine number fifty, and Arab clubs eleven. |
| April 19, 1927 | Correspondence from Organizing Committee of the 1928 Amsterdam Olympics to Yekutieli, rejecting his request for press passes to the Games. |
| September, 1927 | YMCA buys land in West Nikiforieh district of Jerusalem from the Greek Orthodox Church. |
| 1928 | Nicholas Lattof and Frederick Auburn arrive in Jerusalem to work at its YMCA as assistant secretary-general and physical director, respectively. |
| 1928 | Arab Sports Club founded in Jerusalem. |
| 1928 | German Jewish tennis player, Daniel Prenn, claims his first national tennis title of champion, holding it until 1932 when he is stripped of them as the Nazis rise to power. |
| June, 1928 | Yekutieli begins arrangements to send a Jewish football team to Europe. |
| June 14, 1928 | Letter to all member associations of Fédération Internationale de Football Association (FIFA) regarding Yekutieli representing the interests of Palestine football associations abroad. |
| July, 1928 | Foundation stone laid for the new Jerusalem YMCA building. |
| August 14, 1928 | Founding of Palestine Football Association (PFA). |
| 1929 | Fourth Aliyah ends. Approximately 82,000 Jews arrived in Palestine during this wave of immigration. |
| 1929 | Jewish Agency for Palestine established. |
| 1929 | Fifth Aliyah begins, with a surge in immigration of Jews after the Nazi takeover of Germany. |
| April 29, 1929 | Maccabi Palestine's Fifth National Sports Meeting, held in Jerusalem. |
| May 19, 1929 | Lewald and Diem tour US. |
| August 1, 1929 | Wailing Wall/Al Buraq riots, massacre of Jewish residents in Hebron. |
| October 29, 1929 | Stock market crashes in New York. Great Depression and global financial crisis begins. |
| Early 1930 | Karl Ruff, an ethnic German living in Palestine who will go on to found the Nazi Party in the territory, conceives of founding German sport clubs in Palestine. There are six Nazi Party members in Palestine at the time. |

| Date | Event |
|------|-------|
| 1930 | First known effort by Jerusalem YMCA to form a Palestine Olympic Games Association; exactly when in 1930 is unknown. |
| 1930 | About twenty Arab sport clubs (across all sport disciplines) in Palestine. |
| 1930 | Jerusalem YMCA organizes representative tennis championship and Arab members react negatively, contributing to the failure of the Palestine Olympic Games Association. |
| January 2, 1930 | First correspondence from Yekutieli to IOC, on the letterhead of the Sports & Athletics Organization "Maccabi" Palestine Federation. |
| January 20, 1930 | Waldo Heinrichs joins large reception for Edström and Indian Olympic Association at Masonic Lodge in Lahore. |
| January 25, 1930 | Correspondence from Fédération Sportive Féminine Internationale (FSFI) president Alice Milliat to Yekutieli clarifying membership rules and including sport literature. |
| January 29, 1930 | Correspondence from IOC to Yekutieli outlining membership conditions for a national Olympic committee for Palestine. |
| March 4, 1930 | Jerusalem YMCA receives huge bequest from James Jarvie to complete the new building project in Jerusalem (real value in 2019 equivalent more than $10,000,000). |
| October 17, 1930 | Correspondence from Yekutieli to IOC secretary-general Berdez stating Palestine's interest in participating in 1932 Olympic Games in Los Angeles. |
| October 17, 1930 | Correspondence from Provisional Commission for Forming the Palestine Olympic Committee, to IOC. |
| October 20, 1930 | Passfield White Paper on the Wailing Wall/Al Buraq riots. |
| November 11, 1930 | Correspondence from IOC to Provisional Commission for Forming the Palestine Olympic Committee, outlining membership requirements. |
| November 11, 1930 | Correspondence (separate to above), from IOC to Provisional Commission for Forming the Palestine Olympic Committee, stating that participation in the Olympic Games is by countries, not national federation members (affiliated with international federations). |
| December 8, 1930 | Heinrichs offered the role of secretary-general of the new Jerusalem YMCA building. |
| 1931 | Failed Palestine Olympic Games, which the Jerusalem YMCA attempted to organize. |
| February, 1931 | Heinrichs organizes his last Punjab Olympic Games. |
| February 2, 1931 | First correspondence sent about organizing a Maccabi motorcycle tour (from Tel Aviv to London). |
| March 25, 1931 | Heinrichs leaves India for his exploratory trip to Jerusalem and to begin his furlough. |
| April, 1931 | Arab Palestine Sports Federation (APSF) sends out first invitations to Arab clubs to gather for its inaugural meeting. |
| April 6, 1931 | The Heinrichses arrive in Jerusalem to tour the city and consider the job of secretary-general. |

| Date | Event |
|---|---|
| April 14, 1931 | The Heinrichses leave Jerusalem for the United States to complete furlough through the end of the year. |
| April 28, 1931 | Letter to FIFA from PFA regarding Yekutieli as Palestine's delegate to the 1931 Congress. |
| May 13, 1931 | IOC awards Germany the 1936 Summer Olympic Games. |
| May 14, 1931 | IC/YMCA responds to Jerusalem YMCA's 1930 Administrative Report. The report had identified the Zionist Movement as highly politically, financially, and educationally organized and confirms that Zionist sport leaders postponed organizing a joint Palestine Olympic Games Association in 1930 to allow the Arabs to organize. |
| June, 1931 | APSF founded with ten clubs. |
| June, 1931 | Order of Council published in Palestine Gazette recognizing permanent ownership of the Wailing Wall by Muslims. |
| June 12, 1931 | Maccabi motorcycle tour arrives in Dover, England. |
| June 14, 1931 | Maccabi riders welcomed at West Ham Stadium in England at the end of the Maccabi motorcycle tour. |
| July 3, 1931 | Correspondence from Yekutieli to Mayor of Stepney, informing him of beginning preparations for the 1st Maccabiad |
| July 6, 1931 | Jerusalem YMCA writes to IC/YMCA in New York informing them of their coordinated efforts with Arab sports leadership and Hapoel to engage Maccabi on running the Palestine Football Association (to allow for more Arab and Labor sport interests in the organization). On the basis of these agreements, Heinrichs will be elected to the board of the Palestine Football Association. |
| July 31, 1931 | First correspondence from Yekutieli to automobile clubs in North Africa, Europe, and the United States, about planning a transcontinental trip to the 1932 Olympic Games in Los Angeles. |
| August 3, 1931 | First correspondence from Yekutieli to the organizing committee for the 1932 Olympic Games in Los Angeles, about visiting the Games. |
| August 3, 1931 | Correspondence from Yekutieli to Milliat about joining FSFI. |
| August 9, 1931 | Kisch's last day as Chairman of the Palestine Zionist Executive. |
| August 10, 1931 | Chaim Arlosoroff replaces Kisch at the Palestine Zionist Executive/Jewish Agency. |
| September, 1931 | Nazi Party becomes second largest in the Reichstag. |
| October, 1931 | Guru Dutt (G. D.) Sondhi makes his first public announcement about his intentions to form a Western Asiatic Games Confederation and organize a First Western Asiatic Games. |
| November, 1931 | Ruff begins corresponding with the Nazi Party in Germany. He will eventually found the NSDAP branch in Palestine. |
| December 26, 1931 | Founding of the Federation of the Amateur Sports Clubs of Palestine (FASCP). |
| 1932 | Jewish press starts to report extensively on discrimination against Jewish sport personalities in Germany. |
| January 1, 1932 | Formal application from Yekutieli to the IAAF requesting affiliation for Palestine. |
| January 16, 1932 | Correspondence from IAAF to Yekutieli confirming that the application will be accepted in time for the hosting of the 1st Maccabiad in the spring of 1932. |

| Date | Event |
|---|---|
| January 16, 1932 | Correspondence from Fédération internationale de Natation (FINA) to FASCP regarding its affiliation request and FINA's nondiscrimination requirements. |
| March 28, 1932 | First Maccabiad opens in Tel Aviv. |
| May 4, 1932 | Jerusalem YMCA board ratifies its decision to participate against Maccabi on the new cinder track in Tel Aviv (which was built for the First Maccabiad) and to participate in the Syrian Olympic Games. |
| May 6, 1932 | The trials for the Syrian Olympic Games are held in Tel Aviv and organized on that city's new cinder track, built for the Maccabiad. The Jerusalem YMCA agrees to compete in them. |
| May 8, 1932 | Heinrichs arrives in Jerusalem to assume his post as secretary-general of the new Jerusalem YMCA. |
| May 13, 1932 | Yekutieli writes to the Organizing Committee of the 1932 Olympic Games in Los Angeles to inquire about obtaining a press pass. |
| May 14, 1932 | Syrian Olympic Games scheduled in Beirut. |
| May 14, 1932 | Kisch and Heinrichs meet within a week of the latter's arrival in the country. |
| May 10, 1932 | Grand reception at the Fast Hotel to welcome the Heinrichses to Palestine, hosted by the Jerusalem YMCA. |
| June 3, 1932 | Heinrichs meets all the notables of Palestine at Government House on the King's Birthday. |
| June 27, 1932 | Heinrichs holds first meeting with Henrietta Szold on YMCA-Yishuv cooperation, including in sports. |
| July, 1932 | Overseas Department of the German foreign ministry in Hamburg starts encouraging Germans in Palestine to form a local branch of the Nazi Party. |
| July 1, 1932 | Dr. Tawfiq Canaan introduces Heinrichs to the leading residents of the German colony at Rephaim. |
| July 9, 1932 | First meeting between the YMCA, Jerusalem Sports Club, and Maccabi Rehavia's tennis club on forming the Palestine Tennis Association with representation in governance according to equal number of playing members. Meeting held at Jerusalem Sports Club. |
| July 26, 1932 | Heinrichs attends meeting of the YMCA tennis club and is depressed at the vocal opposition to cooperating with Jews, even though Jews constituted a high percentage of the club's members. |
| July 30, 1932 | Summer Olympic Games open in Los Angeles. |
| July 31, 1932 | Nazi Party wins 230 out of 608 seats in the Reichstag elections. |
| August 8, 1932 | Palestine Bulletin criticizes the YMCA for organizing a tennis championship after it had boycotted the tennis events during the Maccabiad. |
| August 12, 1932 | Maccabi Palestine advertises the first meeting of the FASCP in the Palestine Bulletin. It invites all clubs in Palestine to attend and provides the contact address to which to send all requests to enroll as a member. |
| August 13, 1932 | First meeting of the FASCP for all clubs in Palestine convenes. |
| August 13, 1932 | Correspondence from Milliat to Yekutieli in which she agrees to allow FASCP into FSFI and communicates that the FSFI congress must approve the membership decision in September 1932. |

| Date | Event |
|------|-------|
| August 15, 1932 | Maccabi sends a delegate to the Jerusalem YMCA, likely to discuss the Jerusalem YMCA's involvement in FASCP and sport governance for Palestine. |
| August 22, 1932 | Rehavia Tennis Club boycotts the Jerusalem YMCA's tennis championship in retaliation for the boycott of the Maccabiad tennis competition and the attitude of the Association's tennis club toward cooperation with Jews. |
| August 25, 1932 | Hapoel approaches Heinrichs with the invitation to back his candidacy to become the President of the PFA instead of Percy Speed, Maccabi's candidate. |
| August 25, 1932 | Heinrichs attends an all-day meeting of the PFA. Hapoel withdraws from the association, but Heinrichs is still elected as the vice president, representing Arab club interests within the organization (as part of his mandate as secretary-general of the Jerusalem YMCA). |
| September 6, 1932 | Heinrichs attends a meeting of the Jerusalem YMCA's Physical Department Committee to observe and participate in the committee's discussion about joining the FASCP. |
| October 28, 1932 | First possible Nazi touchpoint by way of a low bid to print the YMCA sports map for the new building's dedication (received from Sarona and Syrian Orphanage Press). |
| November 28, 1932 | First and only correspondence from Heinrichs to the IOC in which he enquires about affiliation for Palestine and about the status of the FASCP. |
| December, 1932 | Sondhi writes to his contacts privately, including to Heinrichs, about forming the Western Asiatic Games Confederation and organizing the First Western Asiatic Games. |
| December 14, 1932 | Heinrichs attends his first cabinet meeting of the Va'ad Leumi to discuss cooperation in all matters, including sport. |
| December 20, 1932 | Correspondence from FASCP to the International Committee for Modern Pentathlon, regarding affiliation for Palestine. |
| 1933 | In the first half of the year, all Jewish athletes and officials are expelled from German sport clubs and federations; the MWU relocates its headquarters from Berlin to London. |
| January 1, 1933 | Reply from IOC to Heinrichs, providing him with the history on its correspondence with Yekutieli. |
| January 2, 1933 | Budget cut to Jerusalem YMCA because of the global economic situation. |
| January 30, 1933 | Heinrichs meets for three hours with leading Zionists, including Chaim Arlosoroff, at Emanuel Mohl's house to discuss cooperation. Zionist Executive agrees not to boycott the Jerusalem YMCA. |
| February 8, 1933 | Heinrichs hosts the first open house to support the membership drive of the Association. |
| February 10, 1933 | Jerusalem YMCA Physical Department decides to call for a meeting to found the Palestine Lawn Tennis Association with Jewish clubs. |
| February 21, 1933 | Jerusalem YMCA board has first of many clashes over its constitution, which last for weeks. |
| March 5, 1933 | Franklin D. Roosevelt closes the banks in the US. |

| Date | Event |
|---|---|
| March 6, 1933 | Lewald and Diem called to a meeting with Adolf Hitler and Joseph Goebbels in which Lewald is removed from his post in the German Reich Committee for Physical Exercise. |
| March 9, 1933 | Roosevelt's Emergency Banking Act issued. |
| March 11, 1933 | Fred Ramsey arrives in Jerusalem to work things out with the board before the dedication of the new building. |
| March 15, 1933 | The *New York Times* questions Berlin's hosting rights. |
| March 16, 1933 | Depreciation of the Palestine pound, pegged to British pound sterling, impacts completion of project and payment to contractors shortly before building dedication. |
| March 17, 1933 | Heinrichs starts avoiding the Fast Hotel. |
| March 19, 1933 | German swastika banner hoisted on the Fast Hotel at the German Consulate in Jerusalem for the first time. |
| March 22, 1933 | Dachau concentration camp is opened in Germany. |
| March 23, 1933 | Arlosoroff approaches Heinrichs at the French Consulate to inform him that a leak (in the US) about his cooperation with the Association (by Rev. Everett Clinchy) could cause him trouble. |
| March 27, 1933 | Official invitation sent by Sondhi to Palestine Government requesting that Palestine participate in the First Western Asiatic Games. |
| March 27, 1933 | Yekutieli proposes to FSFI an exception to membership rules based on "heavy & continuous immigration" and "Palestine as the Jewish National Home." |
| March 28, 1933 | Boycott of Jewish businesses in Germany begins. |
| March 29, 1933 | Arlosoroff confirms to Heinrichs and Mohl at the Rotary Club in Jerusalem that he has already received one comeback from the US regarding his cooperation with the Association. |
| April 1, 1933 | Cornelius Schwarz, one month away from joining the Nazi Party in Palestine, is angered by opposition of German Palestinian businesses to the anti-Jewish-business boycott in Palestine. He writes to his son complaining that such German Palestinians should be neutralized. |
| April 1, 1933 | Heinrichs clashes with the board over Jewish teams playing at the dedication's sport events. |
| April 1, 1933 | New York grants the Jerusalem YMCA board permission to occupy the new building. |
| April 5, 1933 | Fritz Rosenfelder, a German Jewish athlete and sport administrator, commits suicide after being expelled from his club. |
| April 5, 1933 | Heinrichs meets with the FASCP, which seems willing to cooperate on all points to incorporate the Jerusalem YMCA. |
| April 7, 1933 | Law for the Restoration of the Professional Civil Service passed in Germany, barring Jews from public positions. |
| April 7, 1933 | Formal invitations sent to all countries, including Palestine, for the First Western Asiatic Games. |
| April 9, 1933 | The dedication exercises for the new Jerusalem YMCA building commence. |

| Date | Event |
|------|-------|
| April 10, 1933 | Ramsey and Heinrichs clash with J. Gordon Boutagy and Canaan over the necessary cuts to the Association's budget at the board meeting. |
| April 14, 1933 | FSFI agrees "that the Israelits [sic] who are permanent residents in Palestine are considered as Palestine citizens." |
| April 18, 1933 | Lord Allenby's address at the dedication is broadcast as the first international broadcast from Palestine, in which he alludes to the emerging dark situation in the world. |
| April 21, 1933 | Board clashes with Heinrichs over Ramsey's demand for appointments to the board from New York. |
| April 21, 1933 | Dr. John R. Mott enforces appointment from New York of members to the Association board. |
| April 24, 1933 | The dedication exercises for the new Jerusalem YMCA building conclude. |
| April 29, 1933 | Ramsey requests copy of the deed to the new Association building in Jerusalem for the International Committee of YMCAs' vault in New York. |
| May 1, 1933 | Heinrichs negotiates reduction in property taxes with the Mayor of Jerusalem to balance the budget. |
| May 2, 1933 | Heinrichs begins to suspect a shift in loyalties from the board, first indications of a plot. |
| May 10, 1933 | Correspondence from Kisch to IOC President Baillet-Latour requesting copy of formal recognition of Palestine Olympic Committee (of which there was none). |
| May 11, 1933 | Heinrichs forced to reduce staff compensation. |
| May 11, 1933 | Heinrichs confirms to New York in his annual report that he has been elected to the Palestine Football Association and that he has also been asked by the Arabs to co-operate with their rival Palestine Amateur Football Federation; he confirms that Arab and Jewish sport clubs participated in a friendly rivalry throughout the dedication's sport events. |
| May 13, 1933 | Yekutieli and Kisch's Palestine Olympic Association founded. |
| May 16, 1933 | Boulos Said suddenly resigns as Treasurer of the Jerusalem YMCA. |
| May 16, 1933 | Julius Jacobs sends invitation to the First Western Asiatic Games to Yekutieli. |
| June, 1933 | Ludwig Buchalter, Hans Kirchner, and Erich Herrmann form the Jerusalem branch of the Nazi Party. |
| June 2, 1933 | Palestinian staff of Jerusalem YMCA depart for the US for their studies (on scholarships procured by Heinrichs). |
| June 2, 1933 | Nazi Minister of Science, Education, and Culture bans Jews from all sport clubs. |
| June 2, 1933 | Albert Abramson leaves Palestine on furlough, leaving Heinrichs exposed with one less ally on the Association board. |
| June 2, 1933 | Heinrichs' brother is approved to assume the role of the associate physical director by the entire board (except for Boutagy) to fill the role left vacant in the Physical Department by the Palestinian staff member who traveled. |
| June 7, 1933 | IOC Session in Vienna at which the German Olympic Committee commits to having Jewish athletes on the German team. Amateur Athletic Union in US remains unconvinced. Indeed, German Jews are only permitted to use public facilities but, not private sport clubs (which were the center of German sport). |

| Date | Event |
| --- | --- |
| June 16, 1933 | Arlosoroff is murdered in Tel Aviv. |
| June 19, 1933 | Major clash between Heinrichs and the board, which refuses to grant Heinrichs the opportunity to attend Arlosoroff's funeral. |
| June 26, 1933 | Constitution finally accepted by membership of the Association after a major push by Heinrichs, Lattof, and Emile Ohan to gather 137 supportive members for the vote at the meeting. |
| July, 1933 | Death of Fritz Rosenfelder is widely reported. |
| July 14, 1933 | The Nazi Party bans all other political parties in Germany. |
| July 15, 1933 | Board decides it is not satisfied with the Association's constitution and reopens the matter. |
| July 29, 1933 | In Germany, the Jewish boy scouts, Maccabi Bavaria, and Jewish War Veterans clubs are dissolved. |
| August 7, 1933 | Conrad Heinrichs has arrived in Jerusalem. |
| August 10, 1933 | Said is back as Treasurer of the Association but refuses to sign checks for Heinrichs. |
| August 22, 1933 | IOC member Clarence Bruce, 3rd Baron Aberdare (Lord Aberdare) sends confidential letter to IOC President Baillet-Latour advising him against affiliation of the Palestine Olympic Committee. |
| August 23, 1933 | Heinrichs notes in his diary that Lattof appears to be afraid of the Association's working committees and wonders why. |
| August 25, 1933 | IOC president replies to Lord Aberdare, confirming that he will coordinate with Hitler personally not to invite Palestine to the 1936 Olympic Games. |
| August 25, 1933 | German Consul Heinrich Wolff supports the Haavara (Transfer) Agreement and is subsequently secretly investigated by Ruff, Buchalter, and Schwarz. |
| September 4, 1933 | Heinrichs begins to prepare the staff for the 1934 budget, which will have drastic cuts. |
| September 11, 1933 | The Jerusalem YMCA's Physical Department Committee holds a very long meeting on affiliating to the FASCP and decides not to affiliate. This decision closes the door to cooperation with Jewish sport on national sport governance. It also opens the door for Yekutieli, who had not yet decided to send a delegation to New Delhi, to consider his options. Maccabi begins discussing going, yet all, except for Yekutieli and one other person, oppose the plan. |
| September 19, 1933 | Cuts to Association salaries, even those funded from New York. |
| September 16, 1933 | Boutagy attacks Heinrichs over contract awards and staff appointments; Heinrichs counters every point, angering Boutagy all the more. |
| September 20, 1933 | Ernst Schneller of the Syrian Orphanage, about to join the Nazi party, takes Heinrichs on a tour of the orphanages workshops. |
| September 22, 1933 | Goebbels takes over entire cultural landscape of Germany, including sports. |
| September 26, 1933 | IOC President Baillet-Latour writes to Yekutieli to inform him that Palestine's affiliation request to the IOC is rejected. |
| September 27, 1933 | Boutagy attacks Heinrichs at the board meeting over the budget cuts required from the US, and for having his brother Conrad present. |

| Date | Event |
| --- | --- |
| September 28, 1933 | Heinrichs records in his diary, "My heart is full of hatred of Boutagy today for the vile manner in which he tries to obstruct every single step of the way" and he notes how Boutagy is trying to provoke him. |
| September 28, 1933 | Yekutieli confirms interest in Sondhi's unofficial inquiry about Palestine joining a new Western Asiatic Games Confederation. |
| October 3, 1933 | Heinrichs negotiates use of the YMCA athletic field with Hapoel. |
| October 5, 1933 | October 1933 budget from Hitler grants 20,000,000 Reichsmarks to the Berlin Olympic Games. |
| October 6, 1933 | Executive committee of the Association meets over the list of sixteen names for the Board, eight each of westerners and Palestinians. |
| October 7, 1933 | Yekutieli attempts to affiliate Palestine to the International Federation of Motocyclist Clubs. |
| October 8, 1933 | Jewish Daily Bulletin reports on the travel of Eissa Bendak to Paris to be trained on how to conduct Nazi propaganda in Palestine; Bendak was "editor of the radical Christian-Arabic bi-weekly "Sowt Es-Shaab" and "was…instrumental in organizing the Arab Fascist Party at Bethlehem." |
| October 10, 1933 | Heinrichs records in his diary that his friendship with Jews and refusal to involve himself in petty Arab rivalries have caused some key board members to dislike him; he identifies Boutagy, Said, and Canaan and characterizes their "lousy underhanded methods, and their carping criticism" as "almost beyond endurance." He also records that Arab Sports Club will begin using the YMCA football field regularly. |
| October 11, 1933 | Heinrichs writes to Francis Harmon continuing to stress that sports is the pathway to cooperation in other fields in Palestine (between Jews and Arabs). |
| October 13, 1933 | Riots occur in Jerusalem and Heinrichs notes in his diary how repression of the Arabs will not work. |
| October 14, 1933 | Hapoel plays on the Jerusalem YMCA field despite the riots. |
| October 22, 1933 | Heinrichs has tea at Haddad's café and notes the pro-German and anti-Jewish attitude in the discussions of war and politics. |
| October 28, 1933 | Arab members of the Association want Heinrichs to cancel a social event at the building because of the riots; he eventually relents. |
| October 28, 1933 | The organizing committee for the First Western Asiatic Games requests a sketch of the flag for Palestine from Yekutieli. |
| October 29, 1933 | Riots arrive in Jerusalem, ships at Jaffa and Haifa refuse to unload their 1,600-1,800 Jewish refugees from Europe. |
| November, 1933 | Nazi Party in Germany lifts restrictions on membership in Nazi Party in Palestine, which immediately begins to expand. |
| November, 1933 | The Jerusalem YMCA board cancels a subscription to a Hebrew newspaper because it is "the organ of an extreme political group." |
| November 3, 1933 | Heinrichs overhears Nazi news of trouble in Tul Karem on radios that the Nazi party had likely smuggled into Palestine. |
| November 6, 1933 | Board clashes with Heinrichs over the employment of Ms. Shapiro (a Jewess) and continues almost weekly pressure against Heinrichs through January 17, 1934. |

| Date | Event |
|------|-------|
| November 8, 1933 | Yekutieli receives the formal invitation to join Western Asiatic Games Confederation. |
| November 16, 1933 | Dr. Iven arrives from the Reich Ministry of Public Enlightenment and Propaganda via Kabul, Afghanistan. |
| November 17, 1933 | Buchalter, head of the National Socialist (NS/Nazi) Group in Jerusalem reports to Ruff, the head of the Nazi Party in Palestine, on the success of the evening with Dr. Iven, and notes that Dr. Herbert Rohrer had become a member. |
| November 17, 1933 | Nazi Overseas Department (*Auslands-Abteilgung*) nominates Ruff as an under-cover NS Agent for Palestine. |
| November 19, 1933 | Start of the newspaper incident at the Jerusalem YMCA. Herbert Liebmann writes to Jan MacDonald about ordering the *Völkischer Beobachter*. |
| November 22, 1933 | Gustavus Kirby of the AAU threatens a boycott resolution at the American Olympic Committee Convention. |
| November 25, 1933 | Heinrichs decides to leave the Jamal's house and move into the Association with his family to balance budgets. |
| November 26, 1933 | Heinrichs records in his diary after a dinner at the Auburns, "I have the constant feeling of their hostility to me personally." |
| November 27, 1933 | Kisch writes to IOC president Baillet-Latour to obtain confirmation of Palestine's affiliation to the IOC. |
| December 1, 1933 | The New York Times reports Sherrill's anti-boycott stance. |
| December 2, 1933 | Berlin Boycott: First *Westland* article comes out on the Berlin boycott issue, implying that the American boycott threat is real and that Germany (likely a euphemism for Goebbels) was in a frenzy. |
| December 3, 1933 | The Jewish Daily Bulletin reports on Maccabi Palestine's invitation to attend the First Western Asiatic Games and the World Women's Games in 1934. |
| December 4, 1933 | Edström backs the Nazi attitude towards the Jews in a letter to Brundage: "They are intelligent and unscrupulous. Many of my friends are Jews so you must not think that I am against them, but they must be kept within certain limits." |
| December 4, 1933 | First compulsory meeting (*Pflichtabend*) for NSDAP Members takes place in Jerusalem (two days before the Nazi newspaper incident blows open). |
| December 5, 1933 | Kisch replies to IOC president Baillet-Latour (after the rejection of Palestine's affiliation request) and notes that the YMCA is not entitled to power within the Palestine Olympic Committee; Kisch claims that Jewish sport represents 90% of the sporting movement of Palestine. |
| December 6, 1933 | MacDonald forwards Herbert Liebmann's letter requesting the Völkischer Beobachter to Heinrichs. |
| December 11, 1933 | Heinrichs records that a conflict with Boutagy and Said leads to Boutagy going "wild." |
| December 17, 1933 | The Jewish Telegraphic Agency publishes its Fair Play article on the Berlin boycott issue. |
| December 23, 1933 | Second *Westland* article is published on the Berlin Games. |

| Date | Event |
|------|-------|
| December 24, 1933 | Lord Aberdare writes to IOC president Baillet-Latour claiming that he was not given a copy of a brochure to edit that was circulated and listed Palestine as a member on page six. Lord Aberdare informs the president that he will try to work with the Colonial Office in London to deal with the matter of affiliation. |
| December 24, 1933 | Lord Aberdare sends his report on the situation of German Jewish athletes and the Berlin Games to IOC president Baillet-Latour. |
| December 27, 1933 | Heinrichs has his first meeting with Herbert Liebmann to discuss his request for the *Völkischer Beobachter*. |
| December 29, 1933 | Rohrer's first reply to MacDonald's circular about the Nazi paper. |
| December 31, 1933 | Nazi membership rosters show that Jerusalem has 42 adult and four Hitler Youth members. All adults seem to be involved in the newspaper incident at the Jerusalem YMCA. |
| January 4, 1934 | Heinrichs drops all his engagements that involve Boutagy. |
| January 5, 1934 | Confirmation that Maccabi Tel Aviv has been appointed to prepare a team for the First Western Asiatic Games. |
| January 8, 1934 | First reports that Wilbert Smith will return to some type of role at the Association; Lattof and Auburn refuse to work with him. |
| January 15, 1934 | Surprisingly smooth meeting of the Jerusalem YMCA board, even though Boutagy had threatened trouble. |
| January 16, 1934 | Heinrichs consults with Dr. Gruelin, who is not a Nazi, about how to handle the reactionary attitude of the Nazis. He arranges to see Rohrer and Liebmann about the *Völkischer Beobachter* that evening. |
| January 17, 1934 | Organizing committee for First Western Asiatic Games requests color sketch of flag by airmail and music score of national anthem. |
| January 17, 1934 | Heinrichs succeeds in getting Miss Shapiro's employment approved, with the exception of Boutagy, Khadder, and Said. |
| January 18, 1934 | Library Committee battle over the *Völkischer Beobachter* in which Canaan feels his honor is affected, and who subsequently resigns. |
| January 20, 1934 | Heinrichs leaves the Jamal's house and stores his goods under the grandstands of the Jerusalem YMCA athletic field. |
| January 22, 1934 | Theodor Fast expresses anger to Heinrichs that the Association is taking away significant business from the Fast Hotel. |
| January 25, 1934 | Heinrichs asks Friedrich Lorenz to get him invited to a meeting of the German members who will gather that evening to discuss their position on the *Völkischer Beobachter*. Heinrichs is not invited and his wife thinks that the Germans are afraid. |
| January 26, 1934 | Lorenz reports to Heinrichs on the meeting of twenty-five Germans and issues their ultimatum. |
| January 28, 1934 | *Jewish Daily Bulletin* reports that negotiations have started with German authorities to admit Palestine to the 1936 Olympiad. |
| January 29, 1934 | First letter from Heinrichs to Frank Slack about Nazi newspaper incident. |
| January 30, 1934 | Heinrichs reports to Bishop Graham Brown regarding Boutagy and Said's behavior. |

| Date | Event |
|------|-------|
| January 30, 1934 | Nazi Germans in Palestine celebrate the first anniversary of the rise of Hitler to power. |
| January 31, 1934 | Rohrer is not available to Heinrichs as agreed to provide him a letter on the *Völkischer Beobachter* affair. |
| February, 1934 | Nazis significantly increase their program of historical topics from the NS viewpoint such as lectures on Austria in German History, the Second Reich, International Jewry and screening films. Compulsory and social meetings also begin taking place at German schools and sports clubs. |
| February 1, 1934 | Overseas organization of the NSDAP restructured. |
| February 1, 1934 | Dr. Hermann Schneller of Syrian Orphanage Press offering 10% discounts for all Nazi printing jobs. |
| February 1, 1934 | Most of the ethnically German Palestinians who are agitating at the Jerusalem YMCA become Nazi Party members on this day. |
| February 3, 1934 | Library Committee meets and decides that the Jerusalem YMCA board must provide guidance on how to select papers. |
| February 3, 1934 | *Westland* publishes its article on Goebbels and the German Maccabi Circle, perhaps encouraging IOC member Schmidt's visit to investigate the sport situation in Palestine. |
| February 4, 1934 | Heinrichs prepares the newspaper memo to be shared at the board meeting the next day. |
| February 5, 1934 | Meeting in which the Association board decides to adopt the Nazi rule that twenty-five members constitutes a decision that overrides a decision of the Board, thereby guaranteeing that the *Völkischer Beobachter* will be ordered and the Association will be split by the departure of the Jewish members; Heinrichs is very bitter about Canaan in particular. |
| February 5, 1934 | Yekutieli receives the formal invitation for Palestine to participate in the Women's World Games in London between 9 and 11 August, 1934. |
| February 8, 1934 | Yekutieli sends the Magen David flag design and HaTikva (now the Israeli national anthem) to the organizing committee of the First Western Asiatic Games. He communicates that he is doing all he can to get a delegation to India. He is only supported by one other person (Kurland) in his convictions that it is important for Palestine to send a delegation. |
| February 9, 1934 | Heinrichs departs Jerusalem for Beirut to take counsel from Bayard Dodge on the *Völkischer Beobachter* problem. |
| February 13, 1934 | Heinrichs details his strategy to Slack (with copies to Mott, Ramsey, Harmon and Gethman). He includes the detailed memo that he had prepared for the board and shares with Slack that he is beginning to take security precautions. |
| February 13, 1934 | Lattof offers to negotiate with the Germans privately. |
| February 14, 1934 | *Meraat Elsherk* newspaper starts publishing attacks against the Jerusalem YMCA. |
| February 15, 1934 | *Jamia Al Arabiyeh* publishes an article declaring that the *Völkischer Beobachter* has not been ordered. Ohan identifies the source as Shukri Salman, who Heinrichs decides to fire. Lattof reports to Heinrichs on his meeting with the Germans, with all hope given up. |

| Date | Event |
|---|---|
| February 15, 1934 | Yekutieli confirms to Sondhi for the first time the expected departure to India of a Palestine team for the First Western Asiatic Games. |
| February 17, 1934 | The Maccabi delegation leaves Palestine for India on the SS *Conte Verde*. |
| February 20, 1934 | *Meraat Elsherk* publishes another attack against the Jerusalem YMCA. |
| February 23, 1934 | Boutagy forces Heinrichs at the board meeting to share the letter that he had written to Bayard Dodge, the Bishop, and Harte. The sub-committee to deal with the newspaper issue is established and comprises Heinrichs, Canaan, Stubbs, and Jamal. It is empowered to negotiate directly with H. Schneller, Rohrer, Gruelin, Liebmann, and Probst Rhein. |
| February 26, 1934 | *Meraat Elsherk* publishes another attack against the Jerusalem YMCA. |
| February 26, 1943 | Sub-committee agrees to meet with the Nazis the next day, after two hours of discussion in Heinrichs' office. |
| February 27, 1934 | First Western Asiatic Games commence. |
| February 28, 1934 | Nazi units in Palestine, including Jerusalem, are upgraded to official Nazi Groups (*Ortsgruppen*) by the Reich. |
| March, 1934 | NSDAP Palestine: Probst Rhein, associated with the YMCA, publishes a call to support Hitler's Winter Relief Organization (*Winterhilfswerk*) (although he never joined the NSDAP). |
| March 1, 1934 | Judge Cressall, a member of the Association board, suggests that Heinrichs should sue *Jamia Al Arabiyeh* newspaper for defamation. |
| March 2, 1934 | *Meraat Elsherk* publishes another attack against the Jerusalem YMCA, with particular focus on Heinrichs (The YMCA and the German Papers: The Heinrichs Hotel). |
| March 3, 1934 | Palestine is appointed, during the first meeting of the Western Asiatic Games Confederation, to host the Fourth Western Asiatic Games. |
| March 3, 1934 | Lattof and Auburn take Heinrichs to the George Williams Room and propose to him that he arrange a temporary recall to New York on finance work (to allow things to calm down). |
| March 3, 1934 | Heinrichs sends Slack (with copies to Mott, Ramsey, Harmon and Gethman) copies of all the articles that have appeared in *Meraat Elsherk* on 2/14, 2/20, 2/20, 2/20, 2/26, and 3/2. |
| March 4, 1934 | Heinrichs cables New York requesting that he be recalled temporarily. |
| March 5, 1934 | Yekutieli writes to IOC member Schmidt that Mustakim has accepted the vice presidency of the Palestine Olympic Committee. |
| March 5, 1934 | Palestine Olympic Committee writes to Schmidt regarding his visit to Palestine and confirms meetings with the Muslim community and Mustakim. |
| March 5, 1934 | Heinrichs withdraws all of his files from his office at the Association. |
| March 6, 1934 | Anti-Nazi rally at Madison Square Gardens is held by American Jewish Congress (with Kirby as a speaker from the AAU). |
| March 6, 1934 | The Association is forced finally to order the *Völkischer Beobachter*. |
| March 8, 1934 | Cable arrives in Jerusalem recalling Heinrichs. |

| Date | Event |
|---|---|
| March 8, 1934 | Heinrichs, Auburn, and Lattof write to Slack explaining why they cabled that Heinrichs be recalled; Auburn will later dispute the reasons why he signed this letter. |
| March 9, 1934 | Slack writes to Ramsey without Heinrichs' knowledge to get Mott's input on Nazis targeting YMCAs in Germany. |
| March 9, 1934 | Jerusalem YMCA board grants Heinrichs leave. |
| March 10, 1934 | Heinrichs reconciles longstanding issues between Lattof and Auburn prior to his departure, to ensure stability. |
| March 11, 1934 | Heinrichs leaves Palestine, never to return. |
| March 12, 1934 | Heinrichs writes to Lattof, Auburn, and Canaan from his ship cabin to calm the waters. |
| March 14, 1934 | Schmidt (of the IOC) visits Palestine to inspect the sport situation in the country ahead of Palestine's anticipated affiliation to the IOC in May 1934. |
| March 17, 1934 | Schmidt of the IOC gives a free, publicized, and public lecture at 9:00 p.m. at Kadima Hall on Nahlat Benjamin Street in Tel Aviv |
| March 18, 1934 | Heinrichs meets Allenby and Mott in London, getting the latter's backing on his stance in the *Völkischer Beobachter* affair. |
| March 21, 1934 | New York raises first inquiry about removing Canaan's power of attorney over the Association building in Jerusalem. |
| March 21, 1934 | Yekutieli writes to Mustakim requesting that he accept the vice presidency of the Palestine Olympic Committee formally (following the meetings with Schmidt of the IOC). |
| March 26, 1934 | Harmon writes to Slack and admits that the YMCA Movement is aware of Hitler's war against it. |
| March 27, 1934 | Ali Bey Mustakim accepts formally the position of vice president of Palestine Olympic Committee. |
| March 28, 1934 | Heinrichs arrives in New York and is met by Slack. |
| April 3, 1934 | Heinrichs drafts the newspaper committee memo for the IC/YMCA and sends it to Slack. He meets with Dimnock, the project manager of the Jerusalem Association's architectural project. He cables Lattof and is still functioning as the secretary-general from New York. |
| April 4, 1934 | Heinrichs speaks for fifteen minutes on the situation in Palestine on NDC. |
| April 6, 1934 | Heinrichs receives a cable from his wife saying that things are quieting down in Jerusalem. |
| April 7, 1934 | Canaan writes to Slack arguing that Heinrichs is incompatible with Jerusalem. |
| April 9, 1934 | Confidential memo on newspaper situation prepared by Heinrichs and Slack for IC/YMCA meeting in May. |
| April 11, 1934 | Heinrichs led to believe that Lattof betrayed him. |
| April 12, 1934 | Heinrichs meets with the associate director of the Jerusalem YMCA's Physical Department in Springfield, Massachusetts (who received his scholarship to study there through Heinrichs, who had also hired him). |

| Date | Event |
| --- | --- |
| April 12, 1934 | Colonial Office, Downing Street confirms to Lord Aberdare that the Palestine Olympic Committee is not representative of all sport in Palestine, just of the Jewish national home in Palestine. |
| April 20, 1934 | Heinrichs receives letter from his brother in Jerusalem documenting that things are getting worse. |
| April 24, 1934 | Secret meeting of the Jerusalem YMCA executive committee is held to oust Heinrichs. |
| April 24, 1934 | Heinrichs receives letter from his wife noting opposition of Canaan to Heinrichs. |
| April 24, 1934 | Edström congratulates Yekutieli on Palestine's results in the First Western Asiatic Games. |
| April 27, 1934 | Heinrichs receives a cable from his wife while he is in Chicago notifying him that the Board has requested his resignation and she calls for an investigation. Heinrichs meets with Fuad Khadder, the other Palestinian staff member on scholarship in the US. |
| April 28, 1934 | Heinrichs goes to Cleveland to meet Fred Ramsey. He is met by Margaret Ramsey, who had been his assistant during his first year in Palestine. Heinrichs and Mr. Ramsey have an all-night meeting about the Jerusalem situation. Everything seems fine to Heinrichs. |
| April 28, 1934 | Ramsey confides privately to Slack that Heinrichs will probably not be going back (without Heinrichs' knowledge). |
| April 29, 1934 | Ramsey's first indication to Heinrichs that the board and secretary-general might not be compatible. |
| April 29, 1934 | Kisch denies (to one Mr. Nadav) his associations with Nazi General Hermann Göring. |
| April 30, 1934 | Heinrichs expresses his first willingness to resign on condition that the principles of the Association are protected. The Nazi newspaper had to go. |
| May 2, 1934 | Auburn writes to Slack and copies Heinrichs, implying that Lattof had somehow set him up. It is still not clear (at all) what actually happened. |
| May 2, 1934 | Yekutieli writes to *Westland* and denies its claims and accuses the paper of falling victim to a deception. |
| May 4, 1934 | Slack writes to Mott, undercutting Heinrichs but acknowledging the financial success that he has made of the Jerusalem YMCA during his tenure there. |
| May 7, 1934 | Heinrichs receives a cable in New York (from Jerusalem YMCA president Bowman) advising him to stay in the US. |
| May 8, 1934 | Heinrichs receives a letter from Lattof and a second from Bowman, the latter of which Heinrichs considers to be a betrayal of their friendship. |
| May 9, 1934 | Heinrichs receives a cable from Fekhri Bey Nashashibi on the morning that Heinrichs is scheduled to meet with the IC/YMCA in New York. Nashashibi calls for an investigation into the actions of the board of the Jerusalem YMCA. |
| May 9, 1934 | IC/YMCA formally appoints Slack and Ramsey as the investigators. |
| May 11, 1934 | Harmon makes first suggestions to Heinrichs that he consider a financial role in New York. |
| May 11, 1934 | Slack and Ramsey provided with aide mémoire to guide their investigation and resolution of the newspaper issue. |

| Date | Event |
|------|-------|
| May 12, 1934 | Dorothy Heinrichs decides to stay in Jerusalem. Slack leaves for Jerusalem. |
| May 14, 1934 | *Westland* responds to Yekutieli, refusing to publish a correction about its claims regarding Kisch. It insists that Kisch was implicated by the German Maccabi Circle. |
| May 15, 1934 | IOC meets at its session in Athens. Germany is confirmed as host of the 1936 Olympic Games. |
| May 16, 1934 | IOC accepts Palestine's membership request to affiliate to the Olympic Movement as a national Olympic committee. |
| May 18, 1934 | First Annual Open Tennis Tournament under the auspices of the (Arab) Amateur Sports Clubs of Palestine is held. |
| May 18, 1934 | The *New York Times* publishes the news that Palestine has been affiliated to the Olympic Movement, but Heinrichs does not record anything related to it in his diary. |
| May 19, 1934 | The IOC formally conveys its recognition of Palestine's affiliation in writing. |
| June 7, 1934 | Heinrichs gives his seventy-fifth lecture on the situation at the Jerusalem YMCA at Prospect Temple in Brooklyn. |
| June 11, 1934 | First cable from Heinrichs' wife about her planned return to Boston on July 8. |
| June 14, 1934 | America withholds acceptance of its invitation to the Olympic Games. |
| June 20, 1934 | Palestine Olympic Committee holds its inaugural meeting. |
| June 22, 1934 | Invitations sent from Organizing Committee in Berlin to Egyptian Olympic Committee and Palestine Olympic Association. |
| June 22, 1934 | Organizing Committee of the Berlin Games writes to German Consul Wolff in Jerusalem confirming that the POC has been recognized by the IOC, Mustakim has become the vice president of the Palestine Olympic Committee, the YMCA promises to cooperate, and that Lord Aberdare confirms that the Secretary of State for the Colonies has approved the recognition of the POC. The Organizing Committee also asks for information on Kisch's personality. |
| June 25, 1934 | IC/YMCA offers Jerusalem YMCA role of secretary-general to Wilbert Smith. |
| June 26, 1934 | Investigators decide that Heinrichs' return to Jerusalem is inadvisable. |
| June 28, 1934 | Harmon requests Heinrichs for a long and unhurried meeting. |
| June 28, 1934 | Kisch Informs the IOC that the POC has held its inaugural meeting. |
| June 30, 1934 | Grover Little breaks the news to Heinrichs that Slack and Ramsey found his return inadvisable. |
| June 30, 1934 | Night of the Long Knives begins in Germany. |
| July, 1934 | High Commissioner Wauchope acknowledges Yekutieli's letter of 11 July regarding his patronage of the 2nd Maccabiad, accepting to be Patron because Maccabi Palestine is an "...altogether non-political organization". |
| July 2, 1934 | Night of the Long Knives concludes in Germany. Estimated range of those killed is between 85 and 1,000 of Hitler's rivals. |
| July 2, 1934 | IC/YMCA's executive committee confidentially approves Heinrichs' transfer without informing him. |

| Date | Event |
|---|---|
| July 5, 1934 | Jewish Telegraphic Agency publishes front-page story about Heinrichs' resignation. |
| July 6, 1934 | *Jewish Daily Bulletin* writes that Heinrichs confirmed that he had resigned because the Jerusalem YMCA's board had wanted to keep a Nazi paper in its library. |
| July 9, 1934 | Heinrichs' family arrives in Boston. |
| July 10, 1934 | Heinrichs writes to Auburn and instructs him to sell his property in Jerusalem. |
| July 20, 1934 | The Heinrichses set sail for Honolulu. |
| August 1, 1934 | Meetings in August in Stockholm between Brundage, Diem, von Halt, Lewald, and Justus Meyerhof (a Jewish member of the Berliner Sports-Club) to discuss the German situation. |
| August 23, 1934 | Conrad Heinrichs returns from Jerusalem to Ohio. |
| September 1, 1934 | Heinrichs departs Honolulu for New York to meet with IC/YMCA. |
| September 11, 1934 | Slack and Ramsey inform Heinrichs that he is out. |
| September 12, 1934 | Memo on settlement of newspaper controversy excludes any reference to Heinrichs. |
| September 26, 1934 | American Olympic Association (AOA) finally accepts its invitation to the Berlin Olympic Games, but the AAU is in disagreement. Palestine withholds. |
| October 1, 1934 | Nazi groups in Jaffa and Sarona merge. |
| October 15, 1934 | Heinrichs receives a letter from Ohan about his being fired, along with Sami Suz and Mike Haddad, for supporting Heinrichs in the newspaper controversy. |
| November 1, 1934 | Rudolf Hess writes a letter to IOC president Baillet-Latour to assure him that new restrictive German laws do not apply to sports clubs. |
| November 4, 1934 | Kisch writes the Organizing Committee of the 1936 Olympic Games and declines Palestine's invitation to participate in the 1936 Games. |
| November 8, 1934 | Smith writes to Slack that Lattof was forced to fire Ohan, Suz, and Haddad, and suggests continued external interests in the Association. |
| November 12, 1934 | Cressall writes to Heinrichs about continued intrigue at the Association in Jerusalem. |
| November 13, 1934 | Heinrichs burns many of his papers from Jerusalem. |
| November 21, 1934 | The New York Times publishes the news of Palestine's boycott of the Olympic Games. |
| November 21, 1934 | Lattof writes a long letter to Harmon in which he discusses the firing of Suz, Ohan, and Haddad. |
| November 30, 1934 | Buchalter reports takeover of *Deutscher Sportverein Jerusalem* by a completely Nazi board and expresses hope for better cooperation between the club and NSDAP. The club might be central to the formation of a Palestinian delegation to the Berlin Olympics, whose football team was captained by the associate physical director of the Jerusalem YMCA's Physical Department, who Heinrichs had hired and sent to Springfield College on a scholarship. |
| December 5, 1934 | Mott expresses his wish that Heinrichs was back in Jerusalem, where problems continue. |

| Date | Event |
|------|-------|
| December 7, 1934 | At its meeting between December 7 and 9, 1934, the AAU protests the AOA decision to go to Berlin. |
| December 21, 1934 | Heinrichs sends his final letter to Slack, copying Mott, Harmon, and Ramsey, terminating his relationship with the Jerusalem situation and calling the Association unsound at its core. |
| January 7, 1935 | Edström writes Yekutieli and questions the wisdom of Palestine's not participating in the 1936 Olympic Games in Berlin. |
| February, 1935 | Sports cooperation with Jews at the Jerusalem YMCA is back to normal, with significant increase in attendance. |
| March 7, 1935 | Searing response from Yekutieli to Edström, which includes the real reasons for Palestine not participating in the 1936 Games. |
| March 7, 1935 | Aberdare declines Yekutieli's invitation to attend the Second Maccabiad in Tel Aviv. |
| March 18, 1935 | The *New York Times* again reports that Palestine has withdrawn from attending the Olympic Games. |
| April 1, 1935 | Second Maccabiad starts with a large delegation from Germany approved by Goebbels. |
| April 2, 1935 | Alvah Miller accepts Jerusalem YMCA secretary-general position. |
| June 20, 1935 | As German Jews are being denaturalized upon their arrival in Palestine, *Palestine Post* reports that if they return to Germany they will be immediately interned in camps for "correction". |
| June 21, 1935 | Jerusalem YMCA's Third Annual Open Track and Field Championship includes Zionist sport officials and athletes. |
| July 11, 1935 | Syrian Orphanage buildings put up for sale. (By 1937 it complains of being located in a neighborhood of fanatical Jews.) |
| September, 1935 | The Reich Federal Sports Association asks all sports clubs to discuss Jewish Question during the month. |
| September 13, 1935 | Brundage travels to Germany to investigate the situation with sport there. |
| September 25, 1935 | German Maccabi withdraws from the 1936 Berlin Olympic Games. |
| October 8, 1935 | AAU again attempts boycott of Berlin Olympics. |
| November 12, 1935 | Letter from Selig Brodetsky to Baillet-Latour included in IOC Bulletin No. 30, Baillet-Latour also publishes a letter in the same bulletin. The two organizations seem to state their final positions, putting on a good face over their dispute regarding the 1936 Berlin Games. |
| December 6, 1935 | Last American boycott attempt within American Olympic Association. |
| February 27, 1936 | Yekutieli writes to Schmidt acknowledging that Schmidt is the reason Palestine was able to become affiliated to the IOC. He asks Schmidt for clarification on the requirements for Kisch to join the IOC's board. |
| March 7, 1936 | IOC member Schmidt confirms to Yekutieli that the IOC has already considered the subject of Kisch becoming a member of its executive commission, but notes that Palestine must compete in an Olympic Games first. |

| Date | Event |
|---|---|
| April, 1936 | Lattof removed from YMCA suddenly. Auburn was on furlough and is also not permitted to return. |
| April 1, 1936 | Kisch writes to Yekutieli regarding how to reply to the IOC's position regarding a Palestine member on the board of the IOC. |
| May 16, 1936 | Lattof family departs Palestine for the US. |
| May 22, 1936 | Kisch reprimands Yekutieli for his ardent Jewish feelings, perhaps because he had discovered that Yekutieli wrote to Edström personally and informed him of Palestine's real reason for boycotting the 1936 Games (although the exact reason for Kisch's displeasure with Yekutieli is unknown). |
| May 27, 1936 | Lattof family arrives in New York. |
| July 30, 1936 | IOC Session in Berlin at which Brundage is elected for the first time to IOC executive commission. |
| August 1, 1936 | Berlin Olympic Games open. Heinrichs attends the ceremony. He does not identify a Palestine delegation in his diary, despite Palestinian claims that a Palestinian football team traveled to Berlin and participated in the football competition. |
| August 13, 1936 | Nazi organized football conference organized by Herr Shreker commences on the sidelines of the Olympic Games at which Lebanon is admitted to FIFA. The physical director of the Jerusalem YMCA, who had studied at Springfield College, claims that he captained a Palestinian football team in Berlin and resided in the Athletes' Village. There is no record of Palestine participating in the official football competition. Was Palestine in attendance at this conference through Nazi channels? |
| August 14, 1936 | Nazi organized football conference on the sidelines of the Olympic Games concludes. |
| August 16, 1936 | Berlin Olympic Games conclude. |
| May 17, 1937 | Western Asiatic Games Confederation writes to Yekutieli and asks Palestine to host the Second Western Asiatic Games. |
| February 21, 1938 | Letter from Kisch to Schmidt about attending the IOC meeting in Alexandria, Egypt between 21 and 23 March, 1938 to discuss participation in Tokyo (but also, it seems, his joining the IOC executive commission). |
| March 21, 1938 | Kisch begins meetings with IOC in Cairo, Egypt about Palestine's participation in the 1940 Olympic Games in Tokyo, Japan and about joining the IOC executive commission. |
| March 23, 1938 | Kisch concludes his meetings with the IOC in Cairo, Egypt. |
| March 27, 1938 | Kisch finalizes *Palestine Diary*. |
| April 20, 1938 | Executive committee of the POC convenes at the San Remo Hotel in Tel Aviv to discuss Palestine's participation in the 1940 Olympic Games in Tokyo; Yekutieli becomes vice president of the Palestine Olympic Committee and Heth becomes its Honorary Secretary, taking over Yekutieli's former role. Kisch transfers POC office to his home in Haifa (from Tel Aviv). |
| April 24, 1938 | Kisch requests Yekutieli to transfer Olympic files to Heth. |
| April 24, 1938 | Kisch informs IOC that he has moved the POC secretariat to Haifa. |
| July 13, 1938 | Lord Aberdare rebukes Yekutieli about "...what was done in Jewish interest...". The source of his anger is not clear. |

| Date | Event |
|------|-------|
| 1939 | Fifth Aliyah ends. Approximately 250,000 Jews arrived in Palestine during this wave of immigration because of the rise of the Nazis in Germany. |
| January 10, 1939 | Edström rebukes Yekutieli for not participating in Berlin and refuses to change fundamental rules to accommodate Palestine. The source of friction is not clear. |
| April 21, 1939 | FASCP hosts its edition of the Palestine Track & Field Championship and its program includes a letter of best wishes from Kisch, as POC president, noting the "great value" of the event "in the eventual selection of representatives of Palestine for the next Olympic Games." |
| September 1, 1939 | Second World War breaks out. |
| September 2, 1939 | Heinrichs manages to get out of Europe on one of the last ships to leave France. |
| September 3, 1939 | Great Britain declares war on Germany and Canaan is immediately arrested in Palestine, along with many others, and interned in camps for those who have close connections with the Germans. |
| 1941 | "Maccabi Troop" of the British army formed. |
| March 1, 1941 | Headquarters British Forces Palestine & Transjordan in Jerusalem reject Yekutieli's request to join a Palestinian Unit of the British army. |
| 1944 | Maccabi Torch Race introduced in Palestine; run annually on the Festival of Lights (Chanukah) since its introduction. |
| April 7, 1943 | Kisch dies in North Africa at Wadi Akarit. |
| May 12, 1945 | First record of the Brigadier Kisch annual memorial international track and field championships. |
| June 29, 1945 | A report of unidentified origin (No. 447/45/App., now housed at the Wingate Institute in Netanya) identifies that the Arab Palestine Sports Federation was re-organized in 1945 with the purpose of serving non-Jewish amateur clubs in Palestine; it identifies the federation's PO Box as 279, Jaffa and that its negotiations for international affiliations are pending). |
| September 18, 1945 | Edström confirms to Yekutieli that he held a meeting in London with Gad Frumkin, who will be the new president of the POC. |
| July 9, 1946 | IAAF responds to the Arab Palestine Sports Federation's request for affiliation, directing it to the existing IAAF-member organization in Palestine (Yekutieli's FASCP in Tel Aviv). |
| July 22, 1946 | Bombing of King David Hotel by Lehi. Jerusalem starts its slide into civil war. |
| January 23, 1947 | Paul Hartman writes to Harold Friermood (in the US) stating that he hopes to arrange a second YMCA delegation to the Olympics in 1948. |
| May 28, 1947 | Hartman writes the Chief Secretary requesting more information on the committee to which the Olympic invitation was sent for the London Olympic Games. |
| June 19, 1947 | Chief Secretary's office responds to Hartmann and provides complete list of current members of POC, including its new President, Frumkin, and James H. H. Pollock. |
| September 13, 1947 | In the lead up to the London Olympic Games, Brundage labels the Jerusalem YMCA's report by Hartman (to Friermood) as "Rapport sur la situation des sports de Palestine" and distributes it to IOC members to inform their discussions regarding Palestine's participation in the St. Moritz Winter and London Summer Olympic Games. |

| Date | Event |
| --- | --- |
| November 29, 1947 | United Nations recommends to partition Palestine into two states, one Jewish, one Arab. |
| January 5, 1948 | Chief Secretary's office blocks POC from traveling to 1948 Winter Olympic Games in St. Moritz, Switzerland on financial technicalities. |
| February 22, 1948 | Arab operatives bomb the central Jewish business district of Jerusalem on Ben Yehuda Street. |
| May 14, 1948 | David Ben Gurion proclaims Israel's independence. |
| May 15, 1948 | Great Britain surrenders the mandate for Palestine. The person overseeing the final loading of trucks in a special zone at Haifa port is Pollock, founding vice president of the Palestine Olympic Committee with Kisch and Yekutieli. |
| July 16, 1948 | IOC telegrams the POC that Palestine will be barred from the 1948 Games in London. |
| July 26, 1948 | Yehoshuah Alouf appeals to Edström, now IOC president, to reconsider barring Palestine from the Games. He notes his discussions with Edström in 1924 at the Olympic Games in Paris. |
| July 27, 1948 | IOC rejects Palestine's London participation request because "...the question is so involved at present..." |
| December 26, 1948 | MWU Congress convenes for first time in Tel Aviv. |
| April 5, 1949 | Olympic Committee of Israel (OCI) writes to the IOC arguing that Lausanne cannot stall Israel's recognition further because the UN Security Council had recommended that Israel be accepted as a member of the United Nations. |
| May 22, 1949 | IOC requests assurance from the OCI that it is against discrimination in sport |
| January 19, 1950 | Edström writes to IOC chancellor Otto Mayer asking him to inform the OCI that a decision regarding their membership will be taken at the IOC Session in Copenhagen, but that there will be no recognition without fulfillment of the IOC's conditions. |
| March 19, 1950 | OCI is reorganized and confirms to the IOC that "...all athletes in our country without distinction of religion or race will be admitted by the national federations of Israel and also recognized by our authority." |
| May 26, 1950 | IOC informs the OCI that it has postponed its recognition. |
| November 2, 1950 | Daniel Ferris reports to Brundage that the OCI claims that Arabs in Israel have been given citizenship and have seemed to satisfy the IOC conditions. |
| March 4, 1951 | OCI adopts its new statutes. |
| April 19, 1951 | Edström proposes to Mayer that Israel be a sleeping member in 1951 and confirms that no Mediterranean Games participation by Israel will be permitted. |
| April 24, 1951 | OCI confirms to IOC the reconstitution of its executive board. |
| May 8, 1951 | IOC postpones recognition of Israel at its session in Vienna because there are two Olympic committees for the country. |
| May 17, 1951 | IOC letter to OCI requests that OCI produce a letter signed by both national Olympic committees in Israel (those associated with Maccabi and Hapoel) confirming their merger into one national Olympic committee for Israel. |
| May 28, 1951 | IOC sends letter to OCI requesting further details on a new, single national Olympic committee. |

| Date | Event |
|------|-------|
| August 29, 1951 | Israeli Consul General in NY writes to its Ministry of Foreign Affairs regarding the need to fix the rift between Hapoel and Maccabi. |
| November 11, 1951 | Maccabi and Hapoel agree to cooperate on forming one Olympic committee for Israel. |
| November 19, 1951 | IOC writes to Betar regarding its claim that it is the appropriate Olympic committee for Israel. |
| November 19, 1951 | IOC writes to the Organizing Committee for the 1952 Olympic Games in Helsinki to inquire if invitations to participate have been sent to either Israel or Palestine. |
| November 22, 1951 | The Organizing Committee for the 1952 Olympic Games in Helsinki confirms to the IOC that it has not sent invitations to either Israel or Palestine. |
| December 19, 1951 | OCI sends letter to IOC confirming the merger of Maccabi and Hapoel national Olympic committees into one committee for Israel. |
| December 22, 1951 | Edström writes to Mayer confirming the merger of the two national Olympic committees in Israel and requests that it be recognized and that the IOC should ignore the affiliation request from Betar. |
| December 31, 1951 | IOC finally sends out its letter recognizing the Olympic Committee of Israel. |
| July 19, 1952 | Yekutieli and the first Israeli delegation to an Olympic Games enters the Olympic stadium in Helsinki, Finland. |
| June 15, 1959 | Heinrichs dies in Middlebury, Vermont. |
| May 9, 1972 | MWU president Gildesgame writes to Yekutieli, congratulating him on his seventy-fifth birthday and confirming a contribution of £2,000 sterling to support Yekutieli's project to clean up the site of the Hasmonean graves at Modi'in. |
| August 26, 1972 | The 1972 Summer Olympic Games open in Munich, Germany with an Israeli delegation comprising thirty athletes, coaches, and officials. |
| September 5, 1972 | Palestinian guerillas of the Black September faction of the Palestine Liberation Organization (PLO) break into the Olympic Village and take 11 members of the Israeli delegation hostage. The American Broadcasting Corporation (ABC), broadcasting the Games via satellite for the first time, covers the incident live for the world. |
| September 6, 1972 | Jim McKay, of ABC, confirms to the world the death of all eleven Israeli hostages. |
| September 7, 1972 | The surviving members of the Israeli delegation to the Games leave Germany for Israel. |
| September 15, 1972 | Milton Stark, of Milton Stark Productions, Ltd., writes to Yekutieli regarding the attack in Munich, and describes it as "a terribly frightening disaster...which will ever remain in the minds of millions thruout [sic] the world...as a dastardly deed." |
| 1978 | The Palestine Liberation Organization forms a reconstituted Arab Palestine Olympic Committee. |
| 1979 | The PLO's reconstituted Olympic committee submits its first application for membership to the IOC from its headquarters in Beirut, Lebanon. |
| 1980 | The PLO's reconstituted Olympic committee attends the 1980 Summer Olympic Games in Moscow for the first time. Israel joined the boycott of the Games and was not present. |

| Date | Event |
|---|---|
| 1981 | The Asian Games Federation, cofounded after the Second World War by Sondhi, is restructured as the Olympic Council of Asia. Its headquarters are moved permanently to Kuwait. |
| 1982 | Israel is excluded from the Olympic Council of Asia. |
| 1982 | Israel invades Lebanon and forces the PLO to withdraw from the country. The headquarters of the Palestine Olympic Committee moves between Baghdad, Kuwait City, and Tunis between 1982 and 1993. |
| September 13, 1993 | Israel and the PLO sign the Declaration of Principles on Interim Self-Government Arrangements (Oslo I Accord) on the White House lawn. |
| September 13, 1993 | The Palestine Olympic Committee sends its application for recognition to the IOC immediately after the signing of the Oslo I Accord. |
| September 17, 1993 | The 101st Session of the IOC opens in Monaco and approves provisional recognition of the new Palestine Olympic Committee. |
| 1994 | Olympic Committee of Israel finally admitted to the European Olympic Committees after twelve years of exclusion from Asia. |
| 1995 | Palestine joins the Olympic Council of Asia. |
| July 19, 1996 | Palestine's first Arab delegation to the Olympics enters the stadium in Atlanta at the 1996 Summer Olympic Games, led by Majid Abu Maraheel, its flag bearer and sole athlete; Palestine participates in each subsequent Summer Olympic Games in Sydney (2000), Athens (2004), Beijing (2008), London (2012), and Rio de Janeiro (2016). |
| 1998 | Palestine admitted to FIFA. |
| 2015 | Boycott effort of Israel in global sport begins in FIFA. |
| 2017 | Palestine Olympic Committee and Palestine Football Association president Major General Jibril Rajoub gives a symbolic red card to Israel at the 65th FIFA Congress in Manama, Bahrain. |
| 2018 | Rajoub encourages fans to burn pictures and the jersey of Argentine football star Lionel Messi, if Messi goes ahead with a friendly against Israel in Jerusalem in the lead-up to the 2018 FIFA World Cup in Russia. Extremely graphic photo mockups of a beheaded Messi are circulated Online. FIFA suspends Rajoub for one year and fines him for "inciting hatred and violence". |

# Endnotes

## Preface

1   Norbert Müller, ed., "3.25 Sport Is a Peacemaker," *Pierre de Coubertin 1863–1937. Olympism: Selected Writings* (Lausanne: International Olympic Committee, 2000), 241.
2   Arnd Krüger and William Murray, eds., *The Nazi Olympics: Sport, Politics, and Appeasement in the 1930s* (Urbana: University of Illinois Press, 2003), 2.
3   David Margolick, "Passing the Torch," *New York Times Sunday Book Review*, 13 July 2008. https://www.nytimes.com/2008/07/13/books/review/Margolick-t.html.
4   Yosef Yekutieli, "Sketch, Original Maccabi Logo," 5-1-10, Joseph Yekutieli 1914–1933, Joseph Yekutieli Maccabi Sport Archives (Tel Aviv, Israel), 1.
5   Theodor Herzl, *The Jewish State* (New York: American Zionist Emergency Council, 1946), 139.
6   Geoffrey Wigoder, ed., *New Encyclopedia of Zionism and Israel K-Z*, vol. 2 of *New Encyclopedia of Zionism and Israel* (Madion, Teaneck, London, and Toronto: Fairleigh Dickinson University Press and Associated University Presses, 1994), 1016.
7   Max Nordau, *Max Nordau to His People* (New York City: Scopus Publishing Company, Inc., 1941), 89.
8   Board of Regents of the University of Nebraska, "Jews, Antisemitism, and Sports in Britain, 1900–1939," in *Emancipation Through Muscles*, ed. Michael Brenner and Gideon Reuveni (Lincoln: University of Nebraska Press, 2006), 143.
9   Wikipedia, "Young Men's Muslim Association," in *Young Men's Muslim Association.* https://en.wikipedia.org/wiki/Young_Men%27s_Muslim_Association.
10  Elwood S. Brown, "Address, Presumably in Antwerp, Belgium at a Meeting in Parallel with the VII Olympiad," Y.USA.9-2-2, Physical Education Program Records, Kautz Family YMCA Archives (Minneapolis, MN), 1.
11  Ibid., 2.
12  Ibid., 3.
13  Ibid.
14  Ibid., 4.

## Chapter 1

1   Yosef Yekutieli, "Essay, the Maccabi-Soldier," 5-1-9, Joseph Yekutieli, no date, Joseph Yekutieli Maccabi Sport Archives (Tel Aviv, Israel).
2   "Oberst Kisch Treibt Politik," *Westland*, 17 March 1934, 4.

3   Yotam Hotam, "'Re-Orient-Ation': Sport and the Transformation of the Jewish Body and Identity," *Israel Studies* 20, no. 2 (June 2015): 65–66.

4   Ibid., 56.

5   Ibid., 66.

6   Ibid.

7   Yekutieli, "Essay, the Maccabi-Soldier."

8   J. Sigfrid Edtsröm, "Correspondence, Boycott of Palestine from 1936 Olympic Games, to Yekutieli," 5-1-30, Joseph Yekutieli 1934–1948, Joseph Yekutieli Maccabi Sport Archives (Tel Aviv, Israel, 1935).

9   Federation of the Amateur Sports Clubs of Palestine, "Correspondence, Boycott of 1936 Olympic Games, from Yekutieli to Edström," ADI.29 0004 FASCP, SYNSO 0001542, The Zvi Nishri Archive for Sports and Physical Education in the Wingate Institute (Netanya, Israel, 1935).

10  Federation of the Amateur Sports Clubs of Palestine, "Minutes of Meeting, Foundational Meeting," ADI 5.27 0002, SYNSO 0052466, The Zvi Nishri Archive for Sports and Physical Education in the Wingate Institute (Netanya, Israel, 1931).

11  Federation of the Amateur Sports Clubs of Palestine, "Correspondence, Boycott of 1936 Olympic Games, from Yekutieli to Edström," 1.

12  Ibid.

13  Ibid.

14  Ibid., 2.

15  Ibid.

16  Ibid., 2–3.

17  Ibid., 3.

18  Norman Bentwich and Michael Kisch, *Brigadier Frederick Kisch: Soldier and Zionist* (Tonbridge, Kent: Tonbridge Printers Ltd., 1966), 91–92.

19  Wigoder, *Encyclopedia*, Vol. 2, 909.

20  "Essay, the History of the Maccabi Organisation—in the Beginning," 4237 British Maccabi, The Weizmann Archives (Rehovot, Israel, 1944), 19.

21  Ibid.

22  Geoffrey Wigoder, ed., *New Encyclopedia of Zionism and Israel A-J*, vol. 1 of *New Encyclopedia of Zionism and Israel* (Madion, Teaneck, London, and Toronto: Fairleigh Dickinson University Press and Associated University Presses, 1994), 603.

23  "Essay, the History of the Maccabi Organisation—in the Beginning," 20.

24  Ibid., 27.

25  Ibid.

26  Allen Guttmann, *The Games Must Go On: Avery Brundage and the Olympic Movement* (New York: Columbia University Press, 1984), 25.

27  Ibid., 24.

28  Ibid., 253–54.

29  Yosef Yekutieli, "Correspondence, European Motorcycle Tour, to Sunbeam Motorcycles, 10 September," 1–40, European Motorcycle Tour 1930–33, Joseph Yekutieli Maccabi Sport Archives (Tel Aviv, Israel, 1930).

30  Ibid., 2.

31  World Union Maccabee Palestine Branch, "Correspondence, Cancellation of Banker's Guarantee After Maccabi Motorcycle Tour, Yekutieli to Royal Automobile Club of Egypt," 1–40, European Motorcycle Tour 1930–33, Joseph Yekutieli Maccabi Sport Archives (Tel Aviv, Israel, 1931), 2.

32  Ibid.

33  Yosef Yekutieli, "Correspondence, European Motorcycle Tour, to Sunbeam Motorcycles, 10 September," 1–40, European Motorcycle Tour 1930–33, Joseph Yekutieli Maccabi Sport Archives (Tel Aviv, Israel, 1930).

34  Ibid.

35  Ibid., 2.

36  World Union Maccabee Palestine Branch, "Maccabi Palestine Bank Guarantee," 1.

37  The Shell Oil Company of Palestine, "Correspondence, Sponsorship Supplies, 25 March, Company to Yekutieli," 1–40, European Motorcycle Tour 1930–33, Joseph Yekutieli Maccabi Sport Archives (Tel Aviv, Israel, 1931).

38  Vacuum Oil Company, "Correspondence, Sponsorship Supplies, 27 March to Yekutieli," 1–40, European Motorcycle Tour 1930–33, Joseph Yekutieli Maccabi Sport Archives (Tel Aviv, Israel, 1931).

39  The Asiatic Petroleum Company, Limited, "Correspondence, Sponsorship Supplies, 17 June, to Yekutieli," 1–40, European Motorcycle Tour 1930–33, Joseph Yekutieli Maccabi Sport Archives (Tel Aviv, Israel, 1931).

40  Physical Culture Institute of Gymnastics and Sport in Palestine, "Correspondence, European Motorcycle Tour, 2 February, Form Letter to Anonymous," 1–40, European Motorcycle Tour 1930–33, Joseph Yekutieli Maccabi Sport Archives (Tel Aviv, Israel, 1931).

41  Ibid.

42  Royal Automobile Club de Belgique, "Correspondence, European Motorcycle Tour," 1–40, European Motorcycle Tour 1930–33, Joseph Yekutieli Maccabi Sport Archives (Tel Aviv, Israel, 1931).

43  Association Internationale des Automobile-Clubs Reconnus, "Correspondence, Affiliation Enquiry of 4 February from Palestine, Secretary General Lt. Col. G. Peron to Yekutieli," 1–40, European Motorcycle Tour 1930–33, Joseph Yekutieli Maccabi Sport Archives (Tel Aviv, Israel, 1931).

44  Automobil-Club der Schweiz, "Correspondence, European Motorcycle Tour," 1–40, European Motorcycle Tour 1930–33, Joseph Yekutieli Maccabi Sport Archives (Tel Aviv, Israel, 1931).

45  Yosef Yekutieli, "Business Card," 5.01 53 Joseph Yekutieli, The Zvi Nishri Archive for Sports and Physical Education in the Wingate Institute (Netanya, Israel).

46  L'Independant, "News Article, Les Motocyclistes Palestiniens à Salonique," 1–40, European Motorcycle Tour 1930–33, Joseph Yekutieli Maccabi Sport Archives (Tel Aviv, Israel, 1931).

47  Ibid.

48  Ibid.

49  Ibid.

50  Jewish Telegraphic Agency, "Palestine Jewish Motor-Cyclists Arrested in Poland Because Visas Expired," JTA Daily News Bulletin, 26 August 1931, 3.

51 *Manchester Evening Chronicle*, "News Article, Arrival of Maccabi Motorcycle Tour," 1–40, European Motorcycle Tour 1930–33, Joseph Yekutieli Maccabi Sport Archives (Tel Aviv, Israel, 1931).

52 "Clipping, Photo of Motorcycle Team with the Lord Mayor of London," 1–40, European Motorcycle Tour 1930–33, Joseph Yekutieli Maccabi Sport Archives (Tel Aviv, Israel, 1931).

53 *Manchester Evening Chronicle*, "News Article, Arrival of Maccabi Motorcycle Tour."

54 Bentwich and Kisch, *Brigadier Kisch*.

55 Ibid., 190.

56 Ibid.

57 Wikipedia, "Battle of Wadi Akarit" (2019). https://en.wikipedia.org/wiki/Battle_of_Wadi_Akarit#Background.

58 Wigoder, *Encyclopedia Vol. 2*, 810.

59 Bentwich and Kisch, *Brigadier Kisch*, 124.

60 Ibid.

61 Wikipedia, "Second Battle of El Alamein," in *Second Battle of El Alamein* (2019). https://en.wikipedia.org/wiki/Second_Battle_of_El_Alamein.

62 Wikipedia, "Second Battle of El Alamein: The Break-In," in *Second Battle of El Alamein* (2019). https://en.wikipedia.org/wiki/Second_Battle_of_El_Alamein#Phase_one:_the_break-in.

63 Wikipedia, "Second Battle of El Alamein: Aftermath," in *Second Battle of El Alamein* (2019). https://en.wikipedia.org/wiki/Second_Battle_of_El_Alamein#Aftermath.

64 Bentwich and Kisch, *Brigadier Kisch*, 181.

65 Ibid.

66 Ibid., 15–16.

67 Ibid., 13–14.

68 Ibid., 13.

69 Ibid., 15.

70 Ibid.

71 Ibid.

72 Ibid., 16.

73 Ibid.

74 Ibid., 17.

75 Ibid.

76 Ibid.

77 Ibid.

78 Ibid., 18.

79 Ibid., 22.

80 Ibid., 47–53.

81 Ibid., 59.

82 Ibid.

83 Ibid., 83.

84 Ibid., 83–84.

85 Ibid., 104.

86 Frederick H. Kisch, *Palestine Diary* (London: Victor Gollancz Ltd, 1938), 246.

87  Wigoder, *Encyclopedia Vol. 1*, 51–52.
88  Ibid., 52.
89  Bentwich and Kisch, *Brigadier Kisch*, 113.
90  Ibid., 118.
91  Ibid.
92  Ibid., 102.
93  Ibid.
94  Ibid., 102–3.
95  Ibid., 113–14.
96  Ibid., 104–5.
97  Ibid., 114.
98  Ibid., 123.
99  Ibid., 191.
100 Ibid.
101 Ibid., 193.
102 Ibid., 195.
103 Ibid., 196.
104 Ibid., 195.
105 Ibid.
106 Waldo H. Heinrichs, "Diary Entries, 17 September to 17 November 1918, Copy Typed by Howard D. Case from the Original Diary," 115, Waldo Huntley Heinrichs Papers, Yale Divinity Library Archives and Manuscripts (New Haven, CT, 1918).
107 Waldo H. Heinrichs, "Diary Entry, 21 May," 115, Waldo Huntley Heinrichs Papers, Yale Divinity Library Archives and Manuscripts (New Haven, CT, 1934), 1.
108 Charles Woolley, *First to the Front: The Aerial Adventures of 1st Lt. Waldo Heinrichs and the 95th Aero Squadron, 1917–1918*, Schiffer Military History (Atlgen, PA: Schiffer Pub., 1999), Cover Title.
109 Waldo H. Heinrichs, "Diary Entry, 13 August," 115, Waldo Huntley Heinrichs Papers, Yale Divinity Library Archives and Manuscripts (New Haven, CT, 1934).
110 Woolley, *First to the Front*, 126.
111 Ibid.
112 Heinrichs, "Case Copy of Heinrichs' 1918 Diary," 3.
113 Ibid.
114 Ibid.
115 Ibid., 4.
116 Ibid.
117 Ibid.
118 The term "Boche" is a French pejorative reference to a person. The origins of the word are not clear. Allies used the term during the First World War and Heinrichs used it in his diary to describe his encounter with the German pilot who shot him down.
119 Heinrichs, "Case Copy of Heinrichs' 1918 Diary," 4.
120 Ibid., 5.
121 Ibid.
122 Ibid.

123 Ibid.
124 Ibid.
125 Ibid.
126 Ibid.
127 Ibid., 6.
128 Ibid.
129 Ibid.
130 Ibid.
131 Ibid.
132 Ibid.
133 Ibid., 7.
134 Ibid.
135 Ibid.
136 Ibid.
137 Ibid.
138 Ibid., 8.
139 Ibid.
140 Ibid.
141 Ibid.
142 Ibid.
143 Ibid., 9.
144 Ibid.
145 Ibid., 11.
146 Ibid., 10.
147 Ibid., 11.
148 Ibid.
149 Ibid., 12.
150 Ibid., 15.
151 Ibid.
152 Ibid.
153 Ibid., 25.
154 Ibid., 17–18.
155 Ibid., 21.
156 Ibid.
157 Ibid.
158 Ibid.
159 Ibid.
160 Ibid., 22.
161 Ibid., 26.
162 Ibid., 32–34.
163 Ibid., 37–38.
164 Ibid., 36.
165 Ibid.
166 Ibid.
167 Ibid., 53.

168 Army of the United States of America, "Certificate, of Honorable Discharge from Service, for Waldo Huntley Heinrichs," 115, Waldo Huntley Heinrichs Papers, Yale Divinity Library Archives and Manuscripts (New Haven, CT, 1919), 1.

169 Waldo H. Heinrichs, "Form, Biographical Information on Jacob Heinrichs, Jr., Filled Out by Waldo Huntley Heinrichs, Sr.," 115, Waldo Huntley Heinrichs Papers, Yale Divinity Library Archives and Manuscripts (New Haven, CT), 1.

170 Ibid.

171 First Baptist Bible School of Newton, "Certificate, Promotion from Primary to Junior Department, of Waldemar Huntley Heinrichs," 115, Waldo Huntley Heinrichs Papers, Yale Divinity Library Archives and Manuscripts (New Haven, CT, 1901), 1.

172 Chestnut Street Public School, "Report Card, Third Grade, of W. H. Heinrichs," 115, Waldo Huntley Heinrichs Papers, Yale Divinity Library Archives and Manuscripts (New Haven, CT), 1.

173 Ibid., 2.

174 Jacob Heinrichs, "Correspondence, 7 December, Death of Brother Edgar, to Heinrichs," 115, Waldo Huntley Heinrichs Papers, Yale Divinity Library Archives and Manuscripts (New Haven, CT, 1910), 1.

175 Dorothy Heinrichs, "Correspondence, Regarding Colonel Frey's Desire not to Make Waldo's Jerusalem Diaries Available to Researchers Yet Because They Could Hurt Some People, to Her Son Junior," Special Collections and University Archives at UMass Amherst (Amherst, MA, 1971), 4.

176 Mason Grammar School, "Report Card, Arithmetic Performance, of W. H. Heinrichs (Sr.)," 115, Waldo Huntley Heinrichs Papers, Yale Divinity Library Archives and Manuscripts (New Haven, CT, June 1905), 1.

177 J. Edgar Heinrichs, "Correspondence, 7 August, to Heinrichs," 115, Waldo Huntley Heinrichs Papers, Yale Divinity Library Archives and Manuscripts (New Haven, CT, 1910), 1.

178 Heinrichs, "Correspondence, 7 December, Death of Brother Edgar, to Heinrichs," 1.

179 Jacob Heinrichs, "Correspondence, 13 December, Death of Brother Edgar, to Heinrichs," 115, Waldo Huntley Heinrichs Papers, Yale Divinity Library Archives and Manuscripts (New Haven, CT, 1910), 2.

180 Jacob Heinrichs, "Correspondence, Autopsy of Brother Edgar, to Rev. Emery W. Hunt," 115, Waldo Huntley Heinrichs Papers, Yale Divinity Library Archives and Manuscripts (New Haven, CT, 1910), 1.

181 Jacob Heinrichs, "Correspondence, 21 April, on Joining Foreign Service of YMCA, to Heinrichs," 115, Waldo Huntley Heinrichs Papers, Yale Divinity Library Archives and Manuscripts (New Haven, CT, 1913), 1.

182 Ibid., 2.

183 *The Pacific Commercial Advertiser*, "Newspaper Article, Coming from Ohio for Important Work, About Waldo Huntley Heinrichs Sr.'s Fellowship Secretary Position at the Honolulu Y.M.C.A.," 115, Waldo Huntley Heinrichs Papers, Yale Divinity Library Archives and Manuscripts (New Haven, CT).

184 Matson, Inc., "Menu, S. S. Lurline Voyage 61 to Honolulu," 115, Waldo Huntley Heinrichs Papers, Yale Divinity Library Archives and Manuscripts (New Haven, CT, 1913).

185 Anonymous, "Newspaper Article, to Begin Work in Honolulu, About Waldo Huntley Heinrichs, Sr.'s Secretary Position at the Honolulu Y.M.C.A," 115, Waldo Huntley Heinrichs Papers, Yale Divinity Library Archives and Manuscripts (New Haven, CT).

186 Stanley High, "Article Reprint, the Most Thrilling Job in the Most Thrilling City on Earth, from Christian Herald," 115, Waldo Huntley Heinrichs Papers, Yale Divinity Library Archives and Manuscripts (New Haven, CT).

187 Waldo H. Heinrichs, "Diary Entry, 31 December," 115, Waldo Huntley Heinrichs Papers, Yale Divinity Library Archives and Manuscripts (New Haven, CT, 1934).

## Chapter 2

1  "Holy Land Emerges from Stagnation: Jews Found Palestine as Devastated as War-Torn France, Says Col. F. H. Kisch," *New York Times*, 28 December 1924, 2.

2  Board of Regents of the University of Nebraska, "Jewish Gymnasts and Their Corporeal Utopia in Imperial Germany," in *Emancipation Through Muscles*, ed. Michael Brenner and Gideon Reuveni (Lincoln: University of Nebraska Press, 2006), 37.

3  Kisch, *Palestine Diary*, 8.

4  Ibid., 21.

5  Ibid., 448–59.

6  Ibid., 448.

7  Frederick Hermann Kisch, "Correspondence, I.O.C. Session in Egypt in March 1938," 5-1-25, Joseph Yekutieli 1960–73, Joseph Yekutieli Maccabi Sport Archives (Tel Aviv, Israel, 1938).

8  Theodor Schmidt, "Correspondence, Kisch Representing Palestine on IOC Board, to Yekutieli," 5-1-30, Joseph Yekutieli 1934–1948, Joseph Yekutieli Maccabi Sport Archives (Tel Aviv, Israel, 1936).

9  Kisch, *Palestine Diary*, 449.

10  Ibid.

11  Ibid., 451.

12  Ibid., 455.

13  Ibid., 458–59.

14  Ibid., 52.

15  Ibid., 54.

16  Ibid., 80.

17  Regina Copilon, "Correspondence, Succoth Sports Meet, to Yekutieli," 5-62-1, Colonel Kisch 1923–44, Joseph Yekutieli Maccabi Sport Archives (Tel Aviv, Israel, 1923), 1.

18  Ibid.

19  Ibid.

20  Ibid.

21  Kisch, *Palestine Diary*, 31.

22  Ibid., 69.

23  Ibid., 95.

24 Ibid., 70.
25 2019 equivalent of USD 22,893,392.
26 2019 equivalent of USD 8,654,818.
27 Kisch, *Palestine Diary*, 70–71.
28 Ibid., 89.
29 Ibid., 91.
30 Ibid., 115.
31 Ibid., 120.
32 Ibid., 131.
33 Guttmann, *The Games Must Go On*, 52.
34 Ibid., 54.
35 Frederick H. Kisch, "Correspondence, 1924 Paris Olympic Games, to the Secretary of the Committee for the Olympic Games in Paris," 5–62–1, Colonel Kisch 1923–44, Joseph Yekutieli Maccabi Sport Archives (Tel Aviv, Israel, 1924), 1.
36 The meetings that the delegation held in Paris would be recalled later at a moment of crisis between the IOC and the Palestine Olympic Association in 1948. One of the meetings that occurred in 1924 probably discussed Palestine's attempt to join the International Amateur Athletic Federation (of which Edström was President). This attempt was rebuffed allegedly on the basis that the Maccabi Movement was not representative of all the sport organizations in Palestine (either Jewish or non-Jewish). Source: Issam Khalidi, *One Hundred Years of Football in Palestine* (Amman: Dar Al-Shorouk for Publishing and Distribution, 2013), 24.
37 Kisch, *Palestine Diary*, 155.
38 Ibid., 158.
39 Ibid.
40 "Holy Land Emerges from Stagnation: Jews Found Palestine as Devastated as War-Torn France, Says Col. F. H. Kisch," 2.
41 Ibid.
42 Kisch, *Palestine Diary*, 183–84.
43 Ibid., 211.
44 Ibid., 233.
45 Ibid., 213.
46 Ibid., 237.
47 "Vienna Jewish Soccer Team Coming to Play Americans: Victor In," *New York Times*, March 28, 1926, 13.
48 Avraham Harman Institute of Contemporary Jewry: The Hebrew University of Jerusalem, "Pride and Priorities: American Jewry's Response to Hakoah Vienna's U.S. Tour of 1926," in *Jews and the Sporting Life: Studies in Contemporary Jewry, an Annual XXIII*, ed. Ezra Mendelsohn (New York: Oxford University Press, 2008), 73.
49 Ibid., 74.
50 Ibid., 75.
51 Jewish Telegraphic Agency, "Saturday Football Playing by Jewish Teams in Palestine Causes Big Indignation Movement Among Jewish Orthodoxy: 2,500 Agudists Threaten to Prevent Forcibly Sale of Tickets: Chief Rabbi Kook Endeavouring to Get Matches Withdrawn: Claim of Broken Promise Not to Play Football on Saturdays," *JTA Daily News Bulletin*, 30 May 1931, 4.

52  Avraham Harman Institute of Contemporary Jewry: The Hebrew University of Jerusalem, "AHICJ Hakoah Vienna," 77.

53  Z. Weizmann, "Correspondence, Palestine Football, to Egyptian Consul in Jerusalem," 4–29–03, Maccabi Egypt 1927–72, Joseph Yekutieli Maccabi Sport Archives (Tel Aviv, Israel, 1926), 1.

54  International Olympic Committee, "Bulletin Officiel, Comité Internationale Olympique," 5–1–16, International Olympic Committee, Joseph Yekutieli Maccabi Sport Archives (Tel Aviv, Israel, 1927).

55  Asaf Grasowsky, Gideon Abulafia, and Yosef Yekutieli, "Circular, Creation of Palestine Football Association, to All Football Associations in Palestine," 5–1–23, Joseph Yekutieli 1916–1935, Joseph Yekutieli Maccabi Sport Archives (Tel Aviv, Israel, 1927), 1.

56  Ibid.

57  Ibid.

58  Ibid.

59  Issam Khalidi, *One Hundred Years of Football in Palestine* (Amman: Dar Al-Shorouk for Publishing and Distribution, 2013), 16.

60  Ibid.

61  Ibid.

62  Ibid., 19.

63  Jerusalem International Young Men's Christian Association, "Map, of Jerusalem and Showing Sports Grounds," Special Collections and University Archives at UMass Amherst (Amherst, MA, 1932–33).

64  Khalidi, *One Hundred Years of Football in Palestine*, 19.

65  Ibid., 20.

66  Ibid.

67  Ibid.

68  Ibid.

69  Ibid., 21.

70  Sports & Athletics Organisation "Maccabi" Palestine Federation, "Memorandum, History, Aims and Aspirations, and Activities," AD 2.001 0002 Maccabi 'Olami Tik 2, SYNSO 0002096, The Zvi Nishri Archive for Sports and Physical Education in the Wingate Institute (Netanya, Israel, 1927), 2.

71  "Correspondence, Jewish Footballer Trip to the USA, to the American Consul in Jerusalem," ADI.29 0007, SYNSO 0001539, The Zvi Nishri Archive for Sports and Physical Education in the Wingate Institute (Netanya, Israel, 1927), 1.

72  John Kiernan, "Sports of the Times," *New York Times*, 26 June 1927, 2.

73  Yosef Yekutieli, "Proposed Budget, Travel of a Jewish Football Team to England, in Yekutieli's Personal Papers," 5–1–10, Joseph Yekutieli 1914–1933, Joseph Yekutieli Maccabi Sport Archives (Tel Aviv, Israel, 1928), 1.

74  2019 equivalent of USD 381,582.

75  2019 equivalent of USD 349,138.

76  Palestine Football Association, "Circular, to All Football Clubs and Associations, Regarding Yekutieli's Foreign Travel," 5–1–10, Joseph Yekutieli 1914–1933, Joseph Yekutieli Maccabi Sport Archives (Tel Aviv, Israel, 1928), 1.

77  Yosef Yekutieli, "Correspondence, Affiliation of Palestine Football Associaton to FIFA, M.C.A.E. Hirschman, Esq," 5-1-23, Joseph Yekutieli 1916–1935, Joseph Yekutieli Maccabi Sport Archives (Tel Aviv, Israel, 1928), 1.

78  Not long afterward, the Hapoel sports movement, which represented the Jewish labor sports movement in Palestine, registered its statutes with the Deputy District Commissioner's Office in Jerusalem. Source: Government of Palestine, "Correspondence, 12108/3939/569, from Deputy District Commissioner's Office Jerusalem Division to Mr. A. Perlstein of Jerusalem Workers Council (Sports Association Hapoel)," IV-244–119, The Pinchas Lavon Institute for Labour Movement Research (Tel Aviv, Israel, 1928), 1. In 1951, Hapoel became central to the Jewish sport movement's effort to re-affiliate to the IOC as Israel. Nine of the eleven athletes murdered in Munich were actually from Hapoel and not Maccabi clubs. Source: Hapoel, "The Establishment of 'Hapoel'," in *The Establishment of "Hapoel"* (2019), https://www.hapoel.org.il/en/The-Establishment-of-Hapoel/. Hapoel was the largest sports movement in Mandate Palestine yet it was somewhat less interested in the Olympics, which it considered a bourgeois festival. Instead, it affiliated with the Socialist Workers' Sport International (SASI). The Betar sports movement, a more militant Zionist movement, was also very active in sports. These three movements' enrollment numbers far exceeded the enrollment of the Arab clubs.

79  "Correspondence, Palestine Football, Sent to the Société Sportif Oriental," 5-1-23, Joseph Yekutieli 1916–1935, Joseph Yekutieli Maccabi Sport Archives (Tel Aviv, Israel, 1928), 1.

80  Ibid.

81  Herbert C. O. Plumer, "Speech, by the High Commissioner of Palestine Field Marshall Lord Plumer, on the Occasion of Laying the Corner-Stone of the Jerusalem International YMCA," Y.USA.9-2-2, International Work in Palestine/Israel, Kautz Family YMCA Archives (Minneapolis, MN, 1928).

82  Kisch, *Palestine Diary*, 247.

83  Wigoder, *Encyclopedia Vol. 2*, 1352–53.

84  Newspaper Enterprise Association, "Photo, Colonel Kisch, War Hero and Diplomat, Arrives," Private Collection (Grand Rapids, MI, 1929), Referred D-E Dept.

85  "Walker Welcomes Zionists' Official: Assures Col. Kisch That Move to Rebuild Palestine is Aid to All the World," *New York Times*, 31 January 1929, 12.

86  Kisch, *Palestine Diary*, 158.

87  Wigoder, *Encyclopedia Vol. 1*, 751.

88  The Palestine Federation for Gymnastics and Athletics "Maccabi", "Programme, Fifth National Sports Meeting," ADI 5.27 0002 Shlomo Arazi, SYNSO 0052466, The Zvi Nishri Archive for Sports and Physical Education in the Wingate Institute (Netanya, Israel, 1929).

89  Tom Segev, *One Palestine, Complete: Jews and Arabs Under the Mandate* (New York: Metropolitan Books, 2000), 301.

90  Wigoder, *Encyclopedia Vol. 2*, 1380.

91  Segev, *One Palestine, Complete*, 325–26.

92  Ibid., 327.

93  Ibid., 317.

94  Ibid., 318.
95  Ibid., 316.
96  Ibid., 317.
97  Ibid.
98  Ibid., 321–23.
99  Ibid., 323.
100 Ibid.
101 Ibid., 324.
102 Ibid., 327.
103 Ibid.
104 Ibid.
105 Ibid., 329–30.
106 "$50,000 for Relief Reaches Palestine: Kisch Cables That First Gift is Aiding Urgent Cases—$100,000 More Being Sent," *New York Times*, 4 September 1929, 9.
107 Ibid.
108 "Security Restored, Relief Leader Says: Kisch Cables That Many Jews in Palestine Are Returning to Their Homes," *New York Times*, 12 September 1929, 4.
109 Joseph M. Levy, "Stronger Guards Patrol Jerusalem: Moslem Holy Day Passes Quietly, Though Disorders Had Been Predicted," *New York Times*, 14 September 1929, 5.
110 "Relief Fund Feeds 8,000 in Palestine: Kisch Cables of Aid Being Given to Refugees in Jerusalem Pending Return to Homes," *New York Times*, 17 September 1929, 3.
111 "Thousands Are Aided by Palestine Fund: Strauss Soup Kitchens Feed 2,000 Daily, F. H. Kisch Reports—$36,552 New Gifts in Day," *New York Times*, 26 September 1929, 9.

## Chapter 3

1  For a brief period of time, the letterhead of Maccabi Palestine used the name Sports & Athletics Organisation [*sic*] "MACCABI" Palestine Federation. This appears to be the name that Maccabi Palestine used in its correspondence with the International Olympic Committee, but it is not clear whether the name was limited to such use.
2  Sports & Athletics Organization, Maccabi, Palestine Federation, "Correspondence, 2 January, NOC Recognition, Yekutieli to Berdez," 0077643, CIO CNO ISR CORR OU MO 01 14 36, Historical Archives Olympic Studies Centre (Lausanne, Switzerland, 1930), Corr. 1930–34.
3  Guttmann, *The Games Must Go On*, 56.
4  Ibid.
5  Ibid., 57.
6  Ibid.
7  Ibid.
8  Ibid.
9  Fédération Sportive Féminine Internationale, "Correspondence, Affiliation Request, Milliat to Yekutieli," 1–39, Women's Olympiad London 1932–34 (4), Joseph Yekutieli Maccabi Sport Archives (Tel Aviv, Israel, 1930), 1.

# Endnotes

10 International Olympic Committee, "Correspondence, 29 January, NOC Recognition, Berdez to Yekutieli," 0077643, CIO CNO ISR CORR OU MO 01 14 36, Historical Archives Olympic Studies Centre (Lausanne, Switzerland, 1930), Corr. 1930–34.

11 Ibid., 1.

12 Jewish Telegraphic Agency, "Jews Urge Equality of Races in Palestine: Agency in Its Closing Session Resolves Against Domination of the Arabs or by Them," *New York Times*, 28 March 1930, 22.

13 Ibid.

14 Ibid.

15 2019 equivalent of USD 55,773,478.

16 Yosef Yekutieli, "Correspondence, European Motorcycle Tour, to Sunbeam Motorcyles, 10 September," 1–40, European Motorcycle Tour 1930–33, Joseph Yekutieli Maccabi Sport Archives (Tel Aviv, Israel, 1930).

17 Yosef Yekutieli, "Correspondence, Palestine Footballer Jeno Stern Amateur Status, Yekutieli to the Honorary Secretary of FIFA," 5-1-23, Joseph Yekutieli 1916–1935, Joseph Yekutieli Maccabi Sport Archives (Tel Aviv, Israel, 1930), 1.

18 Commission Provisoire pour la Formation du Comité Olympique Palestinien, "Correspondence, 17 October, NOC Recognition, Yekutieli and Unidentified Member to Berdez," 0077643, CIO CNO ISR CORR OU MO 01 14 36, Historical Archives Olympic Studies Centre (Lausanne, Switzerland, 1930), 1.

19 International Olympic Committee, "Correspondence, Process for Forming a Palestine Olympic Committee, to the Provisional Committee," 5-1-10, Joseph Yekutieli 1914–1933, Joseph Yekutieli Maccabi Sport Archives (Tel Aviv, Israel, 1930), 1.

20 "Serious Defeat Seen by Jews in Palestine: Leaders Call on High Commissioner to Express Indignation at Government's Stand," *New York Times*, 22 October 1930, 14.

21 Ibid.

22 International Olympic Committee, "Correspondence, 11 November, NOC Recognition, Mayer to Palestine Olympic Committee," 0077643, CIO CNO ISR CORR OU MO 01 14 36, Historical Archives Olympic Studies Centre (Lausanne, Switzerland, 1930), 1.

23 Palestine Olympic Association, "Regulations, Palestine Olympic Association, as Handwritten by Yekutieli," 5-1-10, Joseph Yekutieli 1914–1933, Joseph Yekutieli Maccabi Sport Archives (Tel Aviv, Israel), 1.

24 Palestine Olympic Association, "Regulations, Palestine Olympic Association, as Typed by Yekutieli," 5-1-10, Joseph Yekutieli 1914–1933, Joseph Yekutieli Maccabi Sport Archives (Tel Aviv, Israel), 1.

25 Yosef Yekutieli, "Memorandum, Amendments to the Rules of the Orient Cup," 5-1-10, Joseph Yekutieli 1914–1933, Joseph Yekutieli Maccabi Sport Archives (Tel Aviv, Israel).

26 Eretz Israel Sport Company Ltd., "Memorandum, of Association of a Company Limited by Shares," 5-1-10, Joseph Yekutieli 1914–1933, Joseph Yekutieli Maccabi Sport Archives (Tel Aviv, Israel).

27 Ministry of Foreign Affairs, France, "Correspondence, 18 November, 1932 Olympic Games Participation of Palestine, Berthelot to Unidentified Recipient," 0077643,

CIO CNO ISR CORR OU MO 01 14 36, Historical Archives Olympic Studies Centre (Lausanne, Switzerland, 1930), 1.

28 Wilbert B. Smith, "Correspondence, Profile of Situation in Jerusalem, to Heinrichs," Y.USA.9–2-2, International Work in Palestine/Israel, Kautz Family YMCA Archives (Minneapolis, MN, 1930), 6.

29 Ibid.

30 Ibid.

31 Ibid.

32 Ibid., 7.

33 Ibid.

34 Jerusalem International Young Men's Christian Association, "Project Outline, Political and Religious Significance of Palestine," Y.USA.9–2-2, International Work in Palestine/Israel, Kautz Family YMCA Archives (Minneapolis, MN, 1930), 1.

35 Ibid.

36 Jerusalem International Young Men's Christian Association, "Report, Physical Department for June, July and August," Y.USA.9–2-2, International Work in Palestine/Israel, Kautz Family YMCA Archives (Minneapolis, MN, 1930), 1.

37 Ibid.

38 Fred W. Auburn, "Correspondence, Founding of Jerusalem Tennis League, to Frank V. Slack," Y.USA.9–2-2, International Work in Palestine/Israel, Kautz Family YMCA Archives (Minneapolis, MN, 1930), 1–2.

39 Ibid., 2.

40 The archival source refers to it as "Palestine Olympic Committee". This is not Yekutieli's Palestine Olympic Association, although they seem to have started at around the same time. In 1930, the failure of the intercommunal negotiations to form this association and host the Palestine Olympic Games is what seems to have spurred Yekutieli to write the International Olympic Committee directly.

41 Jerusalem International Young Men's Christian Association, "Report, Physical Department for June, July and August," 1.

42 Ibid.

43 Ibid.

44 Ibid.

45 Nicholas M. Lattof, "Report, Administrative for 1930, Responded to by Slack on 14 May 1931," Y.USA.9–2-2, International Work in Palestine/Israel, Kautz Family YMCA Archives (Minneapolis, MN, 1930).

46 Smith, "Correspondence, Profile of Situation in Jerusalem, to Heinrichs," 3.

47 Nicholas M. Lattof, "What the Young Men's Christian Association Has Meant to Me," Private Collection of the Lattof Family (1978), 1.

48 Ibid.

49 Ibid., 2.

50 Ibid., 2, 4.

51 Ibid., 5.

52 Ibid.

53 Ibid.

54 Ibid.

55  Lattof, "Report, Administrative for 1930, Responded to by Slack on 14 May 1931," 1.
56  Ibid.
57  Ibid.
58  Ibid., 2.
59  Ibid.
60  Ibid.
61  Ibid.
62  2018 equivalent of USD 9,773,625.
63  J. M. Perry, "Correspondence. Transfer of Check for $650,000 for Construction of Jerusalem YMCA, to International Committee of YMCAs of North America and Canada," Y.USA.9–2-2, International Work in Palestine/Israel, Kautz Family YMCA Archives (Minneapolis, MN, 1930), 1.
64  Alvah H. Miller, "Article, Recollections of Archie Harte, from Association Forum and Section Journals," Attallah A. Kidess Collection, The Springfield College Archives and Special Collections (Springfield, MA, 1966), 15–16.
65  At the time, the Jerusalem YMCA was a comparatively small association. Harte's position as secretary was equivalent in authority to that of secretary-general used in later decades.
66  Miller, "Article, Recollections of Archie Harte, from Association Forum and Section Journals," 16.
67  Ibid., 15.
68  Ibid.
69  Ibid., 17.
70  Ibid.
71  Ibid.
72  Ibid.
73  Jerusalem International Young Men's Christian Association, "Project Outline, Political and Religious Significance of Palestine," 1.
74  Ibid.
75  Ibid.
76  Ibid.
77  Fred W. Ramsey, "Correspondence, Relations with Wilbert Smith, to Canaan," Y.USA.9–2-2, International Work in Palestine/Israel, Kautz Family YMCA Archives (Minneapolis, MN, 1930), 1.
78  Ibid.
79  Ibid.
80  The problems between Canaan, Smith, Harte, and New York foreshadow the problems that would arise for Waldo Heinrichs Sr. in the 1930s. The tension between Smith and New York's support for Canaan and the Arab board are also a contributing factor in Smith's refusal to assume the role of secretary-general of the Jerusalem YMCA in 1935. See Wilbert S. Smith, "Correspondence, Reasons for Hesitating to Take up the Role of Senior Secretary in Jerusalem, to Slack," Y.USA.9–2-2, International Work in Palestine/Israel, Kautz Family YMCA Archives (Minneapolis, MN, 1934).
81  Wilbert B. Smith, "Correspondence, Nationality of Candidates for Secretary-General, to Slack," Y.USA.9–2-2, International Work in Palestine/Israel, Kautz Family YMCA Archives (Minneapolis, MN, 1930), 1.

82  Ibid.

83  Ibid.

84  Ibid.

85  Smith, "Correspondence, Profile of Situation in Jerusalem, to Heinrichs," 3.

86  Ibid.

87  Ibid.

88  Smith, "Correspondence, Nationality of Candidates for Secretary-General, to Slack," 1.

89  Ibid.

90  Ibid., 1–2.

91  Ibid., 1–2.

92  Ibid., 2.

93  Frank V. Slack, "Correspondence, Opinion of Candidature of Heinrichs, to Smith," Y.USA.9–2-2, International Work in Palestine/Israel, Kautz Family YMCA Archives (Minneapolis, MN, 1930), 2.

94  Waldo H. Heinrichs, "Diary Entry, 2 May," 115, Waldo Huntley Heinrichs Papers, Yale Divinity Library Archives and Manuscripts (New Haven, CT, 1930).

95  Waldo H. Heinrichs, "Diary Entry, 12 June," 115, Waldo Huntley Heinrichs Papers, Yale Divinity Library Archives and Manuscripts (New Haven, CT, 1930).

96  Waldo H. Heinrichs, "Diary Entry, 7 January," 115, Waldo Huntley Heinrichs Papers, Yale Divinity Library Archives and Manuscripts (New Haven, CT, 1930).

97  Waldo H. Heinrichs, "Diary Entry, 20 January," 115, Waldo Huntley Heinrichs Papers, Yale Divinity Library Archives and Manuscripts (New Haven, CT, 1930).

98  Waldo H. Heinrichs, "Diary Entry, 31 January," 115, Waldo Huntley Heinrichs Papers, Yale Divinity Library Archives and Manuscripts (New Haven, CT, 1930).

99  Waldo H. Heinrichs, "Diary Entry, 8 March," 115, Waldo Huntley Heinrichs Papers, Yale Divinity Library Archives and Manuscripts (New Haven, CT, 1930).

100  Ibid.

101  Waldo H. Heinrichs, "Diary Entry, 9 March," 115, Waldo Huntley Heinrichs Papers, Yale Divinity Library Archives and Manuscripts (New Haven, CT, 1930).

102  Waldo H. Heinrichs, "Diary Entry, 13 March," 115, Waldo Huntley Heinrichs Papers, Yale Divinity Library Archives and Manuscripts (New Haven, CT, 1930).

103  Waldo H. Heinrichs, "Diary Entry, 15 March," 115, Waldo Huntley Heinrichs Papers, Yale Divinity Library Archives and Manuscripts (New Haven, CT, 1930).

104  Waldo H. Heinrichs, "Diary Entry, 29 March," 115, Waldo Huntley Heinrichs Papers, Yale Divinity Library Archives and Manuscripts (New Haven, CT, 1930).

105  Wilbert B. Smith, "Correspondence, Profile of Membership in Jerusalem and Political Relationships with Catholics and Zionists, to Heinrichs," Y.USA.9–2-2, International Work in Palestine/Israel, Kautz Family YMCA Archives (Minneapolis, MN, 1930), 3.

106  Ibid., 4.

107  Waldo H. Heinrichs, "Correspondence, Initial Reply to Job Offer, to Ramsey, Colton, and Slack," Y.USA.9–2-2, International Work in Palestine/Israel, Kautz Family YMCA Archives (Minneapolis, MN, 1930), 1.

108  Ibid.

109  Ibid.

110  Ibid.

111  Ibid.

112  Waldo H. Heinrichs, "Diary Entry, 26 June," 115, Waldo Huntley Heinrichs Papers, Yale Divinity Library Archives and Manuscripts (New Haven, CT, 1930).

113  Heinrichs, "Correspondence, Initial Reply to Job Offer, to Ramsey, Colton, and Slack," 1.

114  Ibid.

115  Ibid.

116  Ibid.

117  Ibid.

118  Wilbert B. Smith, "Correspondence, Opinion of Candidature of Heinrichs, Slack," Y.USA.9-2-2, International Work in Palestine/Israel, Kautz Family YMCA Archives (Minneapolis, MN, 1930), 1.

119  Slack, "Correspondence, Opinion of Candidature of Heinrichs, to Smith," 1.

120  Waldo H. Heinrichs, "Diary Entry, 1 December," 115, Waldo Huntley Heinrichs Papers, Yale Divinity Library Archives and Manuscripts (New Haven, CT, 1930).

121  Waldo H. Heinrichs, "Diary Entry, 7 December," 115, Waldo Huntley Heinrichs Papers, Yale Divinity Library Archives and Manuscripts (New Haven, CT, 1930).

122  Waldo H. Heinrichs, "Diary Entry, 8 December," 115, Waldo Huntley Heinrichs Papers, Yale Divinity Library Archives and Manuscripts (New Haven, CT, 1930).

123  Ibid.

124  Ibid.

125  High, "Article Reprint, the Most Thrilling Job in the Most Thrilling City on Earth, from Christian Herald," 1.

126  Smith, "Correspondence, Profile of Situation in Jerusalem, to Heinrichs."

127  Ibid., 4.

128  Ibid., 5.

129  Ibid.

130  Ibid.

131  Ibid.

132  Frank V. Slack, "Correspondence, Situation in Jerusalem, to Heinrichs," Y.USA.9-2-2, International Work in Palestine/Israel, Kautz Family YMCA Archives (Minneapolis, MN, 1930), 2.

133  Smith, "Correspondence, Profile of Membership in Jerusalem and Political Relationships with Catholics and Zionists, to Heinrichs."

134  Ibid., 1.

135  Ibid., 2.

136  Ibid.

137  Waldo H. Heinrichs, "Diary Entry, 31 December," 115, Waldo Huntley Heinrichs Papers, Yale Divinity Library Archives and Manuscripts (New Haven, CT, 1930).

## Chapter 4

1   Waldo H. Heinrichs, "Diary Entry, 5 January," 115, Waldo Huntley Heinrichs Papers, Yale Divinity Library Archives and Manuscripts (New Haven, CT, 1931).

2  Waldo H. Heinrichs, "Diary Entry, 6 January," 115, Waldo Huntley Heinrichs Papers, Yale Divinity Library Archives and Manuscripts (New Haven, CT, 1931).

3  Waldo H. Heinrichs, "Diary Entry, 8 January," 115, Waldo Huntley Heinrichs Papers, Yale Divinity Library Archives and Manuscripts (New Haven, CT, 1931).

4  Waldo H. Heinrichs, "Diary Entry, 9 January," 115, Waldo Huntley Heinrichs Papers, Yale Divinity Library Archives and Manuscripts (New Haven, CT, 1931).

5  Ibid.

6  Ibid.

7  Waldo H. Heinrichs, "Diary Entry, 10 January," 115, Waldo Huntley Heinrichs Papers, Yale Divinity Library Archives and Manuscripts (New Haven, CT, 1931).

8  Ibid.

9  Ibid.

10  Ibid.

11  Waldo H. Heinrichs, "Diary Entry, 30 January," 115, Waldo Huntley Heinrichs Papers, Yale Divinity Library Archives and Manuscripts (New Haven, CT, 1931).

12  Waldo H. Heinrichs, "Diary Entry, 6 February," 115, Waldo Huntley Heinrichs Papers, Yale Divinity Library Archives and Manuscripts (New Haven, CT, 1931).

13  The Young Men's Christian Association Lahore, "Menu, from 1931 Annual Members' Dinner," 115, Waldo Huntley Heinrichs Papers, Yale Divinity Library Archives and Manuscripts (New Haven, CT, 1931), 1.

14  Ibid.

15  Ibid., 3.

16  Ibid.

17  Ibid.

18  Ibid., 3.

19  Waldo H. Heinrichs, "Diary Entry, 24 March," 115, Waldo Huntley Heinrichs Papers, Yale Divinity Library Archives and Manuscripts (New Haven, CT, 1931).

20  Wilbert B. Smith, "Correspondence, Heinrichs' Visit to Jerusalem and Relationship with Government and High Commissioner, to Ramsey," Y.USA.9–2-2, International Work in Palestine/Israel, Kautz Family YMCA Archives (Minneapolis, MN, 1931), 1.

21  Ibid.

22  Ibid., 2.

23  Waldo H. Heinrichs, "Diary Entry, 4 April," 115, Waldo Huntley Heinrichs Papers, Yale Divinity Library Archives and Manuscripts (New Haven, CT, 1931).

24  Waldo H. Heinrichs, "Diary Entry, 6 April," 115, Waldo Huntley Heinrichs Papers, Yale Divinity Library Archives and Manuscripts (New Haven, CT, 1931).

25  Waldo H. Heinrichs, "Diary Entry, 7 April," 115, Waldo Huntley Heinrichs Papers, Yale Divinity Library Archives and Manuscripts (New Haven, CT, 1931).

26  Ibid.

27  Ibid.

28  Waldo H. Heinrichs, "Diary Entry, 8 April," 115, Waldo Huntley Heinrichs Papers, Yale Divinity Library Archives and Manuscripts (New Haven, CT, 1931).

29  Bayard Dodge, "Correspondence, on Things Being in a Fearful State at the Jerusalem YMCA with the Newspaper Controversy," Y.USA.9–2-2, International Work in Palestine/Israel, Kautz Family YMCA Archives (Minneapolis, MN, 1934), 2.

30  Waldo H. Heinrichs, "Diary Entry, 9 April," 115, Waldo Huntley Heinrichs Papers, Yale Divinity Library Archives and Manuscripts (New Haven, CT, 1931).
31  Waldo H. Heinrichs, "Diary Entry, 11 April," 115, Waldo Huntley Heinrichs Papers, Yale Divinity Library Archives and Manuscripts (New Haven, CT, 1931).
32  Waldo H. Heinrichs, "Diary Entry, 12 April," 115, Waldo Huntley Heinrichs Papers, Yale Divinity Library Archives and Manuscripts (New Haven, CT, 1931).
33  The term "association" in this instance refers to an active membership and full program of activities aligned to the mission of the YMCA Movement.
34  Waldo H. Heinrichs, "Diary Entry, 13 April," 115, Waldo Huntley Heinrichs Papers, Yale Divinity Library Archives and Manuscripts (New Haven, CT, 1931).
35  Waldo H. Heinrichs, "Diary Entry, 14 April," 115, Waldo Huntley Heinrichs Papers, Yale Divinity Library Archives and Manuscripts (New Haven, CT, 1931).
36  Waldo H. Heinrichs, "Diary Entry, 15 April," 115, Waldo Huntley Heinrichs Papers, Yale Divinity Library Archives and Manuscripts (New Haven, CT, 1931).
37  Ibid.
38  Waldo H. Heinrichs, "Diary Entry, 21 April," 115, Waldo Huntley Heinrichs Papers, Yale Divinity Library Archives and Manuscripts (New Haven, CT, 1931).
39  Waldo H. Heinrichs, "Diary Entry, 11 May," 115, Waldo Huntley Heinrichs Papers, Yale Divinity Library Archives and Manuscripts (New Haven, CT, 1931).
40  Government of Palestine, "Official Gazette, Ordinances Pertaining to the Western Wall/Haram-Esh-Sharif," Y.USA.9-2-2, International Work in Palestine/Israel, Kautz Family YMCA Archives (Minneapolis, MN, 1931), 464–68.
41  Louis Stark, "Weizmann Sounds Warning to Britain: Says Valuable Friendships Are 'Squandered' by Attitude Toward Zionist Aims," New York Times, 8 July 1931, 10.
42  "Jewish Olympics Planned. First World-Wide Meet Set for Palestine in 1932," New York Times, 3 February 1931, 35.
43  Ibid.
44  Lionel Shalit, "Correspondence, Arab Sports Clubs in the 1932 Maccabiad, to Weizmann," 4237 British Maccabi, The Weizmann Archives (Rehovot, Israel, 1931), 1.
45  Spelling based on that which appears on the association's letterhead of the time. See Lionel Shalit, "Correspondence, on Letterhead of Bar-Cochba Association, to Weizmann," 4237 British Maccabi, The Weizmann Archives (Rehovot, Israel, 1931).
46  Lionel Shalit, "Correspondence, Conditional Promise to Attend the Reception Given by the Jewish Agency in Honor of the Palestine Motor Cyclists, to Chaim Weizmann," 4237 British Maccabi, The Weizmann Archives (Rehovot, Israel, 1931), 1.
47  Yosef Yekutieli, "Memorandum, First Maccabiah," 2-1-18, First Maccabiad 1932, Joseph Yekutieli Maccabi Sport Archives (Tel Aviv, Israel, 1931).
48  Yosef Yekutieli, "Correspondence, European Motorcycle Tour and First Maccabiad, to Mr. Fox, 23 July," 5-1-23, Joseph Yekutieli 1916–1935, Joseph Yekutieli Maccabi Sport Archives (Tel Aviv, Israel, July 1931), 1.
49  Ibid.
50  Yekutieli, "Memorandum, First Maccabiah," 1.
51  Ibid.
52  Ibid.

53 Ibid., 2.
54 Ibid.
55 Ibid.
56 Ibid.
57 Ibid.
58 Ibid.
59 Ibid., 3.
60 Ibid.
61 Fédération Sportive Féminine Internationale, "Correspondence, Affiliation Request, Milliat to Yekutieli," 1–39, Women's Olympiad London 1932–34 (4), Joseph Yekutieli Maccabi Sport Archives (Tel Aviv, Israel, 1931), 1.
62 Yosef Yekutieli, "Correspondence, Affiliation to FSFI, Yekutieli to FSFI President Milliat" (1931), 1.
63 Yekutieli, "Memorandum, First Maccabiah," 3–4.
64 Ibid., 4.
65 2019 equivalent of USD 4,264,839.
66 Yekutieli, "Memorandum, First Maccabiah," 4.
67 Ibid., 5.
68 Ibid.
69 2019 equivalent of USD 426,520.
70 Bar-Cochba Association, "Souvenir Programme, All-Jewish Athletic Match, Bar-Cochba Association of London Versus Association for Jewish Youth," 2-1-18, First Maccabiad 1932, Joseph Yekutieli Maccabi Sport Archives (Tel Aviv, Israel, 1931), 1.
71 Jewish Telegraphic Agency, "Centuries of Persecution Have Not Prevented Full Physical Development of Our People Mr. D'Avigdor Goldsmid Says at Welcome Reception to Twelve Motor Cyclists Arriving in London from Palestine," *JTA Daily News Bulletin*, 17 June 1931, 8.
72 Joseph Yekutieli, "Correspondence, European Motorcycle Tour, Yekutieli to Mayor of Stepney Morry H. Davis" (1931), 1.
73 Jewish Telegraphic Agency, "Maccabee Asks Damages for Maccabiade Ban," *Jewish Daily Bulletin*, 9 August 1933, 1.
74 Federation of the Amateur Sports Clubs of Palestine, "Minutes of Meeting, Foundational Meeting," 1.
75 Ibid.
76 Waldo H. Heinrichs, "Diary Entry, 13 May," 115, Waldo Huntley Heinrichs Papers, Yale Divinity Library Archives and Manuscripts (New Haven, CT, 1931).
77 Waldo H. Heinrichs, "Diary Entry, 14 May," 115, Waldo Huntley Heinrichs Papers, Yale Divinity Library Archives and Manuscripts (New Haven, CT, 1931).
78 Waldo H. Heinrichs, "Diary Entry, 28 May," 115, Waldo Huntley Heinrichs Papers, Yale Divinity Library Archives and Manuscripts (New Haven, CT, 1931).
79 Lattof, "What the Young Men's Christian Association Has Meant to Me," 11.
80 Jerusalem International Young Men's Christian Association, "Report, Administrative for 1930," Y.USA.9-2-2, International Work in Palestine/Israel, Kautz Family YMCA Archives (Minneapolis, MN, 1930).

81 Ibid., 1.
82 Ibid.
83 The mayor was an early supporter of interfaith cooperation in sports and gave the keynote address at the dedication of the Jerusalem YMCA's tennis courts. Despite the support of the mayor, the Association's tennis club was politicized. In 1932, it had more than twenty Jewish players but withdrew from the First Maccabiad after it had already paid its registration fees. The following year, Maccabi teams boycotted the Association's tennis competition in Jerusalem. Jews felt the long shadow of the Daniel Prenn case in the entire affair. Prenn was Europe's first ranked tennis player. In 1933, he was barred from playing in Germany after the Nazis came to power.
84 Jerusalem International Young Men's Christian Association, "Report, Administrative for 1930," 1.
85 Ibid.
86 Ibid.
87 Ibid.
88 Ibid., 2.
89 Ibid.
90 Ibid.
91 Ibid.
92 Ibid., 2.
93 Jerusalem International Young Men's Christian Association, "Summary, Statement of the Mayor of Jerusalem on the Occasion of the Formal Opening of the Tennis Courts, Attachment to Lattof's Correspondence to Ramsey," Y.USA.9-2-2, International Work in Palestine/Israel, Kautz Family YMCA Archives (Minneapolis, MN, 1931).
94 Nicholas M. Lattof, "Correspondence, Second Annual YMCA Cross Country Championship, Completion of Tennis Courts, and Membership Tally, to Ramsey," Y.USA.9-2-2, International Work in Palestine/Israel, Kautz Family YMCA Archives (Minneapolis, MN, 1931), 2.
95 Ibid.
96 Ibid., 1-2.
97 Waldo H. Heinrichs, "Diary Entry, 2 November," 115, Waldo Huntley Heinrichs Papers, Yale Divinity Library Archives and Manuscripts (New Haven, CT, 1931).
98 Waldo H. Heinrichs, "Memorandum, Endowment Yield and Running Cost of Jerusalem YMCA as Affected by Global Economic Situation, to Harmon and Smith," Y.USA.9-2-2, International Work in Palestine/Israel, Kautz Family YMCA Archives (Minneapolis, MN, 1931).
99 "'Chancellor' Football Cup: Competition Between Troops and Police," *Palestine Bulletin*, 3 December 1931, 4.
100 "Palestine Football League: Palestine Police 3. Hapoel Nil," *Palestine Bulletin*, 7 December 1931, 4.
101 "Boxing in Jerusalem to Night," *Palestine Bulletin*, 11 December 1931, 4.
102 "Police Boxing Championship," *Palestine Bulletin*, 8 December 1931, 4.
103 "Boxing: Second Annual Novice Championship," *Palestine Bulletin*, 10 December 1931, 4.

104 "Y. M. C. A. Autumn Programme," *Palestine Bulletin*, 15 December 1931, 2.

105 "Football," *Palestine Bulletin*, 18 December 1931, 4.

106 "Football: Defeat of Visiting Teams: British Section Police v Petach Tikvah," *Palestine Bulletin*, 20 December 1931, 4.

107 "Football," *Palestine Bulletin*, 21 December 1931, 4.

108 "Football: Semi-Final of Middle East Inter-Unit Cup: Jerusalem Knock Out R.A.F. Aboukir Exciting Game," *Palestine Bulletin*, 24 December 1931, 4.

109 "Football: Two Matches with Same Results," *Palestine Bulletin*, 27 December 1931, 4.

## Chapter 5

1   Heidemarie Wawrzyn, *Nazis in the Holy Land, 1933–1948* (Berlin/Boston: De Gruyter Magnes, 2013), V.

2   Ibid., 4.

3   Ibid., 4–5.

4   Ibid., 4.

5   Ibid., 6.

6   Ibid.

7   Ibid., 89.

8   "Note, on Jacques Goar and His Preparation of an Egyptian Team for the First Maccabiad," 5-1-23, Joseph Yekutieli 1916–1935, Joseph Yekutieli Maccabi Sport Archives (Tel Aviv, Israel, 1932).

9   Jewish Telegraphic Agency, "Palestine Will Permit Unlimited Quota of Athletes to Enter for Jewish Games," *The New York Times*, 7 January 1932, 28.

10  Ibid.

11  Ibid.

12  Fédération Internationale de Natation Amateur, "Correspondence, Affiliation Request for Palestine, from the Honorary Secretary to Yekutieli," ADI.29 0007, SYNSO 0001539, The Zvi Nishri Archive for Sports and Physical Education in the Wingate Institute (Netanya, Israel, 1932), 1.

13  International Amateur Athletic Association, "Correspondence, IAAF Affiliation, President Edström to the Federation of the Amateur Sports Clubs of Palestine," 5-1-10, Joseph Yekutieli 1914–1933, Joseph Yekutieli Maccabi Sport Archives (Tel Aviv, Israel, 1932), 1.

14  Fédération Internationale de Natation Amateur, "Correspondence, Affiliation Request for Palestine, from the Honorary Secretary to Yekutieli."

15  Federation of the Amateur Sports Clubs of Palestine, "Letterhead, Dated and Showing Affiliations at the Time," ADI.29 0004 FASCP, SYNSO 0001542, The Zvi Nishri Archive for Sports and Physical Education in the Wingate Institute (Netanya, Israel, 1932).

16  Fédération Sportive Féminine Internationale, "Minutes, VII Congress in Vienna," 1–39, Women's Olympiad London 1932–34 (4), Joseph Yekutieli Maccabi Sport Archives (Tel Aviv, Israel, 1932).

17  Palestinian Football Association, "Correspondence, Elected Officers of the Association, Honorary Secretary," ADI 5.27 0002, SYNSO 0052466, The Zvi Nishri Archive for Sports and Physical Education in the Wingate Institute (Netanya, Israel, February 12, 1932).

18 "Correspondence, Wauchope's Consent to Be Patron of the 1932 Maccabiad, to Weizmann," 4237 British Maccabi, The Weizmann Archives (Rehovot, Israel, 1932), 1.
19 Ibid.
20 Ibid., 2.
21 Jewish Telegraphic Agency, "Lord Melchett in Palestine," *JTA Daily News Bulletin*, 24 March 1932, 4.
22 Ibid.
23 Ibid.
24 Wigoder, *Encyclopedia Vol. 2*, 926.
25 Yosef Yekutieli, "Essay, Physical Culture in Palestine – Eretz-Israel," 5-1-9, Joseph Yekutieli no date, Joseph Yekutieli Maccabi Sport Archives (Tel Aviv, Israel), 1.
26 Ibid.
27 Adele Berlin, Marc Zvi Brettler, and Michael Fishbane, eds., *The Jewish Study Bible*, Jewish Publication Society (Oxford: Oxford University Press, 2004), 68, 2181.
28 Yekutieli, "Essay, Physical Culture in Palestine – Eretz-Israel," 1.
29 Ibid.
30 Ibid.
31 Ibid.
32 Ibid.
33 Ibid.
34 Ibid.
35 Joseph M. Levy, "Jewish Olympics Open in Palestine: 25,000 Jam Stadium as First Event of Its Kind Gets Under Way in Tel-Aviv," *The New York Times*, 30 March 1932, 22.
36 Ibid.
37 Jewish Telegraphic Agency, "Palestine Maccabiade Opened: 5,000 Maccabee Members March Through Streets of Tel Aviv to Stadium Headed by Mayor Dizengoff on Horseback," *JTA Daily News Bulletin*, 31 March 1932, 5.
38 Ibid.
39 Jewish Telegraphic Agency, "Tel Aviv en Fete for Maccabiade," *JTA Daily News Bulletin*, 30 March 1932, 3.
40 Ibid.
41 Ibid.
42 Levy, "Jewish Olympics Open in Palestine: 25,000 Jam Stadium as First Event of Its Kind Gets Under Way in Tel-Aviv," 22.
43 Jewish Telegraphic Agency, "Tel Aviv en Fete for Maccabiade," 3.
44 Ibid.
45 Excutive of the Zionist Organisation Organisation Department, "Report, of the Organisation Department of the [Zionist] Executive," 4237 British Maccabi, The Weizmann Archives (Rehovot, Israel, March 31,1932), 11.
46 Ibid.
47 Ibid.
48 Ibid.
49 Jewish Telegraphic Agency, "Palestine High Commissioner Presents Cup for Maccabiade Relay Race: Will Attend Closing Ceremony: Egyptian Arab Wins 500 Meters Race," *JTA Daily News Bulletin*, 1 April 1932, 2.

50 Ibid.

51 Jewish Telegraphic Agency, "Miss Koff Scores in Jewish Games," *The New York Times*, 2 April 1932, 21.

52 Jewish Telegraphic Agency, "The Maccabiade," *JTA Daily News Bulletin*, 5 April 1932, 1.

53 Jewish Telegraphic Agency, "Czech Tennis Team Wins. Defeats Poland in Finals of Maccabee Tests in Palestine," *The New York Times*, 5 April 1932, 30.

54 Jewish Telegraphic Agency, "Polish Boxers, Danish Matmen Triumph as Maccabiad Closes," *The New York Times*, 6 April 1932, 16.

55 Jewish Telegraphic Agency, "Miss Koff Scores in Jewish Games," 21.

56 American Consulate of Jerusalem, "Report of the American Consulate in Jerusalem Taken from the National Archives in Washington, DC," 2-1-18, First Maccabiad 1932, Joseph Yekutieli Maccabi Sport Archives (Tel Aviv, Israel, 1932), 17.

57 The Higher Broughton Jewish Literary Society, "Invitation, First Maccabiad, Film Screening," 2-1-18, First Maccabiad 1932, Joseph Yekutieli Maccabi Sport Archives (Tel Aviv, Israel, 1932).

58 American Consulate of Jerusalem, "Report of the American Consulate in Jerusalem Taken from the National Archives in Washington, DC," 7.

59 Jewish Telegraphic Agency, "Jewish Football Club Winning Championship from German Team Attacked and Told to 'Go to Palestine': Revolvers Found by Police on Attackers," *JTA Daily News Bulletin*, 30 May 1932, 2.

60 Ibid.

61 Jewish Telegraphic Agency, "Maccabee Asks Damages for Maccabiade Ban," 1.

62 Ibid.

63 Jewish Telegraphic Agency, "Lord Melchett Arrives in Poland in Interests of Maccabee Association: Is Guest at Reception; Will Be Received by Foreign and Interior Ministers," 3.

64 High Commissioner's Office Jerusalem, "Correspondence, First Maccabiad, Private Secretary to Yekutieli," 5-1-10, Joseph Yekutieli 1914–1933, Joseph Yekutieli Maccabi Sport Archives (Tel Aviv, Israel, 1932), 1.

65 Ibid.

66 "Amateur Sports Federation," *Palestine Bulletin*, 12 August 1932, 4.

67 Ibid.

68 Waldo H. Heinrichs, "Diary Entry, 6 January," 115, Waldo Huntley Heinrichs Papers, Yale Divinity Library Archives and Manuscripts (New Haven, CT, 1932).

69 Waldo H. Heinrichs, "Diary Entry, 7 January," 115, Waldo Huntley Heinrichs Papers, Yale Divinity Library Archives and Manuscripts (New Haven, CT, 1932).

70 Waldo H. Heinrichs, "Diary Entry, 8 January," 115, Waldo Huntley Heinrichs Papers, Yale Divinity Library Archives and Manuscripts (New Haven, CT, 1932).

71 Waldo H. Heinrichs, "Correspondence, $10,000 Gift of Margaret Hopper for Jesus Library, to Bowman," Y.USA.9-2-2, International Work in Palestine/Israel, Kautz Family YMCA Archives (Minneapolis, MN, 1932), 1.

72 2019 equivalent of USD 183,382.

73 2019 equivalent of USD 1,468,844.

74 Waldo H. Heinrichs, "Diary Entry, 3 February," 115, Waldo Huntley Heinrichs Papers, Yale Divinity Library Archives and Manuscripts (New Haven, CT, 1932).

75  Waldo H. Heinrichs, "Diary Entry, 4 February," 115, Waldo Huntley Heinrichs Papers, Yale Divinity Library Archives and Manuscripts (New Haven, CT, 1932).

76  2019 equivalent of USD 9,572.

77  2019 equivalent of USD 24,573.

78  Waldo H. Heinrichs, "Diary Entry, 5 February," 115, Waldo Huntley Heinrichs Papers, Yale Divinity Library Archives and Manuscripts (New Haven, CT, 1932).

79  Ibid.

80  Waldo H. Heinrichs, "Diary Entry, 6 February," 115, Waldo Huntley Heinrichs Papers, Yale Divinity Library Archives and Manuscripts (New Haven, CT, 1932).

81  Waldo H. Heinrichs, "Diary Entry, 13 February," 115, Waldo Huntley Heinrichs Papers, Yale Divinity Library Archives and Manuscripts (New Haven, CT, 1932).

82  Waldo H. Heinrichs, "Diary Entry, 16 February," 115, Waldo Huntley Heinrichs Papers, Yale Divinity Library Archives and Manuscripts (New Haven, CT, 1932).

83  Ibid.

84  Fred W. Ramsey, "Correspondence, 1932 Operating Budget for Jerusalem YMCA, from Ramsey to Heinrichs," Y.USA.9–2 2, International Work in Palestine/Israel, Kautz Family YMCA Archives (Minneapolis, MN, 1932), 1.

85  Ibid., 2.

86  2019 equivalent of USD 427,597 to USD 447,033.

87  Waldo H. Heinrichs, "Diary Entry, 19 February," 115, Waldo Huntley Heinrichs Papers, Yale Divinity Library Archives and Manuscripts (New Haven, CT, 1932).

88  Waldo H. Heinrichs, "Diary Entry, 10 March," 115, Waldo Huntley Heinrichs Papers, Yale Divinity Library Archives and Manuscripts (New Haven, CT, 1932).

89  Ibid.

90  Waldo H. Heinrichs, "Diary Entry, 20 March," 115, Waldo Huntley Heinrichs Papers, Yale Divinity Library Archives and Manuscripts (New Haven, CT, 1932).

91  Waldo H. Heinrichs, "Diary Entry, 30 March," 115, Waldo Huntley Heinrichs Papers, Yale Divinity Library Archives and Manuscripts (New Haven, CT, 1932).

92  Waldo H. Heinrichs, "Diary Entry, 28 March," 115, Waldo Huntley Heinrichs Papers, Yale Divinity Library Archives and Manuscripts (New Haven, CT, 1932).

93  Ibid.

94  Waldo H. Heinrichs, "Diary Entry, 29 March," 115, Waldo Huntley Heinrichs Papers, Yale Divinity Library Archives and Manuscripts (New Haven, CT, 1932).

95  Nicholas M. Lattof, "Report, of the Board of Directors of the Jerusalem YMCA Regarding 1932 Syrian Olympics," Y.USA.9-2-2, International Work in Palestine/Israel, Kautz Family YMCA Archives (Minneapolis, MN, 1932), 1.

96  Ibid.

97  Ibid., 2.

98  Ibid.

99  International Committee of Young Men's Christian Associations, "Minutes, International Committee Meeting," Y.USA.9-2-2, International Work in Palestine/Israel, Kautz Family YMCA Archives (Minneapolis, MN, 1932), 1.

100 Waldo H. Heinrichs, "Diary Entry, 7 April," 115, Waldo Huntley Heinrichs Papers, Yale Divinity Library Archives and Manuscripts (New Haven, CT, 1932).

101 Waldo H. Heinrichs, "Diary Entry, 14 April," 115, Waldo Huntley Heinrichs Papers, Yale Divinity Library Archives and Manuscripts (New Haven, CT, 1932).

102 Waldo H. Heinrichs, "Diary Entry, 17 April," 115, Waldo Huntley Heinrichs Papers, Yale Divinity Library Archives and Manuscripts (New Haven, CT, 1932).

103 Ibid.

104 Ibid.

105 "American to Head Palestine Y. M. C. A.: W. H. Heinrichs Will Sail Tuesday to Take Charge of $1,000,000 Building in Jerusalem. 20 Nationalities Served," *New York Times*, 17 April 1932, 2.

106 Ibid.

107 Waldo H. Heinrichs, "Diary Entry, 19 April," 115, Waldo Huntley Heinrichs Papers, Yale Divinity Library Archives and Manuscripts (New Haven, CT, 1932).

108 Ibid.

109 Francis S. Harmon, "Correspondence, on the Commencement of the New Secretary's Journey to the Hold Land, to Heinrichs," Y.USA.9-2-2, International Work in Palestine/Israel, Kautz Family YMCA Archives (Minneapolis, MN, 1932).

110 Heinrichs, "Diary Entry, 19 April."

111 Waldo H. Heinrichs, "Diary Entry, 20 April," 115, Waldo Huntley Heinrichs Papers, Yale Divinity Library Archives and Manuscripts (New Haven, CT, 1932).

112 Ibid.

113 Ibid.

114 George Khadder, "Minutes, of the Meeting of the Board of Directors of the Jerusalem YMCA on May 4," Y.USA.9-2-2, International Work in Palestine/Israel, Kautz Family YMCA Archives (Minneapolis, MN, 1932), 1.

115 Ibid.

116 Ibid.

117 Waldo H. Heinrichs, "Diary Entry, 7 May," 115, Waldo Huntley Heinrichs Papers, Yale Divinity Library Archives and Manuscripts (New Haven, CT, 1932).

118 Waldo H. Heinrichs, "Diary Entry, 8 May," 115, Waldo Huntley Heinrichs Papers, Yale Divinity Library Archives and Manuscripts (New Haven, CT, 1932).

119 Ibid.

120 2019 equivalent of USD 333.

## Chapter 6

1 Waldo H. Heinrichs, "Diary Entry, 22 August," 115, Waldo Huntley Heinrichs Papers, Yale Divinity Library Archives and Manuscripts (New Haven, CT, 1932).

2 Waldo H. Heinrichs, "Diary Entry, 18 May," 115, Waldo Huntley Heinrichs Papers, Yale Divinity Library Archives and Manuscripts (New Haven, CT, 1932).

3 Waldo H. Heinrichs, "Diary Entry, 10 May," 115, Waldo Huntley Heinrichs Papers, Yale Divinity Library Archives and Manuscripts (New Haven, CT, 1932).

4 Waldo H. Heinrichs, "Diary Entry, 12 May," 115, Waldo Huntley Heinrichs Papers, Yale Divinity Library Archives and Manuscripts (New Haven, CT, 1932).

5 Waldo H. Heinrichs, "Diary Entry, 14 May," 115, Waldo Huntley Heinrichs Papers, Yale Divinity Library Archives and Manuscripts (New Haven, CT, 1932).

6 Waldo H. Heinrichs, "Diary Entry, 17 May," 115, Waldo Huntley Heinrichs Papers, Yale Divinity Library Archives and Manuscripts (New Haven, CT, 1932).

7 Waldo H. Heinrichs, "Diary Entry, 26 May," 115, Waldo Huntley Heinrichs Papers, Yale Divinity Library Archives and Manuscripts (New Haven, CT, 1932).

8   Heinrichs, "Diary Entry, 17 May."

9   Ibid.

10   Heinrichs, "Diary Entry, 18 May."

11   Ibid.

12   Wawrzyn, *Nazis in the Holy Land, 1933–1948*, 8–9.

13   Ibid., 109.

14   Ibid., 160.

15   Ibid., 109.

16   Ibid., 110.

17   Ibid.

18   Waldo H. Heinrichs, "Diary Entry, 20 May," 115, Waldo Huntley Heinrichs Papers, Yale Divinity Library Archives and Manuscripts (New Haven, CT, 1932).

19   Ibid.

20   Ibid.

21   Ibid.

22   Waldo H. Heinrichs, "Correspondence, Confirmation of Arrival and Priorities, to Ramsey," Y.USA.9-2-2, International Work in Palestine/Israel, Kautz Family YMCA Archives (Minneapolis, MN, 1932), 1.

23   2019 equivalent of USD 21,995.

24   Heinrichs, "Correspondence, Confirmation of Arrival and Priorities, to Ramsey," 2.

25   Waldo H. Heinrichs, "Diary Entry, 21 May," 115, Waldo Huntley Heinrichs Papers, Yale Divinity Library Archives and Manuscripts (New Haven, CT, 1932).

26   Jerusalem International Young Men's Christian Association, "Minutes, of Meeting of Board of Jerusalem YMCA Held on 23 May 1932," Y.USA.9-2-2, International Work in Palestine/Israel, Kautz Family YMCA Archives (Minneapolis, MN, 1932), 1.

27   Ibid.

28   Ibid., 2.

29   Waldo H. Heinrichs, "Diary Entry, 23 May," 115, Waldo Huntley Heinrichs Papers, Yale Divinity Library Archives and Manuscripts (New Haven, CT, 1932).

30   Waldo H. Heinrichs, "Diary Entry, 24 May," 115, Waldo Huntley Heinrichs Papers, Yale Divinity Library Archives and Manuscripts (New Haven, CT, 1932).

31   Waldo H. Heinrichs, "Diary Entry, 31 May," 115, Waldo Huntley Heinrichs Papers, Yale Divinity Library Archives and Manuscripts (New Haven, CT, 1932).

32   Ibid.

33   Ibid.

34   Ibid.

35   Waldo H. Heinrichs, "Diary Entry, 1 June," 115, Waldo Huntley Heinrichs Papers, Yale Divinity Library Archives and Manuscripts (New Haven, CT, 1932).

36   Ibid.

37   Waldo H. Heinrichs, "Diary Entry, 2 June," 115, Waldo Huntley Heinrichs Papers, Yale Divinity Library Archives and Manuscripts (New Haven, CT, 1932).

38   Waldo H. Heinrichs, "Diary Entry, 3 June," 115, Waldo Huntley Heinrichs Papers, Yale Divinity Library Archives and Manuscripts (New Haven, CT, 1932).

39   Ibid.

40   Waldo H. Heinrichs, "Diary Entry, 5 June," 115, Waldo Huntley Heinrichs Papers, Yale Divinity Library Archives and Manuscripts (New Haven, CT, 1932).

41  Waldo H. Heinrichs, "Diary Entry, 6 June," 115, Waldo Huntley Heinrichs Papers, Yale Divinity Library Archives and Manuscripts (New Haven, CT, 1932).

42  Waldo H. Heinrichs, "Diary Entry, 13 June," 115, Waldo Huntley Heinrichs Papers, Yale Divinity Library Archives and Manuscripts (New Haven, CT, 1932).

43  Waldo H. Heinrichs, "Correspondence, Operating Budget of New YMCA Building, to Colleagues," Y.USA.9–2-2, International Work in Palestine/Israel, Kautz Family YMCA Archives (Minneapolis, MN, 1932).

44  Waldo H. Heinrichs, "Diary Entry, 16 June," 115, Waldo Huntley Heinrichs Papers, Yale Divinity Library Archives and Manuscripts (New Haven, CT, 1932).

45  2019 equivalent of USD 153,776.

46  2019 equivalent of USD 256,293.

47  2019 equivalent of USD 214,965.

48  2019 equivalent of USD 384.

49  Waldo H. Heinrichs, "Diary Entry, 15 June," 115, Waldo Huntley Heinrichs Papers, Yale Divinity Library Archives and Manuscripts (New Haven, CT, 1932).

50  Waldo H. Heinrichs, "Diary Entry, 20 June," 115, Waldo Huntley Heinrichs Papers, Yale Divinity Library Archives and Manuscripts (New Haven, CT, 1932).

51  Waldo H. Heinrichs, "Diary Entry, 17 June," 115, Waldo Huntley Heinrichs Papers, Yale Divinity Library Archives and Manuscripts (New Haven, CT, 1932).

52  Waldo H. Heinrichs, "Correspondence, Commemorative Portrait of James Jarvie and Notable Gifts Book, to James Turner," Y.USA.9–2-2, International Work in Palestine/Israel, Kautz Family YMCA Archives (Minneapolis, MN, 1932).

53  Waldo H. Heinrichs, "Diary Entry, 27 June," 115, Waldo Huntley Heinrichs Papers, Yale Divinity Library Archives and Manuscripts (New Haven, CT, 1932).

54  Waldo H. Heinrichs, "Diary Entry, 26 June," 115, Waldo Huntley Heinrichs Papers, Yale Divinity Library Archives and Manuscripts (New Haven, CT, 1932).

55  Ibid.

56  Waldo H. Heinrichs, "Diary Entry, 30 June," 115, Waldo Huntley Heinrichs Papers, Yale Divinity Library Archives and Manuscripts (New Haven, CT, 1932).

57  2019 equivalent of USD 98,628.

58  Waldo H. Heinrichs, "Diary Entry, 1 July," 115, Waldo Huntley Heinrichs Papers, Yale Divinity Library Archives and Manuscripts (New Haven, CT, 1932).

59  Waldo H. Heinrichs, "Diary Entry, 2 July," 115, Waldo Huntley Heinrichs Papers, Yale Divinity Library Archives and Manuscripts (New Haven, CT, 1932).

60  Waldo H. Heinrichs, "Diary Entry, 5 July," 115, Waldo Huntley Heinrichs Papers, Yale Divinity Library Archives and Manuscripts (New Haven, CT, 1932).

61  Ibid.

62  Ibid.

63  Waldo H. Heinrichs, "Diary Entry, 9 July," 115, Waldo Huntley Heinrichs Papers, Yale Divinity Library Archives and Manuscripts (New Haven, CT, 1932).

64  Waldo H. Heinrichs, "Diary Entry, 18 July," 115, Waldo Huntley Heinrichs Papers, Yale Divinity Library Archives and Manuscripts (New Haven, CT, 1932).

65  Ibid.

66  Waldo H. Heinrichs, "Diary Entry, 26 July," 115, Waldo Huntley Heinrichs Papers, Yale Divinity Library Archives and Manuscripts (New Haven, CT, 1932).

67  Waldo H. Heinrichs, "Diary Entry, 29 July," 115, Waldo Huntley Heinrichs Papers, Yale Divinity Library Archives and Manuscripts (New Haven, CT, 1932).

68  Waldo H. Heinrichs, "Diary Entry, 3 August," 115, Waldo Huntley Heinrichs Papers, Yale Divinity Library Archives and Manuscripts (New Haven, CT, 1932).

69  Waldo H. Heinrichs, "Diary Entry, 4 August," 115, Waldo Huntley Heinrichs Papers, Yale Divinity Library Archives and Manuscripts (New Haven, CT, 1932).

70  "Letter to the Readers LXIV: Sport in Palestine," *Palestine Bulletin*, 8 August 1932, 2.

71  "Y. M. C. A. Tennis Championships," *Palestine Bulletin*, 8 August 1932, 4.

72  "Letter to the Readers LXIV: Sport in Palestine," 2.

73  Ibid.

74  Ibid.

75  Waldo H. Heinrichs, "Diary Entry, 8 August," 115, Waldo Huntley Heinrichs Papers, Yale Divinity Library Archives and Manuscripts (New Haven, CT, 1932).

76  Waldo H. Heinrichs, "Diary Entry, 9 August," 115, Waldo Huntley Heinrichs Papers, Yale Divinity Library Archives and Manuscripts (New Haven, CT, 1932).

77  Waldo H. Heinrichs, "Diary Entry, 15 August," 115, Waldo Huntley Heinrichs Papers, Yale Divinity Library Archives and Manuscripts (New Haven, CT, 1932).

78  Heinrichs, "Diary Entry, 22 August."

79  Waldo H. Heinrichs, "Diary Entry, 25 August," 115, Waldo Huntley Heinrichs Papers, Yale Divinity Library Archives and Manuscripts (New Haven, CT, 1932).

80  Waldo H. Heinrichs, "Diary Entry, 27 August," 115, Waldo Huntley Heinrichs Papers, Yale Divinity Library Archives and Manuscripts (New Haven, CT, 1932).

81  Waldo H. Heinrichs, "Diary Entry, 2 September," 115, Waldo Huntley Heinrichs Papers, Yale Divinity Library Archives and Manuscripts (New Haven, CT, 1932).

82  Waldo H. Heinrichs, "Diary Entry, 5 September," 115, Waldo Huntley Heinrichs Papers, Yale Divinity Library Archives and Manuscripts (New Haven, CT, 1932).

83  Waldo H. Heinrichs, "Diary Entry, 6 September," 115, Waldo Huntley Heinrichs Papers, Yale Divinity Library Archives and Manuscripts (New Haven, CT, 1932).

84  Ibid.

85  Waldo H. Heinrichs, "Diary Entry, 13 September," 115, Waldo Huntley Heinrichs Papers, Yale Divinity Library Archives and Manuscripts (New Haven, CT, 1932).

86  Waldo H. Heinrichs, "Correspondence, Lord Allenby's Visit and the Dedication Ceremony, to Ramsey," Y.USA.9-2-2, International Work in Palestine/Israel, Kautz Family YMCA Archives (Minneapolis, MN, 1932), 2.

87  Waldo H. Heinrichs, "Correspondence, on Relations with the Latin Patriarchate and the Zionists, to Smith," Y.USA.9-2-2, International Work in Palestine/Israel, Kautz Family YMCA Archives (Minneapolis, MN, 1932).

88  Ibid.

89  Louis Parlisina, "Correspondence, on the Evil Nature of Protestantism and the Work of the YMCA, to Clergy and Laymen of the Latin Church of Jerusalem," Y.USA.9-2-2, International Work in Palestine/Israel, Kautz Family YMCA Archives (Minneapolis, MN, 1932), 1.

90  Ibid.

91  Ibid.

92  Waldo H. Heinrichs, "Diary Entry, 16 September," 115, Waldo Huntley Heinrichs Papers, Yale Divinity Library Archives and Manuscripts (New Haven, CT, 1932).

93  Waldo H. Heinrichs, "Diary Entry, 28 September," 115, Waldo Huntley Heinrichs Papers, Yale Divinity Library Archives and Manuscripts (New Haven, CT, 1932).

94  Waldo H. Heinrichs, "Diary Entry, 28 October," 115, Waldo Huntley Heinrichs Papers, Yale Divinity Library Archives and Manuscripts (New Haven, CT, 1932).

95  Wawrzyn, *Nazis in the Holy Land, 1933–1948*, 12.

96  Waldo H. Heinrichs, "Diary Entry, 7 November," 115, Waldo Huntley Heinrichs Papers, Yale Divinity Library Archives and Manuscripts (New Haven, CT, 1932).

97  Waldo H. Heinrichs, "Diary Entry, 8 November," 115, Waldo Huntley Heinrichs Papers, Yale Divinity Library Archives and Manuscripts (New Haven, CT, 1932).

98  Ibid.

99  Ibid.

100  Waldo H. Heinrichs, "Diary Entry, 9 November," 115, Waldo Huntley Heinrichs Papers, Yale Divinity Library Archives and Manuscripts (New Haven, CT, 1932).

101  Waldo H. Heinrichs, "Diary Entry, 11 November," 115, Waldo Huntley Heinrichs Papers, Yale Divinity Library Archives and Manuscripts (New Haven, CT, 1932).

102  Waldo H. Heinrichs, "Diary Entry, 21 November," 115, Waldo Huntley Heinrichs Papers, Yale Divinity Library Archives and Manuscripts (New Haven, CT, 1932).

103  Waldo H. Heinrichs, "Diary Entry, 22 November," 115, Waldo Huntley Heinrichs Papers, Yale Divinity Library Archives and Manuscripts (New Haven, CT, 1932).

104  Ibid.

105  Ibid.

106  Ibid.

107  Ibid.

108  Waldo H. Heinrichs, "Diary Entry, 23 November," 115, Waldo Huntley Heinrichs Papers, Yale Divinity Library Archives and Manuscripts (New Haven, CT, 1932).

109  Ibid.

110  2019 equivalent of USD 12,815.

111  Heinrichs, "Diary Entry, 23 November."

112  Waldo H. Heinrichs, "Diary Entry, 24 November," 115, Waldo Huntley Heinrichs Papers, Yale Divinity Library Archives and Manuscripts (New Haven, CT, 1932).

113  Jerusalem International Young Men's Christian Association, "Correspondence, 28 November, NOC Recognition, Heinrichs to Berdez," 0077643, CIO CNO ISR CORR OU MO 01 14 36, Historical Archives Olympic Studies Centre (Lausanne, Switzerland, 1932), 1.

114  Waldo H. Heinrichs, "Diary Entry, 29 November," 115, Waldo Huntley Heinrichs Papers, Yale Divinity Library Archives and Manuscripts (New Haven, CT, 1932).

115  Waldo H. Heinrichs, "Diary Entry, 5 December," 115, Waldo Huntley Heinrichs Papers, Yale Divinity Library Archives and Manuscripts (New Haven, CT, 1932).

116  Waldo H. Heinrichs, "Diary Entry, 7 December," 115, Waldo Huntley Heinrichs Papers, Yale Divinity Library Archives and Manuscripts (New Haven, CT, 1932).

117  Ibid.

118  Waldo H. Heinrichs, "Diary Entry, 8 December," 115, Waldo Huntley Heinrichs Papers, Yale Divinity Library Archives and Manuscripts (New Haven, CT, 1932).

119  Waldo H. Heinrichs, "Diary Entry, 14 December," 115, Waldo Huntley Heinrichs Papers, Yale Divinity Library Archives and Manuscripts (New Haven, CT, 1932).

120 Ibid.

121 Waldo H. Heinrichs, "Diary Entry, 19 December," 115, Waldo Huntley Heinrichs Papers, Yale Divinity Library Archives and Manuscripts (New Haven, CT, 1932).

122 Ibid.

123 Ibid.

124 Waldo H. Heinrichs, "Diary Entry, 20 December," 115, Waldo Huntley Heinrichs Papers, Yale Divinity Library Archives and Manuscripts (New Haven, CT, 1932).

125 Ibid. Underline as in the original.

126 Ibid.

## Chapter 7

1 More than seventy years after the end of the Second World War, it is becoming increasingly difficult to remember and understand why the global order is arranged in the manner that it is. Managing a change process to update the order is fraught with danger, because the system serves as a cork to prevent the type of explosive slaughter witnessed between 1939 and 1945. Attempting to change this order radically is even more dangerous.

2 Wawrzyn, *Nazis in the Holy Land, 1933–1948*, 4.

3 Ibid., 135.

4 Ibid.

5 Ibid., 95.

6 Lattof, "What the Young Men's Christian Association Has Meant to Me," 14.

7 Wikipedia, "Early Timeline of Nazism," in *Early Timeline of Nazism* (2019). https://en.wikipedia.org/wiki/Early_timeline_of_Nazism#1933.

8 Ibid.

9 Ibid.

10 Ibid.

11 Ibid.

12 Guttmann, *The Games Must Go On*, 62.

13 Ibid., 65.

14 Richard D. Mandell, *The Nazi Olympics* (New York, New York: The Macmillan Company, 1971), 57–58.

15 Guttmann, *The Games Must Go On*, 63.

16 Ibid., 63–64.

17 Mandell, *The Nazi Olympics*, 44.

18 Guttmann, *The Games Must Go On*, 64.

19 Ibid., 62.

20 Ibid., 65.

21 Ibid.

22 Ibid.

23 Ibid.

24 Ibid.

25 Mandell, *The Nazi Olympics*, 58.

26 Guttmann, *The Games Must Go On*, 66.

27 Ibid.

28  Ibid.
29  Clarence Napier Bruce, "Correspondence, August, NOC Recognition, Lord Aberdare to Baillet-Latour," 0077643, CIO CNO ISR CORR OU MO 01 14 36, Historical Archives Olympic Studies Centre (Lausanne, Switzerland, 1933), 1.
30  Mandell, *The Nazi Olympics*, 58.
31  Ibid., 59.
32  2019 equivalent of approximately USD 91,703,463.
33  Guttmann, *The Games Must Go On*, 65.
34  Ibid., 67.
35  "Sherrill Explains View on Olympics: Asserts Proposed Boycott Would Stir Up Anti-Semitic Feeling in America," *New York Times*, 1 December 1933, 12.
36  "Olympisches Ehrenwort," *Westland*, 2 December 1933, 1.
37  National Gallery of Canada, "Siegfried Thalheimer Fonds: Finding Aid," in *Siegfried Thalheimer* (2019). https://www.gallery.ca/library/ngc040.html.
38  "Olympisches Ehrenwort," 1.
39  Guttmann, *The Games Must Go On*, 69.
40  Ibid.
41  Jewish Telegraphic Agency, "Acts of Nazis Mock Pledge of Fair Play to Jewish Athletes: Diplomats Watching for Legal Disavowal of Promise to Let Jews Compete," *Jewish Daily Bulletin*, 17 December 1933, 1.
42  "Kommt Amerika Zur Olympiade!" *Westland*, 23 December 1933.
43  Guttmann, *The Games Must Go On*, 67.
44  Wawrzyn, *Nazis in the Holy Land, 1933–1948*, 25.
45  Wigoder, *Encyclopedia Vol. 1*, 536.
46  Ibid.
47  Ibid.
48  David B. Green, "This Day in Jewish History 1933: The Murder of Chaim Arlosoroff. The Mystery of Who Assassinated This Pre-State Leader of the Zionist Movement Remains Unresolved," *HaAretz*, June 16, 2013. https://www.haaretz.com/jewish/.premium-1933-the-murder-of-chaim-arlosoroff-1.5280334.
49  Ofer Aderet, "Was Magda Goebbels' Father Jewish?", *HaAretz*, August 21, 2016. https://www.haaretz.com/world-news/europe/.premium-was-magda-goebbels-father-jewish-1.5427433.
50  Waldo H. Heinrichs, "Diary Entry, 23 March," 115, Waldo Huntley Heinrichs Papers, Yale Divinity Library Archives and Manuscripts (New Haven, CT, 1933).
51  Wawrzyn, *Nazis in the Holy Land, 1933–1948*, 65–66.
52  In late 1932 or early 1933, this press had printed the Jerusalem sport map that the Jerusalem YMCA distributed at its April dedication.
53  Waldo H. Heinrichs, "Diary Entry, 20 September," 115, Waldo Huntley Heinrichs Papers, Yale Divinity Library Archives and Manuscripts (New Haven, CT, 1933).
54  Waldo H. Heinrichs, "Diary Entry, 6 December," 115, Waldo Huntley Heinrichs Papers, Yale Divinity Library Archives and Manuscripts (New Haven, CT, 1933).
55  Wawrzyn, *Nazis in the Holy Land, 1933–1948*, 186.
56  Ibid.
57  Jewish Telegraphic Agency, "From Bethlehem to Paris Arab-Christian Editor Goes to Get Nazi Instructions," *Jewish Daily Bulletin*, 8 October 1933, 1.

58  Ibid.

59  Waldo H. Heinrichs, "Diary Entry, 22 October," 115, Waldo Huntley Heinrichs Papers, Yale Divinity Library Archives and Manuscripts (New Haven, CT, 1933).

60  Waldo H. Heinrichs, "Diary Entry, 29 October," 115, Waldo Huntley Heinrichs Papers, Yale Divinity Library Archives and Manuscripts (New Haven, CT, 1933).

61  Waldo H. Heinrichs, "Diary Entry, 3 November," 115, Waldo Huntley Heinrichs Papers, Yale Divinity Library Archives and Manuscripts (New Haven, CT, 1933).

62  Wawrzyn, *Nazis in the Holy Land, 1933–1948*, 13.

63  Ibid.

64  Ibid., 14.

65  Ibid., 6.

66  Deutsche Sportsverein Jerusalem, "List, of Board Members of German Sports Club Jerusalem," 526/15 כ, 67.1/3 - 1530 - Sport 1928 to 1939, Israel State Archives (Jerusalem, Israel, 1936), 1.

67  Wawrzyn, *Nazis in the Holy Land, 1933–1948*, 6.

68  Ibid., 7.

69  Ibid., 8.

70  Indian Olympic Association, "Correspondence, First Western Asiatic Games, Sondhi to the Private Secretary to the High Commissioner for Palestine," 1–36, First Western Asian Games 1933–1934, Joseph Yekutieli Maccabi Sport Archives (Tel Aviv, Israel, 1933).

71  Julius Jacobs, "Correspondence, First Western Asiatic Games, to Yekutieli, 16 May," 1–36, First Western Asian Games 1933–1934, Joseph Yekutieli Maccabi Sport Archives (Tel Aviv, Israel, 1933).

72  Ibid.

73  British Mandate for Palestine, "Arabic and Middle Eastern Electronic Library: Official Gazette of the Government Palestine," in *Palestine Gazette* (Arabic and Middle Eastern Electronic Library, 1933), 316. http://findit.library.yale.edu/images_layout/fullviewnoocr?parentoid=15537434.

74  British Mandate for Palestine, "Arabic and Middle Eastern Electronic Library: Official Gazette of the Government Palestine," in *Palestine Gazette* (Arabic and Middle Eastern Electronic Library, 1933), 538. http://findit.library.yale.edu/images_layout/fullviewnoocr?parentoid=15537434.

75  Julius Jacobs, "Correspondence, First Western Asiatic Games, to Yekutieli, 16 May," 1–36, First Western Asian Games 1933–1934, Joseph Yekutieli Maccabi Sport Archives (Tel Aviv, Israel, 1933).

76  Palestine Olympic Association, "Protocol, Foundation Meeting of the Palestine Olympic Association," 0077643, CIO CNO ISR CORR OU MO 01 14 36, Historical Archives Olympic Studies Centre (Lausanne, Switzerland, 1933), Corr. 1930–34.

77  They were joined by Zvi Nishri, chairman of the FASCP, Alex Epstein, and A. Poper from the Palestine Fencing Association; Walter Frankl, a representative of the FASCP's athletics section to the IAAF (headed by the IOC's executive board member Edström); Mr. Weigler from FASCP's swimming and water polo section affiliated with FINA; Arazi and Danin from FASCP's motorcyclists section to be affiliated with FICM; and David Almagor from FASCP's boxing section affiliated with FIBA.

78  Palestine Olympic Association, "Foundation Meeting of POA."

79  Ibid.

80  Ibid.

81  Palestine Olympic Association, "Correspondence, CIO Receipt 6241 on NOC Recognition, Yekutieli to Berdez," 0077643, CIO CNO ISR CORR OU MO 01 14 36, Historical Archives Olympic Studies Centre (Lausanne, Switzerland, 1933), Corr. 1930–34.

82  International Olympic Committee, "Bulletin Officiel, Comité Internationale Olympique, 8me année n° 24," 5–1–16, International Olympic Committee, Joseph Yekutieli Maccabi Sport Archives (Tel Aviv, Israel, 1933), 5.

83  Yosef Yekutieli, "Correspondence, First Western Asiatic Games, to Honorary Secretary Sondhi of the Indian Olympic Association," 1–36, First Western Asian Games 1933–1934, Joseph Yekutieli Maccabi Sport Archives (Tel Aviv, Israel, 1933).

84  Indian Olympic Association, "Correspondence, 472/313 First Western Asiatic Games, Sondhi to Yekutieli," 1–36, First Western Asian Games 1933–1934, Joseph Yekutieli Maccabi Sport Archives (Tel Aviv, Israel, 1933).

85  Indian Olympic Association, "Correspondence, 471/312 First Western Asiatic Games, Sondhi to Yekutieli," 1–36, First Western Asian Games 1933–1934, Joseph Yekutieli Maccabi Sport Archives (Tel Aviv, Israel, 1933).

86  Federation of the Amateur Sports Clubs of Palestine, "Correspondence, First Western Asiatic Games, Honorary Secretary Yekutieli to Honorary Secretary Sondhi of the Indian Olympic Association," 1–36, First Western Asian Games 1933–1934, Joseph Yekutieli Maccabi Sport Archives (Tel Aviv, Israel, 1934).

87  Ibid.

88  International Olympic Committee, "Correspondence, 9 June, NOC Recognition, Baillet-Latour to Yekutieli," 0077643, CIO CNO ISR CORR OU MO 01 14 36, Historical Archives Olympic Studies Centre (Lausanne, Switzerland, 1933), Corr. 1930–34.

89  Guttmann, *The Games Must Go On*, 66.

90  Bruce, "Correspondence, August, NOC Recognition, Lord Aberdare to Baillet-Latour," 1–2.

91  Henri de Baillet-Latour, "Correspondence, 25 August, NOC Recognition, Baillet-Latour to Lord Aberdare," 0077643, CIO CNO ISR CORR OU MO 01 14 36, Historical Archives Olympic Studies Centre (Lausanne, Switzerland, 1933), Corr. 1930–34.

92  Ibid.

93  Jewish Telegraphic Agency, "German Jewish Athletes Officially Forbidden to Attend Prague Maccabiade," *Jewish Daily Bulletin*, 25 August 1933, 1.

94  Frederick H. Kisch, "Correspondence, CIO Receipt 6448 on NOC Recognition, Kisch to Baillet-Latour," 0077643, CIO CNO ISR CORR OU MO 01 14 36, Historical Archives Olympic Studies Centre (Lausanne, Switzerland, 1933), Corr. 1930–34.

95  International Olympic Committee, "Correspondence, 26 September, NOC Recognition, Baillet-Latour to Palestine Olympic Association," 0077643, CIO CNO ISR CORR OU MO 01 14 36, Historical Archives Olympic Studies Centre (Lausanne, Switzerland, 1933), Corr. 1930–34.

96 Jewish Telegraphic Agency, "Maccabee Movement Vital to Jewry, Says Viscountess Erleigh," *Jewish Daily Bulletin*, 8 October 1933.

97 First Western Asiatic Games Championships, "Correspondence, 28 October, First Western Asiatic Games, Sondhi to Yekutieli," 1–36, First Western Asian Games 1933–1934, Joseph Yekutieli Maccabi Sport Archives (Tel Aviv, Israel, 1933), 2.

98 Ibid.

99 Frederick H. Kisch, "Correspondence, NOC Recognition, Kisch to Baillet-Latour, 27 November," 0077643, CIO CNO ISR CORR OU MO 01 14 36, Corr. 1930–1934, Historical Archives Olympic Studies Centre (Lausanne, Switzerland, 1933), 1–2.

100 Ibid.

101 Jewish Telegraphic Agency, "Jew, Arab Athletes to Compete in India: Palestine Maccabee Unit Invited to Send Team to Western Asiatic Olympics," *Jewish Daily Bulletin*, 3 December 1933, 3.

102 Ibid.

103 Guttmann, *The Games Must Go On*, 69.

104 Clarence Napier Bruce, "Correspondence, 24 December, NOC Recognition, Lord Aberdare to Baillet-Latour," 0077643, CIO CNO ISR CORR OU MO 01 14 36, Historical Archives Olympic Studies Centre (Lausanne, Switzerland, 1933), 1–2.

105 Clarence Napier Bruce, "Note Titled 'Jewry and the Next Olympiad', Forwarded with Correspondence from 24 December 1933, to Baillet-Latour," 6529, CIO MBR-ABERD-CORR, Historical Archives Olympic Studies Centre (Lausanne, Switzerland, 1933), Correspondence de Clarence Aberdare 1930 à 1957 Securité: DG1.

106 Ibid., 5.

107 Ibid.

108 Ibid.

109 Ibid., 6.

110 Ibid., 4–5.

111 Ibid., 4.

112 Waldo H. Heinrichs, "Diary Entry, 3 January," 115, Waldo Huntley Heinrichs Papers, Yale Divinity Library Archives and Manuscripts (New Haven, CT, 1933).

113 Ibid.

114 Ibid.

115 Jerusalem International Young Men's Christian Association, "Constitution, Suspended on 15 July 1933," Y.USA.9-2-2, International Work in Palestine/Israel, Kautz Family YMCA Archives (Minneapolis, MN, 1933), 6.

116 Ibid., 22.

117 Ibid.

118 Heinrichs, "Diary Entry, 3 January."

119 Waldo H. Heinrichs, "Diary Entry, 4 January," 115, Waldo Huntley Heinrichs Papers, Yale Divinity Library Archives and Manuscripts (New Haven, CT, 1933).

120 Waldo H. Heinrichs, "Correspondence, Disagreement Over Constitutional Crisis, to Smith," Y.USA.9-2-2, International Work in Palestine/Israel, Kautz Family YMCA Archives (Minneapolis, MN, 1933).

121 Ibid., 2.

122 Ibid.

123 The presence of a large, ardent Bolshevik-aligned group of Arab members at the Jerusalem YMCA underscores the degree to which politics was interwoven into the Arab positions in sport. Heinrichs identified the leader of this Bolshevik faction as Isa Hazon and referred to his followers as "the young irreconcilables." See Waldo H. Heinrichs, "Diary Entry, 22 November," 115, Waldo Huntley Heinrichs Papers, Yale Divinity Library Archives and Manuscripts (New Haven, CT, 1932).

124 Heinrichs, "Correspondence, Disagreement Over Constitutional Crisis, to Smith," 2.

125 Ibid.

126 Ibid., 3.

127 Ibid., 2.

128 Ibid., 3–4.

129 Ibid., 3–4.

130 Lattof, "What the Young Men's Christian Association Has Meant to Me," 6.

131 Heinrichs, "Correspondence, Disagreement Over Constitutional Crisis, to Smith," 4.

132 Ibid.

133 Ibid.

134 Ibid., 4–5.

135 Ibid., 4.

136 Ibid., 6.

137 Ibid., 7.

138 Waldo H. Heinrichs, "Diary Entry, 31 January," 115, Waldo Huntley Heinrichs Papers, Yale Divinity Library Archives and Manuscripts (New Haven, CT, 1933).

139 Wigoder, *Encyclopedia Vol. 2*, 896.

140 Heinrichs, "Diary Entry, 31 January."

141 Waldo H. Heinrichs, "Diary Entry, 8 February," 115, Waldo Huntley Heinrichs Papers, Yale Divinity Library Archives and Manuscripts (New Haven, CT, 1933).

142 Waldo H. Heinrichs, "Diary Entry, 10 February," 115, Waldo Huntley Heinrichs Papers, Yale Divinity Library Archives and Manuscripts (New Haven, CT, 1933).

143 High, "Article Reprint, the Most Thrilling Job in the Most Thrilling City on Earth, from Christian Herald," 9.

144 Waldo H. Heinrichs, "Correspondence, Non-Proselytizing Nature of Jerusalem YMCA, to Mott," Y.USA.9–2-2, International Work in Palestine/Israel, Kautz Family YMCA Archives (Minneapolis, MN, 1933).

145 Ibid., 1.

146 Ibid., 2.

147 Waldo H. Heinrichs, "Correspondence, Misrepresentation of Jerusalem YMCA in the Jewish Daily Bulletin, to Wise," Y.USA.9–2-2, International Work in Palestine/Israel, Kautz Family YMCA Archives (Minneapolis, MN, 1933), 1.

148 Ibid., 1–2.

149 Waldo H. Heinrichs, "Diary Entry, 4 March," 115, Waldo Huntley Heinrichs Papers, Yale Divinity Library Archives and Manuscripts (New Haven, CT, 1933).

150 Waldo H. Heinrichs, "Diary Entry, 5 March," 115, Waldo Huntley Heinrichs Papers, Yale Divinity Library Archives and Manuscripts (New Haven, CT, 1933).

151 Ibid.

152 Waldo H. Heinrichs, "Diary Entry, 8 March," 115, Waldo Huntley Heinrichs Papers, Yale Divinity Library Archives and Manuscripts (New Haven, CT, 1933).

153 Waldo H. Heinrichs, "Diary Entry, 9 March," 115, Waldo Huntley Heinrichs Papers, Yale Divinity Library Archives and Manuscripts (New Haven, CT, 1933).

154 Waldo H. Heinrichs, "Diary Entry, 11 March," 115, Waldo Huntley Heinrichs Papers, Yale Divinity Library Archives and Manuscripts (New Haven, CT, 1933).

155 Waldo H. Heinrichs, "Diary Entry, 16 March," 115, Waldo Huntley Heinrichs Papers, Yale Divinity Library Archives and Manuscripts (New Haven, CT, 1933).

156 Ibid.

157 Jerusalem International Young Men's Christian Association, "Report, of the Sub-Committee Appointed to Investigate Claims on the Owner from the General Contractor, Signed by Canaan and Abramson," Y.USA.9-2-2, International Work in Palestine/Israel, Kautz Family YMCA Archives (Minneapolis, MN, 1933), 1.

158 Ibid., 3.

159 Ibid., 6-7.

160 Ibid., 8-9.

161 At this time, Yekutieli was busy affiliating the FASCP to the Comité International du Pentathlon Moderne Olympique. Source: Comité International du Pentathlon Moderne Olympique, "Correspondence, Requesting Copy of Rules for Palestine, to Yekutieli," ADI.29 0007, SYNSO 0001539, The Zvi Nishri Archive for Sports and Physical Education in the Wingate Institute (Netanya, Israel, 1933).

162 Waldo H. Heinrichs, "Diary Entry, 17 March," 115, Waldo Huntley Heinrichs Papers, Yale Divinity Library Archives and Manuscripts (New Haven, CT, 1933).

163 Heinrichs, "Correspondence, Non-Proselytizing Nature of Jerusalem YMCA, to Mott," 2.

164 Fred W. Ramsey, "Correspondence, Journey to Jerusalem for Dedication, to Mott," Y.USA.9-2-2, International Work in Palestine/Israel, Kautz Family YMCA Archives (Minneapolis, MN, 1933), 2.

165 Waldo H. Heinrichs, "Diary Entry, 1 April," 115, Waldo Huntley Heinrichs Papers, Yale Divinity Library Archives and Manuscripts (New Haven, CT, 1933).

166 Fred W. Ramsey, "Correspondence, Permission-to-Occupy Letter with Safeguards, to Board of Directors of the Jerusalem YMCA," Y.USA.9-2-2, International Work in Palestine/Israel, Kautz Family YMCA Archives (Minneapolis, MN, 1933), 1.

167 Ibid., 2.

168 Ibid.

169 Ibid.

170 Ibid., 3.

171 Ibid.

172 Ibid.

173 Ibid.

174 Emile's younger brother Fuad, upon Waldo's nomination, received a YMCA scholarship to study in the United States. Fuad eventually married Fred Ramsey's daughter, Margaret, who was Waldo's personal secretary during his first year in Jerusalem. Source: Nicholas M. Lattof. "What the Young Men's Christian Association Has Meant to Me." Private Collection of the Lattof Family, 1978, 12.

175 Emile A. Khadder, "Correspondence, Origins of Friction in the Jerusalem YMCA, to Ramsey," Y.USA.9–2-2, International Work in Palestine/Israel, Kautz Family YMCA Archives (Minneapolis, MN, 1933), 1–4.

176 Heinrichs, "Diary Entry, 1 April."

177 Waldo H. Heinrichs, "Diary Entry, 5 April," 115, Waldo Huntley Heinrichs Papers, Yale Divinity Library Archives and Manuscripts (New Haven, CT, 1933).

178 Ibid.

179 Jerusalem International Young Men's Christian Association, "Memorandum, Dedication Exercises Associated with the New Building," Y.USA.9–2-2, International Work in Palestine/Israel, Kautz Family YMCA Archives (Minneapolis, MN, 1933), 1.

180 Ibid., 1–2.

181 Ibid., 1.

182 Ibid., 2.

183 Ibid.

184 Waldo H. Heinrichs, "Diary Entry, 9 April," 115, Waldo Huntley Heinrichs Papers, Yale Divinity Library Archives and Manuscripts (New Haven, CT, 1933).

185 Waldo H. Heinrichs, "Diary Entry, 10 April," 115, Waldo Huntley Heinrichs Papers, Yale Divinity Library Archives and Manuscripts (New Haven, CT, 1933).

186 Waldo H. Heinrichs, "Diary Entry, 12 April," 115, Waldo Huntley Heinrichs Papers, Yale Divinity Library Archives and Manuscripts (New Haven, CT, 1933).

187 Waldo H. Heinrichs, "Diary Entry, 13 April," 115, Waldo Huntley Heinrichs Papers, Yale Divinity Library Archives and Manuscripts (New Haven, CT, 1933).

188 Ibid.

189 Waldo H. Heinrichs, "Diary Entry, 18 April," 115, Waldo Huntley Heinrichs Papers, Yale Divinity Library Archives and Manuscripts (New Haven, CT, 1933).

190 Berlin, Brettler, and Fishbane, *Jewish Bible*, 1307–8.

191 International Committee of Young Men's Christian Associations of Canada and the United States, "Bulletin, First International Broadcast from Jerusalem, April 18, 1933," Y.USA.9–2-2, International Work in Palestine/Israel, Kautz Family YMCA Archives (Minneapolis, MN, 1933).

192 Ibid.

193 Fred W. Ramsey, "Memorandum, Copy of Lord Allenby's Dedication Address, to Harmon," Y.USA.9–2-2, International Work in Palestine/Israel, Kautz Family YMCA Archives (Minneapolis, MN, 1933), 3–4.

194 *Palestine Post*, "Article, New YMCA Buildings Dedicated," Y.USA.9–2-2, International Work in Palestine/Israel, Kautz Family YMCA Archives (Minneapolis, MN, 1933), 5.

195 John R. Mott, "Correspondence, Appointment of Eight Members to the Board of the Jerusalem YMCA, to Ramsey," Y.USA.9–2-2, International Work in Palestine/Israel, Kautz Family YMCA Archives (Minneapolis, MN, 1933), 1.

196 Ibid.

197 Ibid. Underline as in the original.

198 Fred W. Ramsey, "Correspondence, Request for Copy of Deed of Title from Land Registry Office of Jerusalem, to Abramson," Y.USA.9–2-2, International Work in Palestine/Israel, Kautz Family YMCA Archives (Minneapolis, MN, 1933).

199 Waldo H. Heinrichs, "Diary Entry, 30 April," 115, Waldo Huntley Heinrichs Papers, Yale Divinity Library Archives and Manuscripts (New Haven, CT, 1933).

200 Waldo H. Heinrichs, "Diary Entry, 1 May," 115, Waldo Huntley Heinrichs Papers, Yale Divinity Library Archives and Manuscripts (New Haven, CT, 1933).

201 Waldo H. Heinrichs, "Diary Entry, 16 May," 115, Waldo Huntley Heinrichs Papers, Yale Divinity Library Archives and Manuscripts (New Haven, CT, 1933).

202 Ibid.

203 Waldo H. Heinrichs, "Diary Entry, 14 May," 115, Waldo Huntley Heinrichs Papers, Yale Divinity Library Archives and Manuscripts (New Haven, CT, 1933).

204 Jerusalem International Young Men's Christian Association, "Report, 1932–1933 Annual Administration Report of Jerusalem International YMCA, Signed by Heinrichs," Y.USA.9-2-2, International Work in Palestine/Israel, Kautz Family YMCA Archives (Minneapolis, MN, 1933), 5.

205 Waldo H. Heinrichs, "Diary Entry, 2 June," 115, Waldo Huntley Heinrichs Papers, Yale Divinity Library Archives and Manuscripts (New Haven, CT, 1933).

206 Ibid.

207 Waldo H. Heinrichs, "Diary Entry, 17 June," 115, Waldo Huntley Heinrichs Papers, Yale Divinity Library Archives and Manuscripts (New Haven, CT, 1933).

208 Waldo H. Heinrichs, "Diary Entry, 19 June," 115, Waldo Huntley Heinrichs Papers, Yale Divinity Library Archives and Manuscripts (New Haven, CT, 1933).

209 Ibid.

210 Ibid.

211 Waldo H. Heinrichs, "Diary Entry, 15 July," 115, Waldo Huntley Heinrichs Papers, Yale Divinity Library Archives and Manuscripts (New Haven, CT, 1933).

212 Waldo H. Heinrichs, "Cable, Confirmation of Appointment System of Board of Directors and the Revised Constitution of the Jerusalem YMCA Passing, to Ramsey," Y.USA.9-2-2, International Work in Palestine/Israel, Kautz Family YMCA Archives (Minneapolis, MN, 1933).

213 2019 equivalent of USD 246,569.

214 Waldo H. Heinrichs, "Diary Entry, 10 August," 115, Waldo Huntley Heinrichs Papers, Yale Divinity Library Archives and Manuscripts (New Haven, CT, 1933).

215 The Clark Collection would become a major focus of Heinrichs' time and attention in the autumn of 1933 and his focus on it is one possible reason for his not having understood the brewing Nazi trouble (until it erupted in early December).

216 Heinrichs, "Diary Entry, 10 August."

217 Waldo H. Heinrichs, "Diary Entry, 17 September," 115, Waldo Huntley Heinrichs Papers, Yale Divinity Library Archives and Manuscripts (New Haven, CT, 1933).

218 Waldo H. Heinrichs, "Diary Entry, 16 September," 115, Waldo Huntley Heinrichs Papers, Yale Divinity Library Archives and Manuscripts (New Haven, CT, 1933).

219 Waldo H. Heinrichs, "Diary Entry, 27 September," 115, Waldo Huntley Heinrichs Papers, Yale Divinity Library Archives and Manuscripts (New Haven, CT, 1933).

220 Heinrichs' relationship with Boutagy does, indeed, become his worst relationship. There is no concrete explanation for why it got so bad. Certainly, there were personality conflicts. But if Boutagy was associated with the Palestinian Germans agitating at the Jerusalem YMCA, this could also explain what appears to have

been the irreconcilable nature of their relationship. In the Israel State Archives, there is one postcard that references a "Boutagy" in a meeting at the home of the founder of the Nazi Party of Palestine; however, it is not clear if this was J. Gordon Boutagy. Source: Karl Goebel, "Correspondence, Postcard About an Event to Be Held on November 3, 1934 for Which a Nazi Songbook Was Needed, from Goebel to Karl Ruff Requesting One Boutagy [not clear if it is J. Gordon Boutagy] to Drop Off the Nazi Songbook at Goebel's Address," 823/17- מ, Karl Ruff, Landesvertrauensmann der N.S.D.A.P. für Palästina, in Haifa—Correspondenz 1934–1935, Israel State Archives (Jerusalem, Israel, 1934).

221 Waldo H. Heinrichs, "Diary Entry, 3 October," 115, Waldo Huntley Heinrichs Papers, Yale Divinity Library Archives and Manuscripts (New Haven, CT, 1933).

222 Heinrichs, "Diary Entry, 6 December."

223 Waldo H. Heinrichs, "Diary Entry, 10 October," 115, Waldo Huntley Heinrichs Papers, Yale Divinity Library Archives and Manuscripts (New Haven, CT, 1933).

224 Ibid.

225 Waldo H. Heinrichs, "Correspondence, Progress in Cooperation with Arab and Jewish Sport Clubs, to Harmon," Y.USA.9-2-2, International Work in Palestine/Israel, Kautz Family YMCA Archives (Minneapolis, MN, 1933), 2.

226 Waldo H. Heinrichs, "Diary Entry, 13 October," 115, Waldo Huntley Heinrichs Papers, Yale Divinity Library Archives and Manuscripts (New Haven, CT, 1933).

227 Waldo H. Heinrichs, "Diary Entry, 14 October," 115, Waldo Huntley Heinrichs Papers, Yale Divinity Library Archives and Manuscripts (New Haven, CT, 1933).

228 Ibid.

229 Ibid.

230 Waldo H. Heinrichs, "Diary Entry, 28 October," 115, Waldo Huntley Heinrichs Papers, Yale Divinity Library Archives and Manuscripts (New Haven, CT, 1933).

231 Ibid.

232 Waldo H. Heinrichs, "Diary Entry, 31 October," 115, Waldo Huntley Heinrichs Papers, Yale Divinity Library Archives and Manuscripts (New Haven, CT, 1933).

233 Ibid.

234 Waldo H. Heinrichs, "Diary Entry, 6 November," 115, Waldo Huntley Heinrichs Papers, Yale Divinity Library Archives and Manuscripts (New Haven, CT, 1933).

235 Waldo H. Heinrichs, "Diary Entry, 7 November," 115, Waldo Huntley Heinrichs Papers, Yale Divinity Library Archives and Manuscripts (New Haven, CT, 1933).

236 Waldo H. Heinrichs, "Diary Entry, 8 November," 115, Waldo Huntley Heinrichs Papers, Yale Divinity Library Archives and Manuscripts (New Haven, CT, 1933).

237 Waldo H. Heinrichs, "Diary Entry, 9 November," 115, Waldo Huntley Heinrichs Papers, Yale Divinity Library Archives and Manuscripts (New Haven, CT, 1933).

238 Waldo H. Heinrichs, "Diary Entry, 12 November," 115, Waldo Huntley Heinrichs Papers, Yale Divinity Library Archives and Manuscripts (New Haven, CT, 1933).

239 Ibid.

240 Waldo H. Heinrichs, "Diary Entry, 17 November," 115, Waldo Huntley Heinrichs Papers, Yale Divinity Library Archives and Manuscripts (New Haven, CT, 1933).

241 Waldo H. Heinrichs, "Diary Entry, 19 November," 115, Waldo Huntley Heinrichs Papers, Yale Divinity Library Archives and Manuscripts (New Haven, CT, 1933).

242 Waldo H. Heinrichs, "Diary Entry, 20 November," 115, Waldo Huntley Heinrichs Papers, Yale Divinity Library Archives and Manuscripts (New Haven, CT, 1933).

243 2019 equivalent of USD 2,861.

244 Waldo H. Heinrichs, "Diary Entry, 25 November," 115, Waldo Huntley Heinrichs Papers, Yale Divinity Library Archives and Manuscripts (New Haven, CT, 1933).

## Chapter 8

1 Wikipedia, "Early Timeline of Nazism," in *Early Timeline of Nazism* (2019). https://en.wikipedia.org/wiki/Early_timeline_of_Nazism#1934.

2 Ibid.

3 Ibid.

4 Ibid.

5 Wawrzyn, *Nazis in the Holy Land, 1933–1948*, 20.

6 Ibid.

7 Ibid., 7.

8 Ibid.

9 Ibid., 1.

10 Ibid., 150–201.

11 Ibid., 17.

12 Ibid.

13 Ibid., 7.

14 Ibid., 6.

15 Ibid., 48.

16 Ibid., 11–12.

17 Ibid., 11.

18 Ibid., 21.

19 Ibid., 17.

20 Ibid., 18.

21 Ibid.

22 Ibid., 34.

23 Ibid., 33–34.

24 Ibid., 81.

25 Federation of the Amateur Sports Clubs of Palestine, "Correspondence, 5 January, First Western Asiatic Games, Yekutieli to Sondhi," 1–36, First Western Asian Games 1933–1934, Joseph Yekutieli Maccabi Sport Archives (Tel Aviv, Israel, 1934).

26 Henry Ludwig Mond, "Correspondence, British Empire Games, to Chaim Weizmann," 4237 British Maccabi, The Weizmann Archives (Rehovot, Israel, 1934), 1–2.

27 First Western Asiatic Games Championships, "Correspondence, 16 January, First Western Asiatic Games, Sondhi to Yekutieli," 1–36, First Western Asian Games 1933–1934, Joseph Yekutieli Maccabi Sport Archives (Tel Aviv, Israel, 1934).

28 Western Asiatic Games Committee, "Official Report, First Western Asiatic Games," 1–36, First Western Asian Games 1933–1934, Joseph Yekutieli Maccabi Sport Archives (Tel Aviv, Israel, 1934), 29.

29 First Western Asiatic Games Championships, "Correspondence, 16 January, First Western Asiatic Games, Sondhi to Yekutieli," 1.

30  Western Asiatic Games Committee, "Official Report, First Western Asiatic Games," 28.
31  First Western Asiatic Games Championships, "Correspondence, 16 January, First Western Asiatic Games, Sondhi to Yekutieli," 1–2.
32  Ibid., 3.
33  First Western Asiatic Games Championships, "Correspondence, First Western Asiatic Games, Honorary Secretary Sondhi to Honorary" (1934), 1.
34  Ibid.
35  Jewish Telegraphic Agency, "Palestine Seeks Entry in Berlin 1936 Olympics," *Jewish Daily Bulletin*, 28 January 1934, 1.
36  Western Asiatic Games Committee, "Official Report, First Western Asiatic Games," 47.
37  Aside from the Western Asiatic Games, in early February, Yekutieli received an invitation from the Women's Amateur Athletic Association in England to participate in the Women's World Games. These games would take place in London between August 9 and 11, 1934. Yekutieli was also juggling his responsibilities at the Palestine Football Association, which would be fielding teams in conjunction with the Levant Fair in Tel Aviv as part of the Tel Aviv Levant Fair Cup. Source: Palestine Football Association, "Correspondence, Presentation of Yekutieli on Behalf of Association in Relation to the Levant Fair, Form Letter from the Honorary Secretary General," ADI.29 0007, SYNSO 0001539, The Zvi Nishri Archive for Sports and Physical Education in the Wingate Institute (Netanya, Israel, 1934), 1. Yekutieli was also negotiating the participation contracts with football clubs overseas, including with the Association of Football Clubs in Soviet Russia. Source: Yosef Yekutieli, "Correspondence, Proposal to Play Football in Palestine, to the Director of the Association of Football Clubs in Soviet Russia," ADI.29 0007, SYNSO 0001539, The Zvi Nishri Archive for Sports and Physical Education in the Wingate Institute (Netanya, Israel, 1934), 1. For these reasons, Yekutieli was unable to go to the First Western Asiatic Games. Nonetheless, he arranged the entire delegation to India.
38  Federation of the Amateur Sports Clubs of Palestine, "Correspondence, First Western Asiatic Games, from Honorary Secretary Yekutieli to Honorary Secretary Sondhi," 1–36, First Western Asian Games 1933–1934, Joseph Yekutieli Maccabi Sport Archives (Tel Aviv, Israel, 1933), 1–2.
39  Organising Committee of the First Western Asiatic Games, "Programme, First Western Asiatic Games," ADI 5.27 0002, SYNSO 0052466, The Zvi Nishri Archive for Sports and Physical Education in the Wingate Institute (Netanya, Israel, 1934).
40  Jewish Telegraphic Agency, "Palestine Athlete Runs 25 Miles in 3' 15'," *Jewish Daily Bulletin*, 25 February 1934, 7.
41  First Western Asiatic Games Championships, "Correspondence, 16 January, First Western Asiatic Games, Sondhi to Yekutieli," 1.
42  "Note, First Western Asiatic Games, Typed Note (Possibly by Yekutieli) Titled '50 Years Ago!!!'," 1–36, First Western Asian Games 1933–1934, Joseph Yekutieli Maccabi Sport Archives (Tel Aviv, Israel, 1984).
43  *Jerusalem Post*, "News Clipping, an Olympic Odyssey, 50-Year Anniversary of Participation in the First Western Asiatic Games," 1–36, First Western Asian Games 1933–1934, Joseph Yekutieli Maccabi Sport Archives (Tel Aviv, Israel, 1984), 6.

44  Wikipedia, "Flag of Mandatory Palestine," in *Flag of Mandatory Palestine* (2019). https://en.wikipedia.org/wiki/Flag_of_Mandatory_Palestine.

45  Ibid.

46  *Jerusalem Post*, "An Olympic Odyssey," 6.

47  2019 equivalent of USD 2,488.

48  *Jerusalem Post*, "An Olympic Odyssey," 6.

49  Ibid.

50  Ibid.

51  Ibid.

52  Ibid.

53  S. H. Haskell, "Correspondence, First Western Asiatic Games, to Dizengoff," 1–36, First Western Asian Games 1933–1934, Joseph Yekutieli Maccabi Sport Archives (Tel Aviv, Israel, 1934).

54  *Jerusalem Post*, "An Olympic Odyssey," 6.

55  Ibid.

56  Ibid.

57  Ibid.

58  Ibid.

59  Ibid.

60  Ibid.

61  Western Asiatic Games Committee, "Official Report, First Western Asiatic Games," 13.

62  Hotam, "'Re-Orient-Ation,'" 57.

63  Western Asiatic Games Committee, "Official Report, First Western Asiatic Games," 14.

64  Ibid., 18.

65  Ibid., 20.

66  Ibid., 1.

67  Ibid., 37.

68  Ibid., 26.

69  Ibid., 27.

70  Ibid., 35–36.

71  Ibid., 47.

72  Ibid.

73  Ibid.

74  Ibid., 47–48.

75  Ibid., 48.

76  Ibid.

77  Ibid.

78  Ibid.

79  Ibid.

80  Ibid.

81  Ibid.

82  Ibid., 49.

83  Ibid.

84  Ibid.

85  *Jerusalem Post*, "An Olympic Odyssey," 6.

86 Western Asiatic Games Committee, "Official Report, First Western Asiatic Games," 50.
87 Ibid.
88 Ibid.
89 Ibid. Persia participated only with an administrative delegation and hosted the inaugural meeting of the Western Asiatic Games Confederation. It did not participate in the First Western Asiatic Games with athletes.
90 Ibid., 2.
91 Ibid., 3.
92 Ibid., 52.
93 Ibid., 53.
94 Ibid.
95 Ibid., 53–54.
96 Ibid., 45.
97 Ibid.
98 Ibid., 56.
99 Ibid.
100 Ibid.
101 Ibid.
102 Ibid., 57.
103 Ibid., 58.
104 Lal was another of Heinrichs' friends from Lahore. The Lals had picnicked under the deodars with the Heinrichses and Sondhis not long before Waldo received "the call" for Jerusalem.
105 Western Asiatic Games Committee, "Official Report, First Western Asiatic Games," 64.
106 Ibid.
107 Ibid.
108 Ibid.
109 Ibid., 65.
110 Ibid., 65–66.
111 Ibid., 66.
112 Ibid., 69.
113 Ibid., 40.
114 Ibid.
115 Ibid.
116 Ibid., 42.
117 Ibid.
118 Ibid.
119 Ibid., 41.
120 Ibid., 43.
121 Ibid.
122 Ibid., 41.
123 Ibid., 79.
124 Ibid., 80.

125 Ibid., 81.
126 Anonymous, "Correspondence, First Western Asiatic Games, Typed Letter (Probably from Almagor, Team Manager), to Yekutieli," 1–36, First Western Asian Games 1933–1934, Joseph Yekutieli Maccabi Sport Archives (Tel Aviv, Israel, 1934), 1–2.
127 Western Asiatic Games Committee, "Minutes, Innaugural Meeting of First Western Asiatic Games Committee," 1–36, First Western Asian Games 1933–1934, Joseph Yekutieli Maccabi Sport Archives (Tel Aviv, Israel, 1934).
128 Waldo H. Heinrichs, "Diary Entry, 3 March," 115, Waldo Huntley Heinrichs Papers, Yale Divinity Library Archives and Manuscripts (New Haven, CT, 1934).
129 Yadvinder Singh Mahendra Bahadur, "Correspondence, 5 March, First Western Asiatic Games, to Almagor," 1–36, First Western Asian Games 1933–1934, Joseph Yekutieli Maccabi Sport Archives (Tel Aviv, Israel, 1934).
130 Organising Committee for the First Western Asiatic Games, "Correspondence, 7 March, First Western Asiatic Games, Sondhi to Yekutieli," 1–36, First Western Asian Games 1933–1934, Joseph Yekutieli Maccabi Sport Archives (Tel Aviv, Israel, 1934).
131 Federation of the Amateur Sports Clubs of Palestine, "Correspondence, Invitation to Participate in the Levant Fair's Sport Activities, to Di Angelo," ADI.29 0007, SYNSO 0001539, The Zvi Nishri Archive for Sports and Physical Education in the Wingate Institute (Netanya, Israel, 1934).
132 Yosef Yekutieli, "Correspondence, Visit of Dr. Theodor Schmidt to Palestine; to Unknown Recipient," 5-1-11, Joseph Yekutieli 1934–1948, Joseph Yekutieli Maccabi Sport Archives (Tel Aviv, Israel, 1934).
133 Jewish Telegraphic Agency, "Palestine Seeks Entry in Berlin 1936 Olympics," 1.
134 "Göbbels und die Makkabäer," Westland, 3 February 1934, 2.
135 Yekutieli, "Correspondence, Visit of Dr. Theodor Schmidt to Palestine; to Unknown Recipient."
136 Ibid.
137 Waldo H. Heinrichs, "Diary Entry, 17 March," 115, Waldo Huntley Heinrichs Papers, Yale Divinity Library Archives and Manuscripts (New Haven, CT, 1934).
138 "Oberst Kisch," Westland, 4.
139 Colonial Office, "Correspondence 37331/34, NOC Recognition, Wilhams to Lord Aberdare," 0077643, CIO CNO ISR CORR OU MO 01 14 36, Historical Archives Olympic Studies Centre (Lausanne, Switzerland, 1934), Corr. 1930–34.
140 Ibid., 1–2.
141 Ibid., 2–3.
142 Frederick H. Kisch, "Correspondence, Kisch's Alleged Communications with Nazi General Göring, 29 April," 5-62-1, Colonel Kisch 1923–44, Joseph Yekutieli Maccabi Sport Archives (Tel Aviv, Israel, 1934).
143 Yosef Yekutieli, "Correspondence, An die Redaktion 'Westland', to Westland," 5-1-23, Joseph Yekutieli 1916–1935, Joseph Yekutieli Maccabi Sport Archives (Tel Aviv, Israel, 1934), 1.
144 Ibid.
145 Ibid.
146 Ibid., 2.

147 Ibid., 1.

148 Ali Mustakim, "Correspondence, 27 March, NOC Recognition, to Yekutieli," 0077643, CIO CNO ISR CORR OU MO 01 14 36, Historical Archives Olympic Studies Centre (Lausanne, Switzerland, 1934), Corr. 1930–34.

149 Federation of the Amateur Sports Clubs of Palestine, "Correspondence, 3 May, NOC Recognition, Yekutieli to Berdez," 0077643, CIO CNO ISR CORR OU MO 01 14 36, Historical Archives Olympic Studies Centre (Lausanne, Switzerland, 1934), Corr. 1930–34.

150 Ibid.

151 Yosef Yekutieli, "Correspondence, NOC Recognition, to Schmidt, 3 May," 5–1–23, Joseph Yekutieli 1916–1935, Joseph Yekutieli Maccabi Sport Archives (Tel Aviv, Israel, 1934), 1–2.

152 Jerusalem Inter-School Sports Executive Committee, "Programme, Tenth Jerusalem Inter-School Sports Programme," ADI 5.27 0002, SYNSO 0052466, The Zvi Nishri Archive for Sports and Physical Education in the Wingate Institute (Netanya, Israel, 1934).

153 Ibid., 2.

154 *Westland*, "Correspondence, Regarding the Correspondence of 2 May, to Yekutieli," 5–1–30, Joseph Yekutieli 1934–1948, Joseph Yekutieli Maccabi Sport Archives (Tel Aviv, Israel, 1934).

155 Associated Press, "Jewish Body Asks Olympic Inquiry," *New York Times*, 18 May 1934, 32.

156 The article also reported that the American Jewish Congress requested that the IOC investigate Germany further before deciding to allow the Games to proceed. In what appears to be a curious editorial mistake, the newspaper reported that the Christian Olympic committee of the territory had been recognized.

157 International Olympic Committee, "Correspondence, 19 May, NOC Recognition, Baillet-Latour to Kisch," 0077504, CIO CNO ISR RECON OU MO 01 14 36, Historical Archives Olympic Studies Centre (Lausanne, Switzerland, 1934), Recon. Palestine (Israël) 1934.

158 International Olympic Committee, "Official Bulletin, Addresses of National Olympic Committees, as Published Officially by International Olympic Committee," 5–1–16, Joseph Yekutieli 1927–1937, Joseph Yekutieli Maccabi Sport Archives (Tel Aviv, Israel, 1934), 5.

159 Ibid., 11.

160 Palestine Olympic Association, "Minutes, Palestine Olympic Association's First Meeting," 5–1–11, Joseph Yekutieli 1934–1948, Joseph Yekutieli Maccabi Sport Archives (Tel Aviv, Israel, 1934).

161 Ibid., 1.

162 Ibid.

163 Palestine Olympic Association, "Correspondence, 1936 Berlin Olympic Games; Kisch to the President of the Organizing Committee of the XI Olympiad," 5–1–11, Joseph Yekutieli 1934–1948, Joseph Yekutieli Maccabi Sport Archives (Tel Aviv, Israel, 1934).

164  The Palestine Olympic Association, "Correspondence, Recognition by the IOC and the Inaugural Meeting Held on 20 June 1934, to the Editor of *Palestine Post*," ADI 5.27 0002, SYNSO 0052466, The Zvi Nishri Archive for Sports and Physical Education in the Wingate Institute (Netanya, Israel, 1934).

165  Palestine Olympic Committee, "Correspondence, 28 June NOC Recognition and Inaugural Meeting, Kisch to Baillet-Latour," 0077504, CIO CNO ISR RECON OU MO 01 14 36, Historical Archives Olympic Studies Centre (Lausanne, Switzerland, 1934), Recon. Palestine (Israël) 1934.

166  Palestine Olympic Association, "Correspondence, 1936 Berlin Olympic Games; Kisch to the President of the Organizing Committee of the XI Olympiad."

167  "Germany Expects 3,000 in Olympics," *New York Times*, 21 November 1934, 24.

168  Edtsröm, "Correspondence, Boycott of Palestine from 1936 Olympic Games, to Yekutieli."

169  Clarence Napier Bruce, "Correspondence, 7 March, Second Maccabiad, to Yekutieli," 1–118, Maccabi Yisrael 1926–37, Joseph Yekutieli Maccabi Sport Archives (Tel Aviv, Israel, 1935).

170  Ibid.

171  Federation of the Amateur Sports Clubs of Palestine, "Correspondence, Boycott of 1936 Olympic Games, from Yekutieli to Edstrom," 3.

172  Associated Press, "Palestine Out of Olympics," *New York Times*, 18 March 1935, 22.

173  Jewish Telegraphic Agency, "Reich Maccabi 'Withdraws' from Olympics," *Jewish Telegraphic Agency Latest Cable Dispatches*, 25 September 1935, 1.

174  Ibid.

175  International Olympic Committee, "Bulletin Officiel, Comité Internationale Olympique, 10me année n° 30," 5-1-16, International Olympic Committee, Joseph Yekutieli Maccabi Sport Archives (Tel Aviv, Israel, 1935), 6.

176  Ibid.

177  Ibid.

178  Frederick H. Kisch, "Correspondence, 12 February, Discussing Correspondence to Schmidt of IOC and Destroying Other Material Sent for Review, Kisch to Yekutieli," 5-62-1, Colonel Kisch 1923–44, Joseph Yekutieli Maccabi Sport Archives (Tel Aviv, Israel, 1936).

179  Yosef Yekutieli, "Correspondence, Palestine Membership on Executive of IOC, Yekutieli to Schmidt," 5-1-25, Joseph Yekutieli 1960–73, Joseph Yekutieli Maccabi Sport Archives (Tel Aviv, Israel, 1936).

180  Ibid.

181  Theodor Schmidt, "Correspondence, Kisch Representing Palestine on IOC Board, to Yekutieli, 7 March," 5-1-30, Joseph Yekutieli 1934–1948, Joseph Yekutieli Maccabi Sport Archives (Tel Aviv, Israel, 1936).

182  Palestine Olympic Committee, "Correspondence, Membership on IOC Executive, Kisch to Yekutieli," 5-1-30, Joseph Yekutieli 1934–1948, Joseph Yekutieli Maccabi Sport Archives (Tel Aviv, Israel, 1936).

183  Frederick H. Kisch, "Correspondence, 12 February, Discussing Correspondence to Schmidt of the IOC and Destroying Other Material Sent for Review, to Yekutieli, 12 February," 5-62-1, Colonel Kisch 1923–44, Joseph Yekutieli Maccabi Sport Archives (Tel Aviv, Israel, 1936).

184 International Amateur Athletic Federation, "Correspondence, Boycott of Palestine from 1936 Olympic Games, Edström to Yekutieli," 5-1-30, Joseph Yekutieli 1934–1948, Joseph Yekutieli Maccabi Sport Archives (Tel Aviv, Israel, 1939).

**Chapter 9**

1 Waldo H. Heinrichs, "Diary Entry, 16 January," 115, Waldo Huntley Heinrichs Papers, Yale Divinity Library Archives and Manuscripts (New Haven, CT, 1934).
2 Wawrzyn, *Nazis in the Holy Land, 1933–1948*, 184–85.
3 Ibid., 184–85.
4 Ibid., 178–79.
5 Waldo H. Heinrichs, "Diary Entry, 18 January," 115, Waldo Huntley Heinrichs Papers, Yale Divinity Library Archives and Manuscripts (New Haven, CT, 1934).
6 Waldo H. Heinrichs, "Diary Entry, 19 January," 115, Waldo Huntley Heinrichs Papers, Yale Divinity Library Archives and Manuscripts (New Haven, CT, 1934).
7 Waldo H. Heinrichs, "Diary Entry, 22 January," 115, Waldo Huntley Heinrichs Papers, Yale Divinity Library Archives and Manuscripts (New Haven, CT, 1934).
8 Wawrzyn, *Nazis in the Holy Land, 1933–1948*, 178–79.
9 Waldo H. Heinrichs, "Diary Entry, 25 January," 115, Waldo Huntley Heinrichs Papers, Yale Divinity Library Archives and Manuscripts (New Haven, CT, 1934).
10 Wawrzyn, *Nazis in the Holy Land, 1933–1948*, 178–79.
11 Waldo H. Heinrichs, "Diary Entry, 26 January," 115, Waldo Huntley Heinrichs Papers, Yale Divinity Library Archives and Manuscripts (New Haven, CT, 1934).
12 Waldo H. Heinrichs, "Diary Entry, 29 January," 115, Waldo Huntley Heinrichs Papers, Yale Divinity Library Archives and Manuscripts (New Haven, CT, 1934).
13 Waldo H. Heinrichs, "Correspondence, First Notification of the Newspaper Incident, to Slack," Y.USA.9-2-2, International Work in Palestine/Israel, Kautz Family YMCA Archives (Minneapolis, MN, 1934), 1–2.
14 Waldo H. Heinrichs, "Diary Entry, 30 January," 115, Waldo Huntley Heinrichs Papers, Yale Divinity Library Archives and Manuscripts (New Haven, CT, 1934).
15 Waldo H. Heinrichs, "Diary Entry, 31 January," 115, Waldo Huntley Heinrichs Papers, Yale Divinity Library Archives and Manuscripts (New Haven, CT, 1934).
16 Waldo H. Heinrichs, "Memo, on the German Newspaper Question in the Library Committee, as Prepared for Slack and Attached to Heinrichs' Correspondence to Him of 13 February," Y.USA.9-2-2, International Work in Palestine/Israel, Kautz Family YMCA Archives (Minneapolis, MN, 1934), 1–2.
17 Waldo H. Heinrichs, "Diary Entry, 4 February," 115, Waldo Huntley Heinrichs Papers, Yale Divinity Library Archives and Manuscripts (New Haven, CT, 1934).
18 Waldo H. Heinrichs, "Diary Entry, 5 February," 115, Waldo Huntley Heinrichs Papers, Yale Divinity Library Archives and Manuscripts (New Haven, CT, 1934).
19 Amin Jamal, "Minutes, of the Meeting of the Board of Directors of the Jerusalem YMCA on February 5, 1934," Y.USA.9-2-2, International Work in Palestine/Israel, Kautz Family YMCA Archives (Minneapolis, MN, 1934), 1.
20 Waldo H. Heinrichs, "Diary Entry, 6 February," 115, Waldo Huntley Heinrichs Papers, Yale Divinity Library Archives and Manuscripts (New Haven, CT, 1934).
21 Waldo H. Heinrichs, "Diary Entry, 8 February," 115, Waldo Huntley Heinrichs Papers, Yale Divinity Library Archives and Manuscripts (New Haven, CT, 1934).

22  Ibid.
23  Waldo H. Heinrichs, "Diary Entry, 9 February," 115, Waldo Huntley Heinrichs Papers, Yale Divinity Library Archives and Manuscripts (New Haven, CT, 1934).
24  This hotel was frequented by Germans and even used during the Second World War by the German government for meetings between their delegate Werner Otto von Hentig and local Arab leaders in Syria and Lebanon. Source: Götz Nordbruch, *Nazism in Syria and Lebanon: The Ambivalence of the German Option, 1933–1945* (London and New York: Routledge Taylor & Francis Group, 2009), 96. A single postcard from this hotel in the Israel State Archives dated October 18, 1934 (after the Nazis forced Heinrichs to depart for the United States) connects a "Boutagy" to the leader of the Nazi Party in Palestine. Source: Karl Goebel, "Correspondence, Postcard About an Event to Be Held on November 3, 1934 for Which a Nazi Songbook Was Needed, from Goebel to Karl Ruff Requesting One Boutagy [not clear if it is J. Gordon Boutagy] to Drop Off the Nazi Songbook at Goebel's Address," 823/17-2, Karl Ruff, Landesvertrauensmann der N.S.D.A.P. für Palästina, in Haifa— Correspondenz 1934–1935, Israel State Archives (Jerusalem, Israel, 1934). Original text: "*Original baldige Zusendung bitte ich, am besten sie lassen es bei Boutagy abgeben unter meiner Adresse.*" The sender of the postcard, Karl Goebel, wrote to Karl Ruff about an upcoming Nazi event scheduled for November 3. He described a "German evening" for which they needed a songbook (*Liederbuch*) from the National Socialist Movement. Goebel informed Ruff that he had been instructed by the Nazi administration to approach him and, among other discussions about Nazi policy, hoped to receive the Nazi songbook quickly. Goebel told Ruff that it would be best to have it dropped off at/with [one] Boutagy under Goebel's address.
25  Waldo H. Heinrichs, "Diary Entry, 10 February," 115, Waldo Huntley Heinrichs Papers, Yale Divinity Library Archives and Manuscripts (New Haven, CT, 1934).
26  Waldo H. Heinrichs, "Diary Entry, 12 February," 115, Waldo Huntley Heinrichs Papers, Yale Divinity Library Archives and Manuscripts (New Haven, CT, 1934).
27  Waldo H. Heinrichs, "Diary Entry, 13 February," 115, Waldo Huntley Heinrichs Papers, Yale Divinity Library Archives and Manuscripts (New Haven, CT, 1934).
28  Waldo H. Heinrichs, "Correspondence, Strictly Confidential on the German News-paper Question in the Library Committee, to Slack," Y.USA.9-2-2, International Work in Palestine/Israel, Kautz Family YMCA Archives (Minneapolis, MN, 1934).
29  Ibid., 2–3.
30  Ibid., 3.
31  Ibid.
32  Heinrichs, "Memo, on the German Newspaper Question in the Library Committee, as Prepared for Slack and Attached to Heinrichs' Correspondence to Him of 13 February."
33  Jerusalem International Young Men's Christian Association, "Memo, on the German Paper Question in the Library Committee," Y.USA.9-2-2, International Work in Palestine/Israel, Kautz Family YMCA Archives (Minneapolis, MN, 1934), 3.
34  Ibid., 5.
35  Ibid., 5–7.
36  Ibid., 7.

37 Waldo H. Heinrichs, "Diary Entry, 23 February," 115, Waldo Huntley Heinrichs Papers, Yale Divinity Library Archives and Manuscripts (New Haven, CT, 1934).
38 Waldo H. Heinrichs, "Diary Entry, 24 February," 115, Waldo Huntley Heinrichs Papers, Yale Divinity Library Archives and Manuscripts (New Haven, CT, 1934); Heinrichs, "Diary Entry, 24 February."
39 Waldo H. Heinrichs, "Correspondence, in Continuation to His Letter of 13 February Regarding the Newspaper Controversy, to Slack," Y.USA.9–2-2, International Work in Palestine/Israel, Kautz Family YMCA Archives (Minneapolis, MN, 1934).
40 Ibid.
41 Waldo H. Heinrichs, "Diary Entry, 26 February," 115, Waldo Huntley Heinrichs Papers, Yale Divinity Library Archives and Manuscripts (New Haven, CT, 1934).
42 Waldo H. Heinrichs, "Diary Entry, 27 February," 115, Waldo Huntley Heinrichs Papers, Yale Divinity Library Archives and Manuscripts (New Haven, CT, 1934).
43 Waldo H. Heinrichs, "Diary Entry, 28 February," 115, Waldo Huntley Heinrichs Papers, Yale Divinity Library Archives and Manuscripts (New Haven, CT, 1934).
44 The political agenda of *Meraat Elsherk* as a historical newspaper in Mandate Palestine has been hard to pin down. According to the web site of the Israel State Archives, its owners participated in founding new parties and organizations in the territory. Whether they were involved in the founding of the Nazi Party is unclear. But the paper certainly appears to have served as a Nazi mouthpiece in the case of the *Völkischer Beobachter* affair at the Jerusalem YMCA.
45 Waldo H. Heinrichs, "Diary Entry, 1 March," 115, Waldo Huntley Heinrichs Papers, Yale Divinity Library Archives and Manuscripts (New Haven, CT, 1934).
46 Heinrichs, "Diary Entry, 3 March."
47 Waldo H. Heinrichs, "Correspondence, in Continuation to His Letter of 24 February Regarding the Newspaper Controversy, to Slack with Translations of *Meraat Elsherk* Newspaper Articles Attached," Y.USA.9–2-2, International Work in Palestine/Israel, Kautz Family YMCA Archives (Minneapolis, MN, 1934), 1.
48 Waldo H. Heinrichs, "Memo, Translated Copies of Press Articles on the Growing Newspaper Controversy," Y.USA.9–2-2, International Work in Palestine/Israel, Kautz Family YMCA Archives (Minneapolis, MN, 1934), 1–2.
49 Ibid., 2.
50 Ibid., 3.
51 Ibid.
52 Ibid., 4; Heinrichs, "Memo, Translated Copies of Press Articles," 4.
53 Heinrichs, "Memo, Translated Copies of Press Articles," 4.
54 Waldo H. Heinrichs, "Correspondence, Requesting a Cable Be Sent Recalling Heinrichs to New York for Three Months Finance Work, to Slack," Y.USA.9–2-2, International Work in Palestine/Israel, Kautz Family YMCA Archives (Minneapolis, MN, 1934).
55 Waldo H. Heinrichs, "Diary Entry, 5 March," 115, Waldo Huntley Heinrichs Papers, Yale Divinity Library Archives and Manuscripts (New Haven, CT, 1934).
56 Waldo H. Heinrichs, "Diary Entry, 6 March," 115, Waldo Huntley Heinrichs Papers, Yale Divinity Library Archives and Manuscripts (New Haven, CT, 1934).
57 Waldo H. Heinrichs, "Diary Entry, 7 March," 115, Waldo Huntley Heinrichs Papers, Yale Divinity Library Archives and Manuscripts (New Haven, CT, 1934).

58 Heinrichs, Diary Entry, 6 March.
59 Waldo H. Heinrichs, "Diary Entry, 9 March," 115, Waldo Huntley Heinrichs Papers, Yale Divinity Library Archives and Manuscripts (New Haven, CT, 1934).
60 Frank V. Slack, "Correspondence, on the Need to Bring Heinrichs Back from Jerusalem for His Own Sake, to Ramsey," Y.USA.9-2-2, International Work in Palestine/Israel, Kautz Family YMCA Archives (Minneapolis, MN, 1934).
61 Waldo H. Heinrichs, "Diary Entry, 11 March," 115, Waldo Huntley Heinrichs Papers, Yale Divinity Library Archives and Manuscripts (New Haven, CT, 1934).
62 Waldo H. Heinrichs, "Diary Entry, 12 March," 115, Waldo Huntley Heinrichs Papers, Yale Divinity Library Archives and Manuscripts (New Haven, CT, 1934).
63 Ibid.
64 Waldo H. Heinrichs, "Diary Entry, 13 March," 115, Waldo Huntley Heinrichs Papers, Yale Divinity Library Archives and Manuscripts (New Haven, CT, 1934).
65 Heinrichs, "Diary Entry, 17 March."
66 Dodge, "Correspondence, on Things Being in a Fearful State at the Jerusalem YMCA with the Newspaper Controversy," 1-2.
67 Waldo H. Heinrichs, "Diary Entry, 18 March," 115, Waldo Huntley Heinrichs Papers, Yale Divinity Library Archives and Manuscripts (New Haven, CT, 1934).
68 Waldo H. Heinrichs, "Diary Entry, 20 March," 115, Waldo Huntley Heinrichs Papers, Yale Divinity Library Archives and Manuscripts (New Haven, CT, 1934).
69 Waldo H. Heinrichs, "Diary Entry, 21 March," 115, Waldo Huntley Heinrichs Papers, Yale Divinity Library Archives and Manuscripts (New Haven, CT, 1934).
70 Ibid.
71 Frank V. Slack, "Correspondence, on Removing the Power of Attorney from Canaan, to Ramsey," Y.USA.9-2-2, International Work in Palestine/Israel, Kautz Family YMCA Archives (Minneapolis, MN, 1934).
72 Waldo H. Heinrichs, "Diary Entry, 27 March," 115, Waldo Huntley Heinrichs Papers, Yale Divinity Library Archives and Manuscripts (New Haven, CT, 1934).
73 Tawfiq Canaan, "Correspondence, the Weak Power of Judgement of Heinrichs, Sent on 7 April 1944 to Slack," Y.USA.9-2-2, International Work in Palestine/Israel, Kautz Family YMCA Archives (Minneapolis, MN, 1934), 1-2.
74 Francis S. Harmon, "Correspondence, Arranging a Meeting with Heinrichs and Slack to Discuss the Newspaper Controversy, to Heinrichs and Slack," Y.USA.9-2-2, International Work in Palestine/Israel, Kautz Family YMCA Archives (Minneapolis, MN, 1934), 1-2.
75 Waldo H. Heinrichs, "Diary Entry, 28 March," 115, Waldo Huntley Heinrichs Papers, Yale Divinity Library Archives and Manuscripts (New Haven, CT, 1934).
76 Waldo H. Heinrichs, "Diary Entry, 30 March," 115, Waldo Huntley Heinrichs Papers, Yale Divinity Library Archives and Manuscripts (New Haven, CT, 1934).
77 Waldo H. Heinrichs, "Diary Entry, 2 April," 115, Waldo Huntley Heinrichs Papers, Yale Divinity Library Archives and Manuscripts (New Haven, CT, 1934).
78 E. R. Leibert, "Transcript, of Heinrichs' N.B.C. Address Broadcast Over Station WZJ from 4:00 to 4:30 PM Eastern Standard Time on 4 April 1934," Y.USA.9-2-2, International Work in Palestine/Israel, Kautz Family YMCA Archives (Minneapolis, MN, 1934).

79  Waldo H. Heinrichs, "Diary Entry, 3 April," 115, Waldo Huntley Heinrichs Papers, Yale Divinity Library Archives and Manuscripts (New Haven, CT, 1934).

80  Waldo H. Heinrichs, "Diary Entry, 6 April," 115, Waldo Huntley Heinrichs Papers, Yale Divinity Library Archives and Manuscripts (New Haven, CT, 1934).

81  Waldo H. Heinrichs, "Diary Entry, 18 April," 115, Waldo Huntley Heinrichs Papers, Yale Divinity Library Archives and Manuscripts (New Haven, CT, 1934).

82  Waldo H. Heinrichs, "Diary Entry, 20 April," 115, Waldo Huntley Heinrichs Papers, Yale Divinity Library Archives and Manuscripts (New Haven, CT, 1934).

83  Ibid.

84  Waldo H. Heinrichs, "Diary Entry, 24 April," 115, Waldo Huntley Heinrichs Papers, Yale Divinity Library Archives and Manuscripts (New Haven, CT, 1934).

85  Waldo H. Heinrichs, "Diary Entry, 27 April," 115, Waldo Huntley Heinrichs Papers, Yale Divinity Library Archives and Manuscripts (New Haven, CT, 1934).

86  Waldo H. Heinrichs, "Diary Entry, 28 April," 115, Waldo Huntley Heinrichs Papers, Yale Divinity Library Archives and Manuscripts (New Haven, CT, 1934).

87  Ibid.

88  Fred W. Ramsey, "Correspondence, Regarding Urgent Cable from Heinrichs That the Board Had Asked for His Resignation, to Slack," Y.USA.9–2-2, International Work in Palestine/Israel, Kautz Family YMCA Archives (Minneapolis, MN, 1934).

89  Waldo H. Heinrichs, "Diary Entry, 30 April," 115, Waldo Huntley Heinrichs Papers, Yale Divinity Library Archives and Manuscripts (New Haven, CT, 1934).

90  Waldo H. Heinrichs, "Diary Entry, 1 May," 115, Waldo Huntley Heinrichs Papers, Yale Divinity Library Archives and Manuscripts (New Haven, CT, 1934).

91  Fred W. Auburn, "Correspondence, on the Rationale Behind Heinrichs' Departure, to Slack," Y.USA.9–2-2, International Work in Palestine/Israel, Kautz Family YMCA Archives (Minneapolis, MN, 1934), 2.

92  Ibid., 3.

93  Waldo H. Heinrichs, "Diary Entry, 5 May," 115, Waldo Huntley Heinrichs Papers, Yale Divinity Library Archives and Manuscripts (New Haven, CT, 1934).

94  Ibid.

95  Waldo H. Heinrichs, "Diary Entry, 6 May," 115, Waldo Huntley Heinrichs Papers, Yale Divinity Library Archives and Manuscripts (New Haven, CT, 1934).

96  Waldo H. Heinrichs, "Diary Entry, 7 May," 115, Waldo Huntley Heinrichs Papers, Yale Divinity Library Archives and Manuscripts (New Haven, CT, 1934).

97  Waldo H. Heinrichs, "Diary Entry, 8 May," 115, Waldo Huntley Heinrichs Papers, Yale Divinity Library Archives and Manuscripts (New Haven, CT, 1934).

98  Waldo H. Heinrichs, "Diary Entry, 9 May," 115, Waldo Huntley Heinrichs Papers, Yale Divinity Library Archives and Manuscripts (New Haven, CT, 1934).

99  Jerusalem Inter-School Sports Executive Committee, "Programme, Tenth Jerusalem Inter-School Sports Programme."

100  Ibid., 9.

101  Ibid., 14.

102  Heinrichs, "Diary Entry, 20 January."

103  Waldo H. Heinrichs, "Diary Entry, 10 May," 115, Waldo Huntley Heinrichs Papers, Yale Divinity Library Archives and Manuscripts (New Haven, CT, 1934).

# Endnotes

104 Waldo H. Heinrichs, "Diary Entry, 11 May," 115, Waldo Huntley Heinrichs Papers, Yale Divinity Library Archives and Manuscripts (New Haven, CT, 1934).

105 Francis S. Harmon, "Correspondence with Aide Mémoire and Confidential Memorandum, Concerning Jerusalem Newspaper Incident, to the Members of the International Committee of YMCAs," Y.USA.9-2-2, International Work in Palestine/Israel, Kautz Family YMCA Archives (Minneapolis, MN, 1934), 1.

106 Ibid., 2.

107 Ibid., 4.

108 Ibid.

109 International Committee of Young Men's Christian Associations of Canada and the United States, "Aide Memoire, as Carried by Ramsey and Slack to Jerusalem," Y.USA.9-2-2, International Work in Palestine/Israel, Kautz Family YMCA Archives (Minneapolis, MN, 1934), 2.

110 Ibid., 4.

111 Ibid.

112 International Committee of Young Men's Christian Associations of Canada and the United States, "Memorandum, Confidential on Interracial and Interreligious Tension in the Jerusalem YMCA, Attached to Harmon's Correspondence of 6 April 1934," Y.USA.9-2-2, International Work in Palestine/Israel, Kautz Family YMCA Archives (Minneapolis, MN, 1934), 2.

113 Ibid.

114 Wawrzyn, *Nazis in the Holy Land, 1933–1948*, 184–85.

115 International Committee of Young Men's Christian Associations of Canada and the United States, "Memorandum, Confidential on Interracial and Interreligious Tension in the Jerusalem YMCA, Attached to Harmon's Correspondence of 6 April 1934," 2.

116 Ibid., 3.

117 Ibid., 5

118 Ibid

119 Waldo H. Heinrichs, "Diary Entry, 12 May," 115, Waldo Huntley Heinrichs Papers, Yale Divinity Library Archives and Manuscripts (New Haven, CT, 1934).

120 Waldo H. Heinrichs, "Diary Entry, 13 May," 115, Waldo Huntley Heinrichs Papers, Yale Divinity Library Archives and Manuscripts (New Haven, CT, 1934).

121 Ibid.

122 Waldo H. Heinrichs, "Diary Entry, 15 May," 115, Waldo Huntley Heinrichs Papers, Yale Divinity Library Archives and Manuscripts (New Haven, CT, 1934).

123 Ibid.

124 Waldo H. Heinrichs, "Diary Entry, 16 May," 115, Waldo Huntley Heinrichs Papers, Yale Divinity Library Archives and Manuscripts (New Haven, CT, 1934).

125 Waldo H. Heinrichs, "Correspondence, Procedure for Negotiations, to Ramsey," Y.USA.9-2-2, International Work in Palestine/Israel, Kautz Family YMCA Archives (Minneapolis, MN, 1934), 1.

126 Waldo H. Heinrichs, "Diary Entry, 17 May," 115, Waldo Huntley Heinrichs Papers, Yale Divinity Library Archives and Manuscripts (New Haven, CT, 1934).

127 Waldo H. Heinrichs, "Diary Entry, 18 May," 115, Waldo Huntley Heinrichs Papers, Yale Divinity Library Archives and Manuscripts (New Haven, CT, 1934).

128 Waldo H. Heinrichs, "Diary Entry, 20 May," 115, Waldo Huntley Heinrichs Papers, Yale Divinity Library Archives and Manuscripts (New Haven, CT, 1934).
129 Associated Press, "Jewish Body Asks Olympic Inquiry," 32.
130 Waldo H. Heinrichs, "Diary Entry, 19 May," 115, Waldo Huntley Heinrichs Papers, Yale Divinity Library Archives and Manuscripts (New Haven, CT, 1934).
131 International Olympic Committee, "Correspondence, NOC Recognition, Baillet-Latour to Kisch, 19 May," 0077504, CIO CNO ISR RECON OU MO 01 14 36, Recon. Palestine (Israël) 1934, Historical Archives Olympic Studies Centre (Lausanne, Switzerland, 1934).
132 "Sie Kommen — Sie Kommen Nicht!," *Westland*, 19 May, 1934.
133 Waldo H. Heinrichs, "Diary Entry, 7 June," 115, Waldo Huntley Heinrichs Papers, Yale Divinity Library Archives and Manuscripts (New Haven, CT, 1934).
134 Waldo H. Heinrichs, "Diary Entry, 8 June," 115, Waldo Huntley Heinrichs Papers, Yale Divinity Library Archives and Manuscripts (New Haven, CT, 1934).
135 Waldo H. Heinrichs, "Diary Entry, 11 June," 115, Waldo Huntley Heinrichs Papers, Yale Divinity Library Archives and Manuscripts (New Haven, CT, 1934).
136 Waldo H. Heinrichs, "Diary Entry, 12 June," 115, Waldo Huntley Heinrichs Papers, Yale Divinity Library Archives and Manuscripts (New Haven, CT, 1934).
137 Frank V. Slack, "Correspondence, Offering Jerusalem YMCA Secretary General Position to Wilbert Smith, to Smith," Y.USA.9-2-2, International Work in Palestine/Israel, Kautz Family YMCA Archives (Minneapolis, MN, 1934).
138 Fred W. Ramsey and Frank V. Slack, "Radiogram, the Inadvisable Return of Heinrichs, to New York," Y.USA.9-2-2, International Work in Palestine/Israel, Kautz Family YMCA Archives (Minneapolis, MN, 1934).
139 Waldo H. Heinrichs, "Diary Entry, 28 June," 115, Waldo Huntley Heinrichs Papers, Yale Divinity Library Archives and Manuscripts (New Haven, CT, 1934).
140 Waldo H. Heinrichs, "Diary Entry, 30 June," 115, Waldo Huntley Heinrichs Papers, Yale Divinity Library Archives and Manuscripts (New Haven, CT, 1934).
141 Francis S. Harmon, "Cable, on Approval to Transfer Heinrichs, to Slack," Y.USA.9-2-2, International Work in Palestine/Israel, Kautz Family YMCA Archives (Minneapolis, MN, 1934).
142 Francis S. Harmon, "Correspondence, Securing Heinrichs' Promise Not to Do Anything Precipitous, to Slack," Y.USA.9-2-2, International Work in Palestine/Israel, Kautz Family YMCA Archives (Minneapolis, MN, 1934).
143 Jewish Telegraphic Agency, "Jerusalem 'Y' Official Quits in Nazi Clash," *Jewish Daily Bulletin*, 5 July 1934, 1, 8.
144 Ibid., 1.
145 Jewish Telegraphic Agency, "Jerusalem 'Y' Official Upheld by Secretary," *Jewish Daily Bulletin*, 6 July 1934, 7.
146 Waldo H. Heinrichs, "Diary Entry, 9 July," 115, Waldo Huntley Heinrichs Papers, Yale Divinity Library Archives and Manuscripts (New Haven, CT, 1934).
147 Waldo H. Heinrichs, "Diary Entry, 13 July," 115, Waldo Huntley Heinrichs Papers, Yale Divinity Library Archives and Manuscripts (New Haven, CT, 1934).
148 Waldo H. Heinrichs, "Diary Entry, 20 July," 115, Waldo Huntley Heinrichs Papers, Yale Divinity Library Archives and Manuscripts (New Haven, CT, 1934).

149 Waldo H. Heinrichs, "Diary Entry, 23 July," 115, Waldo Huntley Heinrichs Papers, Yale Divinity Library Archives and Manuscripts (New Haven, CT, 1934).

150 Waldo H. Heinrichs, "Diary Entry, 24 July," 115, Waldo Huntley Heinrichs Papers, Yale Divinity Library Archives and Manuscripts (New Haven, CT, 1934).

151 Waldo H. Heinrichs, "Diary Entry, 30 July," 115, Waldo Huntley Heinrichs Papers, Yale Divinity Library Archives and Manuscripts (New Haven, CT, 1934).

152 Waldo H. Heinrichs, "Diary Entry, 1 August," 115, Waldo Huntley Heinrichs Papers, Yale Divinity Library Archives and Manuscripts (New Haven, CT, 1934).

153 Waldo H. Heinrichs, "Diary Entry, 7 August," 115, Waldo Huntley Heinrichs Papers, Yale Divinity Library Archives and Manuscripts (New Haven, CT, 1934).

154 2019 equivalent of USD 12,061.

155 Waldo H. Heinrichs, "Diary Entry, 15 August," 115, Waldo Huntley Heinrichs Papers, Yale Divinity Library Archives and Manuscripts (New Haven, CT, 1934).

156 Waldo H. Heinrichs, "Diary Entry, 19 August," 115, Waldo Huntley Heinrichs Papers, Yale Divinity Library Archives and Manuscripts (New Haven, CT, 1934).

157 Ibid.

158 Waldo H. Heinrichs, "Diary Entry, 24 August," 115, Waldo Huntley Heinrichs Papers, Yale Divinity Library Archives and Manuscripts (New Haven, CT, 1934).

159 Ibid.

160 Waldo H. Heinrichs, "Diary Entry, 1 September," 115, Waldo Huntley Heinrichs Papers, Yale Divinity Library Archives and Manuscripts (New Haven, CT, 1934).

161 Ibid.

162 Waldo H. Heinrichs, "Diary Entry, 3 September," 115, Waldo Huntley Heinrichs Papers, Yale Divinity Library Archives and Manuscripts (New Haven, CT, 1934).

163 Waldo H. Heinrichs, "Diary Entry, 5 September," 115, Waldo Huntley Heinrichs Papers, Yale Divinity Library Archives and Manuscripts (New Haven, CT, 1934).

164 Waldo H. Heinrichs, "Diary Entry, 9 September," 115, Waldo Huntley Heinrichs Papers, Yale Divinity Library Archives and Manuscripts (New Haven, CT, 1934).

165 Ibid

166 Waldo H. Heinrichs, "Diary Entry, 10 September," 115, Waldo Huntley Heinrichs Papers, Yale Divinity Library Archives and Manuscripts (New Haven, CT, 1934).

167 Waldo H. Heinrichs, "Diary Entry, 11 September," 115, Waldo Huntley Heinrichs Papers, Yale Divinity Library Archives and Manuscripts (New Haven, CT, 1934).

168 Francis S. Harmon, "Memorandum, Report on the Settlement of Newspaper Controversy in Jerusalem Y.M.C.A," YUSA 9-2 2, International Work in Palestine/ Israel, Kautz Family YMCA Archives (Minneapolis, MN, 1934).

169 Harmon, "Memorandum, Report on settlement," 2.

170 Waldo H. Heinrichs, "Correspondence, on the Settlement of the Newspaper Controversy, to Dorothy Heinrichs," 115, Waldo Huntley Heinrichs Papers, Yale Divinity Library Archives and Manuscripts (New Haven, CT, 1934), 1.

171 Ibid., 2.

172 Not a relative of the author's paternal ancestors, who lived in Jerusalem during this period.

173 Heinrichs, "Correspondence, on the Settlement of the Newspaper Controversy, to Dorothy Heinrichs," 2.

174 Ibid., 3.
175 Ibid.
176 Ibid.
177 Ibid., 4.
178 Ibid.
179 Ibid.
180 Ibid.
181 Ibid., 5.
182 Ibid.
183 Ibid., 6.
184 Ibid.
185 Waldo H. Heinrichs, "Diary Entry, 26 September," 115, Waldo Huntley Heinrichs Papers, Yale Divinity Library Archives and Manuscripts (New Haven, CT, 1934).
186 Ibid.
187 Waldo H. Heinrichs, "Diary Entry, 2 October," 115, Waldo Huntley Heinrichs Papers, Yale Divinity Library Archives and Manuscripts (New Haven, CT, 1934).
188 Waldo H. Heinrichs, "Diary Entry, 4 October," 115, Waldo Huntley Heinrichs Papers, Yale Divinity Library Archives and Manuscripts (New Haven, CT, 1934).
189 Waldo H. Heinrichs, "Diary Entry, 13 October," 115, Waldo Huntley Heinrichs Papers, Yale Divinity Library Archives and Manuscripts (New Haven, CT, 1934).
190 Francis S. Harmon, "Correspondence, Regarding Resignation of Waldo H. Heinrichs, to Friend in North America of the Jerusalem YMCA," Y.USA.9-2-2, International Work in Palestine/Israel, Kautz Family YMCA Archives (Minneapolis, MN, 1934).
191 Waldo H. Heinrichs, "Diary Entry, 28 October," 115, Waldo Huntley Heinrichs Papers, Yale Divinity Library Archives and Manuscripts (New Haven, CT, 1934).
192 Stephen S. Wise, "Correspondence, on Position Taken in the Newspaper Controversy to Heinrichs," Y.USA.9-2-2, International Work in Palestine/Israel, Kautz Family YMCA Archives (Minneapolis, MN, 1934).
193 Waldo H. Heinrichs, "Correspondence, on Enjoying Very Much Becoming a Casualty of the Newspaper Incident, to Wise," Y.USA.9-2-2, International Work in Palestine/Israel, Kautz Family YMCA Archives (Minneapolis, MN, 1934).
194 Waldo H. Heinrichs, "Diary Entry, 13 November," 115, Waldo Huntley Heinrichs Papers, Yale Divinity Library Archives and Manuscripts (New Haven, CT, 1934).
195 Heinrichs, "Correspondence, on Enjoying Very Much Becoming a Casualty of the Newspaper Incident, to Wise."
196 Wilbert S. Smith, "Correspondence, on Lattof's Role in the Dismissal of Ohan, Suz and Haddad, to Slack," Y.USA.9-2-2, International Work in Palestine/Israel, Kautz Family YMCA Archives (Minneapolis, MN, 1934).
197 Wawrzyn, *Nazis in the Holy Land, 1933–1948*, 82.
198 "Manifest, SS *Excalibur*, Documenting the Arrival of the Lattof Family in New York," Private Collection of the Lattof Family (1936).
199 Frank V. Slack, "Correspondence, Regarding the Final Decision Not to Allow Lattof or Auburn to Return to Jerusalem, to Nicholas Lattof," Y.USA.9-2-2, International Work in Palestine/Israel, Kautz Family YMCA Archives (Minneapolis, MN, 1936).

200 Wawrzyn, *Nazis in the Holy Land, 1933–1948*, 109–10.

201 Waldo H. Heinrichs, "Diary Entry, 20 November," 115, Waldo Huntley Heinrichs Papers, Yale Divinity Library Archives and Manuscripts (New Haven, CT, 1934).

202 Waldo H. Heinrichs, "Diary Entry, 21 November," 115, Waldo Huntley Heinrichs Papers, Yale Divinity Library Archives and Manuscripts (New Haven, CT, 1934).

203 Waldo H. Heinrichs, "Diary Entry, 5 December," 115, Waldo Huntley Heinrichs Papers, Yale Divinity Library Archives and Manuscripts (New Haven, CT, 1934).

204 Paul E. F. Cressall, "Correspondence, on the Intention of the Christian Arabs to Take Control of the YMCA, to Heinrichs," Y.USA.9–2-2, International Work in Palestine/Israel, Kautz Family YMCA Archives (Minneapolis, MN, 1934).

205 Nicholas M. Lattof, "Correspondence, Excerpts Prepared by Harmon from One of Lattof's Correspondences on the Emerging Situation in Jerusalem After Heinrichs' Departure," Y.USA.9–2-2, International Work in Palestine/Israel, Kautz Family YMCA Archives (Minneapolis, MN, 1934).

206 Ibid., 1.

207 Waldo H. Heinrichs, "Correspondence, Disagreeing That He Has Embarassed the International Committee in Any Way, to Slack," Y.USA.9–2-2, International Work in Palestine/Israel, Kautz Family YMCA Archives (Minneapolis, MN, 1934).

208 Heinrichs, "Diary Entry, 31 December."

209 Ibid.

## Chapter 10

1 Jerusalem International Young Men's Christian Association, "Report, of the Acting Secretary-General to the Board of Directors for the Month of February 1935," Y.USA.9–2-2, International Work in Palestine/Israel, Kautz Family YMCA Archives (Minneapolis, MN, 1935), 2.

2 Ibid.

3 Ibid.

4 Federation of the Amateur Sports Clubs of Palestine, The Swimming Association, "Programme, Winter Swimming Championships Under the Patronage of District Commissioner for Jerusalem J. E. F. Campbell," ADI.29 0002 FASCP, SYNSO 0001556, The Zvi Nishri Archive for Sports and Physical Education in the Wingate Institute (Netanya, Israel, 1934).

5 Jerusalem International Young Men's Christian Association, "Report, of the Acting Secretary-General to the Board of Directors Following the Settlement of the Newspaper Controversy," Y.USA.9–2-2, International Work in Palestine/Israel, Kautz Family YMCA Archives (Minneapolis, MN, 1934), 1.

6 Khalidi, *One Hundred Years of Football in Palestine*, 32.

7 Ibid., 32–33.

8 Ibid., 32–33.

9 Organizing Committee of the XI Olympic Games in Berlin 1936, "Correspondence, Number 2373/34 L/M on Palestine Olympic Committee and Kisch, to General Consul Wolff," 526/15-פ. 67.1/3 - 1530 - Sport 1928 to 1939, Israel State Archives (Jerusalem, Israel, 1934), 1.

10 Ibid., 2.

11  Ibid.

12  "Correspondence, Number Nr.Sport.3/34 on Palestine Olympic Committee and Kisch," 526/15- פ. 67.1/3 - 1530 - Sport 1928 to 1939, Israel State Archives (Jerusalem, Israel, 1934), 1.

13  Organizing Committee of the XI Olympic Games in Berlin 1936, "Correspondence, Number 2661/34 L/M on Palestine Olympic Committee Decision to Attend the Games," 526/15-פ. 67.1/3 - 1530 - Sport 1928 to 1939, Israel State Archives (Jerusalem, Israel, 1934), 2.

14  Organizing Committee of the XI Olympic Games in Berlin 1936, "Correspondence, Number OK. 4358/34 L/M on Palestine Olympic Committee Decision Not to Attend the Games," 526/15-פ. 67.1/3 - 1530 - Sport 1928 to 1939, Israel State Archives (Jerusalem, Israel, 1934), 1.

15  Reichsminister für Volksaufklärung und Propaganda, "Correspondence, Number II 2864/3/1. K I on Team from Germany for Maccabi Games," 526/15-פ. 67.1/3 - 1530 - Sport 1928 to 1939, Israel State Archives (Jerusalem, Israel, 1935).

16  Sherwood Eddy had volunteered for thirty-five years with the YMCA Movement and was considered a leading lay leader and missionary in the United States. After his time with the YMCA, Eddy became a disciple of Reinhold Niebuhr, one of the leading American intellectuals of the time. This gives us an idea of the circles in which Heinrichs was circulating. Eddy spent a significant amount of time in India and Heinrichs joined him on two summer trips that Eddy organized to Europe in 1936 and 1939 to assess the situation in Europe. Both Eddy and Heinrichs were early and strong critics of Hitler and Nazism. Source: Jewish Telegraphic Agency, "Sherwood Eddy Summarizes Nazi Peril," *Jewish Daily Bulletin*, 1 October 1933, 6.

17  Waldo H. Heinrichs, "Diary Entry, 19 June," 115, Waldo Huntley Heinrichs Papers, Yale Divinity Library Archives and Manuscripts (New Haven, CT, 1936).

18  Waldo H. Heinrichs, "Diary Entry, 27 June," 115, Waldo Huntley Heinrichs Papers, Yale Divinity Library Archives and Manuscripts (New Haven, CT, 1936).

19  Waldo H. Heinrichs, "Diary Entry, 1 July," 115, Waldo Huntley Heinrichs Papers, Yale Divinity Library Archives and Manuscripts (New Haven, CT, 1936).

20  Waldo H. Heinrichs, "Diary Entry, 3 July," 115, Waldo Huntley Heinrichs Papers, Yale Divinity Library Archives and Manuscripts (New Haven, CT, 1936).

21  Waldo H. Heinrichs, "Diary Entry, 12 July," 115, Waldo Huntley Heinrichs Papers, Yale Divinity Library Archives and Manuscripts (New Haven, CT, 1936).

22  Waldo H. Heinrichs, "Diary Entry, 25 July," 115, Waldo Huntley Heinrichs Papers, Yale Divinity Library Archives and Manuscripts (New Haven, CT, 1936).

23  Ibid.

24  Waldo H. Heinrichs, "Diary Entry, 30 July," 115, Waldo Huntley Heinrichs Papers, Yale Divinity Library Archives and Manuscripts (New Haven, CT, 1936).

25  Waldo H. Heinrichs, "Diary Entry, 31 July," 115, Waldo Huntley Heinrichs Papers, Yale Divinity Library Archives and Manuscripts (New Haven, CT, 1936).

26  Ibid.

27  Paul Hartman, "Correspondence, Regarding Plans to Form a Delegation for the 1948 Olympic Games in London, to Unknown Recipient but, Presumably Friermood," Y.USA.9–2-2, International Work in Palestine/Israel, Kautz Family YMCA Archives (Minneapolis, MN, 1947).

28  Attallah Alexander Kidess, "CV of Attallah Alexander Kidess," Kidess CV, 528, Attallah A. Kidess Papers, Springfield College Archives and Special Collections (Springfield, MA, 1960–80).

29  *Springfield Student*, "Article, International Center to Be Created on Springfield Campus," Attallah A. Kidess Collection, The Springfield College Archives and Special Collections (Springfield, MA, 1965).

30  Khalidi, *One Hundred Years of Football in Palestine*, 33.

31  Ibid.

32  *Springfield Sunday Republican*, "Article, SC Vice-President Well-Known Educator and Olympic Athlete," Attallah A. Kidess Collection, The Springfield College Archives and Special Collections (Springfield, MA, 1961), 20C.

33  "Notes, on Interview with Ted Kidess on Friday, December 8, 1961," Attallah A. Kidess Collection, The Springfield College Archives and Special Collections (Springfield, MA, 1961).

34  *Springfield Union*, "Article, International, Not National Teams, Are Advocated for Olympic Games: Would Regain Spirit, Promote Better World Understanding SC Panel is Told," Attallah A. Kidess Collection, The Springfield College Archives and Special Collections (Springfield, MA, 10 August 1954).

35  Ibid.

36  O. T. Johnston, "Memorandum, Regarding Submittal of the 1936 Budget for the Jerusalem YMCA, to Slack," Y.USA.9–2-2, International Work in Palestine/Israel, Kautz Family YMCA Archives (Minneapolis, MN, 1936).

37  O. T. Johnston, "Correspondence, Regarding the 1936 Budget for the Jerusalem YMCA, to Parker of Central Hanover Bank and Trust Company," Y.USA.9–2-2, International Work in Palestine/Israel, Kautz Family YMCA Archives (Minneapolis, MN, 1936).

38  Wawrzyn, *Nazis in the Holy Land, 1933–1948*, 110.

39  German Consulate Jerusalem, "Correspondence, Number Nr.Spanl 8/36 on Waldemar Fast, to Shaath," 526/15-Ɔ. 67.1/3 - 1530 - Sport 1928 to 1939, Israel State Archives (Jerusalem, Israel, 1936).

40  "List, Olympiadeplakate," 526/15-Ɔ. 67.1/3 - 1530 - Sport 1928 to 1939, Israel State Archives (Jerusalem, Israel, 1936); "List, Olympiadeplakate."

41  Heinrichs, "Correspondence, in Continuation to His Letter of 13 February Regarding the Newspaper Controversy, to Slack."

42  Ibid.

43  Deutsche Sportsverein Jerusalem, "List, of Board Members of German Sports Club Jerusalem, 29 January," 526/15-Ɔ. 67.1/3 - 1530 – Sport 1928 to 1939, (Israel State Archives, Jerusalem, Israel, 1936).

44  *Springfield Union*, "International, Not National Teams."

45  *Springfield Sunday Republican*, "Article, SC Vice-President Well-Known Educator and Olympic Athlete," Attallah A. Kidess Collection, The Springfield College Archives and Special Collections (Springfield, MA, 1961), 20C.

46  *Springfield College Bulletin*, "Article, Distinguished Service Award of the International Relations Council ARAPCS 1979 American Alliance for Health, Physical Education and Recreation, Dr. Attallah A. Kidess (Fifth Annual Presentation),"

Attallah A. Kidess Collection, The Springfield College Archives and Special Collections (Springfield, MA), Vol. 52, No. 3, 7.

47 Dylan Baun, "Lebanon's Youth Clubs and the 1936 Summer Olympics: Mobilizing Sports, Challenging Imperialism and Launching a National Project," *The International Journal of the History of Sport* 34, no. 13 (2018): 1347–65. https://doi.org/10.1080/09523367.2017.1388230. Article received from Dylan Baun via email with web link on 24 April, 2019.

48 Ibid., 1351.

49 Ibid., 1352–53.

50 Ibid., 1352–53.

51 Ibid., 1352–53.

52 Ibid., 1352–53.

53 Robert Fisk, *Pity the Nation* (New York: Touchstone, 1990), 65.

54 Ibid.

55 Ibid., 73.

56 Western Asiatic Games Federation, "Correspondence, Assignment of Palestine to Host the Second West Asian Games, from Sondhi to Yekutieli," 1–37, Second West Asian Games 1937–38 (4), Joseph Yekutieli Maccabi Sport Archives (Tel Aviv, Israel, 1937).

57 Yosef Yekutieli, "Correspondence, Cancellation of Second West Asian Games, to Sondhi," 1–37, Second West Asian Games 1937–38 (4), Joseph Yekutieli Maccabi Sport Archives (Tel Aviv, Israel, 1938).

58 Maccabi World Union, "Correspondence, Maccabi-Hapoel Tension, from Brodetsky to Shertok," ADI.10 0023 Maccabi Hapoel, SYNSO 0001771, The Zvi Nishri Archive for Sports and Physical Education in the Wingate Institute (Netanya, Israel, 1937).

59 Lee M. Terrill, "Report, Administrative and Inclusive of 1937," Y.USA.9–2-2, International Work in Palestine/Israel, Kautz Family YMCA Archives (Minneapolis, MN, 1938), 5.

60 Frederick H. Kisch, "Correspondence, I.O.C. Session in Egypt in March 1938, Kisch to Schmidt," 5-1-25, Joseph Yekutieli 1960–73, Joseph Yekutieli Maccabi Sport Archives (Tel Aviv, Israel, 1937).

61 Frederick H. Kisch, "Correspondence, IOC President's Visit to Palestine, to Yekutieli, 12 December," 5–62-1, Colonel Kisch 1923–44, Joseph Yekutieli Maccabi Sport Archives (Tel Aviv, Israel, 1937).

62 Ibid.

63 "Correspondence, Kisch Visit to Alexandria to See Baillet-Latour, Yekutieli (?) to Kisch," 5–62-1, Colonel Kisch 1923–44, Joseph Yekutieli Maccabi Sport Archives (Tel Aviv, Israel, 1938), 2.

64 Associated Press, "Palestine to Enter Olympics," *New York Times*, 24 March 1938, 29.

65 Palestine Olympic Association, "Minutes, Palestine Olympic Association, April 1938," 5-1-11, Joseph Yekutieli 1934–1948, Joseph Yekutieli Maccabi Sport Archives (Tel Aviv, Israel, 1938).

66 Ibid.

67 Palestine Olympic Committee, "Correspondence, 24 April, NOC Constitution, Kisch to the Secretary of the IOC," 0077643, CIO CNO ISR CORR OU MO 01

14 36, Historical Archives Olympic Studies Centre (Lausanne, Switzerland, 1938), Corr. 1937–48.

68 Waldo H. Heinrichs, "Correspondence, on Meeting with Bowman in London, to Dorothy Heinrichs," 115, Waldo Huntley Heinrichs Papers, Yale Divinity Library Archives and Manuscripts (New Haven, CT, 1939).

69 Waldo H. Heinrichs, "Diary Excerpt, 22 August," 115, Waldo Huntley Heinrichs Papers, Yale Divinity Library Archives and Manuscripts (New Haven, CT, 1939).

70 Waldo H. Heinrichs, "Correspondence, Italian War Preparations, to His Father and Mother," 115, Waldo Huntley Heinrichs Papers, Yale Divinity Library Archives and Manuscripts (New Haven, CT, 1939).

71 Ibid.

72 Waldo H. Heinrichs, "Correspondence, Sinking of the SS *Athenia*, to His Father and Mother," Y.USA.9-2-2, Waldo Huntley Heinrichs Papers, Yale Divinity Library Archives and Manuscripts (New Haven, CT, 1939).

73 Wawrzyn, *Nazis in the Holy Land, 1933–1948*, 109–15.

74 Khaled Nashef, "Tawfik Canaan: His Life and Works," *Jerusalem Quarterly File* 20, no. 16 (2002): 20–21. https://www.palestine-studies.org/sites/default/files/jq-articles/16_canaan_2.pdf.

75 Ibid.

76 Wawrzyn, *Nazis in the Holy Land, 1933–1948*, 99.

77 Nashef, "Tawfik Canaan," 20–21.

78 Ibid., 20–21.

79 Jerusalem International Young Men's Christian Association, "List, of Officers and Religious Demographic Data of Membership of YMCA," Y.USA.9-2-2, International Work in Palestine/Israel, Kautz Family YMCA Archives (Minneapolis, MN, 1940).

80 Jerusalem International Young Men's Christian Association, "Correspondence, Open Track and Field Meet, to Sports Secretary Hapoel," IV 211 303, The Pinchas Lavon Institute for Labour Movement Research (Tel Aviv, Israel, 1942).

81 O. Lifczis, "Correspondence, 30 April, General Meeting, Lifsciz to Goar," 4–29–03, Maccabi Egypt 1927–72, Joseph Yekutieli Maccabi Sport Archives (Tel Aviv, Israel, 1947).

82 Headquarters British Forces Palestine and Transjordan, "Correspondence, Rejection of Request to Serve in a Commissioned Rank in a Palestine Unit, to Yekutieli," 5–1–30, Joseph Yekutieli 1934–1948, Joseph Yekutieli Maccabi Sport Archives (Tel Aviv, Israel, 1941).

83 Alvah L. Miller, "Correspondence, Regarding the Appointment of Palestinian Representatives of Slack in the Event the German Army Reaches Palestine, to Slack," Y.USA.9-2-2, International Work in Palestine/Israel, Kautz Family YMCA Archives (Minneapolis, MN, 1941).

84 Ibid.

85 Jerusalem International Young Men's Christian Association, "Report, Excerpts from the 1945 Report of the Secretary-General to the Annual General Meeting," Y.USA.9-2-2, International Work in Palestine/Israel, Kautz Family YMCA Archives (Minneapolis, MN, 1945), 3.

86 Waldo H. Heinrichs, "Diary Entry, 11 July," 115, Waldo Huntley Heinrichs Papers, Yale Divinity Library Archives and Manuscripts (New Haven, CT, 1941).

87 Waldo H. Heinrichs, "Diary Entry, 21 August," 115, Waldo Huntley Heinrichs Papers, Yale Divinity Library Archives and Manuscripts (New Haven, CT, 1941).

88 Waldo H. Heinrichs, "Diary Entry, 7 December," 115, Waldo Huntley Heinrichs Papers, Yale Divinity Library Archives and Manuscripts (New Haven, CT, 1941).

89 Waldo H. Heinrichs, "Diary Entry, 6 January," 115, Waldo Huntley Heinrichs Papers, Yale Divinity Library Archives and Manuscripts (New Haven, CT, 1942).

90 Waldo H. Heinrichs, "Diary Entry, 17 January," 115, Waldo Huntley Heinrichs Papers, Yale Divinity Library Archives and Manuscripts (New Haven, CT, 1942).

91 Waldo H. Heinrichs, "Diary Entry, 20 January," 115, Waldo Huntley Heinrichs Papers, Yale Divinity Library Archives and Manuscripts (New Haven, CT, 1942).

92 Waldo H. Heinrichs, "Diary Entry, 13 May," 115, Waldo Huntley Heinrichs Papers, Yale Divinity Library Archives and Manuscripts (New Haven, CT, 1942).

93 Waldo H. Heinrichs, "Diary Entry, 7 June," 115, Waldo Huntley Heinrichs Papers, Yale Divinity Library Archives and Manuscripts (New Haven, CT, 1942).

94 Waldo H. Heinrichs, "Correspondence, Nostalgia for Palestine, to Dorothy Heinrichs," 115, Waldo Huntley Heinrichs Papers, Yale Divinity Library Archives and Manuscripts (New Haven, CT, 1942), 1.

95 Waldo H. Heinrichs, "Diary Entry, 1 September," 115, Waldo Huntley Heinrichs Papers, Yale Divinity Library Archives and Manuscripts (New Haven, CT, 1943).

96 Waldo H. Heinrichs, "Diary Entry, 2 September," 115, Waldo Huntley Heinrichs Papers, Yale Divinity Library Archives and Manuscripts (New Haven, CT, 1943).

97 Waldo H. Heinrichs, "Correspondence, on Spending His Last Nickel to Visit Huntley's Mother at Wellesley Before the First War, to Waldo Huntley Heinrichs, Jr," 115, Waldo Huntley Heinrichs Papers, Yale Divinity Library Archives and Manuscripts (New Haven, CT, 1943).

98 Waldo H. Heinrichs, "Correspondence, Instructions to His Soldier Son on How to Behave in the Millitary, to His Son Waldo Huntley Heinrichs, Jr," 115, Waldo Huntley Heinrichs Papers, Yale Divinity Library Archives and Manuscripts (New Haven, CT, 1943), 1.

99 J. H. L. Wiley, "Correspondence, from the War Department on His Separation from Active Service, to Heinrichs," 115, Waldo Huntley Heinrichs Papers, Yale Divinity Library Archives and Manuscripts (New Haven, CT, 1944).

100 Middlebury College, "Obituary, Titled 'Waldo Huntley Heinrichs July 15, 1891–June 15, 1959', in News Letter, p. 41," Y.USA.9–2-2, International Work in Palestine/Israel, Yale Divinity Library Archives and Manuscripts (Minneapolis, New Haven, CT, 1959), 41.

101 "Brigadier F. H. Kisch Slain in Tunis Action: He Was Chief Engineer of the British Eighth Army," *New York Times*, 15 April 1943, 3.

102 "Montgomery Marks Memory of Officer: Becomes Honorary Chairman of Committee Here," *New York Times*, 22 November 1943, 8.

103 Federation of the Amateur Sports Clubs of Palestine, The Track and Field Committee, "Programme, International Track and Field Championship Palestine 1945," ADI.29 0002 FASCP, SYNSO 0001556, The Zvi Nishri Archive for Sports and Physical Education in the Wingate Institute (Netanya, Israel, 1945).

104 J. Sigfrid Edtsröm, "Correspondence, 1948 London Olympic Games and New President of Palestine Olympic Committee, to Yekutieli," 5-1-30, Joseph Yekutieli 1934–1948, Joseph Yekutieli Maccabi Sport Archives (Tel Aviv, Israel, 1945).

105 International Amateur Athletic Federation, "Correspondence, Affiliation of Palestine Sports Federation, from the IAAF Honorary Secretary to the Palestine Sports Federation," ADI.29 0005 FASCP, SYNSO 0001541, The Zvi Nishri Archive for Sports and Physical Education in the Wingate Institute (Netanya, Israel, 1946).

106 Khalidi, *One Hundred Years of Football in Palestine*, 57–79.

107 Waldo H. Heinrichs, "List, 'Sieges of Jerusalem—Conquerers, Etc.," Y.USA.9-2-2, International Work in Palestine/Israel, Kautz Family YMCA Archives (Minneapolis, MN, 1932).

108 Alvah L. Miller, "Correspondence, Regarding the Closeness of His Relationship with Mantoura and on How Farradj Had Been Particularly Active in the Physical Department, to McClelland," Y.USA.9-2-2, International Work in Palestine/Israel, Kautz Family YMCA Archives (Minneapolis, MN, 1946), 1.

109 Alvah L. Miller and Mildred Miller, "Correspondence, Form Letter for the Holidays Discussing the Calamitous Year in Jerusalem and the Slow Return to Normalcy, to Ed," Y.USA.9-2-2, International Work in Palestine/Israel, Kautz Family YMCA Archives (Minneapolis, MN, 1946).

110 Hartman, "Correspondence, Regarding Plans to Form a Delegation for the 1948 Olympic Games in London, to Unknown Recipient but, Presumably Friermood," 2.

111 Paul Hartman, "Correspondence, Regarding News in the *Palestine Post* That Zionists from Palestine Plan to Send Teams to the London Olympic Games, to Friermood," Y.USA.9-2-2, International Work in Palestine/Israel, Kautz Family YMCA Archives (Minneapolis, MN, 1947).

112 Ibid.

113 Chief Secretary's Office, "Correspondence, Referencing Newspaper Article That Reported Palestine's Invitation to the London Olympic Games, to Gurney," 562/6-ם, Z/Misc/6/47 Olympic Games - 1948 London, Israel State Archives (Jerusalem, Israel, 1947).

114 Alvah L. Miller, "Correspondence, Regarding UN Delegates Descending on the YMCA in Hordes, Porter," Y.USA.9-2-2, International Work in Palestine/Israel, Kautz Family YMCA Archives (Minneapolis, MN, 1947).

115 Ibid.

116 Paul Hartman, "Correspondence, Regarding Reaching Out to the Chief Secretary About an Invitation Being Extended to Palestine to Participate in the London Olympic Games, to Friermood," Y.USA.9-2-2, International Work in Palestine/Israel, Kautz Family YMCA Archives (Minneapolis, MN, 1947).

117 A. G. Antippa, "Correspondence, Recognition of Palestine Olympic Committee by International Olympic Committee and List of the National Committee's Officers, to Paul Hartman," 562/6-ם, Z/Misc/6/47 Olympic Games—1948 London, Israel State Archives (Jerusalem, Israel, 1947).

118 Paul Hartman, "Correspondence, Copy (for Friermood) Regarding the Sport Situation in Palestine with a Handwritten Note on the Reverse Noting That He Had Written the Palestine Olympic Committee Secretary on 16 September Requesting

More Information and That It Should Be Communicated to Avery Brundage That No Reply Had Been Received Through 14 October 1947, Original to Avery Brundage," Y.USA.9–2-2, International Work in Palestine/Israel, Kautz Family YMCA Archives (Minneapolis, MN, 1947).

119 Guttmann, *The Games Must Go On*, 81.

120 Hartman, "Correspondence, Copy (for Friermood) Regarding the Sport Situation in Palestine," 1.

121 Ibid., 3.

122 Ibid., 2.

123 Ibid., 4.

124 Paul Hartman, "Correspondence, the General Situation and the Ben Yehuda Street Bombing, to Friermood," Y.USA.9–2-2, International Work in Palestine/Israel, Kautz Family YMCA Archives (Minneapolis, MN, 1948), 1.

125 Associated Press, "Haganah Says Germans Aid Arabs," *New York Times*, 27 December 1947, 8.

126 I. M. Brin, "Correspondence, F/EW/2/48 Rejection of Request for Release of Swiss Francs to Cover Expenses of Palestine Olympic Delegation to St. Moritz, for Chief Secretary of Palestine Government to Gentlemen at I. L. Feuchtwanger Bank, Ltd," 5846/42-נ, F/EW/2/48 Defence (Finance) Regulations—Olympic Games 1948 at St. Moritz, Israel State Archives (Jerusalem, Israel, 1948).

127 John Burkhart, "Memorandum, Jerusalem YMCA Becomes International Relief Center," Y.USA.9–2-2, International Work in Palestine/Israel, Kautz Family YMCA Archives (Minneapolis, MN, 1948).

128 Alvah L. Miller, "Correspondence, Jewish Atrocities and the Flight of the Arab Residents of Palestine, to McClelland," Y.USA.9–2-2, International Work in Palestine/Israel, Kautz Family YMCA Archives (Minneapolis, MN, 1948), 1.

129 Burkhart, "Memorandum, Jerusalem YMCA Becomes International Relief Center."

130 Miller, "Correspondence, Jewish Atrocities and the Flight of the Arab Residents of Palestine, to McClelland," 1.

131 US Mission Jerusalem, "Telegram, Stern Group Complaint About Lehi Transport Being Fired Upon from YMCA, to US Mission to the United Nations," Y.USA.9–2-2, International Work in Palestine/Israel, Kautz Family YMCA Archives (Minneapolis, MN, 1948).

132 Ibid., 2.

133 Alvah L. Miller, "Correspondence, Visit to the YMCA by a Group of Haganah Fighters Led by a Former Tennis Player, to McClelland," Y.USA.9–2-2, International Work in Palestine/Israel, Kautz Family YMCA Archives (Minneapolis, MN, 1948).

134 US Mission Jerusalem, "Telegram, Stern Group Complaint About Lehi Transport Being Fired Upon from YMCA, to US Mission to the United Nations."

135 Miller, "Correspondence, Visit to the YMCA by a Group of Haganah Fighters Led by a Former Tennis Player, to McClelland," 1.

136 Alvah L. Miller, "Correspondence, the Final Order to Evacuate Arab Staff from the YMCA," Y.USA.9–2-2, International Work in Palestine/Israel, Kautz Family YMCA Archives (Minneapolis, MN, 1948), 1.

Endnotes

137 Palestine Olympic Committee, "Telegram, 1948 Olympic Games Protest, Hett to Edström," 0077643, CIO CNO ISR CORR OU MO 01 14 36, Historical Archives Olympic Studies Centre (Lausanne, Switzerland, Undated), Corr. 1937–48.
138 Associated Press, "Arabs Balk at Flag of Israel at Games," *New York Times*, 8 July 1948, 28.
139 Jewish Telegraphic Agency, "Olympics Committee Rules Israel Ineligible for Participation in International Games," *JTA Daily News Bulletin*, 25 July 1948, 5.
140 Palestine Olympic Committee, "Correspondence, 16 July, 1948 Olympic Games, Alouf to Edström," 0077643, CIO CNO ISR CORR OU MO 01 14 36, Historical Archives Olympic Studies Centre (Lausanne, Switzerland, 1948), 1–3.
141 International Olympic Committee, "Correspondence, 27 July, 1948 Olympic Games, Edström to Alouf," 0077643, CIO CNO ISR CORR OU MO 01 14 36, Historical Archives Olympic Studies Centre (Lausanne, Switzerland, 1948), Corr. 1937–48.
142 Jewish Telegraphic Agency, "Swedish Head of International Olympics Committee Hit for Disqualifying Israel," *JTA Daily News Bulletin*, 1 August 1948, 4.
143 Palestine Olympic Committee, "Correspondence, 6 August, 1948 Olympic Games, Alouf to Edström," 0077643, CIO CNO ISR CORR OU MO 01 14 36, Historical Archives Olympic Studies Centre (Lausanne, Switzerland, 1948), Corr. 1937–48.
144 Jewish Telegraphic Agency, "Olympic Body Votes to Defer Discussions on Recognizing Sports Federation of Israel," *JTA Daily News Bulletin*, 11 August 1948, 4.
145 Olympic Committee of Israel, "Correspondence, 5 April, NOC Recognition, Heth to Executive Committee of IOC," 0077504, CIO CNO ISR RECON OU MO 01 14 36, Historical Archives Olympic Studies Centre (Lausanne, Switzerland, 1949), Demande de recon. 1949–51.
146 The Green Line, so named because it was drawn in green on the map, was the demarcation line dividing opposing Jewish and Arab forces at the end of the 1948–1949 war when the 1949 Armistice Agreements were signed. It was never accepted as a de jure border by any side of the conflict.
147 Olympic Committee of Israel, "Correspondence, NOC Recognition, Heth to Executive Committee of IOC, 5 April," 0077504, CIO CNO ISR RECON OU MO 01 14 36, Demande de recon. 1949–1951, Historical Archives Olympic Studies Centre (Lausanne, Switzerland, 1949).
148 International Olympic Committee, "Correspondence, 20 January, NOC Recognition, Mayer to Olympic Committee of Israel," 0077504, CIO CNO ISR RECON OU MO 01 14 36, Historical Archives Olympic Studies Centre (Lausanne, Switzerland, 1950), Demande de recon. 1949–51.
149 J. Sigfrid Edström, "Correspondence, 18 January, NOC Recognition, Edström to Mayer," 0077504, CIO CNO ISR RECON OU MO 01 14 36, Historical Archives Olympic Studies Centre (Lausanne, Switzerland, 1950), Demande de recon. 1949–51.
150 Israeli Olympic Committee, "Correspondence, 19 March, NOC Recognition, Heth to IOC Headquarters," Isr. OC, 0077504, CIO CNO ISR RECON OU MO 01 14 36, Historical Archives Olympic Studies Centre (Lausanne, Switzerland, 1950), Demande de recon. 1949–51.

151 Daniel J. Ferris, "Correspondence, NOC Recognition for Israel, to IOC Vice-President Avery Brundage," 5-1-11, Joseph Yekutieli 1934–1948, Joseph Yekutieli Maccabi Sport Archives (Tel Aviv, Israel, 1950), 1.

152 J. Sigfrid Edström, "Correspondence, 12 March, NOC Recognition, Edström to Mayer," 0077504, CIO CNO ISR RECON OU MO 01 14 36, Historical Archives Olympic Studies Centre (Lausanne, Switzerland, 1951), Demande de recon. 1949–51.

153 J. Sigfrid Edström, "Correspondence, 19 April, NOC Recognition, Edström to Mayer," 0077504, CIO CNO ISR RECON OU MO 01 14 36, Historical Archives Olympic Studies Centre (Lausanne, Switzerland, 1951), Demande de recon. 1949–51.

154 Jewish Telegraphic Agency, "Hapoel and Maccabi Conclude Pact on Sports Activities in Israel," *JTA Daily News Bulletin*, 22 October 1951, 6.

155 International Olympic Committee, "Correspondence, 19 November, NOC Recognition, Mayer to Liberman," 0077504, CIO CNO ISR RECON OU MO 01 14 36, Historical Archives Olympic Studies Centre (Lausanne, Switzerland, 1951), Demande de recon. 1949–51; International Olympic Committee, "IOC."

156 J. Sigfrid Edström, "Correspondence, 22 December, NOC Recognition, Edström to Mayer," 0077504, CIO CNO ISR RECON OU MO 01 14 36, Historical Archives Olympic Studies Centre (Lausanne, Switzerland, 1951), Demande de recon. 1949–51.

157 International Olympic Committee, "Correspondence, 31 December, NOC Recognition, Mayer to Merged Olympic Committee of Israel," 0077504, CIO CNO ISR RECON OU MO 01 14 36, Historical Archives Olympic Studies Centre (Lausanne, Switzerland, 1951), Demande de recon. 1949–51.

158 Organizing Committee of the XV Olympiad Helsinki, "Accreditation Card, 1952 Helsinki Olympic Games, Accreditation of Joseph Yekutieli," 5-1-1, Joseph Yekutieli 1929–79, Joseph Yekutieli Maccabi Sport Archives (Tel Aviv, Israel, 1952).

**Chapter 11**

1 Then Israeli Minister of Foreign Affairs.

2 Then Member of the Executive Council of the Palestine Liberation Organization (PLO).

3 Then Foreign Minister of the Russian Federation.

4 Then US Secretary of State.

5 Then Chairman of the Executive Council of the PLO.

6 Then Prime Minister of Israel.

7 Then President of the United States of America.

8 International Olympic Committee, "Correspondence, 25/94/JMG/Jel, to Al Koudoua," D42/004–30G, 4333 CIO CNO-PALES-RECON, Historical Archives Olympic Studies Centre (Lausanne, Switzerland, 1994), 1.

9 Palestine Olympic Committee, "Correspondence, Assignment of Tunisia to Handle Palestine Olympic Matters, to Samaranch," D42/004–30G, 4333 CIO CNO-PALES-RECON, Historical Archives Olympic Studies Centre (Lausanne, Switzerland, 1993), 1.

10 Olympic Council of Asia, "Correspondence, Recognition of Palestine Olympic Committee, to Al Koudoua," D42/004–30G, 4333 CIO CNO-PALES-RECON, Historical Archives Olympic Studies Centre (Lausanne, Switzerland, 1993), 1.

11 The International Olympic Committee required the Palestine Olympic Committee to change its logo as one of the conditions for its provisional recognition as a member of the Olympic family.

12 Palestine Olympic Committee, "Correspondence, Following the Signing of the Oslo Accords and Regarding Recognition of Palestine Olympic Committee, Including Board Members and List of 15 National Federations, to Samaranch from Ali," D42/004–30G, 4333 CIO CNO-PALES-RECON, Historical Archives Olympic Studies Centre (Lausanne, Switzerland, 1993), 1.

13 Ibid.

14 Ibid.

15 Ibid.

16 Ibid., 1–2.

17 Guttmann, *The Games Must Go On*, 67–68.

18 ABC Sports, *Our Greatest Hopes, Our Worst Fears* (Private Collection, 2002).

19 Ibid.

20 Ibid.